ASPECTS OF UFOS AND ALIENS

Reports of similar UFO and alien interactions around the world, and the unofficial and military responses.

Moira McGhee

Published by INUFOR - Independent Network of UFO Researchers

Aspects of UFOs and Aliens

Reports of similar UFO and alien interactions around the world, and the official and military responses.

Copyright © 2021 by Moira McGhee. All rights reserved. Printed in Australia. No part of this book may be reproduced in any manner whatsoever without written permission.

For information address:
INUFOR, PO Box 169, Katoomba NSW 2780, AUSTRALIA

INUFOR books may be purchased for business, educational, or sales promotional use. For information please write:
INUFOR, PO Box169, Katoomba NSW 2780, AUSTRALIA

INUFOR web sites:
www.independentnetuforesearchers.com.au
www.facebook.com/inufor
Email:
ind.net.ufo.res@bigpond.com

FIRST INUFOR PAPERBACK EDITION PUBLISHED IN DECEMBER 2021

ISBN 978-0-9587-045-6-4

ASPECTS OF UFOS AND ALIENS

CONTENTS

	Introduction	1
1	Ours or Theirs? - Part One	7
2	Ours or Theirs? - Part Two	33
3	Behind the Iron Curtain. – Part One	75
4	Behind the Iron Curtain – Part Two	101
5	Up into the Air. - Part One	125
6	Up into the Air. – Part Two	148
7	Aliens Among Us.	172
8	Alien Encounters. – Part One	201
9	Alien Encounters. – Part Two	227
10	Come Fly With Me.	247
11	Telepathy, Channelling and Compulsions	256
12	Out in Space	277
13	Amerindians	306
14	South-East Asia	326
15	The Children Remembered.	347
16	Of Schools and Trains	368
17	What Really Happened?	387
	Epilogue	400

INTRODUCTION

The concept of life in the Universe is not new. In the 4th Century BC, Greek Philosopher Metrodorus said; *"To consider the Earth as the only populated world in infinite space is as absurd as to assert that in an entire field of millet, only one grain will grow."*

The March 1972, '*London Daily Telegraph*' published an interesting article by Kenneth Gatland on the search for life in the Universe. It inadvertently demonstrated the varying points of view within the scientific community.

He quoted Dr. Ehricke of the Space Division, North American Rockwell Corporation, who said; *"I believe encounter with an alien civilisation will be an elevating or a dangerous experience, stimulating and interesting in any case, but not degrading on the grounds that it refutes the cherished, but not very plausible postulate that we are of a unique quality.*

'There are those, of course, who say we, as mere mortals, have no business questioning the secrets of the Universe. I cannot imagine a more foreboding, apocalyptic vision than the fate of mankind possessed with cosmic powers and condemned to solitary confinement on one small planet.'

Professor Zdenek Kopal, from the University of Manchester was definitely against any contact with extraterrestrials; '*A thousand, or ten thousand years of evolutionary difference is just nothing on cosmic scales; and the chance that we could come across another civilisation in the Universe at approximately the same level of development – and with which we could affect some kind of intellectual understanding – are therefore vanishingly small. And such being the case, what gain could we hope to derive from contacts with hypothetical civilisations which are likely to be removed, not thousands, but millions of years from our level?*

'Certainly the risks entailed in such an encounter would vastly exceed any possible interest – let alone benefit, and could easily prove fatal. Therefore, should we ever hear that 'Space Phone' ringing in the form of observational evidence, which may admit no other explanation, for God's sake let us not answer, but rather make ourselves as inconspicuous as we can to avoid attracting attention...'

Sometimes scientists are very non-committal, and give mixed messages. In 2002, SETI Director, Jill Tartar said she didn't believe that aliens have been 'abducting Aunt Sally', but admitted that there have been attempts to find ships that might be on long-term stations in our solar system. An extraterrestrial presence was not impossible, and anything hidden in places such as the asteroid belt or Saturn's rings, would be virtually indistinguishable from other objects.

By the 1950s and 60s, many scientists were already becoming less sceptical and more outspoken. Physics Professor Charles Maney, from Defiance College, Ohio, concluded an intensive, unbiased study by saying; "I am convinced that there is massive documental evidence confirming UFO reality. Their tremendous speed, intricate manoeuvres, unique shapes, and other outstanding features indicate they are not made on Earth."

In 1954, 'The American Weekly' reported that, after completing a study for the West German government, Professor Hermann Oberth had concluded; *"I have examined all the arguments supporting and denying the existence of flying saucers, and it is my belief that UFOs do exist, are very real, and are spaceships from another, or more than one other solar system.*

"They are probably manned by intelligent observers who are members of a race carrying out long-range scientific investigation of the earth for centuries....I think they have possibly been sent out to conduct systematic, long-range investigations, first of men, animals, vegetation, and more recently of atomic centres, armaments and centres of armament production."

At a press conference in January 1957, retired Rear Admiral Delmer Fahrney, once head of the US Navy's guided missile program, said; "There are objects coming into our atmosphere at very high speeds. No agency in this country or Russia is able to duplicate, at this time, the speeds and accelerations which radar and observers indicate these flying objects are able to achieve."

He told reporters that he had no information or preconceived ideas as to whether the unidentified objects were from outer space, but they involved "a tremendous amount of technology of which we have no knowledge."

Australian Air Marshall, Sir George Jones, who was Chief of Air Force Staff during World War II, admitted to once seeing a craft he could not identify. He stressed that the object was travelling very fast, in a purposeful way. He had reported it, but wished there had been other witnesses. He was loath to talk about it publicly, for fear people would think he was either an incompetent witness, or getting a little screwy in the head.

In his book, *'Confrontations'*, Dr Jacques Vallèe concludes; .... *'UFOs seem to represent an alien force that anticipates our own scientific developments by decades, mocking our efforts to identify its nature and its long-term intentions. Understandably, the military establishment does not feel comfortable with the disclosure of our weakness any more than the scientific establishment feels inclined to confessing its ignorance.'*

What is the purpose of some of the more benign beings who have visited our planet? British investigator, Tony Dodd, asked this question and received the following message; *'Our presence has been in your skies for hundreds of earth years, but through our cloaking devices you have been unable to observe us. As your cosmic evolution has developed, the time has arrived for you to understand the existence and presence of other life in your universe, thus resulting in us making our presence known to you. Our choice of contacts has been governed by the ability of their spiritual minds to comprehend this contact without anxiety or aggression.'*

In his book, *'Alien Base'*, Timothy Good discusses a 'Filipino' pianist, Bobby, who had a meeting and contact with human looking visitors and their landed craft in 1962.

The message they gave him encapsulated the important communications received by other witnesses, but was far more critical of humans, and their treatment of this world and its inhabitants.

'We come to your planet, not for a visit, but to deliver a message which may well serve as a warning to mankind. We cannot and must not reveal from which planet, star or moon we come from, because of the imminent danger of your people contriving all possible means and resources to conquer space, and eventually to try and conquer us, although we could fight back and wipe out your mean and selfish humanity.

'Within your planet, there is continuous strife among nations for power and domination, and within every nation there is dissention and dissatisfaction among the masses. Within a family and family relations there is still enmity, intrigue and conspiracies, and within an individual's mind there is still a

continuous struggle between good and bad, evil and purity, generosity and selfishness. Why? Because there is so much selfishness on your planet, meanness, cruelty, wickedness and evil; more than good, purity and generosity.

'Observe carefully the great mass of humanity killing each other through centuries of war and strife. And for what purpose? For power and domination; the intense desire to dominate and subjugate... There are thousands of good people on your planet, but the mean and selfish humanity outnumbers the good by millions and millions.

'Unless there is a radical change, starting now, from an individual's mind, within a family and family relations, within a nation and between nations, your people will all be destroyed by their own selfishness for power and domination. Not until your humanity is completely wiped out will there ever be peace on Earth. The danger of atomic war between nations is imminent....It may not be now, it may be centuries from now, but the end will still come. There is no turning back for your people. Some day you will all be wiped out by your own greediness, and if a few good people live through, then they will propagate and breed an unselfish humanity, and no longer will there be a continuous strife between nations, within a family and family relations, and within an individual mind. There will be peace on Earth at last.

'There is a great and possible danger, too, that your humanity's intense desire to conquer, eventually seeking power and domination over the other planets, will only mean a complete massacre for Earthmen, because other planets will retaliate with terrifying power and force, only because of their fear of your selfish humanity coming to their planets and spreading greed and evil around. This is our message. Transmit it and let humanity beware.'

I have been involved with UFO and alien research for over forty-five years, and still don't have all the answers.

In 1998, my friend, Australian researcher John Auchetll, from PRA Victoria, spoke very aptly about the difficulties involved in UFO investigations; "...You may have also found, as we have over the years, that everyone wants to do 'field research', without doing all the paperwork, long work hours, and without facing up to the disappointment caused by the many dead ends.

"Just about everyone who wants to help us, either does not have a car, or has work commitments. Most will not travel twenty kilometres from their home, or will not face the facts that they may have to stay overnight and repeatedly visit the same location, (over many days at a remote place), using up their free time, and to their surprise, at their own cost."

New Zealand's Fred and Phyllis Dickenson also succinctly summed up the problems facing UFO investigators and researchers; *'It has not been an easy road for those taking the initiative in this study – the years have been time consuming, frustrating but extremely fascinating, and in a way, rewarding. The pit-falls have been many and the answers to endless questions as to whom, why, what and wherefore of their appearance, still unfortunately remains rather obscure.*

'Sometimes it appears to many in this work to be like treading warily and carefully down an unending one-way street, never knowing what one will find next. Certainly, there are those who claim "they know", but do they?.....They never seem to prove their reasoning or points of view to everyone's satisfaction! All sorts of theories and patterns have emerged, yet no true researcher can afford to be dogmatic about his or her conclusions. Have you noticed that as soon as one thinks the answer is found, something else turns up to change it?'

Over the years, UFO and alien research has been a massive patchwork quilt analysis by the military, government scientists and departments, volunteer organisations and individual investigators all over the world.

Each one of us 'does our bit'. However individually we only have a small piece of the jigsaw. In this book I have searched for sighting reports, from other parts of the world, which share some similarities to my own investigations.

I have concentrated mainly on incidents from the 'early years', before our skies were full of drones and unknown terrestrial prototypes. In so far as entities are concerned, I discuss cases which usually involve 'humanoids' or the 'little guys', where the witness or contactee has conscious memory of the encounter. Recollections of the 'taller Grays', usually require regressive hypnosis.

Many of the objects and craft reported are not necessarily extraterrestrial. Sometimes it is difficult to determine – a task complicated by governments subtly encouraging a belief in 'flying saucers' rather than admitting to or exposing their own secret advanced technology.

Sometimes, we can only weigh-up the evidence and make a judgement on 'the balance of probabilities'. If only **one** incident is of extraterrestrial origin, mankind is on the brink of a new awakening and serious self-appraisal.

CHAPTER ONE

OURS OR THEIRS?

PART ONE

Many times witnesses cannot really be sure if an unidentified craft is one of their own country's new secret prototype aircraft, a spy plane from a foreign country, or something truly alien. Sometimes, we will never know. In the early days, it was relatively easy to judge, but as the years went by, determining from where an unidentified craft originated became complicated.

Any society advanced enough to travel the galaxy would have sophisticated machines – smooth, seamless, silent, hovering craft which are incredibly fast. Compare this description with some of the craft reported by witnesses. These more terrestrial objects have seams or rivets, exhaust gases or flames, legs to land on, a ladder to climb out, and often a 'clumsy' and noisy modus operandi.

We also have to remember that the general public are often not aware of our own craft and innovations until long after they have been in experimental and clandestine use. Sometimes, it is only in hindsight that we realise some of the craft reported were actually our own.

No country is going to allow a potential rival to know the full extent of its arsenal. A new craft or weapon is not going to be flown across hostile skies, allowing an enemy to capture and replicate it. Neither is it going to be flaunted in full view of one's own citizens, many of whom may give full details to the local media!

Why then, do unidentified, technologically superior craft openly traverse our skies, detected by radar and in full view of the public and our military and commercial airlines?

A classic example is the use of unmanned drones. Most people think they came into existence about thirty years ago. Wrong! British group -'Contact International' – reported that Lockheed Skunk Works Project manufactured thirty-eight D21 unmanned drones sixty years ago, and in 1963 connected them with a 'mother-ship' aircraft. The first flight apparently took place in December 1964, and three official missions were scheduled for 1967.

The D21 were essentially a small spy craft, designed to overfly the target country, and then return to a friendly nation, where it would eject its camera in flight, before self-destructing at a low altitude. The photographs and other data would be recovered mid-air by a C-130 recovery system.

However, similar objects were seen before our first official launch of these 'mother-ships'. Donald Keyhoe recounted a report from July 1952, when several witnesses saw an elliptical shape craft flying over Culver City, California. It stopped and hovered, and two small discs were launched from the starboard side. They circled the area for a few minutes, before returning to the 'mother-ship', which climbed straight up, at tremendous speed, and vanished.

Another three similar incidents were reported from Europe in September and October. Large cigar-shaped craft, accompanied by several smaller spinning discs, were seen over Denmark, Norway, Sweden and Germany.

American group CRIFO detailed a multi-witness event, from the Rockford area, in April 1955. A mysterious object in the sky was reported and jets were sent up to intercept it. They fired, causing the intruder to explode, however, just before the explosion, a smaller, round object shot out of the side of the 'parent' craft. It flew horizontally past the jets, then turned on its edge and disappeared straight up into the sky.

In Australia, in September 1972, a Kempsey greengrocer was driving his truck to Armidale. He had stopped at the top of a hill, to check his load, when he saw an enormous cigar-shaped craft in the sky. He estimated it to be several thousand feet above the ground, and many times bigger than a Boeing 707.

For ten minutes he watched as small flying-saucer type objects flew out from either end, and grouped in an arrow-like formation before heading south-east. Once they were out of sight, the large craft speedily ascended, and was out of sight within seconds.

In *'Contact Down Under'*, I mention Garry, who lived on the NSW South Coast. In September, during the late 1960s he saw a huge object, 'at least a mile long, and several stories high', which hovered off the coast while a multitude of small discs, glowing orange, came out. They slowly moved over the houses, as if monitoring or mapping them, before returning to the larger ship, which then moved further to the north, before repeating the process. Were they in fact our own, and not extraterrestrial?

Although we are unable to determine the origin of these craft, it stands to reason that our early experimental prototypes would have been developed over the years.

Pilot, and Air Force veteran, Rufus Drake, wrote about two interesting incidents which occurred in the early 1950s. Both included details which suggested that smaller extraterrestrial craft operated out of larger 'mother-ships'.

In 1952, Lt. Col. William Anderson was flying his F-94 out of Andrews AFB, Maryland, when he was diverted to the Virginia tidewater region, where a crash had been reported.

He circled above what looked like a saucer-shaped craft, buried in the mud flat. There appeared to be some activity around the wreck, although to his knowledge, no rescue crew or helicopter had arrived.

He was low on fuel, and after returning to base, he noticed a flurry of activity. Later, he learned that when the chopper arrived, they found that the saucer's crew had been rescued by an identical disc. The abandoned craft and debris were apparently recovered and brought back to a guarded hanger at Andrews.

Drake went on to quote aviation writer Jerome Candless, who wrote about a second crash in 1953. The Air Force stated that Franciszek Jareacki, a Polish pilot, had defected and landed his MIG-15 jet fighter on the Danish island of Bornholm. Before the Americans could retrieve it, for political reasons, the Danes returned it to Poland.

Candless believed this was just a 'cover-story', as a member of the ATIC team at Nellis advised him that the craft had arrived on the East Coast in April 1953.

'It was a perfect saucer, 30.3 feet in diameter, with thickness ranging from one foot around its circumference to nine feet at its centre. It had a raised cockpit, similar to that of a fighter plane, and an enclosed area beneath, five by five by seven feet. Its propulsion system had been totally destroyed and most of the instrumentation and wiring, although involving familiar materials, was almost incomprehensible.

'No one ever seriously believed this was an interstellar star ship. The feeling was, it was a small craft designed to operate from a mother ship in orbit around

the Earth. Judging from its dimensions, and the battered wreckage of acceleration couches, it was designed to carry two crew members, apparently with human-like limbs, but considerably smaller than human beings. It took months of work to redesign the thing so a human pilot could fit into it.

'......There was exhaustive debate at Nellis over whether the thing could be flown. Metallurgy experts understood the composition of the machine, and actually identified new alloys that we had under development, but nobody could figure out what held it up.'

Throughout history, from the days of ancient times, there are reports of airborne objects which we are certain did not originate on this Earth. Many well known cases have already been written about, some of which I have already included in previous books. Some lesser known events are still being unearthed.

Researcher, Harold Wilkins, found a manuscript from mediaeval England, and there is no doubt what was being described: At Ampleforth, near York, in 1290. Dom. Henricus, the Abbot of the monastery, was saying grace at the Feast of St. Jude. Joannes, a brother monk, came racing in the door, saying there was an amazing portent to be seen outside.

They all rushed out to see 'an awful thing'. *'A nearly circular object of silvery appearance, not unlike a discus (disco quadam haud dissimilis), flying slowly above them all. It excited among all the greatest terror'.*

They felt it was an omen or warning from God, and the abbot blamed Brother Wilfred, whom it was alleged had stolen the sheep they were eating for dinner.

France, like most other countries, has its own history of UFO and alien sightings, some dating back centuries. On August 5th 1608, the inhabitants of the southern city of Nice saw three strange, revolving, luminous craft hovering in the sky above. After a while they slowly descended to the sea, close to the Port. They floated above the water, which was boiling and frothing.

Two beings, with large heads and shiny eyes, came out of one craft, and for two hours they appeared to be diving into the water to waist deep level. They were wearing red and silvery suits, which were linked to the vessel by some sort of a tube. During that time the three craft maintained their position. Once the two entities returned to their craft, all three noisily departed within a few seconds.

The account of this, and subsequent events, is housed in the archives of the city's Library Louise Nucera, and was translated by MUFON's John Tomlinson. Apparently, later that month the three craft appeared off the coast of Genova, in Italy. When soldiers fired cannon balls from the local fortress, one craft flew towards the city, causing mass panic in the population. Several people were killed or injured in the fleeing stampede.

The three craft swiftly departed, however for the next forty days, churches along the Mediterranean coast were full of local parishioners praying.

Nearly two hundred years later, Alencon Police Inspector Liabeuf reported that on 12th June 1790, dozens of peasants, farmers, two mayors and a doctor, amongst other dignitaries, witnessed an amazing event.

A large spherical 'globe', surrounded by flame, and emitting a whistling sound, made some oscillations before slowing and moving towards the top of a hill. It unearthed plants along the slope, and gave off enough heat to set the grass and small trees on fire.

A 'kind of a door' opened, and someone, dressed in a strange tight-fitting suit came out. This person saw all the people, uttered some unintelligible words, and ran into the woods. The sphere silently exploded, throwing pieces everywhere, which burned until they were powder. The mysterious 'man' was never located.

On 18th August 1783, at about 9.45 pm, Dr James Lind, scientist Tiberius Cavallo and artist Thomas Sandby, were gathered together on the terrace at Windsor Castle, when they saw an oblong cloud moving along the horizon.

Underneath the cloud was a spherical, pale blue, brilliantly lit, luminous object, which radiated onto the ground below. It halted, the luminosity increased, and it moved again towards the east, changing direction to eventually disappear in the south-east. Just before it vanished, the craft seemed to separate into a couple of small bodies, and less than two minutes later, the sound of an explosion was heard.

The behaviour of this object was not consistent with that of a meteor. Cavallo's account of the incident was published the next year by the Royal Society, and Sandby made a painting of the object.

In Australia, the late Kenneth Beames told my colleague, Rex Gilroy, of a part-aboriginal man recounting an incident his grandfather mentioned in the 1950s. It appears that the location of this event was known about by local Aborigines as late as the 1930s.

Apparently, a great heavenly 'fire-canoe' landed near the western end of the Blue Mountains' Grose Valley, north of the Blackheath township. The occupants of the 'great canoe' were unable to make it fly again, and they were forced to remain here, living in caves, and surviving as best they could. Said to be grey-skinned, and pygmy-size, they all gradually died.

This was of interest to me, due to later reports of sightings and encounters in the same area, however the beings described then were all of humanoid appearance.

In previous books I have written about sightings before World War II, especially those from the late eighteen and early nineteen hundreds. Although it is obvious these craft were not of Earthly origin, sometimes witnesses, who feared ridicule, waited until their declining years before speaking out.

Extraterrestrial visitors were around well over one hundred years ago, and as occurred in later times, some displayed less than friendly behaviour.

In his book, *'Australian UFOs - Through the Window of Time'*, Rex Gilroy tells of a 1977 meeting with Dave Bradburn from South Australia. In the 1860s, Dave's great grandfather was a drover, mustering cattle on the flat plains of the Robe district. One night, he and his colleagues were camped under the stars. The saw about a dozen silvery, circular, glowing objects, each about fifty feet wide, descend from the sky and hover over the grazing cattle.

The craft then slowly dispersed in various directions, emitting strong light beams from the centre of their undersides. The cattle stampeded far and wide, but after a few minutes, the light beams faded, and the objects gathered together, high in the sky, before increasing speed and flying out of sight to the east.

The next morning, despite an intensive search, over thirty cattle were missing. Some of their hoof impressions had come to a dead stop, as if they had been plucked from the ground.

In the late nineteenth century, there were several sightings, especially in America, that are suspected of being early models of 'airships' or 'dirigibles'. Some reports definitely did not indicate this explanation.

On 22th January 1878, John Martin, a farmer living six miles south of Denison, Texas, described a large, dark saucer-shaped object moving overhead. The editor of the local *'Denison Daily News'* commented that; *'Mr Martin is a gentleman of undoubted veracity, and this strange occurrence, if it was not a balloon, deserves the attention of our scientists.'*

Harold Wilkins wrote about an Oklahoma woman being told of an incident she thought must have occurred in the 1880's. An old man related what had happened when he was a lad, hunting in the nearby hills. He saw a round thing, 'settle down from the sky', on the top of a mountain. He was a little frightened, but climbed up to get a better look.

A strange, big silver 'ball' was sitting in a clearing of some woods, and a piece of the top slid back. Two beings came out, and the old man said they were not as tall as he, and 'nice looking', although rather skinny.

They tried to talk to him, but could not understand each other, and the witness was too scared to say much. The beings got back into the 'ball', and slid the lid shut. Their craft then shot up into the sky and was quickly lost from sight.

My Welsh friend and colleague, Margaret Fry, wrote of an event recounted to Jenny Randles from a witness who was only ten years old in 1901.

One warm, sunny day, he was playing with friends in open ground, at the back of his house, and on his way home he spotted something unusual sitting on the grass verge. It looked like an oblong house, with a door and small turret.

Two small, three feet tall, human-looking beings emerged. They were dressed in green-blue, close fitting uniforms, with helmets which had two wires sticking up on either side.

They then returned to their 'hut', which suddenly became surrounded by an electrical, glowing arc. It made a loud 'whooshing' noise, and swooped into the air over the rooftops. The last he saw of it was a pulsating light.

Margaret also wrote about an occurrence from the late 1880s, when young Willie, from the Llyn Peninsular, was collecting firewood for his mother. He had stacked it at the side of the road, where his mother was to pick it up. As he waited for her, he could hear a funny whistling noise coming from the nearby Whistling Sands.

He made his way down to the beach, and a 'huge black thing' landed near him. Two little men, dressed like 'doctors', came out of a door and walked towards him. They grabbed Willie and carried him back to their craft. Willie said they were talking, but he couldn't understand the words.

The craft had gone 'straight up', and landed he knew not where. They immediately took him to 'a great big building', where, whilst everyone was smiling and friendly, they put him on a table and 'took something from him'.

His mother found the firewood, but Willie was missing for a week. A search was conducted, and everyone thought he had been drowned, resulting in a Memorial Service being planned. Suddenly, he walked through the door looking different. He seemed to be in a trance, with a rough appearance and long hair.

When his story became known, there was much disbelief and 'ragging' until a man from Aberdaron came into the pub and said that he had also seen the strange craft as it rose into the sky from Saron Beach.

'*The Sydney Morning Herald*', 23rd March 2005, detailed an event which occurred in August 1914, during the First World War. Following the Battle of Mons, the British forces were retreating, and the 'Guards' units were the last to withdraw. They became lost in the fog, and with bullets flying everywhere, were fearful of stumbling into the German lines.

Suddenly, they saw a warm glow ahead, out of which appeared a being in a flowing robe, sandals, and a gold band around 'her' hair. The apparition beckoned to the soldiers, who followed. When they reached the road they were supposed to follow, the 'angel' disappeared. I have often wondered if their rescuer was really an angel, or an intervening extraterrestrial?

Researcher Harold Wilkins discussed an unusual case from 1920, when it was unlikely that we had any comparable craft. In June of that year, some duck shooters were out, at dawn, on the Texas shore of the Gulf of Mexico.

Suddenly, four silver discs appeared in the sky. They were each about thirty feet in diameter, and resembled large plates 'slicing one behind the other through the sky'. Their colour alternated between an orange and green/blue glow. Suddenly, they changed direction, and with amazing speed, ascended sharply into the sky, and disappeared inland in the direction of Austin, Texas.

Researchers Jerome Clark and Lucius Farish wrote an interesting article, *'UFOs of the Roaring Twenties'* where they documented several other similar sightings from that decade.

In November 1925, two farm-boys saw an object, one hundred feet away. It was shaped like a soup bowl turned upside down, and flew, at some speed, over a field four miles northwest of Milton North Dakota. It was about 25-30ft in diameter, with a polished metal appearance, and beaming five rays of light onto the ground fifteen feet below. It was unlikely any terrestrial power had such a craft at that time.

The same applies to what Richard Sweed saw, on October 18th 1927, when he was driving through the outskirts of Bakersfield, California. A bluish-gray disc, about sixty feet in diameter, with a row of round windows around the edge, was sitting on the ground not far away. After a few minutes it rose into the air at a 45-degree angle, and flew off making a slight humming-whooshing sound.

Six months later, Floyd Dillon was driving along a rough road near Yakima, Washington. At the top of a slight rise, he saw a domed, hexagonal, metallic object about seventy-five feet above the ground. It moved slowly, and was a drab, olive colour, about twenty-two feet wide and seven feet high, with a smooth, rounded underside. He could see rivets at the edge of each side of the craft, and a metallic framed window, through which he could see the upper torso of a man in a dark blue uniform.

The occupant stared at Floyd, and the object suddenly rotated, flew across the road, and took off at a tremendous speed. Ours or theirs? We will never know.

The *'MUFON Journal'* wrote about an incident which apparently occurred in Tarpon Springs, Florida, in 1929.

An old Greek sponge diver was underwater, in his traditional diver's suit and helmet, when he was disturbed by a silver, saucer-shaped disc, with lights on. It passed him, underwater, then came back again, as if monitoring his actions.

There were no other boats in the area, and although his colleagues wouldn't believe him, he never changed his account of the incident.

Jenny Randles wrote about an event on 13th November 1939, when 'Mr F. Price' was doing essential war work on what was to become an airfield in Gloucestershire, England. Every Monday morning as he drove from London to spend the week at his worksite, he would pass a deserted farm.

This day, he became aware of a high-pitched humming sound, and saw a strange object hovering over a field behind the farmhouse. It was dull grey and bell-shaped, with dark shadings, or window-like patches in a line, part of the way up the body, and a greenish light emanating from underneath.

'Price' got out of his car to watch, but within two minutes, the beam of light retracted, and the object tilted at an eighty degree angle and silently moved away.

One woman reported another mysterious object which she, her father, and many adult witnesses, saw in September 1939, from the small East Coast town of Skerries. It was an orange-coloured, circular globe, about 150 ft in diameter. Travelling at about half a mile to one side of the islands, for over thirty minutes it slowly moved up and down a five mile stretch of the coastline. The next day, World War II was declared between Britain and Germany.

Another evening, at about 6pm, a woman, from the town, along with several children, saw an object which resembled 'a line of railway coaches in the sky'. It was completely silent, at a low altitude, and slowly disappeared out of sight behind a hill.

Were these alien, or were they Nazi spy-craft which some researchers insist existed? British researcher, Nick Redfern, unearthed some FBI documents, one of which detailed a man's visit to their Miami office on 26th April 1967.

'Sometime during 1943, he graduated from the German Air Academy, and was assigned as a member of the Luftwaffe on the Russian Front. Near the end of 1944, he was released from this duty, and was assigned as a test pilot to a top secret project in the Black Forest of Austria.

He described seeing, during this time, a saucer-shaped object, about twenty-one feet in diameter. The craft was radio controlled, with several jet engines around the exterior portion, which revolved around a stationary centre dome.

'It was his responsibility to photograph the object while in flight. He asserted he was able to retain a negative of a photograph he made at 20,000 feet. According to him, the aircraft was designed and engineered by a German engineer, whose whereabouts is unknown to him. He also assumed that the secrets pertaining to this aircraft were captured by Allied Forces. He said this type of aircraft was responsible for the downing of at least one American B-26 airplane.

'He has become increasingly concerned because of the unconfirmed reports concerning a similar object and denials that the United States has such an aircraft. He feels such a weapon would be beneficial in Vietnam, and would prevent the further loss of American lives, which was his paramount purpose in contacting the Federal Bureau of Investigations.'

British intelligence agencies had interviewed many former prisoners of war, who also described unusual and radical aircraft in the vicinity of German and Russian airfields and military installations.

It has been well documented in the past that German scientists, before and during World War II, had been designing 'disc' technology – often referred to as 'flying pancakes'. (I have often wondered about the source of inspiration and knowledge of these gifted scientists.) One German prototype was the Alexander Lippisch designed disc-shaped Messerschmitt AS-6. After the war, Lippisch's work was improved upon to design more advanced jet powered versions, including the circular winged F-6 Skyray jet fighter.

Many plausible claims have been made concerning the Third Reich also back-engineering crashed alien discs, including one from Northern Italy in 1933. (See *'The Alien Gene'*). Some years ago, the Italian TV station, *'Rai Due'*, interviewed the editors of the magazine *'UFO Notizziario'* (UFO Messenger). They claimed that in 1933 Mussolini founded a secret group, headed by G. Marconi, to examine the UFO phenomena. During their studies, from 1933 to 1940, they collected many photographs and documents, one of which mentions some kind of UFO landing near Milano. This explains a strange speech Mussolini made in 1941, suggesting that the USA should worry more about an extraterrestrial attack than the Axis forces.

A lesser known case, researched by Polish researcher Robert Lesniakiewicz, involves a UFO which crashed into a field in German occupied Czernica in 1937. The wreckage was immediately seized by SS-troops and taken to Jelenia

Gora, where there were uranium deposits and ongoing nuclear research. A year later, several leading German physicists, who later worked on Nazi nuclear research, attended a top secret meeting, presumably in regards to the crashed UFO, which was delivered to an underground facility in 1943.

Besides the Vril, Hannebu and V-7 disc, one prototype, just about ready for mass production, was the GO-229 V3, a jet-powered combat aircraft with stealth capabilities. Another prototype, allegedly only flown once, was the Kugelblitz, which combined the principle of an aircraft with a round symmetrical plane. It had direct gyroscopic stabilisation, employing an ejector-gun using grisou and a gelatinous organic-metallic fuel for total-reaction turbine. It had added remote control vehicle take-off, infrared seeking equipment and static firing systems. Some historians have disputed the descriptions of the Kugelblitz, and say it wasn't a flying disc at all, rather an experimental anti-aircraft rocket. To prevent its capture, it was destroyed when allied forces crossed the Rhine.

The Germans had already utilised various 'gases' in their new airborne weapons, and were experimenting with liquid oxygen as a component in new turbine engines. Even before World War I, they were developing the 'porous sinterization of metals' for use in certain aircraft.

Controversial author, Vladimir Terziski, claimed in his book *'UFO Secrets of the Third Reich'*, that the German Secret Societies had 'alien tutors' who secretly co-operated with certain German scientists in the late 1920s. Terziski suggested that they were far more advanced in anti-gravity and space travel than we realised. He mentions, among other projects, an anti-gravity circular craft, the RFZ-1, constructed in 1942/3.

At the end of the war, there was a race to capture the Nazi's advance military and aeronautical technology, and the Americans, British and Russians were not about to disclose, for good reasons, what they had grabbed.

Sir Roy Fadden, who headed the British Ministry of Aircraft technical mission to Germany in 1945 said; "I have seen enough of their designs and production plans to realise that if they had managed to prolong the war some months longer, we would have been confronted with a set of entirely new and deadly developments in air warfare."

It must be remembered that most of what was captured from Germany were advanced concepts, plans and designs. Many experts believe that very few prototypes were ever actually built, however they had many types of guided missiles in various stages of production and development, and were advancing in magnetic and jet propulsion.

Many German scientists willingly relocated to the United States, and enjoyed lucrative employment and conditions there. Were they also involved in producing advanced craft – perhaps reverse engineered? Most possibly.

The Nazis, like many modern super-powers, tended to compartmentalise their scientific aerospace and weapons research, and hide it in diverse, scattered locations, many of which were later occupied by the Soviets. The Allies were quite correct in the assumption that the Russians had also captured some of the advance technology and scientists.

Renato Vesco, was attached to the Italian Air Ministry, and had worked with the Germans at the Fiat Lake Garda secret installation during World War II. In August 1969, he published an article in the *'Argosy'* magazine. He was quite adamant that all the reported unidentified craft were the result of British, Canadian and Australian improvements on the original German technology.

This doesn't explain the American concern about unidentified objects invading their air space. The Air Force commissioned an *'Intelligence Report No. 100-203-79'*, which was dated 10th December 1948, and de-classified in 1985.

It is a very lengthy document, which relies on 'expert and reliable' witnesses to various sightings of unknown craft. Most 'unidentified' reports, classified as 'foreign', come from pilots and air traffic controllers during 1947/8. It is of interest that there was absolutely no mention of any incident at Roswell in 1947, Los Angeles in 1942, or any other purported crashes and retrievals.

In April 1949, a detachment of US Navy personnel and scientists released an instrumental weather balloon from fifty-seven miles north-west of the White Sands Proving Ground. Unexpectedly, a flat, white elliptical object was also spotted, crossing its path. There was no stream of light, nor sign of an exhaust trail or evidence of a propulsion system.

Commander Robert McLaughlin said its altitude was approximately fifty-six miles. It was about 105 feet in diameter, and travelling at about five miles per second, against the direction of the upper atmosphere wind. Suddenly, it swerved abruptly upwards, gaining an increased altitude of another twenty-five miles, before disappearing at an elevation of twenty-nine degrees.

McLaughlin estimated that it would have produced a gravitational force of more than 20G's when it made this manoeuvre, more than any human could withstand. Was this craft alien, or one of our own secret prototypes? We will never know.

In the 1950s, *'Der Kurrier'* newspaper wrote of regular appearances of unidentified objects, flying at great height over occupied Berlin. This nearly always happened on cloudless nights, usually between 10pm and 11pm, and their tremendous speeds, and lightning changes of course, led experts to believe that they were not piloted by any human agency.

In the first couple of decades following World War II, there were many scientists, engineers and self-made entrepreneurs who claimed they had invented saucer-shaped craft and new methods of propulsion. Some appeared to have genuine innovative ideas, and others were considered to be just 'crackpots'!

In 1949, Maryland State Police located some unusual artefacts in an abandoned Baltimore tobacco barn. Their inventor, Jonathan Caldwell, had suddenly and mysteriously disappeared, along with his wife and son, during the winter of 1940. They had left all their personal possessions, which were scattered around the house

There were two dusty 'contraptions' inside the barn. One had a little fuselage, and above it a rotating disc and propeller blades. The other looked like a round 'cheese-box', big enough for four persons, with propellers above and below. A mechanic, who had helped Caldwell, said a smaller model of the prototype had flown, but they were unable to develop the more powerful motor needed for the craft itself.

Had they ever flown? An article in *'The Times'* on 22nd August 1949, said Air Force Captain Belk, and his special investigative office, were anxious to contact Caldwell regarding his experiments with flying discs in the late 1930s. They were eager to discover his engineering innovations, and thought he might have gone elsewhere, and other unknown people had developed and flown 'new planes along these lines.'

In 1955, researcher Harold Wilkins wrote a rather sensational book *'Flying Saucers on the Moon'*. Obviously, he had not, at that time, heard about Roswell or the other alleged previous saucer crashes, which were not widely known until the 1990s. He did, however, write the following transcription of a speech given by Mr. Joe Rohrer, at a Chamber of Commerce luncheon on July 12th 1952.

'Other reports, confirmable or otherwise, have reached me. They are fairly sensational, but probably would not come within a British High Court Rules of Evidence:

'A little man from a saucer is being tenderly cared for in the 'incubator room' at San Diego, while cadavers of two saucer pilots are being dissected by surgeons of the US Army-Air Force (Medical Division). A Californian air pilot told me that, in 1942, he had been right inside a giant saucer, and seen giant fly-wheels sheathed in metal skins, and found that the motive force came from electric-static turbines, whose fly-wheels create an electro-magnetic field of force, creating tremendous speeds. The little saucer men have smaller bone structures than earth men, but the bones are proportionally heavier, and their stomachs smaller.'

The only problem with this report is that whilst the saucer's technology seems a little primitive for alien technology, the pilots definitely seemed to be alien.

Wilkins also received a letter from a correspondent in Oklahoma, who claimed third hand information about a saucer, from another planet, which crashed in the Arizona desert in 1950. Our radar had purportedly brought it down. Three 'little fellows' had died, and the fourth was being kept alive in a pressure chamber, somewhere in California. He was only three feet tall, and they were teaching him to read, write and understand, by showing him pictures.

Before one jumps to the conclusion that these events never happened, it must be remembered that the Army lost control the same day the US Air Force was founded on September 18th 1947. This happened just a few weeks after a spate of UFO sightings and shortly after 'Roswell'. One of the reasons later given was that there was an 'admin battle' within the Army for control of aviation. One wonders if the Army, miffed at being usurped, divulged any information at all?

Another report mentions several suspected Nazi prototypes, plus the doubtful possibility of domestic innovations produced by Britain and a couple of US private companies. Special attention is given to Dr.Geunther Bock, who had been in charge of Germany's flying-wing program at the end of World War II. He was now working with the Soviets, and had given the Russians all the German aerospace and secret craft plans.

I received an edited copy of this report from MUFON's Walt Andrus, and as he noted, whilst there were vague references to an interplanetary origin for the saucers, the main concern was that the German scientists in the USSR had developed and perfected the technology. It was stressed that this was the most probable explanation, and all possible action must be taken to avoid the Soviets gaining technical superiority. The Department of the Air Force were so concerned that in September 1950 they ordered all copies of the report to be destroyed. This was supposedly done in the October, but luckily some copies survived.

Often, with the assistance of 'relocated' German engineers, the 'Super-Powers' continued the research and development of many projects, including the curved wing craft and 'flying pancakes'. The plans and designs for the craft were classified in 1962, and remained so until 1999 when they were declassified to 'restricted distribution'. *'Popular Mechanics'* obtained copies through a Freedom of Information application.

The RAAF files contained a then 'Secret' memo, dated 28th January 1959, from the Australian Military Mission in Washington USA. Titled 'Flying Saucer Avrocar', it detailed how the US Army had developed a 'flying saucer'. It described the 'Avrocar' and had photographs of the vehicle attached. It was a 'two man, gas turbine engine circular disc'.

Although the Canadian Minister of Defence announced that the tests of the AVRO were a failure, many people suspected that it was successfully developed in secret. In 1956, Capt. Edward Ruppelt, who was involved with 'Project Blue Book', claimed that only two Avro-type discs were in existence. They never strayed 'but a few miles' from Edwards Air Force Base, where they were housed.

In a letter dated 13th February 1956, he confirmed that assertion, and said it would probably be several years before this AVRO shaped aircraft ever flew.

Ruppelt later wrote; *'We had no evidence whatever that the saucers are some super-secret US development. On the contrary, we had specific disclaimers from the top Air Force, Army, Navy and Department of Defense officials. Ordinary horse sense is against this theory. If the US has flying saucers that can perform the way saucer-sighters describe them, why would the government be pouring billions of dollars into conventional – and inferior – planes?*

'We also have no evidence that the saucers are of foreign manufacture. Again, logic opposes such a belief. The chief suspect in the 'foreign saucer' theory is Russia. Why would Russia try out such a revolutionary device over the US when it has vast stretches of land behind the Iron Curtain, where the test could be conducted in complete secrecy? Any man-made device is certain to fail sooner or later. The more complex the device, the higher the failure probability.'

He stated that there were no known crashes. Either he had not been advised of the many well-documented crash reports, or he was maintaining official secrecy. He went on to say; *'This may bring you to the possibility that the saucers are craft from outer space. As staggering as the implications may be, to my mind this is the most acceptable theory – if the saucers exist. There is no other alternative.'*

It is not known if all research and development projects led to a successful outcome. In 1956, the Aeronautical Systems Division of the US Air Force was devising a typical 'flying saucer' known as Project 1794. It was designed to land vertically, cover a range of over 1,000 nautical miles, and have a top speed of Mach 4. Officially, conventional planes reached Mach 3 in September 1956, and Mach 4 five years later in March 1961.

In the early days, scientist Townsend Brown had been experimenting with anti-gravity, and after the war, the DOD contractors, including Bell Aircraft, General Electric, Glen L. Martin, Sperry Rand and others were working to achieve this. Later, through a series of mergers, Glen L. Martin became the more prominent Martin-Lockheed Company.

How successful were they? We don't know, but in the early 2000s, according to *'Jane's Defense Weekly'*, Boeing's 'Gravity Research for Advanced Space Propulsion' was still investigating various theories and technologies.

Certainly by the1960s we were starting to develop comparable craft, albeit not so sophisticated or advance as the 'visitors'. In most of the developed countries, hundreds of patents were being lodged for new craft and technologies.

In 1971, a well respected US researcher was visiting a BSRA associate, a Marine sergeant and Vietnam veteran, at Camp Pendleton. He spoke of his time at Edwards Air Force Base, in 1967, when a fighter pilot friend, knowing his interest in UFOs, took him to a hanger, using his uniform and security card to get them both into the upstairs offices. He pulled aside some curtains to the side window, which looked down on a more secure hanger floor.

There was a 30ft saucer-shaped aircraft sitting on high landing gear. It was perfectly circular, with sharp edges sloping up to a domed cockpit area in the centre. It was probably capable of carrying two or three people.

Service personnel were moving around the craft, and they looked like normal human beings, wearing the usual Air Force blue coveralls. His friend said he thought that they were our own saucers, and had often seen these disc-shaped craft operating from specially camouflaged underground hangers at night.

When they parted, the pilot reminded the Marine that nothing was to be said about where they went, or what was seen. If the Marine did divulge anything, he would deny it.

This makes one wonder about a report given to the Toulon police, on October 17th 1954, by local cafe owner Alphonse Rappellini.

'I was motor-cycling between Hyères and Toulon, on the Mediterranean Coast, when I saw a being step out from a disc-shaped saucer. He was dressed in some sort of overalls. I said to him; "Are you from Mars? He said; 'No, French." With me was my engineering friend Monsieur Ottovinni, who will corroborate what I say. The being asked where he was, and when told, made a rapid vertical ascent in his disc.'

Only three weeks later, on November 7th, a taxi driver, Francesco Tanda, and motorcyclist, Gianni Camaboau, gave Sardinian police separate identical reports. A discoid silver saucer, about fifteen feet in diameter, with a turret top, and a 'port' of what looked like thick glass, had landed in a field on the slopes of Mt. Ortowene.

Gianni got such a fright, he fell off his bike. Francesco was a little braver, and got out of his taxi and walked towards the saucer. As he approached, it took off at high speed, emitting a whistle. That same afternoon several witnesses on the other side of the mountain reported seeing a disc in flight.

The military and their design and development corporations are very guarded about their latest developments in aerial technology. Private corporations do not have to account to the public or inquisitive politicians. It can be a couple of decades before we discover that what we thought was a UFO was in fact secretive new technology.

Today we know there is a multitude of exotic craft, mostly of earthly origin, in our skies. The military possess all kinds of 'goodies', including the most sophisticated Stealth bombers and fighter planes, Black Hawke Helicopters, Eurofighter Typhoons, and all manner of circular disc-shaped craft. They boast the latest electronics, and formidable weaponry. Given our accelerated scientific advancement, who knows what the 'US Space Force' and other world powers have up their sleeves?

While I do not dispute what witnesses report or have experienced, one has to ask how much was alien, and how much of very human origin? I suspect that many, (certainly not all), of the strange craft, seen over the last century, were in fact experimental prototypes being tested by one or more of our own foremost nations. Often, years later, when reviewing earlier sightings, they can be explained as products of our own secret research and development.

However, in the 1950s, it is unlikely the majority of saucers seen were of earthly origin. As one researcher pointed out, why didn't we use them to save lives in Korea, and why did we keep building conventional planes and rockets? Why would we risk international antagonism by operating such craft all over the world?

Certainly, in those days high ranking US officials were already documenting their opinions.

In a 1952 memorandum by Air Intelligence Commander Boyd, he wrote; 'The objects sighted may possibly be from another planet...at the present time there is nothing to substantiate this...but the possibility is not being overlooked. Intense research is being carried out by Air Intelligence...The Air Force is attempting, in each instance to send up jet interceptor planes.'

Later that year another memorandum, to the CIA, from H. Caldwell, Assistant Director of Scientific Intelligence, stated; 'Sightings of unexplained objects at great altitude, and travelling at high speeds in the vicinity of major US defence installations, are of such nature that they are not attributable to natural phenomena or known types of aerial vehicles.'

In later years, when Ronald Reagan was President of the USA, he was sent a letter from Justice for Military Personnel, a group comprised of active and retired military and government officers. They were petitioning for full public disclosure of the reality and existence of UFOs, noting that: 'in the interests of national security we all took part in intentionally misleading the nation, manipulating the press, the courts and most politicians.' They did not attempt to define the origin or intent of these craft except to note that we were defenceless against their advanced technology.

Copies of this letter, in its entirety, were sent to the major UFO research organisations and included in some major publications including the '*Simply Living*' magazine. It was comprehensive in both the wrongful acts they had been forced to make, and the dangers to uninformed military and aviation personnel. Obviously the authorities did not wish then, or even now, to make any public disclosure, although it may have prompted some limited briefing to a privileged few.

Some scientists have expressed concern about a possible alien attack on Earth, and in 2006 collaborated on the book '*An Introduction to Planetary Defense – A Study of Warfare Applied to Extra-Terrestrial Invasion.*' The authors – Drs. Taylor, Boan, and Powell are all qualified and respected in the field of space science and technologies. (Why publish this if they did not believe in a possible alien threat?)

Sometimes, without being really sure, we can assume that perhaps what was observed were our own prototypes. In October 1968, several witnesses in Lakeland, Florida, saw a strange disc, thirteen feet wide and eight feet high, hovering above a palm tree near the house. A few days later, on the 1st November, three farmers and the staff of the Philippines Communication

Satellite ground station near Manila, reported seeing a white, low-slung saucer-shaped vehicle landing and taking off nearby.

In both the Florida and Philippines cases the occupants, seen inside the transparent dome of these craft, were described as being Caucasian in appearance and wearing white, tight fitting 'flying suits' with glass-like or plastic headgear – more like human engineers of the day than alien visitors!

The same doubt can be accorded to some crashes at about the same time. Was the debris a downed satellite, one of our own malfunctioning prototypes, or indeed an unfortunate alien who had crashed?

On 3rd August 1967, an object recovered from Sudan in the Middle East was, due to its size and composition, most probably of earthly origin. Maybe the same can be said of four objects which fell in March 1968 in Nepal, although one had a 'nose-cone'.

The Nepalese government requested American assistance in returning them to their country of origin. The US complied, but never advised Nepal as to the identity or origin of the objects. When investigator, Clifford Stone, tried to obtain more information, some twenty-three years later, he was told the matter was classified at a high level, and the Defence Intelligence Agency didn't wish to give out any information regarding that case.

Ben Rich, who was aerospace Skunk Works director from 1975 to 1991 was once reputed as saying; "Some are ours, some are 'theirs', and some are hand-me-downs!" In 1993, during a lecture to his peers, he stated; "Anything you can imagine, we already know how to do."

He had worked on some of the most exotic and technologically advanced covert new craft, but was unable to divulge much due to secrecy obligations. During his lecture he commented that we have the capability to travel to the stars and 'take ET home'. The technologies are locked up in black projects, and 'it would take an act of God to ever get them out to benefit humanity'.

Ben Rich pointed out that to travel faster than the speed of light would require something other than chemical propulsion. He admitted that then, in 1993, theoretical physicists were devising new propulsion technologies.

He died of cancer, approximately three years later. A week before his passing, he made the following comment to Jim Goodall, during a telephone call: "Jim, we have things out in the desert that are fifty years beyond what you could possibly comprehend. If you have seen it on Star Wars or Star Trek, we've been there, done that, or decided it was not worth the effort."

Even by 1965, it was reported that at least forty-six unclassified projects, concerned with anti-gravity, were being undertaken by various agencies in the United States alone. It is logical to assume there was a lot more classified research being undertaken at the same time. Many other countries would also have been experimenting with secret prototypes.

By that time most US 'classified' projects and prototypes were farmed out to private corporations, who were not subject to Congressional oversight or 'Freedom of Information' legislation.

In the February 1987 military magazine, *'Gung-Ho'*, there was an article titled 'Unfunded Opportunities', (UFO), which said;

'As for 'Unfunded Opportunities', these are problems dealing with technology levels so advanced that one Air Force officer involved in the SR-71 development said; "We are flight testing vehicles that defy description. To compare them conceptually to the SR-71 would be like comparing Leonardo da Vinci's parachute design to the space shuttle.

'Other officers are similarly emphatic about the nature of these new systems; "We have things that are so far beyond the comprehension of the average aviation authority as to be really alien to our way of thinking," said one retired Colonel.

'Rumour has it some of these systems involve force-field technology, gravity drive systems and flying saucer designs. Rumour further has it that these designs are not necessarily of Earth human origin – but of who might have designed them or helped us do it, there is less talk.

"Let's just put it this way", explained one retired Lockheed engineer. "We have things flying around in the Nevada desert that would make George Lucas drool."

Many humans prefer to regard our own progress as absurd fantasy, and assume new technology as something impossible or alien. It is often difficult for the average person to comprehend scientific concepts and theories.

Let us go back just one hundred and fifty years. There were no microwaves, radios, CDs, televisions, DVDs, or holograms. The electronic and digital revolution, with its computers, I-Pads, the internet and mobile phones, was unheard of. Most people travelled with a horse and cart or carriage. Aeroplanes, rockets, satellites, radar, lasers and nuclear energy were way in the future, and the medical profession had yet to discover antibiotics, X-Rays, stem cells, DNA and IVF.

Even in more recent years, plasma shields, particle beam weapons, and quantum computers and physics were the province of science fiction. Atomic–resolution microscopes, which can physically image and move atoms, leading to the nanotechnology revolution, is beyond the comprehension of most people. Today, these innovations are a reality.

Until recently, our modern astronomers had not even gained the knowledge our ancient ancestors possessed. Only one hundred years ago nobody would believe that, within a short few decades, we would land on the Moon, send countless probes into outer space, and plan to set up a base on Mars. In fact, in August 1948, the *'Science Digest'* wrote; *'Landing and moving around on the moon offers so many serious problems for human beings that it may take science another two hundred years to lick them.'*

Some years later, in 1956, Dr Richard Wooley, the British Astronomer Royal, demonstrated the official lack of technological vision when he said; "Space travel is utter bilge!" A year later the Russians launched Sputnik I into orbit.

Not to be deterred from his stubborn beliefs, he then pronounced that man would never set foot on the Moon. At that time NASA was already designing the Saturn V rocket which, in 1969, would take Apollo II, along with Armstrong, Collins and Aldrin, to the surface of our rocky companion.

Now, and in the past, these inhibiting beliefs and mindsets seem to be one of the human failings which have often stifled progress. The New Zealand Space Research Group, published an interesting extract from an 1873 Boston Newspaper; *'A man, about 46 years of age, giving the name of Joshua Coppersmith, has been arrested in New York for attempting to extort funds from ignorant and superstitious people, by exhibiting a device which he says will convey the human voice any distance over metallic wires, so it will be heard at the other end.*

'He calls the instrument a telephone, which is obviously intended to imitate the word 'telegraph' and win confidence of those who know of the success of the latter instrument, without understanding the principles on which it is based.

'Well informed people know that it is not possible to transmit the human voice over wires as may be done with dots and dashes and signals of the Morse Code. Even if it were possible to do so, the thing would be of no practical value anyhow.

'The authorities who apprehended this criminal are to be congratulated, and it is hoped that his punishment will be prompt and fitting that it may serve as an example to other schemers of no conscience, who enrich themselves at the expense of their fellow creatures.'

Given the prevailing attitude, it is surprising we made any progress at all!

Pity poor Arnold Kruckman, the newspaper reporter who witnessed the first successful flight of the Wright brothers at Kitty Hawk N.C., in 1903. He was jubilant that he had got the scoop of the new century, and telegraphed his editorial bosses on the *'New York World'*.

He sat back, awaiting the accolades, but when the paper arrived, his story was nowhere to be found. His editors informed him that they didn't publish it because they didn't believe it.

He later became the aeronautical editor for the same paper, and often told his friends at the National Press Club how he missed out on being remembered in the annals of journalistic history.

Due to our own massive technological advances during the twentieth century, only those craft seen during the earlier decades are less likely to be of earthly origin. Often alien craft were silent, where our own made some noise, with jet exhausts or obvious appendages, but this couldn't be taken for granted.

Not all unidentified craft, seen near the end of World War II, originated from the Third Reich or her opponents. In the summer of 1944, an offensive action was occurring in the Loreto and Castelfidaro area of Italy.

Antony Szachnowski, fighting with the Allied Armed Forces, said that at about 10am, in an almost cloudless sky, there suddenly appeared an egg-shaped, metallically glistening, motionless object. Immediately, his Regiment's anti-aircraft guns opened up a barrage of fire. The shells were bursting below the object, and then came a 'Cease Fire' order.

They were astonished to realise the German batteries were also shelling the same object. Apparently both sides thought it was an enemy secret weapon. After a while, the Germans also stopped firing. The object remained motionless for a minute or more, then tilted about fifty degrees, and suddenly shot speedily upwards, disappearing into the blue, Italian skies.

There were other reports which were clearly not the 'Foo Fighter' balls of light. In September 1944, a German pilot in a Messerschmitt jet, encountered a fast moving cylindrical object. It was more than three hundred feet long.

A similar craft had been seen over two years earlier, when Hauptmann Fischer landed at a secret base in Norway. He was asked to go up and identify the intruder, and reported an enormous, streamlined craft, about three hundred feet long, and fifty feet in diameter. It stayed horizontal for a moment, then rose vertically and disappeared at great speed.

Both sides of the War were privately concerned about these objects, and started their own clandestine investigations. Their first thoughts were that it was some form of enemy espionage, but this was obviously not the case.

In 1944, the Luftwaffe set up a centre, known as 'Sonderburo No 13' to collect the data. By the end of hostilities it had an impressive amount of information, but had not reached any definite conclusion.

In 1943, the British, who had already received advice from double agents that the craft were not German, set up an inquiry under Lieutenant General Massey. In 1944 'Project Massey' was officially 'classified'.

Whilst some researchers have suggested that the many UFOs, seen just after World War II, were the results of German or our own prototypes, this hardly seems likely.

To start with, given the number of reports, there would have to be large manufacturing plants turning out these craft. Germany, Italy, Spain and Russia's capabilities were decimated by the war, and Japan was under complete surveillance.

Retired Colonel Hardasty had a slightly different opinion, which he voiced in an article for the *'American Scientific'* in March 1954.

'I am convinced that the Chinese were incapable of producing aircraft such as I observed in Korea. But it was common knowledge that the Russians were engaged in the development of extremely sophisticated aerial hardware during the Korean War.

'My sources, which I am not at liberty to divulge at the moment, have suggested that Russian high-performance aerospace vehicles were in fact already in experimental operation during the Korean conflict, and used to spy on both US operations and those of their own nominal allies.

'What better vehicle could there be for spy missions, than a virtually noiseless, high-speed aircraft equipped with long-range cameras, highly manoeuvrable, and capable of such a rapid rate of climb as to create the illusion of total disappearance when a hasty retreat from ground or aerial observation is necessary.'

There are many cases where strange craft may not have been extraterrestrial, however any possible secret prototypes would be precious, and few and far between. No country would risk flying them in large numbers over their own or enemy territory.

CHAPTER TWO

OURS OR THEIRS?

PART TWO

Strange, unidentified craft, and their occupants, have been seen all over the world. Were they theirs or ours?

AUSTRALIA

In Australia, 'Way out West' is getting into 'frontier territory', an enormous area - sparsely populated and arid, with fearsome dry summers. It is an ideal, isolated region to test all manner of secret 'prototypes', and extends from South and Western Australia into similar terrain in New South Wales, Queensland and the Northern Territory.

One would think that if we did have experimental prototype testing grounds in Australia, there were bound to be some accidents or crashes. Unfortunately, there is scant information in this regard.

In *'Contact Down Under'*, I have mentioned a few vague reports, but nothing really substantial. Another researcher mentioned hearing about a case from June or July in 1947, when an unidentified object supposedly crashed in a cane field. It came to rest after cutting a long path through the cane. It was reported that a week later, the object was apparently taken away by an American warship.

In 1989, another witness, from Hervey Bay in central Queensland, told me that an old guy, who was passing through, said that some sort of a UFO had crashed into the side of a mountain, about twenty miles away; "A lot of 'armed forces fellows' appeared, and no-one was allowed within five miles of the area."

Also, again in Queensland, a Maryborough couple endured a very unpleasant experience in June 1980. Around 1am, a large, silvery-glowing object silently sped towards the earth, and, illuminating the whole area, crashed in a bright explosion on their isolated paddock.

Early the next morning, two plain-clothes 'officers' knocked on their door, and they were told that the 'explosion' was nothing more than a large meteorite.

For their 'safety' they were to take a change of clothes and toiletries, and would be moved to another unspecified location until a search was completed.

A van took them to an isolated property in Gympie, where they remained for two days under the watchful eyes of several men, who were introduced as being 'officers' of an unnamed Government organisation.

Before they had left, they saw at least a dozen overall-clad 'workmen', with metal detectors, or Geiger-counters, swarming over their property. After two days they were returned home, and told to forget about the affair, and tell no-one about it. They would later, under pressure, sell the property, and move elsewhere.

Eyewitnesses who had seen the object come crashing down, advised the media. Initial radio reports were quickly silenced, and after publishing it as 'front page news', the local newspaper had to replace it with another story.

The Alice Springs' *'Centralian Advocate'*, 5th February 1954, published a report and sketch from a man who had been photographing Mount Gillen on 15th January. An enormous round-looking craft had suddenly appeared from behind Gillen. It appeared to be silent, and about 150ft in diameter.

He said it went high, then dropped quite low between the mountain and the town. It was moving very slowly, almost hovering at one stage, and that is when he took a photo. Before he could get any more shots, the saucer moved off very fast, and gaining speed moved high in the sky in a westerly direction.

The newspaper had already received reports from several other witnesses who had seen a fast object streaking overhead at the same time. The 'Advocate' could not persuade the witness to part with his photograph, and I can understand his reluctance, given later instances of the authorities confiscating photos.

That same year, three young men were driving near the West Australian border when they photographed a UFO which was pacing their vehicle. Shortly after, a RAAF light aircraft suddenly landed nearby. Two officers emerged and asked if they could 'borrow' the film. It was never returned.

WOOMERA - SA

Woomera is situated in the desert to the north of the Nullabor Plain, and adjacent to the Maralinga nuclear testing range. Originally, Woomera's Prohibited Area covered 270,000 square miles. Later it was reduced to 127,000 square miles. It was, and still is, an ideal place for all manner of both public and secret projects.

During September and October 1957, three atomic weapons were tested at Maralinga. Much of this is still a 'Commonwealth Prohibited Area'. Photographer, Derek Murray, reported that about one month after the tests, a silver-blue, metallic, flat –based, domed-saucer was seen silently hovering over the area. It had portholes or windows of some sort, and remained there for fifteen minutes before speeding up and away at a fantastic speed.

The Woomera Base was always a top secret facility where the military tested rockets, missiles, bombs and all kinds of classified 'goodies'. On 3rd February 1997, *'The Daily Telegraph'* reported that a US company was proposing a 15-18yr program which involved launching a series of low-cost, low-Earth orbit, reusable communication satellites. The plan included stages of the rocket falling back to earth cushioned by airbags.

There were many reports of 'bogies', (unauthorised air traffic), some of which I detailed in *'Contact Down Under'*. Needless to say, the official 'findings' were nearly always a conventional explanation, no matter how improbable.

Obviously, in the past, personnel and civilians associated with the Base were not satisfied with the government 'whitewash'. What was most significant was that a Woomera UFO group had been formed in the 1960s called the 'Scientific, Technical and Astronomical Research Society', (STARS). The 'powers to be' were not happy when they received reports completed on 'STARS' forms, rather than official documentation. Senior personnel actively discouraged the 'UFO Club', and its activities gradually dwindled out by 1974.

Other military personnel were also seeing 'unauthorised' craft in the sky. Often their senior officers actively attempted to dissuade or discredit their reports. I would never have known of this following incident had I not been at a government training college in the 1980s, and one of the witnesses, a fellow student, confided in me.

"I was with another Army serviceman, on patrol duty at Woomera in the 1960s. As we drove along the perimeters, making a routine security check, we spotted a large cigar shape object, hovering over the electrical cables. It was making a strange noise, and I got the impression it was drawing power from the lines. My hair stood on end, as if there was a strange magnetism in the air. In fact, as I am talking to you, the hair on the back of my neck is standing on end, just like it did that day".

Upon their return to base, they were subjected to three days of interrogation, and less than subtle intimidation; "At first they suggested we had been drinking, but once we proved our sobriety, they changed their tactics and said we must have been mistaken, and should withdraw our reports. We remained adamant in our testimony until eventually the Base Commander released us back to normal duty. He warned us never to discuss the matter with anyone again."

Australian researcher, Debbie Payne, wrote about a clandestine meeting she had with a man, 'Bob', who was a Department of Defence employee. His duty was also to patrol the Woomera perimeter fences, and do guard duty, mostly at night.

It was a clear night when he and a RAAF officer were out in the utility, and stopped to have a cigarette. They saw four gold balls of light, two coming from one direction, and two from the other. They were near the G-range, where the Japanese had their telescopes.

The objects converged, at a central point near the ground, then shot up straight into the sky before taking on a silvery appearance. 'Bob', who had only been at Woomera for a short time, was fascinated. The Air Force officer didn't seem to be concerned, and said they could be 'ours' or 'theirs' – who knew!

These 'spheres' appeared regularly for about three weeks. Mostly they were yellow/orange balls of light, which sometimes had beams of light emanating from them. Other objects were seen travelling at incredible speed, and sometimes lights would circle and hover over the base buildings. Locals also complained about them 'becoming a pest' and how one nearly ran a truck off the road.

One night they followed 'Bob' home, and on another occasion, as he was crossing the golf course, he was confronted by a silver disc, low to the ground. It was about four-and-a-half metres long, and two metres high, with a row of pulsating rectangular lights at the centre, and a bank of yellow lights that rose out of the top of the craft. When 'Bob' started asking questions, he was warned about discussing it any further.

At that time there were other strange sightings in the vast outback. Were these objects 'aliens' or our own prototypes? The *'Daily News'*, February 9th 1968, contained a report from police constable George Pike and the witness, Peter Stephens.

At 10am Peter was out on his tractor, ploughing a field at Koorda. Suddenly his dog took off, and Peter saw an orange-red circular object, moving just above the ground, less than 600 yards away. It was about five feet high, and didn't have any visible lights, windows or portholes.

The strange craft was travelling at about 25 to 30 mph, and disappeared in a south-westerly direction over a neighbour's property. Although the neighbour, D. MacQuarie, did not see the object, he noted that at the same time, his dogs surprisingly refused to accompany the workmen on a trip to check the water points.

FAR WEST OF NSW

Broken Hill, a major 'outback city was created from an 'artificial oasis', and is basically a 'mining town'. Wilcannia – 'just down the road' by Australian standards – is also close to the opal-fields at White Cliffs and was once a key inland river-port in the days of paddle steamers. The areas all around Broken Hill, Wilcannia and other nearby districts, are relatively close to the border with South Australia and possible testing grounds for all manner of 'things unknown'.

One sighting, unlikely to be a prototype, was recounted to my colleague, Rex Gilroy, by Mr 'Snowy' Collins and his wife. On 17th November 1929, they were camped in a paddock, just outside the western town of Gilgandra. They awoke to discover a strange 'round, oval structure' resting in a nearby paddock.

After a while, it emitted a loud rushing sound, and slowly began to rise into the air. It began to fly horizontally over the fields, before picking up speed and 'zooming away at a tremendous pace'.

We cannot be sure as to the origin of another saucer sighted, one night, by a soldier at Wagga Wagga Army Camp in 1950. He was on guard duty at the gate, when a large, circular craft, with flashing lights around its centre, descended and hovered silently, just above him.

He ran to the guardhouse, and raised the alarm. At least two other soldiers rushed out, and they all watched as the craft rose swiftly into the sky and flew off.

In February 1951, members of the Central Australian Unmatjera Aboriginal tribe saw two shiny circular objects, about nine to fifteen metres in diameter, landed on the ground. A very small man-like being, in a shiny suit, was seen to transfer from one object to the other. Both craft then made a buzzing sound and took off.

On 2nd February 1954, the Sydney *'Daily Telegraph'* reported that an aboriginal drover, at Todd River Downs, was 'blown-off' his horse when a spherical object, emitting smoke, had passed overhead, leaving both horse and rider terrified.

Artist Pro Hart, along with some friends, watched four or five dish shaped objects fly over a dry lake bed at Wilcannia in 1968. Both he and a colleague took photos. His mate was silly enough to show it to RAAF officers, who promptly 'confiscated' it for security reasons, something they had done with quite a few UFO photos taken in the area. Pro Hart had lost his, but he had studied it closely, and was able to paint his 'Saucerscape' art-work from memory, and committed the sighting to canvas. He later donated the painting to the tourist information centre as it was getting too much attention in his Broken Hill gallery.

Pro Hart later told journalist Gregg Ker; "Several years before, when I was an army corporal at the Broken Hill camp, I, along with several soldiers, saw several unidentified objects fly over. They did a U-turn over the drive-in, where some people blew their horns, and then went back over the town. They weren't rockets – no wings.

"They follow cars, my sister used to cop it. It's a bit frightening. **I don't believe they are extraterrestrial, rather they are secret surveillance flights by aircraft so sophisticated our governments won't tell us about them."**

Of course the RAAF and Woomera denied all knowledge and responsibility, and the local police, although they received sighting reports 'from time to time' said there was no evidence of secret aircraft on clandestine missions.

It certainly is apparent that the authorities wanted to keep some incidents 'under wraps' in the years following World War II. One cannot discount their paranoia, in confiscating all photographic evidence, as an indication they may have been testing a new prototype 'saucer'.

(This was also happening in the US. On July 7th 1947, William Rhodes, a free-lance scientist, took two photos of a 'flying saucer', which were subsequently published by the local Arizona *'Republic'* newspaper. A week later, he was visited by two FBI agents and an intelligence officer from Hamilton Field, California.

At that time the public were not aware of the Roswell incident, and Rhodes willingly gave them the photos, which the 'authorities' later refused to return.)

'The Australian Saucer Record', (Vol3-P13), reported a case in Eucla WA on 3rd April 1954, when three young men were followed for 80kms by a saucer shape object with portholes. They had five cameras and took ninety-two pictures before reporting the incident to local police. The 'authorities' took their cameras and returned them – minus all film.

Only six days later, on the 9th April, between 8am and 9am, several reports were received from Kapunda, Winkie and Kilburn in South Australia. Witnesses included a school teacher, children and several residents. All had seen a round, silver disc, with a 'circle of lights around it'. It was originally seen travelling silently to the north, but then came down low, travelling very fast, and making a tremendous roar as it passed overhead. Finally, other witnesses watched it in the sky for about five minutes. It then turned sharply on its side and disappeared.

A senior police officer told me of an elderly country lady – now deceased – who saw a traditional 'flying saucer', during daylight hours, near Wilcannia, in Western NSW, in the 1940s, just after WW II. She claimed that after reporting the sighting to the 'authorities', she received a letter from the Air Force confirming the report, and warning her not to tell anyone about the craft. The police officer attested to having seen the letter, which appeared to be genuine.

In 1953, John and Kevin were driving on the road leading into Wilcannia, when they suddenly became aware that something was hovering above them.

"We got quite a start." John said, "We were travelling in an open jeep and looked up. We were astounded to see a 20ft saucer type craft directly above our heads! The hull appeared to be metallic, like satin finish stainless steel. We could see, from an angle, that there was a turret with round portholes on top, and four "ball-like" objects suspended underneath.

"We pulled up and jumped out. It was still motionless, and Kevin was able to photograph it. Maybe it knew what we were doing –I don't know – but suddenly it streaked off across the sky at unbelievable speed and was out of sight within about three seconds"

When the roll of film was developed it showed a really clear image of the strange object they saw. Kevin was so excited he wrote to the Army about the incident, but never received a reply. He then, in hindsight, made the 'mistake' of sending a second letter to the RAAF. Without warning he received a visit from an Air Force officer, who promptly confiscated the film, leaving Kevin with only one print.

Another resident of Broken Hill had also seen a very similar object in daylight hours. He had drawn a sketch which John confirmed as being almost identical to the saucer he and Kevin had seen.

A husband and wife were also near Wilcannia in 1956 when they saw an object like the ones reported in 1953. It was hovering stationary in the sky. The witness grabbed his box camera, and despite his shaking hands and the low shutter speed, the snaps developed quite well, albeit not very clear.

The couple also received a visit from an RAAF officer who confiscated both the negatives and the prints. Country folks are not silly! They had heard what happened to Kevin's photos, and did not tell the Air Force they had a second film. They kept it a secret for ten years before allowing the press to publish it.

Another case is very interesting if considered along with our 1953 and 1956 reports - *'Disclosure Australia'* unearthed an interesting case from the Department of Civil Aviation files. Mr. Keith Weston of Mena Murtee Station, eighteen miles NW of Wilcannia, claimed that in late 1954 he saw a large, saucer shaped object, and took three photographs which were developed at the homestead.

He claimed the object, which was three hundred feet across, came from the direction of Netalia Station, hovered over the woolshed at an altitude of about 500ft, and departed with a loud clanking/explosion sound.

The matter was investigated by DCA, however a couple of weeks later an internal memo, dated the tenth of November, was placed on the file claiming – 'a Mrs Weston, asks your department to drop the matter, as is it a faked snapshot, which was taken to have a joke with someone in Wilcannia, and the matter has gone too far.'

However, adding a little mystery and speculation to this report, is a further internal memo, some two weeks later, dated 23rd November, from their head office .- 'If the photographs are genuine, they will be of considerable interest, and a request has been received from American 'Service' source for copies.' Now why was it a Mrs Weston who wanted to drop the matter, and not Keith? Was she being truthful, and what did she mean by it had 'gone too far'? If there was no 'pressure' on her, and they had been 'faked' as claimed, why were they still considered genuine, and why did the Americans want them?

After a few years, many residents were hesitant to speak out.

AUSTRALIAN HIGHWAY CHASE

Eddy was a 76 year old grandfather, and a respected citizen of his country town in Western NSW, when he contacted us following an interview we had on his local regional radio station.

It was about 8.30pm on a pleasant Saturday evening in 1959. Eddy was only twenty, and he was driving down the Cobb Highway from Ivanhoe to Wilcannia, in Western N.S.W.

"I was about forty miles from Wilcannia when, suddenly, through the open window of my 'ute', I saw a light ahead at the right hand side of the road. As I approached, I was astonished to see a strange craft on the ground, near the telegraph lines. It was round, about thirty feet long and twenty feet in diameter, and was supported by short, two feet, legs. It was a silver colour, with at least four brightly lit portholes, with rounded corners, down the side.

"As I neared this thing, it rose about six feet above the ground and hovered motionless. A multitude of sparks was spurting from the base to the ground. I recall being amazed that they did not ignite the dry grass underneath."

Fear overcame curiosity, and Eddy decided to "get the hell out of there", but when he tried to accelerate, his vehicle would not respond. Terrified he continued slowly down the highway with the object following by his side.

"It was as if it had some magnetic hold on my 'ute'," he recalled. The nightmare continued for the next half mile, when suddenly the object broke away and sped off to the horizon. Once the strange craft had departed, Eddy regained complete control of his vehicle and sped into Wilcannia, still in a state of shock.

"My mates wouldn't believe me, and said I must have been drinking before I left Ivanhoe. I insisted I 'hadn't touched a drop' but they still laughed despite the fact that other Wilcannia residents had reported a strange daylight object only a few hours earlier."

When Eddy returned home on Sunday, he was sure his relatives would be more supportive; "Maybe they were scared of unwanted attention from the authorities, but they refused to listen to me, and insisted that I mention it to no-one, saying it would give people a bad impression of me, and could relate unfavourably on other members of the family."

Eddy commented to me; -"It's a long time to remain silent about something like this, but now I'm older, and I feel I have, at last, found someone who may believe me."

BROKEN HILL 1962

Bryson Brown was only sixteen years old when he and a mate had just left Broken Hill to drive to Menindee.

"We saw this unusual object hovering beside the road, and stopped to look. It didn't make any noise, but we could hear a very slight 'whistling' sound. It was disc shaped – a purple/green colour. It was rather creepy. My friend said he had seen the same thing another night, and we should get out of there. It didn't take me long to understand why he was nervous, - that damn 'disc' followed us for nearly seventy miles!"

In October, the same year, Ellen Sylvester, a high school teacher, was travelling with her three children, across the border in South Australia, near Adelaide. It was dusk, and her nine year-old son drew her attention to an unusual object landed on a level area nearby.

It was reflecting the light of the setting sun, oval in shape, with windows all around. There was a light around the rim, and it was standing on three legs. The children said they could see someone inside.

It was like no plane they had ever seen before, so they stopped, and curiously watched for about forty minutes. After a while, a man got out, coming down some steps to the ground. He was about six feet tall, and was wearing a type of helmet.

He spent some considerable time 'working' on one of the objects' 'legs', as if he was having difficulties getting it to retract. Eventually, he seemed to have had some success, and returned to the craft, which started to move slowly up and away. It then picked up speed, and then disappeared, 'incredibly fast', in a northerly direction.

Researcher Colin Norris tape-recorded a detailed interview he later conducted with the entire family.

In the mid-1970s Jill and Derek, friends of mine, were driving south, with their two children, through the isolated area of Springs Creek, heading towards Broken Hill. He was an expert witness, having worked as a nuclear physicist for thirty years, and not quick to put his reputation on the line to pronounce something an 'unidentified object'.

"At 3pm - (I checked my watch) – we saw this object, motionless to the left and just above the top of a clump of trees about one km away. It was a 'fat' grey cigar shape, about fifty metres across – it could have been a saucer on edge. It had red, yellow and green pulsating lights at the right end. I got my wife, son and daughter to verify what I was seeing, as their long distance vision is better than mine.

"I stopped the car, got out and took a photo with my 35mm SLR camera. Using the car odometer as an accurate measure, I drove point two of a kilometre down the straight road. I stopped and took another photo using the car roof as a steady, the idea being that with trigonometry, I could work out the angles, distances and thus the size of the object. (There was no discernible noise.)

"It was as clear as could be, sharply defined edges, and we watched for thirty minutes until suddenly, 'like a switch' it was gone. It was a clear sunny day, and I was quite excited at the photos I had taken – they should be good! As soon as we got home, on the north coast, I put them into the photo processing agent in town, where they were on-forwarded to the main laboratory.

"A week later I eagerly picked them up to find the photographs of the object were missing. Two frames had been removed from the cut film sections and replaced with blank frames. Microscopic examinations showed the edges did not match at all!"

This was the same notorious company that was responsible for all the other instances of negatives being removed from films and photographs. When asked on his 'report form' if there was any photographic evidence, Derek wrote ; 'Yes – the Government has it!'

Perhaps an incident on August 24th 1967, cannot be so easily attributed to our own prototypes. Peter Norris, from VFSRS interviewed the witness from this unusual encounter.

'Mr Hunter' was travelling from Sydney to Melbourne on his motorbike, when an intense, bluish-white light, came from above and nearly blinded him. He stopped and took off his goggles. About 100ft away, on a grass clearing, sloping gently down from the road, was a metallic object hovering a couple of feet off the ground.

It resembled two saucers, one inverted over the other, and was about thirty feet wide and fifteen feet high. The bottom half was mostly a dark grey colour, and the upper half, which had a small dome on the top, resembled a highly polished chrome.

He looked away, and when he returned his gaze to the craft, he was startled to see two figures standing beside it. They were about five feet tall, and wearing opaque helmets and silvery overalls, which covered both their hands and feet. 'Hunter' took a couple of steps forward, and the beings responded by doing the same.

When one of the 'men' raised his arms and beckoned, 'Hunter' took fright, and jumped on his motorbike. As he sped off down the road, he heard a faint hum. Looking up, he could see the object, surrounded by a pink glow, following him at an estimated height of about 100 to 200 feet.

The area was remote, with no other cars or farmhouses in sight, but he nervously pulled up at the side of the road again. The object then tilted at a 45 degree angle, changed colour to a deep red, and shot up into the air, disappearing at tremendous speed.

In Australia's vast outback, there are some incidents which are most likely 'alien'. My friend and colleague, Glennys McKay, referred to a 1999 Queensland case in a 2001 email.

'The Min Min lights we experienced two years ago, while travelling from Mt Isa toward Boulia - we were followed for some distance. When we stopped the lights seemed to stop, they were about the level of the top of our motor-home. When we stopped at Mitchelton, they stopped over the windmill, and were stationary for some time before going out.

'We had a police friend stationed out that way, and two of them were investigating cattle duffing on an outer station when they were followed. The lights kept about ten feet away as they rode their horses. I was told the locals just take them in their stride.

'Having spoken to some Aboriginal elders at Dejarra, I was told about an abduction many years ago, when an eight-year-old girl was taken from the river bank. It was witnessed by the family and those sitting around. The girl was returned seven days later. This turned into a police case, as they felt at the time there was foul play.

They told the police she was taken by the 'little people', with big heads, that often visit late at night. It sure is an interesting place way out west!'

Sometimes it is the normal 'human-type' behaviour of UFO occupants which makes us wonder as to the origin of strange craft and their occupants. Timothy Good discussed this incident which occurred at Guyancourt, twenty kilometres from Paris, France, in July 1950.

Claude Blondeau was about to go inside, to retire for the night, when he saw two greyish discs hovering above the ground twenty metres away. A thick, oval hatch opened at the bottom of each one, and two 'men', of average height, emerged. They had no 'headgear', and were wearing dark blue or brown flying-suits. Using their 'bare hands' and no tools, they appeared to be replacing a number of 'plates' on the underside of each disc.

Claude approached them, and asked if they had to make a forced landing? One replied, in rather halting French; "Yes, but not for long."

Claude peeked through one open hatch, and got a brief view of the interior of a round cabin with a control column and several panels around a central chair. He asked what the various apparatus was for, and got the curt answer – "Energy' – before the two men jumped back into their respective discs and closed the hatches.

The entire incident had only taken a couple of minutes. The rectangular portholes became luminous, and the two discs tilted on end before accelerating upwards at a very high speed.

DOROTHY KILGALLEN

Dorothy Kilgallen, a well known American journalist, had more than a passing interest in UFOs. On 15th February 1954, her syndicated column stated; *'Flying saucers are regarded of such vital importance that they will be the subject of a special hush-hush meeting of the world's military heads next summer.'*

When in the UK, she sent the following cable to an International News Service;

22nd May 1955; *'I can report today on a story which is positively spooky, not to mention chilling. British scientists and airmen, after examining the wreckage of one mysterious flying ship, are convinced these strange aerial objects are not optical illusions or Soviet inventions, but are flying saucers which originate on another planet.*

'The source of my information is a British official of Cabinet rank, who prefers to remain unidentified; "We believe, on the basis of our inquiry thus far, that the saucers were staffed by small men – probably under four feet tall. It's frightening, but there is no denying the flying saucers come from another planet."

'The official quoted scientists as saying a flying ship of this type could not have possibly been constructed on Earth. The British Government, I learned, is withholding an official report on the 'flying saucer' examination at this time, possibly because it does not want to frighten the public.

'When my husband and I arrived here for a short vacation, I had no premonition that I would be catapulting myself into the controversy over whether flying saucers are real or imaginary...

'In the U.S. all kinds of explanations have been advanced, but no responsible official of the U.S. Air Force has as yet intimated the mysterious flying ships had actually vaulted from outer space.'

We will never know who her confidant was, or to which incident she was referring. Dorothy Kilgallen had reported on many controversial political subjects, and she died, from a suspicious 'overdose', not long after.

Gordon Creighton, one of Britain's most respected investigators, believed her informant was Lord Mountbatten, whom she met at a cocktail party. He was certainly interested in the subject, and was once advised by a groundsman that a strange object had landed on his estate early one morning.

In 1996, British researcher Jenny Randles suggested that the following crash retrieval may have been the basis for the information Dorothy Kilgallen received.

In the summer of 1952, the *'Zeitung'* newspaper reported that Norwegian jets, on exercise over Spitzbergen, spotted a large metallic disc which was badly damaged, and had obviously crashed in the snow. That evening several ski-fitted flying boats located the wreckage, and landed on the icy waters near it.

The 125ft diameter, silver coloured metallic craft, which was buried in the snow and ice, was emitting radioactive frequencies of 934 Hertz. It was constructed from an unknown thin, but extremely strong, lightweight, metallic material and appeared to have been powered by a ring of forty-six jets on the outer rim.

A 'plexiglass' domed compartment in the centre contained a mass of remote controlled equipment. The disc was dismantled and taken to Narvik for examination by the experts.

Foreign symbols on the inside of the device were at first mistakenly thought to be Russian. Perhaps this was a Soviet prototype? Later examination proved that this was not the case. Head of the inquiry, Colonel Gernod Darnhyl stated that the disc 'had not been built by any country on earth'. The 'official' line was that the 'symbols' were Russian, and that it had come from the Soviet Union, crashing due to 'receiver failure'.

Darnhyl noted that the British and Americans were involved in the investigation, and it was reported that parts of the craft had been sent to Britain for further analysis. Unconfirmed reports stated that small burned bodies had been found in the wreckage.

In 1994 Gordon Creighton published an article by respected researcher, and former Jesuit priest, Salvador Freixedo. It discussed contacts between US Presidents and aliens, and while I don't intend to reproduce it all here, there was one section which outlined an event I had never heard of before.

The Americans also had a habit of obscuring the facts and evidence when it came to sighting reports. One can never be sure whether a craft was of earthly or alien origin. One such report only came to light after 'Project Blue Book' closed in 1969.

Just after dawn, on 23rd November 1957, a US Air Force Lieutenant, whose name was withheld, was driving near Tonopah, Nevada, when his car engine cut-out. He could hear a high pitch whining sound, and got out of his vehicle to see four silver shaped objects sitting on the desert about nine-hundred feet away.

Each one was about fifty feet in diameter and ten feet high, with smaller transparent domes, and a dark band rotating around the rim. The officer approached the craft, but when he was about fifty feet away, they emitted an unbearably loud whining sound and lifted off the ground, disappearing behind some hills. Each object had left three small marks on the ground, which corresponded with the 'landing gear' the witness had observed.

When the Blue Book file was finally released the explanation given was 'psychological factors'. Attached to the report was a handwritten memo, obviously written by Blue Book staff in 1957; *'The damage and embarrassment to the USAF would be incalculable if this officer allied himself to the host of 'flying saucer' writers who provide the Air Force with countless charges and accusations. In this instance the USAF would have no effective rebuttal or evidence to disprove any unfounded charges.'*

Wilbur (Wilbert) Smith, an electrical engineer, was initiator and head of Canada's unofficial 'Project Magnet' from 1950-54. One of his ambitions was to harness the energy of the Earth's magnetic field. The aim of this study was to learn as much as possible about UFOs and use this data to duplicate their performance.

The extent of his scientific research and findings was far more detailed than many realised. An in-depth analysis can be found in Major Donald Keyhoe's book *'Flying Saucers from Outer Space'*.

Wilbur also elaborated on some of the reasons for his research; *"When we do get all the answers, it will be a tremendous thing – and we'd better get them before Russia does. Magnetically powered discs would be terrible weapons. Their range would be unlimited, and their speeds would be far beyond anything we've even dared hope for. They'd make perfect guided missiles, and they could easily carry A-bomb warheads – perhaps even the H-bomb, when we get it.'*

Wilbur had already learned, from a meeting between Canadian scientists and engineers with an American physicist in Washington, that flying saucers certainly existed. In 1961 he commented: "I showed to Admiral Knowles (US Navy, Ret.) the small piece of a flying saucer which the USAF kindly loaned me for examination. That was July of 1952." He was instructed not to return it to the USAF, instead it went to 'a highly classified group'.

While Wilbur was unable to ascertain that these saucers operated on 'magnetic principles', he did get confirmation that scientists had not been able to duplicate their performance, and they did not originate on this planet.

Wilbur was certainly knowledgeable enough to identify most aeronautics developed on Earth. In July 1960, his group recovered a much larger mass, about three thousand pounds, of unidentified metal. He did not say where this sample had come from, or how it was obtained.

'We have done a tremendous amount of detective work on this metal...We have something that was not brought to this Earth by plane, nor by boat, nor by any

helicopter. We are speculating that what we have is a portion of a very large device which came into this Solar System – we don't know when – but it had been in space a long time before it came to Earth; we can tell that by the micrometeorites embedded in the surface...We have it, but we don't know what it is.'

Until his premature death in 1962, when Wilbur was working on an anti-gravity device, he struggled to define the nature and technology of UFOs. My colleague, Rosemary Decker, was also friends with Wilbur Smith. Rosemary helped by providing contact and liaison with witnesses and contactees, who provided many valuable observations, insights and information. She said Wilbur did not admit to any direct contact with the Visitors, but Rosemary suggested some had occurred. He confirmed being involved with others in mind-to-mind telepathic communications, and also spread a similar message as that given to Adamski by Orthon.

In a lecture given in Ottawa, Canada, on 31st March 1958, Wilbert Smith explained how, over his years of investigation, his attitude and beliefs had changed from that of a sceptic scientist, to a new understanding of life and the universe.

'It soon became apparent that there was a very, and quite large, gap between this alien science and the science in which I had been trained....There followed a period of soul searching in which many doubts were raised...The inevitable conclusion was that it was all real enough, that the alien science was definitely alien, and possible even forever beyond our comprehension......

'The science which has been passed to us by these people from elsewhere, explains in a manner in which we have been quite unable to do, why the saucers behave as they do, and how it is that they can do things which to us are virtually impossible. The science and the performance check perfectly. Again we have been told where our scientific ideas are wrong or inadequate. Experiments have been suggested and carried out, and in every case the alien science has been vindicated.

'So another approach was also tried – the philosophical – and here the answer was found in all its grandeur. I will not go into details on the many revisions in ideas and basic thinking beyond stating that the people from outside displayed great patience and understanding in overcoming the prejudices and misinformation I had spent many years accumulating.

'I began, for the first time in my life, to realise the basic ONENESS of the Universe and all that is in it – science, philosophy, religion, substance, energy are all facets of the same jewel, and before any one facet can be appreciated, the form of the jewel itself must be perceived.'

Wilbur's address was quite lengthy, and very profound and moving. He went into lengthy explanations of the alien philosophies and science. He also noted how the visitors wished to help and guide us, but could not interfere in our affairs.

In the 1950s, unusual craft were being seen all over the world.

EAST GERMANY

In 1952, Oscar Linke, the former mayor of Gleimershausen, and his daughter, eleven year-old Gabriella, were going home when the tyre on his motorcycle blew out near Hasselbach. They were pushing the motorbike, and walking towards the town, when Gabriella spotted something on the ground, about 140 metres away. Oscar thought it might be a young deer, but when he drew near, he realised it was two men, stooping over something.

They were wearing some form of shiny metallic clothing, and one had a lamp on the front part of his body, which lit up at regular intervals. Oscar crept closer, and looked over a small fence to see a large object resting on the ground. He said it looked like a huge metal frying pan, about fifteen metres in diameter. There were two rows of holes on its periphery, and on the top was a black conical tower, about three metres high.

Oscar said; "At that moment, my daughter, who had remained a short distance behind, called me. The two men must have heard her voice because they immediately jumped on the conical tower and disappeared inside.

"Now, the side of the object, on which the holes had been opened, began to glitter. Its colour seemed green, but later turned to red. At the same time I heard a slight hum. While the brightness and hum increased, the conical tower began to slide down into the centre of the object, which then began to rise slowly from the ground and rotate like a top."

He thought the cylindrical plant (conical tower) had gone down from the top of the object, through the centre, and now appeared from its bottom, on the ground. The craft was surrounded by a ring of flames, and when it rose a few feet, the 'cylinder' disappeared back into the centre and came back out the top.

"The rate of climb had now become greater. At the same time my daughter and I heard a whistling sound.....and the object rose to a horizontal position, turned towards a neighbouring town, and then, gaining altitude, it disappeared to the north, over the forests in the direction of Stockheim.

"I would have thought that both my daughter and I were dreaming if it were not for the following element involved. When the object had disappeared, I went to the place where it had been. I found a circular opening in the ground, and it was quite evident it was freshly dug. It was exactly the same shape as the conical tower."

Many other local people also related seeing the object, and a nearby shepherd had thought he was looking at a 'comet', moving away at a low altitude from where Oscar and Gabriella had been standing.

Oscar was afraid he and his daughter had seen something which may have been a new classified government prototype, and he was scared that the Soviet secret police would seek him out and arrest him. After escaping from East Germany, along with his wife and six children, Oscar and his daughter made sworn statements to West Berlin intelligence officers, who allowed the family to stay in the American Zone.

They passed the information on to the CIA, where it remained classified for many years before the file was released. Although this incident occurred in approximately 1952, perhaps the authorities were concerned that the Russians had already developed some new flying contraption of military significance.

This possibility was certainly given further consideration when Georgia Senator, Richard Russell, reported what he had seen when travelling through the Soviet Union in 1955.

On the evening of October 4th, he was with his Aide, Colonel Hathaway, and another companion, on a train in the Transcaucasia region. Through the window he noticed a large, yellowish-colour, disc-shaped object, about thirty feet in diameter, slowly ascending as a flame shot from underneath it. The craft had two lights on the top portion, which remained stationary while the outer section seemed to spin. The craft raced north, in front of the train, crossing over the tracks ahead.

A second disc then appeared, following the same path as the first. A railway employee rushed into their compartment, shut the curtains, and ordered everybody not to look outside. As soon as they arrived in Prague, the three witnesses went to the United States embassy and reported it to the air attaché. The report was not declassified until 1985.

SCOTLAND

Most British ufologists are well aware that our own new prototypes were being tested in remote areas of the country, but just how advanced were they in mid-1955?

One night, about 7.30pm, Maurice Brazier, a mechanic with the Scottish Forestry Commission, was driving along a bleak, desolate road near Balmaclellan. He saw a light on the hillside and at first assumed it was an oncoming car. Then, realising it was a large, illuminated airborne object, thought it must be a mountain rescue helicopter unit.

It was neither of these. As it came closer, Brazier was astonished that the craft was about sixty feet long, elliptical in shape, with bluish lights along the side. He had seen wartime service in the R.A.F., and knew this was no conventional plane.

He was scared, but stopped his van and jumped out. The UFO was at an altitude of no more than forty feet, and when it was twenty yards away from him, it banked to his left. He was then able to see that it had the appearance of a huge, double saucer, with lights along the outer rim which revolved clockwise.

He notified the local police, who only started to believe him after they were convinced he was sane and sober. Since then, there have been other reports of mysterious craft in the area.

NEW ZEALAND

In *'Contact Down Under'* and *'The Alien Gene'*, I wrote about UFOs and alien activity in New Zealand, especially in the 1950s and 60s.

In March 1960 Mrs. N. was lying in bed which was close to the window at the front of her house, twenty miles down the Wairau Valley. At about 11.30pm, glow of green light seemed to come from behind her home, and within a short time it lit up the entire bedroom. She got up, looked through the window, and was astounded to see an object over the house, and slightly to one side.

It was a large, circular shaped disc, made of silvery metal, and about thirty-five feet in diameter. At the centre was a 'sort of glowing canopy', with a diameter of about ten feet, and shining a strong blue-green light. It was travelling slowly and silently, at about thirty miles per hour.

Mrs N. watched in amazement. The craft came within fifty feet of her window, level with the tops of some young pine trees, which were only about thirty feet high.

What was unusual about this sighting was that the object was travelling on edge, and looked like a huge coin rolling on its rim, slowly revolving in the direction of its travel. It slowly passed out of sight, over a nearby hill, and the glow finally receded.

Apparently the strange craft left no traces behind, the animals did not appear to be affected, and there were no scorch marks on the ground. Mrs N. was not really interested in UFOs, and thinking people would treat it as a joke, it was only by chance she mentioned it to one of the researchers.

By 1972, it was more probable that some craft were of earthly origin. One clear July night that year, a woman in Lower Hutt, was in her second-storey bedroom, unable to get to sleep. At 2am she noticed that the area outside her open window was turning a peculiar blue colour. The light, which was accompanied by a sound like a 'spinning top', intensified until the whole room lit up.

She got up, went to the window, and then froze with fear. Hovering over the neighbouring block of flats was a strange craft, about thirteen feet in diameter, and shaped like an inverted soup plate. It appeared to be bluish-grey metal, with a clear dome on top, and flame coloured lights under the outer rim.

The object seemed to be was suspended mid-air, and she could clearly see two figures inside. They looked like normal human males, and were wearing shining light blue satin-type suits, but no helmets. She could only see their heads and shoulders, and the arms of one who was apparently controlling the craft.

The being on the far side of the dome turned to the other who had his back to the witness. He said something, and then laughed. After hovering for a short while, the craft suddenly shot straight up into the air and disappeared south-west over the Wainuiomata Hill.

The witness was so scared that the strange object and occupants may return, rather than notify anyone, she climbed back into bed, and pulled the blankets over her head.

Hans Petersen related the following event, which occurred on the other side of the world in Denmark in 1959.

The witness said that not far from his neighbour's farm is a pond, about half a mile in diameter. It was Winter, and the ice over a foot thick, so the children used to skate on it. One night a bright light came out of the sky, and crashed through the ice and into the water.

The next morning the farmer saw a perfect round hole, sheared as neatly as cut glass, in the middle of the ice. The following day the hole had not frozen over, so he thought he had better notify the police. When the hole was still there a week later, the government was called in.

The authorities fenced off the area, and erected a crane over the pond. The locals were astonished when a shiny metallic disc, about thirty feet in diameter, was pulled out. It was hastily 'covered-up' and transported to the city, and nothing was ever mentioned about it afterwards.

In 1956 there was a well documented incident involving a Navy four-engine Super Constellation flying across the Atlantic towards Newfoundland.

The crew could see a huge disc, larger than their transport plane, hurtling towards them. It turned, and from a distance of only one hundred yards, paced the Super Constellation for a short while before tilting upwards, accelerating and rapidly vanishing. They described the strange craft as being at least thirty feet thick in the centre, with a blurred glow, which could have been lights, around the rim.

When they arrived at Gander airport, they learned that an object, close to their plane, had also been detected on radar. The pilot was interrogated by officials, but was not given any answers to his questions.

Five days later he was summoned to a meeting with a top government 'scientist', who showed him several photographs. When the pilot identified one as being the same as the craft which had been on a collision course, before pacing him, he naturally started asking many questions. The 'scientist' put the photos back into his briefcase and left without further comment. So what did the government actually know?

Jerome Clark wrote about a similar situation the next year. On November 6th 1957, Olden Moore was driving near Montville Ohio, when a glowing disc, fifty feet in both diameter and height, landed on the roadside.

He stopped his car, and got out, watching the strange craft for fifteen minutes. He left to get his wife, but when they returned, the object had gone. Police and Civil Defence investigated the site, and found both 'footprints' and radioactivity.

A few days later Moore 'disappeared', and when he returned, refused to say where he had been. He later told researchers that Air Force officers had flown him to Washington DC. They kept him incommunicado and questioned him several times. Eventually, after he signed a form swearing him to secrecy, they showed him footage of UFOs seen from a military aircraft, and said that UFOs seemed to be of interplanetary origin.

Investigator, Willy Smith, reported on a similar scenario which unfolded in Uruguay in 1972. The Isla de Lobos, a small island off the coast, was home to an important lighthouse. Its care and upkeep was the responsibility of the Navy, who kept a small garrison of four or five men stationed there.

At 10.10pm on 28th October, Corporal Fuentes left his colleagues in the main house, to check on the generators at the base of the lighthouse. He had only gone a short way, when he noticed, further on, some unusual lights, which shouldn't be there. He returned to the house, and without alerting the other men, got his pistol from his room.

He proceeded back up the hill, and saw that the lights were part of a metallic, 'bowl-shaped' object, with 'legs' underneath. It had a diameter of about five metres, with a dome and antenna on top, and a rectangular aperture or door, from which three entities descended.

Two of them were about 5ft tall, and the third closer to 6ft. They were all wearing close fitting black rubber suits, and Fuentes felt that he must have interrupted their proposed mission. They all climbed back into their craft which emitted a humming noise, swiftly rose to a height of about forty-five metres, then silently shot off, at tremendous speed, to the south-east.

Fuentes reported the incident to his senior officer, and after they had returned to the mainland, he was summoned to a higher ranking authority to report the incident.

The officer, to whom he had related the details, disappeared into an office where two men from the American Embassy were waiting. After a while, someone came out and showed him several drawings. After Fuentes identified one as being closest to the craft he had seen, he was dismissed, without ever seeing or speaking to the American visitors.

Although there have been several cases of unidentified craft temporarily 'setting down' on military bases or airstrips, we cannot automatically assume that they were alien, perhaps they had an earthly origin. Not only could they have been foreign intruders, on a spying mission, perhaps they were our own prototypes being tested, more safely, over local facilities

In September 1959, the *'A.P.R.O Bulletin'* published an account of a 1957 Brazilian incident which was investigated by D. Olavo Fontes.

At 2am on November 4th, on the coast of Sao Paulo State, at San Vicente, the Army Fortress Itaipa was quiet and peaceful. No enemies existed to present any threat, and two guards were on routine duty on top of the military fortifications.

Suddenly their reverie was interrupted by a bright light which was rapidly approaching from over the Atlantic Ocean. It stopped abruptly over the base, and hovered about one hundred and fifty feet above the highest cannon turrets. Its strong orange glow illuminated the ground below.

It was the size of a large airplane, but round and shaped like a disc, and made a distinct humming noise, which the sentries had only noticed when it was hovering overhead. At first the two soldiers did not sense any threat, but after about one minute, the humming sound increased, and an intolerable wave of extreme heat engulfed them.

The one sentry became disorientated, and collapsed, unconscious, on the ground. The other soldier, affected by the intense heat, ran in all directions, screaming with fear. Eventually he found shelter underneath one of the heavy cannons.

The rest of the garrison, woken by the cries of their terrified comrade, were confused about what was happening, and automatically raced towards their battle-stations. A few seconds later, the entire electrical system to the fortress failed, including their own emergency generators. The base, along with all its weapons and back-up systems, was helpless.

Soldiers and their officers were running blindly through darkened corridors when the lights came back on. They all raced outside in time to see an orange light climbing vertically above the base. It then moved away through the sky at incredible speed.

One sentry was still unconscious on the ground, and the other was found hiding in a dark corner. His colleagues said he was mumbling and crying, obviously 'entirely out of his mind'. Both soldiers were taken to the infirmary with second degree burns to their bodies, and in deep nervous shock.

The next day the Army Colonel, in charge of the base, placed the area under martial law, and forbade anyone to speak of the incident. Intelligence officers soon arrived to commence an investigation, and after a few days Brazilian Air Force officers appeared on the scene. They were accompanied by American officers from the US Army Military Mission.

The two injured sentries were taken by a military plane to the Army's Central Hospital, where they were kept under tight security. All attempts to contact them, or even determine their medical condition, proved unsuccessful. The 'security ring' built by Army Intelligence was impenetrable.

Still in South America, but this time in the country of Argentina, were other mysterious cases.

In 1962, Luis Harvey, the airport manager at Cambá Punta, in the north-east Province of Corrientes, was told that an unannounced aircraft was about to land.

He ran out, and saw a luminous object circling above at high speed. Although it had not responded to any signals, the ground-crew prepared for a landing.

Instead of actually touching down, the object descended and hovered, for three or four minutes, a few feet above the runway. It was a revolving spherical body which emitted blue, green and orange flashes. When airport officials tentatively approached, the object climbed back into the sky and 'vanished at staggering speed'.

Argentine authorities initiated an intense investigation, and newspapers were quite forthcoming with their views; - *'The arrival of this interplanetary craft, on an aerodrome in the Province of Corrientes – a fact that cannot be disputed, given the manner of its appearance and the calibre of the eyewitnesses - serves to strengthen the view that there may be Space Peoples' bases somewhere in our country, in view of the great number of recent sightings.'*

Four months later, Buenos Aires newspapers reported that the Argentine Air Force was investigating an incident where a saucer had landed, at 2.15am, on one of the main runways at the Ezezia International Airport. It was intensely luminous, and sitting only two thousand meters from the main control tower.

The two officers in charge of the Flight Control Tower, Sénors Besutti and Alora, were concerned, and said that they were expecting the arrival of a Pan-American DC8, and the behaviour of the UFO was something they 'had to watch most carefully'.

When the giant passenger plane arrived, the mysterious object rose straight into the sky, to an estimated height of five or six hundred meters, then 'made off at vertiginous speed'.

Britain also had its share of inexplicable events. In December 1963, attention was centred on the Cosford R.A.F. training camp, near Wolverhampton in England. The hangers only contained small Chipmunk training craft, and the airfield was usually closed overnight. Just after 9.30pm, two young students had returned after their passes had expired, and climbed over a fence to discreetly make their way back to the barracks. They sighted a bright, dome-shaped object come down from the sky and land between the railway line and a hanger. It was about twenty feet wide by thirty feet high, white with an orange centre, and emitted a green beam, which swept around in searchlight fashion.

When they saw a 'trapdoor in the upper part open', they ran in fear to tell their commanding officer.

By the time the Camp Commander arrived, the object had vanished, however an inquiry was immediately instigated. A few days later, a Vulcan plane landed at the station, which was also an unusual occurrence. Several British researchers investigated this case, and in his book, *'Cosmic Crashes'* Nick Redfern suggests that later, part of the UFO may have been quietly removed from the base.

Authorities later claimed that the incident never happened, and that the two witnesses were either drunk or perpetrating a hoax. They ignored a report from a local British Railway signalman who had also witnessed the incident from his box.

Researcher Wilfrid Daniels later spoke to the Chaplain from the R.A.F. Station, who attested to the characters of the two young witnesses, and said that they were sane and sensible young men, who genuinely believed what they saw that night.

However, this was not the first incident at Cosford. In 1996, Paul Stokes, a witness in his sixties came forward to describe events which had happened in 1952, when he was also a young trainee at the camp.

It was about 7pm, and after dinner, he had returned to his accommodation block. Suddenly he heard his fellow students calling everybody to come outside and "look at this!"

Just beyond the base was a nearby field, above which could be seen a bright white light, shaped like two saucers, moving from left to right. Paul climbed on top of an old air raid shelter to get a better look, and noticed that the silent object was now hovering in one spot.

His comrades took fright, and started running back into the billet, but he remained in position, hoping the strange object would come closer. After about thirty seconds, it moved away and disappeared behind some trees.

Paul returned to his billet, and thought no more about it, but the next morning, when attending the regular early parade, he had difficulty in remembering who he was or his correct place in the parade.

As he went on to serve in the R.A.F., he saw and heard of other inexplicable craft in the sky, many of which were also detected on radar. In about 1955, while stationed at R.A.F. Stradishall, near Newmarket, he and his colleagues saw three bright white, unidentified objects moving slowly, in formation, across the sky.

Disc shaped, like two saucers placed face-to-face, they were about three hundred yards away, and at an altitude of about five hundred feet. When they reached the perimeter of the base, they changed direction slightly, as if to avoid passing directly over the installation. After about fifteen minutes they were lost from view behind some nearby barracks. The next day, radar operators denied detecting the objects on their screens.

Later in the year, he and several other servicemen were walking back to camp, when they saw three more similar objects passing slowly across the sky. This time he did not report the sighting.

Do Cosford, and the nearby RAF Shawbury, have some connection with UFOs – be they earthly or alien? On 30th and 31st March 1993, there were reports from personnel, and the military police, of a UFO flying slowly over both bases. It was making an unpleasant, low frequency humming sound, and fired a beam of light at the ground, before shooting off to the horizon in seconds. It was travelling faster than any RAF jet.

Researcher, Nick Pope, obtained RAF documentation which concluded that; 'In summary, there would seem to be some evidence, on this occasion, that an unidentified object (or objects) of unknown origin was operating over the UK.

On 22nd March 1966, an Air Force electronics engineer, Eddie Laxton, was driving to work along an isolated part of Highway 70, near the Texas-Oklahoma border.

He suddenly slammed on his brakes when a massive object, 22 metres long and 25 metres high, with a small tail and stabilizers, and four brilliant lights on one side, landed on the road ahead. It appeared to be illuminated inside, and had a three foot diameter 'plastic bubble in front'.

There was a small open doorway, two by four feet, which emitted white light. A 'being', about 5'9" tall, who looked totally human, came down a small metal ladder, and was using something like a flashlight to examine the underside of the craft.

Eddie noticed that the 'man', who had a light complexion, looked about thirty years old and was wearing green coveralls and a peaked cap. The 'being' was obviously not aware of anyone's presence until Eddie got out of his car. He immediately retreated back up the ladder, and the craft 'started up', making some noise, as it lifted about fifty feet off the ground and sped away.

When he got to the Air Force Base, Eddie reported the incident, noting another witness had seen the craft speeding away. Although senior officers asked a lot of questions, and examined the landing spot with various instruments, they didn't swear Eddie to secrecy or forbid him from speaking about the incident.

In 1968, Brazilian researcher, Irene Granci, spoke of an incident which occurred in September, at Duque de Caxias. One night, just after midnight, 'Mrs K.' had got up to make a cup of coffee, and saw a light outside. Thinking it was her neighbours, coming home late again, she looked outside to see three strange men, quietly talking under the central avocado tree. She could not hear what they were saying, but they looked quite normal, with human features and about the height of her husband. They were wearing close fitting garments, covered by some sort of plastic.

What seemed strange, was the fact that each was encased in a beam of light, which came down from over their heads. Looking up, she saw, over the yard, and just above the surrounding rooftops, a large round object, which was spinning clockwise, and whose diameter was much bigger than her forty metre yard. It was emitting beams, which resembled powerful headlights.

She thought she must have made a noise, because suddenly, they were sucked up, within the beam, into a metal, aluminium-like bowl at the bottom surface of the craft. The craft made a shrill noise, like 'electronic music', the spinning increased, and the UFO flew off at a moderate speed.

On 18th June 1972, Darrell Totten, from San Bernardino, California, stopped at the scene of a minor traffic accident, to see if he could help. There were other people gathered there, but all were staring upwards, watching a strange, circular craft moving quickly around the sky. It was a weird orange-yellow colour, which changed to a bluish-white when it gained altitude.

One of the spectators, who had seen a similar craft before, claimed that he had been told by Air Force personnel that it was a highly secret craft, which should not be talked about. Three uniformed US Airmen, who were also on the scene, said they would be in a position to know, and had heard nothing about it.

Darrell turned his attention to the accident, and was told that earlier, the 'thing' they had been watching had harassed a family of four, swooping on their pick-up camper and trailer until it ran off the isolated dirt road. As the crowd moved a couple of boulders, and pushed the camper and trailer out of the ditch, the 'thing' swooped down, several times, low over the scene.

The family's two young daughters were hysterical, and it turned out that the afternoon before this accident, the strange disc had been 'hanging around', but when they reported it to the local deputy sheriff, he told them that they were 'imagining things'.

On May 9th 1985, Douglas Oliver was on his motorbike, and travelling along the British A580 East Lancashire Road between Liverpool and Oldham. At 4.30am he pulled over to have a cigarette, and could hear a humming noise coming from a nearby field. Curious, he walked about thirty feet into the field, and could see a silvery-white glow about one hundred feet further on.

Two figures, each about five feet tall approached him, and when they paused about eight feet away, he could see them quite clearly. They were a man and a woman, and both had short blond hair, and looked like 'perfect human beings'. Their lurex-type ski-suits seemed to sparkle from the lights of the craft and his motorbike. Around their waists they had a wide belt, with an 'egg-shaped canister thing' on the right hand side.

Douglas backed away a little, and asked the woman where had they come from? She told him that they were from another Solar System, and he shouldn't be afraid. They had just stopped to make some minor adjustments to their ship, which she explained was powered by magnetic fields and gravitational pull. They walked back to their craft, the humming noise increased, and a silvery, cigar-shaped object took off at tremendous speed on a forty-five degree angle.

Later, Douglas made the mistake of ringing Manchester Airport to ask if any aircraft had been around at that time, but none had.

On 13th July, Douglas, who had told nobody of the incident, was home alone. Just after 11am, there was a knock on the door. Two men were there, both in their early forties, and except for their white shirts, dressed in black including their shoes and hats. Their car, parked outside, was also black.

They told him that they knew of his encounter and his call to the airport. For his own safety, he should 'say nothing to anybody'. Douglas became angry, asked why they were threatening him, and told them to "**** off". Some days later, he received a visit from an Air Force officer who gave him some similar advice.

It was after this that Douglas, who had no previous knowledge of UFOs, heard about BUFORA, and told Norman Oliver about the incidents.

Sometimes, unidentified craft can be so large, that they are unlikely to be of earthly origin. The 'visitors' had told contactees that these enormous craft were for travelling through space. Smaller discs were used for transport and observation within our atmosphere.

In 1954, the US Navy tracked an enormous machine circling over 80,000 feet above Washington. This happened several times, however all the Air Force jets could do was to circle helplessly beneath it. It did not seem hostile, and after a while climbed swiftly out of sight. The government was anxious to avoid any publicity, fearing there would be mass panic at the suggestion of an 'alien invasion'.

'Flying Saucer Review' received an interesting report from a former member of the RAF, who had waited for the expiry of any 'secrets' embargo, and now he was getting old, felt it was time to speak out.

In August 1949, he participated in 'Operation Bulldog', which was an exercise designed to test British radar and defence capabilities. The witness, who didn't give his own name, identified all the other officers who were on duty that particular day at the RAF Sandwich Radar ACI in Kent.

They, and other radar stations, tracked an enormous object, which was over the English Channel before turning northwards towards the Thames Estuary. It was at an altitude of fifty thousand feet, travelling at 3,000mph, with a calculated size of close to twenty thousand tons, and an echo similar to a large passenger or freighter ship. When it approached Bampton Radar Station it suddenly increased speed and headed upwards. It vanished from their screens after it reached an altitude of one hundred thousand feet.

In those days there were no known aircraft of that size, or capable of such speed. They were all summoned to a meeting with the Commanding Officer, who reminded them of the Official Secrets Act. They were to forget about the occurrence, and not mention it to anyone outside of the RAF.

The servicemen and officers on duty had meticulously recorded every detail, but the following evening they noticed that the incomplete Duty Watch Book had disappeared, and had been replaced with a brand new one.

Around about the same time, in the USA, there were a series of sightings, from August 1949 to March 1950, known as the 'Norwood Searchlight Incident'. Len Stringfield wrote about a church festival, in the winter of 1950, at Norwood, Ohio.

The locals had acquired an Army surplus searchlight, which one of their parishioners, a military man, shone into the sky during special occasions. The priest said that several times the enormous beam picked up a tremendous object in the sky. He claimed an unnamed scientist had estimated it as being ten thousand feet in diameter, and said it was probably too high up for jets to be scrambled.

One night, five objects had been seen coming out of the larger craft. A large number of photographs had been taken, and many witnesses had seen the object from different locations.

Major Donald Keyhoe, in his book, *'Aliens from Space'*, also mentions 'gigantic' craft.

On the night of February 15th 1965, an airliner chartered by the Defense Department, was flying over the Pacific on its way to Japan. Three enormous, glowing objects descended from the sky, veered to the side, and paced the plane from a distance of five miles. After a few minutes, the craft moved upwards, accelerated to 1,200 knots and disappeared within a few seconds.

On July 18th 1967, scientists at the Soviet Astronomical Station, near Kazan, reported an enormous crescent shape craft that passed overhead. At an estimated diameter of five to six hundred metres, it was at least eight times larger than any known aircraft, and 'glowed orange', which made the witnesses wonder if it was emitting jet-like exhausts. Similar craft were seen again, at least three times later that year.

In the 2000 edition of the *'IUFOPRA Newsletter'*, Kathy Crinion published an article by Dr Richard Boylan, where he wrote about the astronauts on Apollo 10 seeing an extraterrestrial 'Monolith', similar to, but smaller than the one in Arthur C. Clarke's movie '2001'.

He said it appeared to be some form of 'communication beacon', and claimed that in 1972, a secret military version of the Space Shuttle used a 'shuttle arm' to retrieve it. The object was then brought back to Earth for further study. Apparently, many of the scientists later died of cancer.

Were there enormous alien 'mother-ships' out in space? Maybe so! In 1989 the unmanned Russian probe, Phobos 2, arrived in Martian orbit, and transmitted its images back to Earth. Just before its demise, it had photographed a gigantic, cylindrical object near or on the surface. It was huge, and estimated to be some fifteen miles long.

The Phobos probes contained complicated guidance and recording systems, however Phobos 2 had an additional laser, LIMA-D, which was designed to cause a mini-explosion on the surface, and gather data on the evaporated substances. *'Aviation Week & Space Technology'* magazine reported that the Kaliningrad Control Centre were sure that just after Phobos 2 ceased transmitting, it had hit something, and gone into a spin.

Another interesting case occurred in about 1977. The details only became available to me some years later, and the pilot 'Trevor' (a pseudonym) did not wish to make any public comment at that time.

Trevor was a pilot for British Caledonian Airways, and was taking a 747 cargo plane from London to South America. Just off the coast of Africa, Trevor and the other four crew members noticed an enormous object on their radar screen. It appeared to be on the same altitude as the 747 and directly on their flight path. They couldn't believe the size the screen was displaying. They contacted

Algiers for verification, and were told that Algiers' radar didn't extend that far. They were given permission to alter course, but Algiers noted that there shouldn't be anything else in that airspace.

As they approached the area, Trevor and the crew were dumbfounded to see an unbelievable object which corresponded to the readings on the radar screen. It was silver in colour, with no windows, and hovering like an airborne fortress. As they came closer it moved around to the side, enough to give the 747 room to pass. Trevor claimed it was like something out of 'Science Fiction'. The craft seemed to have doors along the side, as if it might have been some form of cargo vessel.

It remained stationary, and did not interfere or communicate with their plane as they flew along the full length – at least **twenty miles**. The crew maintained a stunned silence during the entire encounter. After they had passed the object, the pilot followed Standard Operations Procedures, which entailed opening a small safe box, and handing report forms to the witnesses. Once the reports were completed they were locked back into the box, and the crew instructed to say nothing about what they had seen.

As soon as they landed back in Britain, the crew and locked safe were escorted back to a RAF Base, or similar government establishment. They said they were treated well, but virtually 'imprisoned' none-the-less. The witnesses were separated, and then questioned individually. Each was told they had seen a 'weather balloon', and would have to 'sign this' before they could leave. After three days they wanted to 'get out' and complied with the request.

If the crew's estimate of the size of this object is correct, it is extremely unlikely it originated on Earth. One can only speculate as to its resemblance to the reported 'mother-ships', and it was conveniently over the ocean, out of range of our ground-based radar systems.

In the 1990s, the RAF tracked an unidentified craft, 'as big as a battleship', over the North Sea. It flew in a zigzag pattern at 30,000km per hour, accelerating to 40,000km before zooming off towards the Atlantic.

In 1996 several independent witnesses along Canada's Yukon Territory, Klondike Highway, reported a craft over Fox Lake that was 'bigger than a football stadium'. It was later calculated as being somewhere between half a mile to over a mile in length.

It was smooth and solid, with an arrangement of coloured lights which illuminated its curved surface. It moved slowly, and at times, had a beam of light which silently swept over the ground below.

Author, Leslie Kean, wrote about one pilot's report in April 2007, when he saw two slow-moving objects whilst flying over the Channel Islands. They were also tracked on radar, and one was estimated as being 'massive' - over a mile long.

Not all giant craft were seen in the upper atmosphere. In January 1981, four workers at the Arizona Morenci copper-smelting plant were terrified when a 'massive spacecraft' swooped down and shone a beam of light on them.

Witness, Larry Morentsen, said that it was 'V-shaped', the size of four football fields. It had twelve small red lights on the edges, and a searchlight in the middle, which shone straight down into the smokestack.

They were not the only witnesses. Two kilometres away, at the Morenci High School, one hundred members of the marching band also reported the object. Director Bruce Smith said; "It was V-shaped and hovering – the biggest aircraft I've ever seen."

Another report came from the Papua New Guinea *'Post Courier'*, on November 15th 1999. An oblong-shaped object, with bright white lights all around, silently approached Pilapila village at about 7pm, and hovered above some tall coconut trees near the beach.

The streetlights dimmed, and some people ran into their houses and locked the doors. The craft was huge, and lit up the ground underneath. It took almost thirty minutes to slowly pass over them, before disappearing over the mountains near Vuvu.

Sometimes too little knowledge can be a dangerous thing. Most people were not aware that by the 1960s it is very likely we had some very secret prototype discs of our own. This could certainly cause confusion in a population who were, at times, encouraged to believe in alien visitation, rather than our own technological advancement.

We may never know the complete truth regarding the following episode-('*True Magazine's Flying Saucers and UFOs Quarterly*' #3 1976)

Investigator James Bonham managed to interview a hunter, who had a very guilty conscience about what he had done in the winter of 1961. He and three friends were returning late one Sunday night from a hunting trip. It was a miserable night, with sleet falling, and they were all very cold.

They suddenly saw a fiery object coming down from the sky, and it landed or touched down about 150 yards away. They stopped at the side of the road, and could see, on the other side of the railway track, an object sitting in the mud. It seemed to be leaning slightly off-centre, and they thought it might be the tail section of a crashed plane. The craft was 'lighted' and they could see four 'people' walking around. As soon as they turned a spotlight on the area, the light from the object went out, but they could still see what they took to be a small plane crash.

They drove back to a small town about twenty minutes away, and persuaded the local police officer to return with them. When they arrived back at the site, despite a search, there was no evidence of any wreckage. The policeman left, and the four hunters, feeling that they were not believed, continued on their way.

Not long after, they saw the craft descending slowly from the sky. It seemed to be in flames, but they all saw it land in a small clearing close to the road. It had a lighted top, and a reddish glow seeping from underneath. They stopped the car, and watched two men who were outside the object. They were about 5ft 6 inches tall, wearing white coveralls.

Two of the hunters stayed in the car, holding a searchlight, while the other two men circled around the UFO occupants, who were heading towards the woods. Nobody will admit who fired the shot, but one of the stalkers fired his rifle, hitting one 'being' in the shoulder. The other 'creature' ran back to his wounded colleague, helped him onto his feet, and yelled out in clear English: "What the hell did you do that for?"

The hunters' intention had been to capture one of these 'aliens' to prove what they had seen. Now, they suddenly realised it may have been an experimental aircraft, and that the wounded figure was an Air Force Officer. They ran back to the car, and sped off as quickly as possible. They were sure they would be arrested, and agreed they would never mention the incident.

Their fears were, to a certain extent, realised the next day. One of the hunters was called into his supervisor's office, where some men were waiting to speak to him. They asked him about the clothes he had been wearing on Sunday, and went to his home, carefully examining his muddy boots. After they departed, the hunter was left totally confused and scared.

It may be never known whether these trigger-happy citizens had accosted a genuine alien 'Visitor', or shot an Air Force officer on a covert saucer-prototype operation. They were lucky, that either way, the government would not want the publicity of a court case!

Nearly twenty years later it was sometimes nigh impossible to determine the origin of a craft, especially if there were both alien and terrestrial facets to the event.

Jenny Randles detailed one such incident, which occurred in November 1980. It was a very wet and windy night when Mario Luisi was walking through a sodden field, by a river, near his home at Burnside in the English Lakes District.

Suddenly he saw a strange object, hovering about three feet above the ground. It was about the size of a helicopter, but had no wings, and glinted in the light of his lantern. He heard a sound, and turned his lantern to see two fair-skinned people, each about six feet tall, wearing dark, skin-tight suits, standing beside an old oak tree.

One of them raised a small pencil-shaped object, and a bright light shot out, shattering the glass in Mario's lantern, and warping and twisting the metal reflector. The beings, a male and a female, stepped forward, and told him they meant no harm, and had come to Earth in peace.

Before climbing a ladder back into their craft, they told Mario he must not tell anyone about the strange symbols on their ship and lapel badges. After a short time, the object shot upwards, leaving a glow in the sky.

The next incident was most definitely terrestrial. On 30th January 2000, a fisherman was in his boat, hauling up crab traps on Farlon Island, about twenty miles off San Francisco on the Californian coast.

He said his dog started to bark furiously, and he looked up to see a huge black triangular object hovering silently overhead. He was hit by a beam of white light, and fell over backwards.

"I grabbed my Ruger 10-22 rifle, loaded with a 100 round banana magazine, and started firing as fast as I could until the clip was empty. I was able to shoot out the light, and while grabbing for a second clip, a hatch opened up on the bottom side of the object.

"Two people leaned down and yelled, "Stop shooting at us, you bloody idiot!"

The object moved off to the south, and he saw a helicopter come out of the top and move in next to his boat. It was about twenty feet above the water, and very close to his vessel. Someone in a side door held up a camera and took a picture of the culprit who was still holding his rifle.

The unmarked black helicopter, which made no noise, then climbed upwards and took off towards the Golden Gate Bridge. The triangular object slowly gained altitude and was last seen still heading in a southerly direction.

He later reflected on the incident; "At first I thought it was an alien UFO, and was genuinely startled by it. However, I now believe it was an experimental military platform for transporting a small fleet of black helicopters that leave and enter out of the top of a huge, silent floating triangle the size of a football field."

In these cases, the witnesses naturally assumed they had mistakenly encountered our own military operating top secret craft. But wait!...How do we know they were not 'visitors' – deliberately giving the impression they were normal humans?

Occasionally, there is an incident which indicates that some people have just been carried away by UFO literature and speculation.

Norman Cohn related a 1954 case from Sinceny, Aisne, in France; Mr S. reported; *'Seeing a silhouette moving in the light of two lamps, I thought I was in the presence of a Martian in the process of repairing his flying saucer. I went to get my gun, and fired at him!'* It turned out to be his neighbour, repairing his motorcar in a nearby field. Fortunately, the shot only damaged the car.

One case, from Dayton, Texas, has always been very contentious. On 29th December 1980, fifty-one–year-old business woman Betty Cash, and fifty-seven-year-old restaurant worker Vickie Landrum, with her seven-year-old grandson Colby, were driving along a road, near Piney Woods, when they encountered a large diamond-shape object, with flames belching from below, hovering silently at treetop level, about 130 feet away over the road ahead.

The interior of their car was flooded with bright light and became unbearably hot, forcing them all to get out. Vickie and Colby were so scared they jumped back into the vehicle, whilst Betty remained outside for about seven to ten minutes. They noticed the flight pattern of the strange craft seemed to be unsteady, in almost a 'staggering' trajectory.

A total of twenty-three twin-rotor Boeing CH-17 Chinook helicopters arrived from all directions, so they assumed the craft must have been military. The helicopters accompanied the object as it rose up into the sky and slowly moved away. Another witness saw the UFO, and three more confirmed sighting the helicopters.

That night they all developed headaches, a reddening of their skin, and nausea and vomiting. Cash was in the worst state. By the morning her face and head were covered by blisters, and her eyes had swollen shut.

All three witnesses suffered from damaged eyes, sores and scarring of the skin, vomiting and diarrhoea, excessive hair loss, and loss of appetite, weight and energy. Cash had more than two dozen hospital stays, and eventually developed breast cancer. Doctors suspected exposure to some form of radiation, and her personal physician, Dr. Brian McClelland said it was a 'textbook case of radiation poisoning'.

Their symptoms and illness continued for years, and their medical bills prompted them to seek compensation from the government. Their claim for damages took years, with the military denying everything. In 1986 the case was thrown out of court on the grounds that the Air Force, Army, Navy or NASA did not own or operate any such craft.

Vickie, Betty and Colby, together with their lawyer and other witnesses were not allowed to present their evidence or utter a word on the matter. Both Betty Cash and Vicky Landrum have since died.

Investigator Graham Birdsall commented that later sources confirmed that the object was alien, but being controlled by a human, military pilot, from the nearby military base, Fort Hood, who was learning to operate the craft under extraterrestrial intelligence and guidance.

MUFON investigator, John Schuessler, who was also a McDonnell Douglas space shuttle engineer, took up their case. He was sure their injuries had been caused by radiation. The only witness he could locate was a pilot who admitted flying one of the helicopters, but refused to identify the brilliant object, calling it 'classified'.

Another researcher claimed he had located a couple of ex-employees from Fort Hood, who confirmed 'test flights' of UFOs. One of them said he was dying of cancer as a result of working with these craft which were stored underground.

It is suggested that, for years, the government knew full well that these craft, be they earthly or alien, were a radiation hazard. The NICAP group in Washington D.C. commented on a case from 13th August 1959.

A former Navy pilot, with over 6,000 flying hours, was in his private plane, heading for New Mexico, when three 'oval-shaped devices', in formation, passed directly in front of his Cessna. They were grey in colour, about eight feet or more in diameter, and identical in shape – like two bowls, one inverted on the other – with the bottom rounded instead of flat.

The strange objects circled his plane, then disappeared behind him. Upon landing at the base, he was hustled into an office and interrogated for about two hours by an Air Force Major. He was told that if anything unusual happened, or if he had any abnormal illness in the next six months, he was to get to a government hospital straight away, and the Air Force would look after him.

There have been many instances, which I have not discussed in this book, of unidentified craft hovering over military bases, often disabling nuclear missiles. One would have to examine each case in detail to determine whether the interference was caused by our own enemy spy incursions or extraterrestrials, who certainly did not like our manufacture of nuclear weapons.

One unusual case, to which we do not have an answer, occurred in the Belgian Congo in 1952. John Schuessler detailed this account, which was contained in the Central Intelligence Agency Report No. W-23602, dated 6 November 1978.

It describes how, in early 1952, two fiery discs glided and hovered over a uranium mine in the southern part of the Belgian Congo. After about ten to twelve minutes, they sped off to the northeast, zigzagging as they went.

Commander Pierre, of the nearby Elisabethville airfield, immediately went out, pursuing the objects in a fighter jet. As he approached the craft, he advised that they were discus-shaped, with a diameter of twelve to fifteen metres. Their metallic colour resembled aluminium, and their outer rims were veiled in fire, and must have been rotating at some speed.

Pierre was unable to catch the intruders, who changed elevation and moved across the sky at incredible speeds. Eventually, they shot off towards Lake Tanganyika. Pierre estimated they were then travelling at about 1,500 kilometres per hour. This technology was far beyond what we were able to accomplish at the time.

It is hard to say, even today, how advanced we are in anti-gravity research – the military-industrial complexes are not about to divulge any secrets.

In 2000, British investigator Graham Birdsall reported that British Aerospace Systems were currently conducting an anti-gravity research venture called 'Project Greenglow'. Apparently it was part of a world-wide research effort that could lead to a revolutionary breakthrough in advanced propulsion systems. Whilst scientists were confident of success, so far the general public has not been advised of any revolutionary breakthroughs, leading to the same questions regarding the origin of advanced craft seen in the skies over the past seventy years!

CHAPTER THREE

BEHIND THE IRON CURTAIN

PART ONE

There is so much we do not know about UFOs and other mysterious events which have occurred in the Soviet Union.

However, the renowned Tunguska incident, which occurred on 30th June 1908, is quite famous. A large object crashed in a remote area of Siberia, causing enormous damage to the surrounding landscape and wildlife. Shock waves were registered in many neighbouring countries.

Witnesses claimed that very bright object had been seen at 8am. It was travelling from east to north, but before crashing and exploding, it changed its trajectory in the sky, which made them doubt it was an asteroid or comet.

In the afternoon they saw a second object, travelling from east to west, near the crash scene, before it flew away. The second craft was huge, described as being approximately five hundred metres long and seventy metres wide.

Over the following years there were a large number of biological mutations in the area. Although most experts thought that the crash site resembled a large nuclear explosion, the level of radioactivity was far lower than average, and not what the scientists had expected.

They also noticed another strange effect, a type of minor 'time distortion' which affected both mechanical and electronic watches at the Tunguska site. The investigators thought that maybe there was some form of energy field which remained at the sites of UFO crashes.

In 1921, one of the first to investigate was Leonid Kulik, of the Russian Meteorological Institute. It was a tough expedition into inaccessible, frozen territory. The population of the region was primitive and thinly scattered, and it wasn't until a later trip in 1928, that he was able to commence any meaningful research. Various differing conclusions were proffered by his colleagues, however they did not find any remnants of a meteor. In 1942 Kulik was killed in World War II, and it wasn't until 1945, and the nuclear explosions at

Hiroshima and Nagasaki, when investigators noticed the similarities to Tungusta.

During the following years there were many scientific expeditions to the area, and many more conflicting theories.

Later, in 1953, Professor Liapunov suggested that we "abandon the concept of a meteorite, and term the object a 'cosmic ship' of extraterrestrial origin." At the same time, another scientist – Kasanzew – indicated his belief that 'inhabitants of another world came into the atmosphere of the Earth in 1908'.

In the mid-1970s, Dr Alexel Zolotov returned from a trip to the Tungus area, and told a *'Tass'* correspondent; *'Our job this summer was to collect samples of permafrost soil, dating back to 1908, and of the trees which survived that unique catastrophe. We are looking forward to a laboratory analysis of these samples which, we hope, will produce new information that will bring us nearer to a final solution to the Tungus mystery.*

'Our investigations in the course of seventeen years seem to confirm our assumption that what took place in the Tungus Taiga was a nuclear explosion. So far, there is not a single fact that would contradict our nuclear hypothesis. Although the Tungus mystery has not yet been fully solved, the study of test samples of rock, soil, plants (wood and moss), and other material evidence leads us to conclude that the explosion of the Tungus cosmic body was of nuclear character or at least was accompanied by nuclear reactions.'

He went on to describe anomalies in the Earth's magnetic field, seismic shock waves, and radioactive levels.

At an International Congress in Frankfurt, which was sponsored by Michael Hesseman, several Russian investigators from a Soviet delegation, discussed their research, however they were still divided as to the cause of the damage.

More recently, several experts, including Dr. Felix Zigel and Dr Alexel Zolotov, had accompanied researchers into the area on several occasions. Zolotov was also still firmly convinced that this was a nuclear-like explosion caused by an alien spacecraft.

At the beginning of the 21st century another group of scientists visited the area, and claimed they found evidence that it had been part of a comet which had crashed all those years ago.

'The Daily Telegraph', dated 13th August 2004, published the following news item; *'MOSCOW; Russian scientists claim to have discovered the wreck of an alien space device at the sight of an unexplained explosion in Siberia almost a hundred years ago.*

'Interfax newsagency said the scientists, who belong to the Tunguska Space Phenomenon Public State Fund, said they found the remains of an extraterrestrial device that allegedly crashed near the Tunguska River in Siberia.

'They also claim to have discovered a 50kg rock which they have sent to the Siberian city of Kasnoyarsk for analysis.' I guess we will never know!

The Russians have always kept a tight lid of secrecy when it comes to unidentified flying objects. Until the early 1960s, the general population were too scared to report UFOs. Such talk was prohibited under penalty of ridicule, or incarceration in a mental hospital.

Russia's leaders were, however, aware of the possibility of extraterrestrial life. Paul Stonehill wrote of one early encounter in 1898, (fifteen years before Russia's first hot-air balloon), when ten-year-old Rita Nukarinen was walking through the forest near Lagoda Lake, not far from St. Petersburg.

Hovering over the treetops was a giant sphere, with humanoid-like beings inside. Nineteen years later, at Karkiyeki, on the shore of Lagoda Lake, a saucer-like object landed near Enni Leitu's house, and several small humanoids descended to the ground.

They insisted on taking her onboard their craft, which took her into space for several hours. During that time, before being returned to Earth, she had telepathic communications with one of the aliens, whom she thought was their leader. Afterwards, she developed psychic talents, including the ability to predict the future and to heal people through ESP.

Author H.G.Wells told of an interesting conversation he had with Lenin in 1920; *"I said to Lenin that the development of human technology might someday change the world situation. The Marxist conception itself would then become meaningless. Lenin looked at me and said; "You are right. I understood this myself when I read your novel 'the Time Machine'.*

"All human conceptions are on a scale of our planet. They are based on a pretension that the technical potential, although it will develop, will never exceed the 'terrestrial limit'. If we succeed in establishing interplanetary communication, all our philosophical, moral and social views will have to be revised. In this case, the technical potential, becoming limitless, would impose the end of the role of violence as a means and method of progress."

Initially Joseph Stalin, having heard of the alleged crash at Roswell, and incidents within the USSR, showed great interest in UFOs. In 1948 he summoned Sergei Korolyov to a meeting, and asked the scientist to investigate the matter for him.

Korolyov eventually reported back that the phenomenon was real, and although UFOs were not manufactured in America, Russia or any other country, they were not a threat. Stalin thanked him for his efforts, and said that other scientists shared the same opinion.

Russian expert Paul Stonehill, detailed how researcher Yuri Stroganov, stated that in early 1955 a special top secret UFO research committee was established within the USSR Ministry of Defence.

In 1956, the heads of the intelligence services from USSR, USA, France and Britain met in Geneva. They reached an agreement about maintaining secrecy regarding the UFO problem. Part of their strategy was to pressure witnesses, including academics and military, into silence, to fabricate earthly explanations for the phenomena, and to infiltrate and disrupt UFO study groups. Special, highly secret agencies, which would co-operate with each other, were to be established in the participating countries.

Timothy Good wrote about a statement made, in 1965, by George Langelaan, an ex-officer of the French Secret Service. He said that the Russians and Americans, (if not the British and French), had collaborated and reached the conclusion that the flying saucers were of extraterrestrial origin.

Victor Marchetti, former executive assistant to the Deputy Director of the CIA also commented; *'If it were concluded that UFOs were not of terrestrial origin, but rather vehicles from outer space, the CIA and US Government, aware that the phenomenon was of a world-wide nature, would seek co-operation in the investigation from Earth's other technically advanced nations, such as the United Kingdom, France Germany and even the USSR.*

'The CIA would function as the US Government's agent, just as the KGB would be the USSR's, MI6 would be the UK's and so on. These agencies.....are quite accustomed to co-operating with each other on matters of mutual interest. Co-operation in the intelligence business is not restricted to allies. There are times when the CIA and KGB have found it advantageous to work together.'

There were probably more diplomatic exchanges between the two major powers than were ever disclosed. One of the reasons could have been divulged by a couple of news broadcasts on the Australian ABC.

On 11th August 1959, they announced that; - *'The heaviest drop in nearly four years was registered yesterday on the New York Stock Exchange. It's reported that the slump reduced the value of all listed shares by a total of about seven thousand million pounds.*

'The decline started with the news of the forthcoming exchange visits between President Eisenhower and Mr, Khrushchev. Reuter blames the reversal on the psychological impact of the belief that there might be a 'thaw' in the 'cold war', with a possible reduction in America's defence effort. The greatest impact fell on defence stocks, including aircraft, missiles and rocket fuels.....'

After the Summit Conference, another news item stated that because Eisenhower's tour of Russia had been cancelled, the Stock Exchange had stabilized.

Gordon Creighton translated many Russian articles, and in 1961, he reported that V. Kamarov, a prominent Soviet astronomer, wrote; *'Present day science has reached a high level of development. It will not be at all surprising if, in the near future, we receive most interesting evidence concerning other civilisations in the universe.'*

Astronomer V. Davydof, similarly speculated about life in the universe, and asked if they had already been here. The same year, the US held a conference on extraterrestrial civilisations at the Greenbank observatory in Virginia.

In 1964 a SETI (Search for Extraterrestrial Intelligence) conference for radio astronomers was held at the Byurakan Astropysical Observatory, where methods of contact were discussed. Astronomer M. Klyatkovo, wrote an article for the influential Russian trade-union journal *'Trad'*. He confirmed the existence of inhabitants of other worlds, and the possibility that they may be trying to communicate with us.

In 1971, the first international SETI conference was held. Participants comprised twenty-eight Soviets, fifteen Americans, (including Carl Sagan and Francis Drake), and four scientists from other nations.

In 1967, scientific writer Alberto Fenoglio, wrote about information given to him anonymously by Soviet citizens, one of whom was a Soviet diplomat, and another an engineer; *'The USSR, with all its war preparations, atomic installations, and air and missile bases, has been observed, just as have the USA and other points of our planet. The Soviet authorities know it and are preoccupied just as much as the Pentagon. Also the personnel of the Soviet Air Force and pilots have been confronted with great discoid objects, mysterious balls of fire and immense flying cigars in the sky. Thousands of people in the towns have also observed them.*

'The UFOs – those mysterious flying objects of unknown origin – have frequently been picked up on radar screens behind the Iron Curtain. In the spring of 1959 they caused alarm, and near panic spread among the radar personnel and the Air Force when the discs appeared, remaining for over twenty-four hours, in the skies over Sverdlovek, General Headquarters for the Missile Tactical Command.

'The pilots of the Soviet Air Force have already opened fire on the flying discs, just as American, British and Canadian pilots have done.'

The 'Western Alliance' powers flew many missions over the Arctic regions, and had frequently encountered strange, unidentified craft. The Russians also patrolled this strategic region, and had often experienced similar phenomena.

In 1956, V. Akkuratov, the 'flag navigator', of the polar aviation service, was flying over Greenland. They broke cloud cover to suddenly see a strange flying vehicle which resembled a 'big, pear-coloured lens, with wavy, pulsating edges.' It was on their port side, and coming close to their course. To avoid a collision, they moved back into the cloud.

Akkuratov said; "After forty minutes of flight, in the direction of Madvezhi Island, the clouds suddenly receded, and as we got into clear sky, we noticed the same flying object to our port. We changed course sharply, and began to approach it. In response, the UFO also changed course, and flew parallel to us at a speed equal to our own. After 15-18 minutes, the object changed its course sharply, surged ahead of us and shot up fast, melting into the blue skies.

"We detected no aerials, superstructure, wings or portholes on the disc. There was neither gas jet exhaust nor a vapour trail, and the speed of its departure was so great that the whole phenomenon seemed something supernatural."

A few years ago, Russian researcher, Valery Uravov, interviewed several high ranking Russians. One, Col.Gen. Gennadij Reshetnikov, spoke of how, in the late 1970s, he flew to the Arctic Circle to investigate reports of UFOs, although he didn't obtain any tangible evidence. Many times he had personally sent up aircraft to investigate unidentified objects, and there had been several cases when they turned out to be mysterious, unknown targets on which the different detecting systems reacted, including their land, sea and air space surveillance

The Soviet Union's official response to the UFO problem altered in 1980. Although they had been paying close attention to the situation for many years, the Ministry of Defence issued an order to every military unit. They were to report any and all UFO sightings.

Retired Russian Colonel Boris Sokolov was placed at the head of the investigation, which continued for the next ten years. Sokolov confirmed that there were numerous reports of UFOs, including over forty from pilots, some of whom crashed during pursuits. After that they were instructed to change course and move away from any aerial intruder.

Solokov also admitted that they were anxious to obtain access to UFO technology, which would give the Russians an advantage. He later said that the search for stealth technology was prompted by the UFOs and commented; *"The military was interested in UFOs for a number of reasons, including the belief that if the secrets of the UFO could be discovered, the Soviets would be able to win the competition against prospective enemies, by incorporating what extraterrestrials knew of velocity, materials – and stealth."*

It must be remembered that, after World War II, the Russians also commandeered many of the German scientists and technicians. They had also been busy developing new technology and 'flying machines'.

In the 1960s there were many excited Russians claiming crashes of alien craft. The Soviet authorities didn't discourage this enthusiasm. In fact they were not

UFOs but their own illegal tests of space-to-earth nuclear warheads, which made one circuit of the globe before being diverted back to earth in Russia. These weapons, dubbed a 'fractional orbit bombardment system' by the Pentagon, were a clear breach of an international treaty banning the existence of orbiting nuclear weapons.

In 1994, Russia announced plans to build 'Ekip' an unmanned 'flying saucer'. The London *'Sunday Times'*, April 24th, published the news, along with a diagram, showing that the proposed prototype would, at eighty-two metres long, be longer than a Boeing 747. Weighing in at five ton, it could carry a two-ton load, and reach a speed of 400mph.

NATO was very concerned when they heard about a secret Russian aircraft, known only as the Article 1.44, built by MIG. They were just as worried when the Soviets unveiled their Sukhol S-37 'Berkuf', (nicknamed 'The Golden Eagle'), at the Moscow Air Show. It was a fighter plane with incredible manoeuvrability and fantastic fire-power. It could out-pace most NATO aircraft.

Weighing twenty-five ton, and made from some 'secret' material, its wings were swept forward, and it could withstand the forces incurred during extremely quick turns. Its advanced tracking and radar system could detect an enemy in excess of a sixty mile range.

One colleague advised me of an interesting triangular ATB – the T-4MS/200 proposed in 1970 by the Russian Sukhoi team. Designed to cruise at a speed of Mach 3.5, the plans were apparently never realised – but who knows now, some fifty years further on? Certainly the Soviets and the Chinese have developed national aerospace industries and have just as many prototypes of their own. Years ago the Russians had the Sukhoi Su-27 Flanker, with advanced avionics which allowed seemingly impossible aerial manoeuvres.

On 5th October 1983, Solokov investigated a serious incident at an ICBM base in the Ukraine. He met the very concerned base commander, who advised that a UFO had been observed near the facility for four hours the previous evening. During that time their control panel had lit up, indicating that the launch codes for the ICBM's had mysteriously been enabled. Fortunately, no missiles were launched, but this prompted Soviet military leaders to advocate sharing UFO information, on a regular basis, with the West. They feared that one day a UFO may trigger a nuclear exchange between the superpowers.

Little has been said about the Soviets' own attempts to discover the ancient secrets of levitation and space flight. According to some researchers, these secrets were preserved in the ancient monasteries in the Himalayas, over their borders with Tibet, Nepal, India and China. During the early to mid-twentieth century, there were many skirmishes between Soviet and Chinese troops in the boundary areas. Both governments would have been anxious to capture and control these locations, and the possible secrets they held.

In 1970, news started to trickle in from ham radio operators, and also press reporters in Hong Kong and Moscow. New Zealand *'SATCU'* researchers gathered some of the reports from their overseas contacts; *'In February 1970, Kasi-Ku, a Japanese radio ham operator, overheard and taped a conversation from channels usually reserved for military aircraft. When the tapes were translated from Russian, the Japanese Press labelled it the 'Vladivostoc Affair.' A MIG pilot apparently lost his life after attacking a UFO, somewhere north of Vladivostoc, over the Sikhote Alin mountain range, facing the Sea of Japan.*

During March of that year, large formations of UFOs were reported over Sakhalin, and rumours of landings were circulating throughout Northern Japan. Russian sailors told of large numbers of planes and military personnel being deployed to cope with the situation.

'In Hong Kong, Chinese refugees from the mainland said villages on both sides of the Sino-Soviet border were being systematically attacked, and that both China and Russia were accusing each other of using 'secret weapons' for this....Red spheres, emitting powerful light beams, had landed, producing men dressed in spacesuits, like Soviet cosmonauts. Meanwhile, Russian witnesses reported UFO pilots with Oriental features. It seemed considerable propaganda was being generated on both sides against possible military invasion.

'Border clashes increased throughout the area, and by mid-April the two countries, as reported by newspapers, were on the brink of war. 'TASS' reported that Russian manoeuvres in the area were being undertaken.,

On 24th April, a Soviet supersonic bomber disappeared en-route to Vladivostoc, and that afternoon anti-aircraft rockets were reportedly fired at 'hundreds of luminous discs' passing over the Mongolian border.

'Moscow's foreign correspondents reported that all military forces were placed on alert on April 26th, and large troop movements into Siberia were declared to

be 'spring training exercises' by Soviet officials... On April 29th, a huge formation of bombers and fighters moved southwards from Siberia into the disputed area.

'The Soviets poured into Mongolia on April 30th, and the Chinese arrived on May 4th. A few days later, the minor wire services in Hong Kong issued a flurry of brief contradictory dispatches. These varied from efforts of a combined project to preparations for battle, and Russian attacks on a secret Chinese base, possibly using atomic bombs.

'Man' magazine claimed that a group of radical college students from East Germany were touring Mongolia at the time of the air strikes. Manfred Goel, their spokesperson, later reported that; "The Soviet Union liquidated a secret flying saucer base, consisting of pyramid-like structures, and miles of underground tunnels, in Northern Mongolia."

'It is reported that the great Siberian-Orient wave of 1970 ceased abruptly after the air strikes...Soviet forces returned to their bases when the objects disappeared from the skies.'

By 1975 the Russians and Americans were participating in joint space ventures. In July, the Apollo and Soyuz capsules locked together for a two day scientific exercise where the astronauts carried out and shared experiments. The venture was hailed as a great step forward, and goodwill for future joint space adventures and exploration.

All over the world, unidentified objects had been seen hovering over Russian, American and other sensitive defence installations, and each suspected the other of having secret craft with a far superior technology.

Russian Prime Minister Kosygin ordered his military on full alert when an enormous blast occurred five kilometres over Novorsibirsk in Siberia. It registered on seismic instruments in both Washington and Moscow.

At first the Russians thought it was a thermonuclear blast, launched by either the United States or China, whom they called 'Asiatic Lunatics'. Kosygin was ready to hit back once he discovered who was responsible.

After a 'hot-line' call to President Carter, who denied any responsibility for the blast, Kosygin rang Felix Zigel, who had been warning of this possible scenario since 1967. He advised that they had been tracing an unidentified flying object over Siberia. He said it was passing some one hundred kilometres north of Norvosibirsk when it suddenly swooped southward in a descending, erratic glide, as though out of control.

In the meantime, Carter had spoken to the Vice-President of China, who insisted they knew nothing of the blast, except for what their listening posts had picked up. They were on full military alert, and warned they would strike back instantly if subjected to atomic attack.

Kosygin ruled out any nuclear accident of their own, and radar scans showed something had swept down from the vicinity of the North Pole over Siberia. Eventually the official Soviet conclusion was that a seismic disturbance had been caused by a meteorite exploding over Novorsibirsk.

In 1976, R. Varlamov an ex-official of the State Committee for Science and Technology, asked Prime Minister Kosygin to organise an official UFO investigation. The request was passed over to the Academy of Science, who promptly refused to comply, saying that the entire subject was 'unhealthy sensationalism'.

The same year, as Soviet dissidents circulated clandestine typewritten essays and statements opposing the government's actions, someone began spreading copies of a five page typed 'lecture' attributed to Felix Zigel. It said that the USSR had over three hundred recorded sightings, and gave examples.

Although Zigel remained silent about the document, it created immense interest and debate, and before long the official youth newspaper, the '*Kosomololskaya Pravda*' denounced the report, and implied that those who spread the flying saucer stories were somehow subversive, indulging in the 'mass culture' of the West, and 'flirting with superstitions and religious impulses manipulated indirectly by the Pentagon'.

During the following years, although some research was privately conducted, and despite public interest, newspapers were too scared to publish reports, and investigators faced government displeasure.

In 1974, I. Hobana and J. Weverbergh wrote an excellent book *'UFOs from Behind the Iron Curtain'* but most of the sightings they were able to document were essentially lights or craft seen at some distance in the sky.

Due to Russia's 'occupation' of Eastern Block countries, very few reports were published during the early years. In 1954 the Soviet newspaper *'Tass'* denounced UFOs as capitalistic propaganda. The Hungarian government had a similar approach, saying that UFOs didn't exist, and that all reports were invented by capitalist warmongers from bourgeois countries who wanted to detract attention away from economic difficulties. However, despite government denials, some reports managed to escape the official veil of secrecy.

Even in the 1950s, UFO reports, especially those involving craft landing behind the Iron Curtain, were few and far between, however Ronald Hamilton discussed one in 1954; *'Towards the end of July last year, the inhabitants of a number of Baltic villages near the Polish-German border, were amazed to see flights of strange saucer-like objects travelling across the sky at great speed. They were in formations varying from two to six in number. These flights continued for seven days and were usually seen about the time of sunrise and sunset.*

'For the first two days the police and military displayed exceptional interest in collating the reports which were coming in from a large area. Suddenly their attitude changed. They denied that anything unusual was happening in the heavens, and said that people who sent in further reports would be prosecuted as imperialistic war-mongers. This threat was enough to silence the reports, but it did not stop the people talking amongst themselves - nor did it stop the objects flying. After a full week of activity there came a lull of a few days, and then, on 29th July, further flights were observed. On the last day of the month one of the machines landed near a village called Walin.

'A group of Poles and two Germans were labouring in a field when their attention was drawn to an object which they saw descending almost vertically and at high speed. When it was near the ground it slowed down, almost to a hover, and then made a gentle landing.

'The group of workers made their way to the scene and stared at the object. A few minutes later, a Polish policeman arrived, took one look at the circular

machine, uttered the Polish equivalent of "Crikey" and dashed off to make a report.

It was estimated that the diameter of the machine was between forty and sixty feet. It had a spherical metal centre, which was entirely closed. On the outside was a large flat circle bearing wide exhaust pipes, similar to those of jet engines. The outer circle was also of metal. The machine appeared to have no crew'

Several parts of the machine had some indecipherable inscriptions, which the witnesses assumed must be Russian. During the excitement, one of the Germans used the opportunity to escape to the West. The rest of the group remained until the policeman arrived with reinforcements. Shortly after, a Russian helicopter landed with several MVD men who immediately cordoned off the area.

Nothing further was heard from the witnesses, and the Russians tried, unsuccessfully, to trace the German worker who had escaped.

Most of the few reports from the Baltic countries were of unidentified lights or craft in the sky, however some are worth mentioning.

Bulgaria

On 10th April 1967, the newspaper *'Rindt Zwei Kurier Sofia'* published reports of unidentified objects being seen in the atmosphere the previous day. There were many witnesses from Sofia who said a conical object flew over the city. It was photographed by journalists and others, and shown on television some days later.

At 5.30pm on 21st July 1967, there were numerous reports from Sofia of an unusual large, trapeze shape, bright blue neon type light. In the middle of the light there was something which looked like a large balloon type object with a dark disc on top. Around it was a phosphorescent green halo, which later changed to an orange shade.

The object moved slowly across the sky, stopped over the city, then moved away, flying against the prevailing wind. It did not influence radar installations or disturb TV reception. The object was officially declared unidentified by the Russian and Bulgarian authorities.

By 2014, having separated from the Soviet Union, discussion about UFOs was not so restricted. During a heated debate, over the role, feasibility and reform of the Bulgarian Academy of Sciences, Deputy Director of the Space Research Institute, Lachezar Filipov, saw his opportunity to make the most of the arguments between Finance Minister Simeon Djankov and President George Parvanov.

Britain's *'Telegraph'* newspaper reported Filipov as claiming the centre was analysing 150 crop circles from around the world. He said; "Aliens are currently all around us, and are watching us all the time. They are not hostile towards us, rather, they want to help us but we have not grown enough in order to establish direct contact with them."

He quoted the Vatican in his assertion that aliens existed, and was certain that humans would establish direct contact within the next ten to fifteen years.

Czechoslovakia.

On November 16th 1959, at about 8pm, a former Air Force fighter-pilot, Commander Duchon, along with a fellow officer – Bezac - was driving to a nearby airfield to supervise some night-flying exercises.

They were ten kilometres from their destination, when the car engine started to stall. As Duchon got out to look under the bonnet, they both spotted a pale sapphire band of light moving quickly across the sky at an altitude of about 600 metres. It seemed to be in the wake of a larger object, but none of their aircraft, not even a jet, could match that speed.

It took a while before the car would start again, and when Duchon and Bezac reached the airfield, they were surprised that no plane had landed there. Other pilots and ground personnel reported that at about 8.05pm a flaming ball had appeared in the sky. It was twice the size of any known bomber, and rotated as it silently zoomed over the airfield at a phenomenal speed.

It then made a ninety degree turn, and shot back across the aerodrome at an altitude of about 1,000 metres. Everyone agreed that no known aircraft could execute such a manoeuvre. The radar operator alerted an emergency aircraft, ready for any such occurrence, but the object had disappeared over the horizon before it was able to take off.

Soon after it returned, and hovered, for about two minutes, low over the runway. Control tower staff and anti-aircraft gun personnel stared in astonishment, and watched through binoculars. They all agreed that the craft resembled a disc or 'saucer', with a glowing band around its diameter, which was at least 150 metres. In a fraction of a second the object then accelerated to an incredible speed and disappeared into the night sky.

During this time unsuccessful attempts had been made to contact it in Russian, English and the International Aviation Code. Later, the surrounding soil and air were tested for radioactivity, but no traces were found.

Sometimes, when there were multiple witnesses, reports were published in the local press. The *'Letectvi Monautika'* carried a story of how, on 1st September 1965, hundreds of people in Kosise had seen red and black glowing spheres hovering over towns and villages.

The next day a witness from Ukerske Hrodiste reported a round object, about twenty metres in diameter, hovering one thousand metres up in the sky. It was a bright orange colour, and after a short while moved quickly away into cloud cover.

Hungary

In the 1990s, Hungary had the benefit of a new Minister of Defense, George Keleti, who was a Member of Parliament and a retired Colonel in the Hungarian Army. Before his political career, he had been a columnist who published UFO cases which had been observed and registered by the Hungarian armed forces.

Although over-flights of military installations may well have been Earthly spy missions, he considered them to be extraterrestrial. In October 1989, a Saturn-shaped UFO had floated over the Taraszentmaria army barracks. In 1994, when speaking of another 1989 incident over the Szolnok military airfield and academy, Keleti said that the aliens had already mapped Szolnok, and we didn't stand a chance in a UFO invasion.

During a 1989 incident at a Hungarian Air Force field in Kecskemet UFOs were seen, and an unsuccessful attempt was made to apprehend aliens on the ground.

Romania

In 1954, Romanian newspapers declared that the United States were trying to create a 'UFO psychosis' in the Romanian people, and it was sentiments such as these that ensured the silence of many witnesses. In later years, some more prominent citizens found the courage to speak out.

It wasn't until 2015 that an elderly George Pârvu, who was a respected geologist and author, told Romanian investigator Dan Farcas about a very disturbing incident that occurred in 1939.

George was just a young lad of nine when he lived in the village of Armâsesti, Iolamita County. It was early one bright, sunny morning in August when he was with four other primary school friends. After playing together in a field, they lay down on the grass, staring at the sky.

Suddenly, they saw an unusual light moving around in the sky. It circled a few times, and grew brighter and larger as it descended and hovered about 75 metres above them. It then dimmed and turned a dull copper colour. Two of the children were frightened, and hid behind the wall of a fountain.

The object landed about 45 metres away. It was shaped like a 'tulip', about five metres high and three metres wide. At the bottom of the object was a 'hollow, circular, inward bump', and a hatch which opened when two little men came out.

They were taller than the children, looked human, but had no hair, large eyes, and very thin, long arms. They were wearing tight fitting, grey, one-piece suits, and one was carrying a 'stick', similar to a thick police baton. As they walked towards the children, George, along with his friends Fânicâ and Marcel, joined hands and also approached the strange visitors.

When they were about seven metres away, the being pointed his 'stick', and the children could not go any further, as if blocked by an 'invisible wall'. The little fellows stared for a few moments, and then bowed low, in oriental fashion, as if greeting the children. They then turned, and marched in unison back to their craft. The whole time, one seemed to be whispering into some kind of small black box, which he was holding in his hand.

They entered their craft, and as soon as the door snapped shut, the ship rose to an altitude of 75 metres, before becoming illuminated and shooting into the sky 'without noise or flame'.

The three children noticed that the 'invisible wall' had gone, and they rushed home to tell their parents. George's father worked at the local railway station, about two-and-a-half kilometres away, and he rushed there to tell him of their strange encounter.

Mr. Pârvu put his hand on George's head, to calm his excited son, and quickly pulled away, saying it was like touching a 'live electric wire.' His father was a little sceptical when George claimed he had encountered 'two devils', and insisted they talk to the local priest on the way home. The priest tried to tell him they must have been 'two angels' but George didn't agree.

When they got home, his mother also didn't believe him, and after lunch, took him down the street to Fânicâ's house. The boy was very sick, could barely speak, and died soon after. They went on to Marcel's home, to discover he was also ill, and vomiting green bile. On impulse, George grabbed him by the hand, and made him run outside. After going about two kilometres, they stopped. Marcel mysteriously felt better, and by the time they returned to the house, both boys felt quite well again.

He saw, in the sky, what he thinks was the same object, on three other occasions in 1944, 1949 and 1954. During the war, he had reported the 1939 incident to a German officer, who advised him not to say anything about it. Later he got the same advice from one of his teachers at the geological faculty of the Romanian Academy.

Antoni Szachnowaki, the Chairman of the Anglo-Polish UFO Research Club, was able to speak more freely about incidents in the Balkans. During a 1963 lecture, he mentioned a great number of sightings over Transylvania, where the Transylvania Alps and Carpathian Mountains form a huge triangle. In the summer of 1953, some villagers became quite scared as UFOs swooped over the ridges and low over their homes.

One apparently landed on a mountain, north of Negoiul. The people fled, and spent the night camping in the church-yard of another village down in the ravine. When they returned, the cattle were huddled together and shivering.

Behind the village was a large circle of scorched grass, with a hole in the middle. Army units and the militia arrived later that day, and any information withheld from the press.

At 10.30pm on 4th August 1967, Bota Octavian, a professor of civil engineering, saw a strange object in the sky. It was a bluish-yellow to rose-yellow light which alternated with movement. It moved up and down, changing both speed and direction frequently.

A year later, at 8.21pm on 17th August 1968, near the Hungarian border, the pilots of an Ilyushin aircraft, and also the crew of a Hungarian plane, reported an oval object which appeared to have its own lighting system.

It was about three metres in diameter, and emitted a strong, bright greenish light. The object, travelling fast in the sky, flew parallel with the plane at an altitude of nearly eight hundred metres. After a while it accelerated out of sight at a speed of 12,000-13,000 kilometres per hour.

The next day Emil Burea and three other witnesses reported a similar object at Cluj. They also said it appeared to have its own lighting system, and shone silver in the sunlight. Unlike the airline witnesses, they estimated its diameter in excess of thirty metres, and took four photographs.

They said the silent object moved slowly at first, changed direction, then accelerated, shot upwards and disappeared, a 'vapour effect' appearing only at that stage.

Two days later, at 9.50pm on 20th August, Florin Iatan, the administrator of the State Orchestra, along with conductor Leonida Brezeanu and his wife, saw a deep-red coloured disc zigzagging across the sky. A yellow star-like light then joined and followed the disc. As they flew off, the disc's colour changed to 'neon white'.

The *'Flying Saucer Review'* published an interesting account received from Florin Gheorghita, its Romanian consultant.

On 20th June 1994, at about 4am, several witnesses heard a terrifying whistling sound, and saw a flashing light three metres above the wheat field. There was an associated severe blast of wind, and as a nearby shepherd worried about his flock of sheep scattering, the powerful blast left him clinging to a bush.

The area was bathed in light, and he could see a round object, like a big transparent dome, with a powerful white light inside. Two individuals were standing on what looked like a sort of balcony in front of a small, open doorway.

One man seemed to be about forty, and appeared to be slim, with a long beard and Asiatic-type eyes. The other also had a beard and moustache. They were wearing earphones and holding what looked like some sort of tubes or instruments. One was speaking into something he was holding in his hand, but the shepherd didn't know what language it was.

When the beings noticed him, the craft moved a short distance away. After two or three minutes, a bluish flame was emitted from the bottom of the saucer, the light went out, and with a loud noise, like a cannon, shot straight up into the air and was gone.

The sheep were scattered over a neighbouring field, and the dog was hiding in the shed and whimpering. Other witnesses had been so frightened they had fled into their houses.

There were two 'rings' in the crops, the inner one was six metres wide, and the outer forty-two metres wide, with a four to six metre 'band'. The stalks in the rounded and outer rings were heavily pressed down, close to the ground, and swirled in an anti-clockwise fashion. In the outer areas, the stems were interwoven or 'plaited' with each in a 'whirlwind' fashion.

No radioactive or magnetic anomalies were detected by Army specialists, and a local laboratory checked soil samples and found 'nothing notable.'

YUGOSLAVIA

As early as 1954, there were mutterings about new Russian technology, as well as US prototypes. In October the Yugoslav Air Force investigated reports from many areas of the country where up to seven flying saucers were seen. The Belgrade Astronomical Observatory saw four of the objects, which travelled to the south-east and returned half an hour later. The Director, Peter Djorkovic, said they were a 'mechanical contrivance', probably some secret weapon of the Americans or Russians'.

Again, on 21st December 1968, at 6.50pm, a group of young astronomers in Belgrade, Yugoslavia, observed what they considered was an unidentified object which travelled across the sky in a south-easterly direction. They watched for about fifteen minutes, and said it was a brightly lit orange-red, with a diameter less than that of the moon.

USSR

In 1965, in the Caucasus, Dr. L. Tshanovich reported seeing, in the sky, a glittering disc with a dome in the form of a cabin.

Two years later, in 1967, the crew of plane IL14 on the Zaparoyi-Volgograd route made a report which was later published in both the *'Soviets Kaia Latvia'* and the *'Veac Nou'*.

They were over the Ukraine when an unidentified object was seen above the plane. The engines cut out and they began to glide downwards. When they were only eight hundred metres from the ground the object disappeared and the aircraft's engines started up again.

In 1978, a huge disc, over sixteen-hundred feet in diameter, appeared over the Emba 11 Air Defense and Anti-missile Testing Range in Kahzakstan. They were testing new missiles, and the commander ordered the troops to fire an anti-ballistic missile at the intruder. It was blown up by a ray from the strange object, and subsequently the Minister of Defense issued a ban on such actions in the future.

CRASHES BEHIND THE IRON CURTAIN

Russian researchers claimed that the first extraterrestrial to be studied was seized on January 21st 1959, after a UFO crash near Gdynia, Poland. There were apparently other crashes in the sixties, and on 17th February 1979, another disc and its occupants crashed near the town of Zhigansk. Later that year, a further craft was found near Lihanova in Ural.

One very detailed report, written by Anton Anfalov and Philip Mantle, was published in VUFORS *'Australian UFO Bulletin'* in June 1998.

In late June, 1966, a geology expedition in Western Siberia, was woken by a loud noise, and saw a blinding bright globe explode in the sky. The trees around their camp site were on fire. As soon as it was daylight, they surveyed the devastation around them, and noticed a semi-circle of flashing lights through the trees.

Raised up, out of a nearby bog, was the streamlined hull of a charred and burnt object. It looked like 'two basins put together, with blinking lights around the rim'. A hatch was ajar, with dense smoke pouring out. Something dark, almost like a 'tentacle', was lying prone near the edge of the hatch.

The men felt sick, their radio and compass were malfunctioning, and fearing radiation they moved away from the area. That night they heard helicopters, and the next morning the object was gone. When they returned to Moscow a KGB officer told them it was a state secret, and they were to say nothing. Many of the expedition died early with some form of radiation illness.

Researchers found other witnesses. Local villagers who had seen and heard the fiery globe come crashing down out of the sky, were also warned not to say anything.

One man, Sergey Petrovich, had been a member of a military helicopter unit at the time. He recalled going to the site where they lifted the saucer out of the bog, and it was transported to some secret military aerodrome. He said the craft was eight to ten metres in diameter, with the coloured lights still flashing around the rim.

He looked into the dark, smoke filled interior, and like the geologists, also saw the dark-brown flipper-type thing leaning out of the hatch. The scientist who accompanied them carefully wrapped it in some kind of polyethylene, and told them to say nothing about it.

He did not know much more after he saw the cargo helicopter leaving with the disc suspended below. Later he heard rumours that there had been some bodies inside, and the whole incident was classified 'top secret'.

Anfalov alleged that before his death, Dr. Troitsky from the USSR Academy of Sciences, said that the Soviet government knew that the UFOs were extraterrestrial in origin, but concealed the truth from the public. People who spoke out were confined to mental institutions.

In early 1996, an interesting article appeared in *People* Magazine. It claimed that the Russian newspapers *Trud* and *Rabochav Tribune* had quoted rumours of another incident which had been 'hushed-up'. Government salvage workers had apparently died mysteriously after being sent to unearth the wreckage of a strange craft,

Believed to be thousands of years old, the object was buried, at a thirty-five-degree angle in dense woods north of Tallinn. It was made of silvery heat resistant material, fifteen metres in diameter, and weighed about two hundred tonnes. Workers dug a three metre trench around the craft, and several died of a paralysing illness whilst taking water samples back to Moscow.

Scientist Nikolay Sochevanov said they couldn't drill through the hull of the craft, even though it appeared to be only two centimetres thick. Eventually a pneumatic pick-hammer and diamond saws managed to break off a piece, and scientists examining the sample claimed there was no doubt the UFO was of extraterrestrial origin.

There were several instances of strange 'artefacts' being unearthed in Russian territories, however it is not conclusive that they were of alien origin. One was a black ball, discovered in 1976 in a ten million year-old clay deposit in Western Ukraine.

The owner of the land had allowed it to be displayed in a local museum until 1979, when the museum's curator took it to Moscow for examination by several scientists from prestigious institutions.

The owner of the 'ball' was angry, and demanded its immediate return, which left the experts just over a week for their assessments. Dr. Rubtsov reported that in the limited time available, they measured, x-rayed and weighed it, but were unable to definitively establish its composition.

The hard egg-shaped shell had a hermetic seal of some sort at the 'butt end', whilst the inner, glassy core was quite a mystery. It was composed of a substance with anti-gravitational (negative mass) properties, a characteristic previously unknown to conventional science.

According to author and investigator, Paul Stonehill, and an article translated by Gordon Creighton, Russia also had several strange craft crashing on its soil. In Stonehill's book, *'Russia's Roswell and Other Amazing Cases from the Former Soviet Union'*, he tells of the crash-landing of a spherical flying object, on a hill top at Dalnegorsk, a small mining town in south-eastern Russia on 29th January 1986.

It was not large, apparently only about three metres in diameter, perfectly round with the appearance of burning stainless steel. It flew slowly and silently parallel to the ground before ascending and descending. It made an abrupt turn, before making a couple of 'jerking' movements and hitting the edge of the cliff. There was no explosion – just a 'powerful impact', which created a small fire on the site.

Apparently CIA documents indicate that there was great interest in the craft fragments which were recovered. Some displayed anti-gravitational properties, and others, when subjected to heat, indicated some elements 'disappearing' only to be replaced by others. The Tomsk experts stated; *'It is impossible for us – in the present day state of our technology – to manufacture this sort of thing.'*

Dr. Vysoky, a specialist in Chemistry, added; *'Without any doubt, this is the product of a very high technology, and such things as these are not natural, and are not of terrestrial origin.'*

Other scientists who disagreed, went on to speculate that they were spy probes from the West, but later suggested that UFOs, seen over the area the next year, were extraterrestrial!

In 1988, Russian engineer and researcher, Nikolai Lebedev, reported on several other later incidents, in the Dalnegorsk area, where witnesses saw strange craft in the sky. On 3rd December, all the passengers on a bus disembarked to watch an unusual light hovering over a nearby mountain.

Paul Stonehill wrote about an incident in 1989, when a UFO, engulfed in flames, crashed in the Tyumen area, near the port of Nida. The UFO and bodies of its crew were supposedly recovered by the Soviet military.

That same year a UFO was reported as having been shot down over the Urals. It was transported by a MJ-26 helicopter to Zhitkur for further analysis.

Vladim Ilyin spoke of a case from the KGB's 'Blue Folder', which was obtained by Pavel Popovitch.

In early August 1987, the Leningrad Military were sent to the north of Karelia, near Vyborg, to guard an unknown object discovered in the countryside. It was fourteen metres long, four metres wide, and two-and-a-half metres high, with no doors or hatches.

All attempts to open it had failed, and the only things they had been able to remove were several strange rods from the stern. The craft was obviously taken away for further examination, however in late September, it was reported to have 'mysteriously disappeared, without a trace', from the hanger where it was being stored.

Russian ufologists Nikolay Subbotin and Emil Bachurin reported another crashed object on 28th August 1991. At 4.45pm, a large craft, six hundred meters long and over one hundred meters wide, was seen over the Caspian Sea and tracked on radar. It was at an altitude of over twenty thousand feet, and travelling more than six thousand miles per hour. It did not respond to radio transmissions or transponder signals.

Nearby facilities had also seen and tracked the object, and it was determined that no rockets or any other vehicles had been launched. Air Defense Command was alerted and two MIG 29 fighters, already in the air, sent on an intercept course. Two more planes were scrambled from the closest base.

When the planes closed in, they could see a large gray, cigar-shaped dirigible, with two circular portholes near the rounded tip in the front. There was what looked like a set of indecipherable green characters or symbols around its tail. The MIGs circled the object, but it did not respond or deviate from its course.

When the Soviet pilots pressed the trigger buttons to fire on the intruder, there was a complete failure of their electrical systems. The cockpit control panels went 'dead' and radio communication was cut off. As their engines began to splutter, the object shot off ahead of them.

Once the Russians regained control of the planes, they discontinued the pursuit, and returned to base. The unidentified craft was tracked on radar, taking a zigzag course back over the Aral Sea, and climbing vertically at an incredible speed before dropping back down to an altitude of just over fourteen thousand feet, which was back over civilian airspace. Everybody breathed a sigh of relief when just before 5.30pm it disappeared from radar.

At the end of September, authorities became aware of rumours circulating among residents of the villages surrounding Karakol. They said a large object had crashed in the mountains to the east. It had fallen out of the sky, and broken into pieces against a craggy hillside near the headwaters of the Sary Dzhaz river.

It was located in the Tien Shan mountains, in the inhospitable Shaitan Mazar region on the border of Kyrgzstan and Kazakhstan – also close to the Chinese border. An enthusiastic group of ufologists made an unsuccessful effort to locate the wreck, but the rough terrain and weather overwhelmed them.

They were told that in November, the Russian Air Force had located the crash site, and attempted to hoist the object out with a helicopter. Apparently they failed when the helicopter crashed.

In June 1992, the SAKKUFON UFO Research Group organised a much better prepared expedition under the leadership of retired Major German Svechkov. They discovered the metallic type object, in two pieces, resting on a long flat plateau. They declared that it was 'obviously from another world', and still generating some form of 'energy field', which made their precision electronic instruments useless.

At a distance, the expeditionary party could see the wreckage of the MI-8 helicopter, but they could find no bodies at either the helicopter or UFO crash sites.

Nikolay Subbotin organised a third team in 1998, and when they were a few kilometres away from the site, they rented a helicopter. The entire area had been bulldozed and cleared of any remaining debris.

The researchers debated as to the origin of this strange craft, wondering if it may have been conducting a spying mission for China or America? It seems unlikely, as miniature spy drones, and other surveillance methods, including satellites were in use by that time.

In 1998 a documentary, *'The Secret KGB UFO Files,'* was broadcast in many countries around the world. It purported to depict the retrieval of a crashed disc, and subsequent autopsy of a dead alien, near Berezovsky in 1969. Was it true, or an elaborate hoax, perhaps State sponsored? I don't know, and maybe never will. There are a lot of convincing arguments from both sides of the debate.

While there were many genuine events, similar to those in the West during the 1960s, a lot of incidents were due to the Soviets testing their own missile warheads, which upon re-entry from low-trajectory orbits, appeared to be UFOs.

On 30/31 March 1993, the Russian satellite launch rocket, Cosmos 2238, came crashing back to earth over Ireland, Wales and the west coast of Britain. It generated a lot of excited UFO reports.

CHAPTER FOUR

BEHIND THE IRON CURTAIN

PART TWO

During the mid to late twentieth century, Western governments were very concerned about UFOs appearing over their top-secret military establishments, often disabling rockets and equipment. However a similar situation was also occurring in the USSR.

British researcher, Gordon Creighton, an ex-diplomat and multi-linguist, obtained details of these incidents in the 1960s and even earlier.

'In the summer of 1962, on a hill near Rybinsk, some 150 km north of Moscow, new rocket batteries were being set up, as part of the defence network of the Soviet capital. A huge disc appeared, at the height of approximately twenty thousand meters, and with it a number of smaller discs. The UFOs took up positions, and appeared to be studying the missile site.

'A nervous battery-commander panicked and gave – unauthorised – the order to fire a salvo at the giant disc. The missiles were fired. All exploded when at an estimated distance of some two kilometres from the target, creating a fantastic spectacle in the sky. A second salvo followed, with the same result. The third salvo was never fired, for at this point, the smaller discs went into action and stalled the electrical apparatus of the whole missile base. When the smaller discs had withdrawn and joined the larger craft, the electrical apparatus was again found to be in working order.'

Gordon Creighton also reported on another incident the same year, when a large ball of fire was seen descending towards a munitions factory. There was a loud explosion, accompanied by 'myriads of intensely luminous small globes'. A great air-blast was felt, and all that remained was a crater where the department manufacturing an automatic device for atomic cannons had been.

Although the Russians were quick to blame 'American saboteurs', they realised that no factory workers had been injured. A few minutes before the explosion, a warning alarm had sounded, and everyone evacuated. A later enquiry established that the position of the interrupter-switch indicated that no-one had activated the alarm.

Astronomers and Scientists.

Sometimes the Soviet academics could bypass the Russian code of silence. At 9.15pm on 26th July 1965, astronomer R.Vitoloniek, and two colleagues at the Latvian Ogra Observatory of Astrophysics Laboratory of the USSR Academy of Science, made the following report, which was substantiated by two other witnesses, I. Melderis and E. Vitoloniek of the Litonia Astronomical Society.

'High in the sky, at an altitude of five kilometres, was a star-like object with a sharp triangular definition. When viewed through a telescope, it appeared as a combination of a central sphere type disc, like a lens with a ball at the central point, with three similar balls revolving around the perimeter.'

It was a very bright, 'dull green colour of ruby' and estimated to be about one hundred metres in diameter. It moved slowly across the sky, and before disappearing from sight, about twenty minutes later, the three smaller balls appeared to 'take off' from the disc.

About one year later, on 17th June 1966, a similar object was seen by geophysicist V. Krilov and a colleague at Elista in the North Caucasus.

On 24th September 1965, astronomer/geologist L. Tshechanovici was high in the mountains in Abhgazia, when he spotted a small disc in the sky. He commented that the object was darting around executing unusual manoeuvres, which were very complicated, and often spiral.

At Kherson, Russia, on 20th October 1966, U. Duginov, the director of the Hydromereorological School, along with fifty other witnesses, saw a pearly, silver colour, saucer-shaped object, at least two times the diameter of the Sun, moving eastwards across the sky.

By the 1980s, all the world's major powers were aware of the presence of UFOs, and speculated as to their origin and intentions.

In November 1985, President Ronald Reagan and Soviet leader Mikhail Gorbachev attended a World Summit Conference in Geneva. Addressing Gorbachev, Reagan famously commented; *"..how much easier his task and mine might be in these meetings that we held if suddenly there was a threat to this world from another species from another planet outside in the universe.*

"We'd forget all the little local differences that we have between our countries, and we would find out once and for all that we really are human beings here on this Earth together."

He is reported as to having made this same speech another four times in the following three years.

On 16th February 1987, Gorbachev was speaking at the Kremlin in Moscow – *"The US President said that if the Earth faced an invasion by extraterrestrials, the United States and the Soviet Union would join forces to repel such an invasion. I shall not dispute the hypothesis, though I think it's early yet to worry about such an intrusion."*

Later that year, on 21st September, Reagan made a very telling statement; *"....Perhaps we need some outside, universal threat to recognise this common bond. I occasionally think how quickly our differences worldwide would vanish if we were facing an alien threat from outside this world.* ***And yet, I ask, is not an alien force already among us..?"***

By 1990, Gorbachev no longer publicly denied the existence of UFOs. On 26th April, when meeting with workers in the Urals, one of them asked about some recent sightings.

He said; *"The phenomenon of UFOs is real, and we should approach it seriously and study it. I know that there are scientific organisations which study this problem."*

In later years, the Russians were a little more forthcoming about UFOs. Again, in May 1990, Gorbachev was reported as saying; "The leaders of our armed services have long recognised UFOs as genuine phenomena, calling for sensitive response. We are alert, but have no reason to believe that these visitors are other than peaceful."

Perhaps this disclosure was due to a well publicised event which occurred at 9pm on 21st March. After multiple witnesses reported mysterious flying discs, a reporter from the Labor Union newspaper, *'Rabochaya Tribuna'*, was given a report and the following declaration by Igor Maltsev, a four star general from the Ministry of Defense.

'We observed a disc-shaped object with a diameter of 300 to 600 feet. It had two pulsating lights on the sides when it flew horizontally. During vertical

movements the object rotated on its axis. It was capable of flying in S-curves, vertically as well as horizontally. It hovered over the ground, then shot off at a speed higher than two or three times that of modern fighter planes. All witnesses agree that with increasing speed the lights blinked faster.

'The object moved at altitudes between 3,000 and 21,000 feet. Its movements were silent and characterised by incredible manoeuvrability. It looked like the law of inertia of mass did not apply to it at all. In other words, they must have overcome the gravitational force of the earth. At present there are no earthly machines capable of performing such feats.

'Sceptics and believers both can take this as an official confirmation of the existence of UFOs. We can only hope that this official acknowledgment will put an end to the enormous speculation about this phenomenon, and affirm beyond all their doubts their presence. We now have good reason to say that sightings of UFOs are not the result of hallucinations, optical illusions or mass hysteria. They were detected by radar, and photographs of the objects have been scrutinised by experts.'

These words must have been a windfall for the media, and the *'Rabochaya Tribune'* recommended that readers *'read these lines carefully...We hope that scientists will now take up the matter and examine the facts systematically. It could be the first step towards solving the mystery.'*

Igor Maltsev, who by then was the Soviet Air Defence Director, also stated; "We had scrambled our jets to observe the craft. Our pilots were ordered not to attack, on the grounds that the discs might possess formidable capacities for retaliation. We obtained many photographs of the UFO – and also registered it on thermal and optical sensors."

These statements must have been a relief to witnesses, who, in the past risked being incarcerated in a mental institution, or at least losing their jobs if they spoke out.

William Burns and MUFON's Harold Burt wrote of an incident on 16th September 1989, which was documented in the local *'Semipalatinsk'* newspaper. It occurred in the skies of Zaostrovka near Russia's permafrost region. Six grey saucers were seen to be in pursuit of another golden disc-shaped craft, which was attempting evasive manoeuvres. Beams of light were being aimed at the golden disc, which was reacting with a similar response.

A Russian helicopter commander, Sichenko, commented that the battle was so intense, the energy generated shut down the local power-grid, and just on dusk, plunged the city into darkness. Eventually the attacking discs surrounded their prey, firing upon it multiple times.

The golden craft slowly descended, eventually coming down and crashing in a bog on a military range about ten kilometres outside the port city. Before leaving, the formation of the six attacking saucers seemed to be flying in a search pattern over the impact area.

One civilian pilot's instruments failed when he flew over the crash site, and Russian investigator, Sobbotin, and his group RUFOR, were not able to access this restricted place until 1990. By this time the area had been totally cleared. Apparently, all members of the military team who had removed the debris suffered serious, if not fatal burns.

In 1992, General Yevgeniy, of the CIS Scientific and Technical Committee, stated; "Our air forces have been recording UFOs and scrambling in pursuit of them since the end of the war against Hitler. The reality of these objects is beyond doubt, but what they are and where they come from is unknown. I am not aware of any overt hostility by the UFOs – and our pilots are ordered always to treat them in a peace-loving manner."

Were any of these strange objects ever apprehended? In his article *'When Pilots See UFOs'*, Steve Gerrard of the Southampton group – SUFOG – wrote of a report in the *'Daily Mail'* 25th June 1990:

'Soviet fighter planes shot down a UFO, but secret police hid the incident, it was claimed yesterday. Scientists attending a conference in Munich said parts of the craft were recovered after it was shot down over the Caucasus Mountains in March 1983. They said a recently leaked picture of the wreckage proved the KGB was hiding something sensational'.

<u>Felix Zigel</u>

One Russian academic, who researched UFOs all his life, often in secret, was astronomer Dr. Felix Zigel. He had graduated from Moscow State University in 1942, and became a lecturer in astronomy and mathematical analysis. In 1948 he became a junior member of the Soviet Academy of Sciences, and in 1963 was appointed to the position of Professor at the Moscow Aviation Institute. He was also responsible for instructing Russian cosmonauts.

He had been involved in researching UFOs since 1955, and along with several colleagues, he formed an informal investigation group. In May 1967, he was elected Deputy President of the 'Initiative Group of UFO Investigators'. Major-General L.Reino, the manager of the House of Aviation and Cosmonautics in Moscow had hosted the inaugural meeting, and helped establish the 'UFO Department of the All-Union Committee of Cosmonautics'. They held their first meeting on 18th October 1967, and 350 people, including the media attended.

Later that year, on 10th November, Zigel appeared on National Television along with Air Force General P. Stolyarov and Navigator V. Akkuratov. Thousands of people contacted them with witness reports, sketches and photographs. The authorities were not happy, and did everything they could to discredit the subject. Later that month Army General A. Ghetman ordered the 'Department' to be disbanded.

Later attempts for investigation and disclosure also failed, and Zigel, along with some eminent scientists and scholars, compiled a book, the *'Inhabited Cosmos'*. While it was at the printers, the publication was halted by government academic Artsimovich, who ordered thirty-two articles deleted as they were 'seditious'. Zigel said that despite his insistent requests, the manuscripts were not returned to him. The heavily censored copy of the book came out in 1972.

Several years before, Russian scientist, Professor Kazantsev caused quite a stir with his book, *'Stages of the Future'*, where he claimed that spaceships from Venus and elsewhere had visited Earth in the distant past.

On 25th May 1977, *'Nostra'*, Paris France, published the following article. (Some of the finer meanings may have been lost in the translation.) It is assumed that this is the same document which was clandestinely distributed in the USSR in 1976.

'UFOs in USSR. – Underground Text of Professor Zigel.'

'Since 1954, scientists from the USSR have begun to feel an interest in UFO problems. We account no more shilly and shallyings and mysterious revulsions of authorities. Sometimes it is common lampoons calling us 'humbugs' and 'agents provocateurs', sometimes a sarcastic smile, sometimes simple threats.

'It has lasted for several years, and is the final interdict which threatens all conscientious researchers who, in spite of that, cannot cast this very important problem aside. It is a fact, which cannot be contested, that in the USSR there is an official prohibition about all that concerns the studies and sightings of UFOs.

Zigel went on to say that all UFO publications have always been forbidden, and are accused of being insidious propaganda used by the United States. He considered that only a minority were in that category. Some of those publications did contain mistakes, misinterpretations and 'mystifications', but some sightings *'were precious and indispensible'*.

'It is really to despise Soviet science that to suspect it to be too infantile to find in a report, dishonesty or mind of cold war. For ten years, almost every month, a pseudo-scientist, guided by authorities, states on wireless, or in newspapers; "No Unidentified Flying Objects have ever been sighted above Soviet territory!" Some pilots, astronomers, professors of Universities and Institutes, some cultured witnesses, quite sincere, are far from this opinion.'

Zigel went on to suggest that a comprehensive, indexed account of over three hundred Soviet sightings should be published in a serious, and non-humorous manner. – *'In spite of some promises and statements, no action has been undertaken to carry through study, classification, and scientific publishing of those numerous mystery cases.'*

Zigel then went on to mention some specific cases; *'The pilot and aircrew of a plane going from Vorkouta to Omsk were categorical: A flying object, circle-shaped, which could not be confused with another aircraft or balloon, escorted their plane during the longer part of the flight. Numerous phenomena could be excluded, however their report was not registered. Similar sightings are very numerous, and it is probable many cases will never be known.*

'.....Another collective statement, and all also quite sincere; on September 24th 1962, aircrew and passengers of TU-104 reported that an oval object, then several other similar objects, turned for a long time around the aircraft. At this time, their statements which were registered, dwelt on the astonishing manoeuvrability and speed of the objects.

'During 1965, in Latvia, a well known astronomer, R. Vitolniek, sighted through a telescope, a make-up in triangle of four sphere-shaped objects. One of them

was in a central position, and perceptibly bigger than the other three. Due to their progressive reduction in size, Vitolniek, and several colleagues, thought that the four spheres were moving off from our planet.

'Ian Mederis, another scientist working with Vitolniek that evening, made immediate calculations and consulted his astronomical maps. He was certain that it was neither satellites nor missiles, however no appropriate action was taken over his report.

'What became of the sightings of Colonel Bykovsky and V.Terechkova? Those astronauts are surely not suspicious! Why haven't Akkoutarov's statements been taken into account? Nobody, including the responsible authorities and official scientists, seem to take notice of these and other reports'

Zigel suggested that there was a 'black-out' established against scientists, who were 'quite sincere and believable people'. He claimed that whenever they enquired about progress on experts' reports concerning statements or photographs, they had 'all too quickly' disappeared or been misappropriated. He wondered if it were better, to escape ridicule, to investigate under an alias.

'Boards of Inquiry no longer exist, are sleeping, or 'temporarily' relieved from their office and competence – often awaiting orders and credits for their research. We put the question – why this artificial silence? What must we think about this abrupt and unforeseeable drop in interest concerning research that we should have to carry on – at all costs.

'It will be necessary, consequently, like in 1959, that UFOs fly over the rocket-launchers of Sverdlovsk, be detected on radar screens, and drive the military crazy, in order that authorities conclude to a threat and come again to a better idea of things.'

In 1976, researcher Henry Gris, published an extensive article in the *'National Enquirer'*. This magazine had an unsavoury reputation for publishing sensational and questionable information, however it is worth taking a look at his report.

Henry Gris claimed to have visited Zigel in Moscow, and was given access to his files, which contained the following information, and had been investigated by respected, high level scientists.

Zigel said that besides artefacts of metal fragments and angel hair being retrieved, two military planes had been downed during one encounter. He declared; *"Based on hundreds on sightings reported by respected people, and actual evidence taken to our laboratories, there's no doubt that extraterrestrial probes have been reconnoitring Russia.*

"On the morning of April 27th 1961, on Lake Onega, north-east of Leningrad, a space probe, coming from another planet, scraped the frozen shoreline, but managed to continue despite some minor damage." The incident was investigated by an army engineer and environmental scientist, who reported back to the government. Witnesses had said that the object was a large, bluish-green oval object, which silently headed east at an enormous speed.

"A highly decorated test pilot claimed he was forced down twice by a UFO," said Dr, Zigel. *"On June 16th 1948, Arkadly Apraksin was flying a jet at 31,000 feet over the Baskunchak area, north of the Caspian Sea, when he spotted a cucumber-shaped object, which was sending out beams of light. The pilot reported the sighting to the air base, and received confirmation that radar had picked up the object. He was ordered to close in on the object, and force it to land – or else open fire on it.*

"When Apraksin got within six miles of the UFO, the beams opened up into a 'fan', and momentarily blinded him. The plane's entire electrical system and his engine went out, but he managed to crash land without any major damage.

"Almost a year later, May 6th 1949, Apraksin was test flying a new plane, when he encountered another cucumber-shaped UFO. Again, from a distance of about six miles, the UFO emitted a beam of light that temporarily blinded the pilot and destroyed the electrical controls." Yet again Apraksin managed to crash land, this time on the bank of the Volga River, twenty-six miles north of Saratov.

In 1981, Zigel was a little more forthcoming regarding the occupants of UFOs. He said there had been at least seven landings of extraterrestrial spacecraft near Moscow between June 1977 and September 1979.

He described occupants similar to those seen in the West, including humanoids who were so similar to us that they could mingle undetected. He then referred to the 'little guys' he called 'aliens' – the three to four feet tall beings who resemble us in some respects, possess relatively large heads, no hair, protruding eyes, set apart, and a pair of nostrils instead of a nose. These two categories he referred to as 'flesh-and-blood extraterrestrials.

He then went on to mention the 'visitors' who are of more concern to myself and other researchers; *'The Spaceships carry crews of robots or androids which possess the ability to disappear and reappear at will, and not being subjected to the physical laws of our planet, seem to be deliberately constructed in order to confound all our notions of space, time and dimensions.'*

On 3rd December 1967, an intensely bright object, beaming several cones of light, was seen by both passengers and crew of a plane approaching Cape Kennedy. They observed it following them for about ten minutes before it zoomed away. At the same time, three Arctic Weather Stations reported a similar object.

In his book *'The Worlds' Greatest UFO Mysteries'* author Nigel Blundell, discussed an incident from the late 1970s. It was initially reported in the *'Pravda'* publication, and Dr. Zigel led the official team of investigators into the case.

'Dr. A. Nikolaev, a respected historical sciences professor, spent three months in hospital recovering from his close encounter. He and three academic colleagues were on a camping holiday in southern Russia, when they came across a metallic, saucer-shaped craft, partly hidden in long grass. One of them threw some stones, which seemed to disappear inside the object.

'All four men then felt a strange force. Dr. Nikolaev was knocked out. The others, though drowsy, dragged him away. Two stayed with him while the third went for help; but both sentries fell asleep.

'When they woke, two three-foot figures, in space suits and helmets, were staring at them. At the first signs of life, the small humanoids scurried back to their craft, vanishing from sight through the hull. The object glowed, then disappeared.'

'Only days later, three other scientists saw an alien craft only sixty-seven miles from Moscow. They too were camping, and that night, in their tents, heard a babble of loud voices. None of them recognised the language, but all felt a sense of unaccountable fear.

'It was half-an-hour before they dared look outside. There stood a shining violet-coloured object, about eighty feet high, looking 'something like a giant electric light bulb.' It rose, swayed slightly, then soared upwards into a fluorescent cloud.

'The next morning the campers found a circle of flattened grass five hundred feet from their tent.....and called in the investigators.'

It must be noted that due to the ridicule given to UFO witnesses in the USSR, it took a lot of courage for respected scientists to report these incidents.

Dr Zigel said he would welcome the day when American and Russian scientists would combine forces to solve the mystery of UFOs once and for all.

Whilst Russian authorities dismissed UFO reports, and kept their files top-secret and firmly closed, they were more than interested in any information they could glean from overseas reports. New Zealand's Henk Hinfelaar reported in 1959 that an organisation called 'VOKS' was actually the 'Society for Cultural Relations between the Soviet Union and Foreign Countries';

'In digging deeper we found that a certain Igor Bogolepov, former Soviet official in Moscow, testified in the hearings on the Institute of Pacific Relations, and divulged re VOKS: - "Actually it was one of the cover organisations from abroad to the Soviet Intelligence."

In my book, *'The Days of the Space Brothers'*, I discuss correspondence, received in 1982, from a purported civilian UFO group in Russia, requesting information re an article I had written. I later discovered that their Novosibisk Post Office Box belonged to the KGB. I later learned of several identical approaches, made at the same time, to newspapers, groups and researchers in both Britain and New Zealand. Obviously the USSR was paying serious attention to the subject!

In 1990, Dr. Jacques Vallee visited Russia and met with some of their leading researchers. In his subsequent book, *'UFO Chronicles of the Soviet Union'*, he told a fascinating story of his experiences in Moscow.

He was especially interested in the reports from the Russian city of Voronezh, three-hundred miles south-east of Moscow, which had been sensationalised by Western newspapers. Later, British researcher Gordon Creighton also made a serious examination of this incident.

On 27th September 1989, less than two weeks after the 'battle of the saucers', at about 7pm, a very bright, flickering, luminous blue ball was seen heading in a northerly direction. It was a craft, about forty-five feet in diameter, and travelling at extraordinary speed at an altitude of about six hundred feet.

It was witnessed by over forty adults and a few schoolchildren, playing football. They reported it was hovering above Yuzhniy Park, when a hatch opened in the bottom section of the sphere. An eight-feet tall being appeared. It was wearing silver-coloured overalls and bronze-coloured boots. The creature seemed to have three eyes, 'and a sort of disc-shaped object on its chest'. It appeared to scan the terrain, and then closed the hatch.

The sphere then came lower, and landed. The being emerged again, and was accompanied by an entity which looked like a robot. *'The alien muttered something, and a luminous rectangle, about two-and-a-half feet by four feet appeared on the ground. It said something else, and the rectangle disappeared. The alien adjusted something on the robot's chest, causing it to walk in a mechanical way.*

'It was at this moment that one of the boys cried out in fear. The alien simply looked at him, and the boy instantly froze, unable to move. The eyes of the alien seemed to be emitting light. Everyone started shouting. Somehow the sphere and the beings vanished on the spot.

'Five minutes later, the sphere and the three-eyed being appeared again, just as strangely as they disappeared. The being now had, at his side, a tube about four feet in length. A sixteen- year- old boy was close to the scene. The alien pointed his 'rifle' toward the teenager, and the boy instantly disappeared. The alien entered the sphere and the sphere flew away, gradually increasing its speed. At the same instant, the vanished teenager reappeared.'

(The case of the disappearing teenager was not without precedent. Welsh researcher, Peter Paget, told of a case in the 1960s. A strange orange light had been seen one night in a field next to a village school in Britian's East Anglia.

The next morning one of the boys found a small 'plastic pistol' in the field, and gave it to the teacher, who put it in her drawer.

That afternoon, one troublesome pupil, Sandra, was chattering so much, the teacher jokingly took the pistol, pointed it at the girl, and said; "gotchya!". Without the other children noticing, Sandra immediately vanished, and after the class was dismissed the teacher just sat there, wondering what to do.

"I was suddenly aware of the figure of a man standing by me, dressed in some kind of 'boiler suit' protective clothing. I assumed he was a parent on his way home from work. He extended his hand, and lying in the palm of which was another 'toy pistol'. Wordlessly, I passed the first one over to him. He examined it briefly, clicked a small ratchet on the side, pointed it towards the corner of the room and pulled the trigger."

Immediately Sandra reappeared, still chattering, and only stopped to leave when she realised it was time to go home. The stranger disappeared into the evening gloom.)

Lev Aksionov and Boris Zverev, from the *'Moscow News'* immediately visited the Voronezh site, and reported that there was a sixty foot circular area, and four holes, set in a rhombus pattern, where the craft had stood. They also interviewed several witnesses, and noticed that some of the children's descriptions and sketches of the craft, aliens and 'robots' coincided to an astonishing degree with the accounts and sketches of children who claimed to have seen landed craft and entities at the village of Konantsevo, near Kharovsk, in Vologda Oblast Province in June 1989.

Foreign newspapers claimed that a Russian aviation engineer, from a nearby factory, had gone to the site with several colleagues. They had examined and measured the landing area and found an 'intense magnetic field'. A local Police-Colonel also commented that whilst she didn't know what it was that happened in the park, the radio-activity at the site was very high.

Many residents, who reported that they had observed UFOs several times between September 23rd and 2nd October, were interviewed by the local police.

'The Soviet researchers also related that eye-witnesses of four landings described not one, but four different kinds of beings who had emerged from the

various UFOs seen at Voronezh. The first kind consisted of ten-foot tall beings with three eyes. Two of the eyes were whitish; the third, in the middle, was red and devoid of a pupil. The second kind was a robot, actually a box with something resembling a head on the top of it.......

'The robot had knobs on its chest. A tall being touched some of the knobs, and the robot began walking in a mechanical way. In ten to twenty minutes the robot returned to the three-eyed beings, who turned it off and carried it back into the sphere....When the UFO rose from the ground, it almost instantaneously became a mere dot and disappeared in the sky.'

Journalists soon flocked to the area, and within days the local Voronezh officials convened an Investigation Committee, comprising scientists and experts.

The *'Moscow Weekly News'* published an intriguing article on 22nd October. Professor Stanislav Kadmenski, who held the Chair of Nuclear Physics at the University of Voronezh, described how he and his colleagues had collected seventeen soil samples at the site, and sent them away for analysis.

He then remarked that if the landing were to be proved, 'it would mean that we would have something to learn about the Special Theory of Relativity', and it would indicate that there exists another sort of physics that is, at present, unknown to us.

This was not the first UFO report from the city of Voronezh. British researcher, Gordon Creighton, reported the following incident which happened, nearly three decades earlier, in the summer of 1962;

'....over the city of Voronezh, a giant cigar, at least 800 meters long, came down to a height of only 2,000 meters, in daylight, and hung there immobile. Thousands saw it, and there was tremendous panic. Suddenly the cigar "began to grow transparent", and then disappeared completely.

'Shortly after this, some fighter aircraft arrived and flew around, evidently searching for it. Seconds after the baffled pilots had departed, the monster was back again "in the same place" above the city. Then a fast jet of flame suddenly shot out from its stern. The cigar began to move, rose steeply into the sky, and vanished at immense speed.'

Villagers in the Voronezh area are still quite superstitious, and researchers didn't quite know what to make of a report in May 1990, from the nearby town of Lipetsk. One night, Vladimir Akhaltsev was driving his milk tanker to the local dairy, when a strange 'ball' followed him along the road.

He speeded up to 100km an hour, but the object still followed him for half-an-hour. When he reached the dairy, the watchman silently pointed to a nearby shop, where it was still hovering. Farmers in three other villages had also seen the craft, and their main concern was 'if thirsty humanoids steal our driver, who is going to deliver the milk?'

In 1974, Canadian milkman, 36 year-old Ron Smith, was also pursued for almost an hour by a craft which resembled a 'giant sea shell'. He originally saw the object resting on the ground behind a barn. Initially, it rose to 500 ft in the air and sped off, soon returning to follow Ron, for almost an hour, around the Minden, Ontario suburbs, as he made his deliveries. It only left after he reached the city limits, and drove into a ditch.

(Elsewhere in the world, there were a couple of other cases of a UFO showing a more morbid interest in our larger, fluid carrying vehicles.

In April 1968, a sanitary collection truck broke down 2km from Hayfield, Victoria. The two drivers were waiting for a tow, when they saw an approaching row of red lights, with a dome and a light on top. They climbed onto the bonnet, to get a better look, but the object suddenly didn't come any closer. Perhaps a load of sewerage was not on its itinerary.

More disturbing was a 1967 Ohio case, related to John Keel by the local school teacher. In early March, the Red Cross Bloodmobile van was driving along Highway 2, near the Ohio River.

The driver, Beau Shertzer and his nurse assistant became hysterical when a large glowing object descended and lowered two long arm-like projections, one on either side of the van. Beau accelerated, but the object remained overhead. The 'arms' appeared to be trying to pick up the whole vehicle. Fortunately, some traffic approached from the opposite direction, and the object withdrew the 'arms' and flew off.)

In *'FSR'* 1990 (Vol 35-3), Gordon Creighton published the translation of a report which appeared in a Russian industrial journal *'Lesnaya Promyshlennost'*.

In June 1966 witness, 'Gennadiy', was fishing in the Kolyvanskiy Lakes near Novosibirsk in Siberia. He suddenly realised all of nature's sounds around him had gone silent, and a field mouse had crept between his knees, as if trying to hide. He noticed a light, and looking around, could see a machine hovering two-to-three metres above the ground, no more than ten metres away.

He said it was about six-to-eight meters long and two meters high, shaped like a 'flattened droplet' and made of a shining, silvery-coloured material, which emitted a faint, dull luminescence. As soon as he spotted it, part of the machine silently 'moved back', (I assume he may have meant a type of sliding door opened), and he could see three seats and a dark control panel divided into squares. There were three men standing in the opening.

He said they were "just like us, everything about them seemed just as it is with us." They were wearing smart casual dress, and were of 'fine physique'. One, who appeared to be the eldest, was standing to the front, and two slighter taller men stood just behind. They had short, fair hair, normal straight noses, and tranquil, 'benevolent-looking' faces. Gennadiy noted they had an air of 'quality – superiority'.

They said: "You won't get away from us so easily...Don't be afraid." When he heard them speak it seemed like a mixture of sound and telepathy. He had the impression they were 'looking at him through his cranium'. They assured him he wasn't asleep or hallucinating, and invited him to ask them questions. The contact lasted about thirty minutes and all three communicated, but the answers were not always specific, and at times they even argued.

They claimed they were the 'Knowers' who are investigating the world. They were with 'you' always and it was not necessary to seek them out. If mankind had a very strong desire to do so, it would be possible to alter the biological program for the life-span. They also advised he should not worry about mankind perishing, as it was their job to make sure it didn't happen.

Gennaldiy realised they were skilfully avoiding direct answers to some questions, and when he asked about the future, one said; "You are tired. You need to rest." He closed his eyes for a moment, and then opened them again. The craft was gone!

Gennaldiy did not speak about this for over twenty years, fearing people would think he was a 'madman.' The incident did not change his life, but Gennaldiy had always felt that one day his secret would be of use. (It is also of interest that this occurred in Siberia, which is an ideal location for concealed bases.)

It would be naive to assume that the humanoid Visitors have only infiltrated and integrated with a couple of countries, and while some societies discuss this, it is not mentioned in Russia. I have some friends from Siberia who talk in hushed tones, and I was surprised at the very public report made by Kirsan Ilyumzhinov in 2010.

Ilyumzhinov, was the leader of Russia's southern region of Kalymkia, which is a small Buddhist area on the shores of the Caspian Sea. He stated, during a television interview, that on 18th September 1997, he heard someone calling him from his Moscow apartment balcony. He went out and saw a 'half-transparent, half tube spaceship'. He went inside, and met human-like beings in yellow spacesuits, who gave him a tour of their craft. Apparently all communication was telepathic, and they advised him they had come to Earth to take samples, and that they were people, just like us.

Although Ilyumzhinov claimed he had witnesses, fellow politician Lebedev, suggested that he should be investigated by President Dmitry Medvedev. Lebedev noted that if this was not just "a bad joke", Illyumzhinov may have "divulged state secrets".

Ilyumzhinov was not the only leading politician to embarrass the Soviet hierarchy. Timothy Good's book, *'Earth – An Alien Enterprise'*, tells of how, in 2012, Dmitry Medvedev, then Russian Prime Minister, was giving a television interview on 7th December that year. Thinking the segment was over, and his microphone was turned off, he made some very revealing comments, which were inadvertently not deleted in the pool signal delivered to Reuters.

Reporters asked him if the President is handed secret files on aliens when he receives the briefcase needed to activate Russia's nuclear arsenal.

His answer was astounding; *'Along with the briefcase of nuclear codes, the president of the country is given a special, top secret 'folder', containing information about aliens who visited our planet....Along with this, you are given a report of the absolutely secret special service that exercises control over aliens on the territory of our country....I will not tell you how many of them are among us, because it may cause panic.'*

He mentioned a Russian documentary, *'The Secret about Men in Black',* which examines testimony that extraterrestrial beings have been established on Earth, and that some are in restricted US military areas with the full knowledge of the Pentagon.

One retired Russian Air Force Colonel said he personally knew of forty cases where Soviet pilots had been ordered to follow the unknown craft, and several had crashed whilst in pursuit.

In 1985 Aeroflot airliner Flight 8852, from Tblisi to Tallinn, was 120km from Minsk when the crew and co-pilot noticed a huge, bright yellowish star. It emitted a thin ray of light which suddenly widened into a blinding cone, followed by two more cones.

Passengers said they were surprised to see the streets below them illuminated. The bright light vanished leaving a green cloud that descended at great speed until it came to a halt behind the plane. The 'cloud' changed shape into a circle, then a square, and finally solidified as a giant wingless aircraft with a 'needle-nose'.

The pilot contacted ground control, who advised the UFO was flying behind him at an altitude of 10,000 metres and a speed of 480km/hr. The object tailed the airliner over Riga and Vilnius all the way to Tallinn, when it eventually disappeared. The radar in all these places picked up two targets. The reality of these objects is beyond doubt, when flight schedules showed only one airborne at the time.

In 1990, Igor Maltsev, Soviet Air Defence Director, said; "We have scrambled our jets to observe the craft. Our pilots were ordered not to attack, on the grounds that the discs might possess formidable capacities for retaliation. We obtained many photographs of the UFO – and also registered it on thermal and optical sensors."

Were any of these strange objects ever apprehended? In his article 'When Pilots See UFOs', Steve Gerrard of the Southampton group – SUFOG – wrote of a report in the *'Daily Mail'* 25th June 1990:

'Soviet fighter planes shot down a UFO, but secret police hid the incident, it was claimed yesterday. Scientists attending a conference in Munich said parts of the craft were recovered after it was shot down over the Caucasus Mountains in March 1983. They said a recently leaked picture of the wreckage proved the KGB was hiding something sensational'.

RUSSIA

Dr Valery Uvarov, of the National Security Academy, St. Petersburg, wrote of an interesting event which occurred on 2nd November 1989.

Truck driver Oleg Kirzhakov, and his offsider Nikolai Baranchikov, were driving from Arkhangelsk to Moscow, when they found the road near Emtza railway station was undergoing repairs. They had to detour down a dirt road in order to reach their destination on time.

After rounding a bend in the road, they noticed a huge 'structure' on the right-hand side, which they initially thought was more construction/repair equipment. When they got within about eighty feet of the object they could see its metallic sheen in their headlights. The truck's motor stalled, and they coasted to a halt around the next bend.

Oleg got out to investigate, and Nikolai remained in the cabin to keep watch and observe. Every time Oleg tried to approach the object, he felt some invisible resistance in the air around him, making it difficult to walk. After some persistence he came close enough to stare at something he was sure was 'not of Earthly origin'.

Thirty feet in front of him was a huge disc, about 130 feet in diameter, with a dome-shaped top. Along the perimeter were some dark holes, and underneath he saw two structures, which he thought were supporting the craft. The far edge of the disc was slightly elevated, and resting on some birch trees, two of which were broken. Oleg could see no signs of life, or any doors or windows on the object, and thought something must have gone wrong. Was some assistance required?

As if an unseen intelligence had read his mind, a glimmering red dotted line appeared in front of him. It morphed into a small transparent screen, upon which several words were written in red. Oleg thought it was asking for 'burning fire', and returned to Nikolai in the truck to get some matches and a bottle of laboratory alcohol, which they used as an anti-freeze in the braking system.

(Although the 'screen' and messages were in front of Oleg at all times, apparently Nikolai couldn't see it. I have spoken to witnesses in Australia, who have also experienced the same type of 'message screen'. It may be inter-dimensional or telepathic.)

Oleg told Nikolai to remain in the truck, and he returned to the shoulder of the road where he gathered some dry leaves and set them on fire. Suddenly the 'resistance' in the air was gone. A passage appeared on the surface of the object. It extended into the interior, forming a corridor, at the end of which was a glimmering, bluish light.

A 'shaft' extended down from the object to the ground, and a black 'mass', which looked like a 'bag or sack', came out of the corridor, slid down the shaft, and took the box of matches. By this time Oleg had fallen into a ditch with terror, and Nikolai's frightened face was pressed against the windshield of the truck.

The 'thing' had returned to the craft by the time Oleg had climbed out of the ditch. He stood there in disbelief, trying to recover his senses, and decided to wait and see what would happen next.

There must have been some form of telepathy in play, because as soon as Oleg thought he would like to observe the disc more closely, the screen reappeared with an invitation for him to enter. He tentatively approached, and noticed several round openings, which he thought may be portholes. A narrow metallic tube came out, just above his head, and when he grabbed hold of it, he suddenly found himself just inside an opening above.

He walked down a corridor, which had oval shaped walls and ceiling. There were no doors, just a shimmering light about twenty feet along at the end. Upon reaching it, he found himself in a large hall, with a domed ceiling and a diameter of about sixty feet. It had a diffused light, and panels of flashing lights along some of the walls. There was a long, straight divan, and a circular crack around the central part of the hall. He thought it may be to allow it rotate, giving access to various controls.

He saw two motionless black 'masses', like the one he had seen outside. They began to move towards him, and he stood still, his mind full of questions. The screen was still in front of him, but the answers appeared in his head before he could read them on the screen.

He was very curious about everything around him, including an oval control panel, and geometric symbols on the upper surface of some lamps. Eventually he got around to asking who they were, and where were they from?

The dome in the hall started to dim, and like a planetarium, a star map appeared on the ceiling. One star began to pulsate and slowly descend, and he was told it was in his galaxy.

He had many more questions, and again the answers appeared in his head before they were on the screen. He learned this was a scout ship, which used electromagnetic fields to fly. They were studying our planet, which they needed as a 'springboard' to the future.

He noticed another two 'masses' had come into the hall, and understood it was time for him to leave. He left the same way as he had come in, and returned to the road. He looked back to see the tube and opening had disappeared. The outer rim and dome had started to silently rotate in opposite directions, and a luminescence surrounded the craft until it resembled a 'ball of light'.

It slowly began to rise, then accelerated and shot out of sight to the north east. By this time there were two other cars on the dirt road, and all the occupants, along with Nikolai, raced over to Oleg. They were full of questions, but he was so overcome and trembling that Nikolai had to drive the rest of the way.

This case is interesting because it does seem possible that Oleg was interacting with alien artificial intelligence during his experience. The 'dark masses' he encountered never seemed to equate to a 'live being'. By 1989 we were more adept at detecting any intrusions into our atmosphere by extraterrestrial craft, and the 'visitors' would certainly have the advanced technology to access our citizens this way.

The second factor in Oleg's testimony is his reference to the 'star map'. In the 1961, Betty and Barney Hill case, (See *The Alien Gene* pp172-4), where the couple were abducted from their car, Betty was also shown a 'star map' which depicted trade routes and other information. She recalled a three-dimensional hologram, which, despite being disputed by some experts, was later verified by the astronomy department of the Ohio State University.

Marjorie Fish, who did the majority of the analysis on Betty's recalled 'star map', was convinced it was genuine and accurate, even to the extent that it contained astronomical bodies which we had not yet documented. Respected scientist and ufologist, Stanton Friedman, wrote an in-depth review supporting Marjorie Fish's analysis. His extensive article can be found in the '*MUFON UFO Journal*' Oct/Nov 2009. A later study and astronomical commentary was contained in *'The Zeta Reticuli Incident'*, by Terence Dickinson.

Not all encounters in Russia were pleasant. Gordon Creighton translated an article from the *'Kazakhstanskaya Pravda'*, 12th November 1994. A night watchman, at a relay station, about two hundred miles from the town of Karatau, in Central Kazakhstan, was alerted, late at night, when his dog started barking and raced outside. There was a 'huge, globe-shaped, luminous machine' standing about fifty metres away.

From what appeared to be an invisible door in the craft, several creatures, who slightly resembled human beings, disembarked. They were wearing skin-tight silver suits, and his dog 'gallantly' attacked them. One of the strangers stretched out his hand. A slim blue ray shot out and touched the dog, which immediately 'froze' and fell silently to the ground.

The witness raced inside, and called the Karatau police station, urging them to - 'Come at once!' Before he could say anymore, the same humanoid appeared in the doorway. A similar blue ray knocked the watchman to the floor.

When the police were about a kilometre away from the relay station, their car engine cut out. When a back-up car was dispatched, the same thing happened. About an hour later, their engines started-up again, and they reached the witness who appeared to be in some 'strange coma'.

They brought him back to the stage where he could recount the entire event. They said that 'the dog never did wake-up', and that a perfect circle of carbonised rock was found at the place where the UFO had landed.

I have always been impressed with the research of Paul Stonehill, Dr. Uvarov and their colleagues. Unfortunately, other early amateur Russian ufologists had a habit of sensationalising some of the sighting reports, and making wild, unsubstantiated claims, and I am hesitant to document some of their reports.

More reliable Soviet officials have confirmed that 'of course UFOs are real', and their country was just as anxious to learn the advanced alien technology.

Before his death, Ukrainian researcher, Anton Anfalov wrote several letters to his Western colleagues. He believed that there was a worldwide UFO conspiracy of silence, in which Russia played a significant part. He claimed that several alien craft had been captured by the Soviets - many were operational, and others back-engineered. They were taken on test flights by a select group of pilots. He also stated that since 1978 the Russians had mastered alien technology quite successfully.

In 1998, Tim Swarz published some of what Anfalov had to say; *'I do not care what you think of me and of my research. I have done my duty to disclose the facts as I know them. What fate lies in store for me because of my revelations, I do not know or care. I do know that I can truly meet my Creator with a clear conscience, knowing that I have done my part to alert humankind to the dangers of alien contact.'*

He believed that the equivalent of America's 'Hanger 18' was located at Military Base 25840 at Odintsovo near Moscow. Further, that Russia had, near the secret village of Zhitkur, an equivalent of America's 'Area 51'. It was manned by Military Unit 73790 on the 4th State Central Test Site, Kapustin Yar, and this was probably where Russia's major secret UFO research centre was located. He contended that this Unit had several alien craft at the disposal of the Russian military and scientists.

He stated that the Soviet Union had also captured several crashed flying saucers, plus some which had been examined and tested, and were fully operational. Since 1978, the technology was understood, and successfully mastered. These alien craft have been used for Russian strategic reconnaissance missions all over the world. Some are piloted by their own officers, and some by remote control.

He confirmed the retrieval of an alien body from the UFO crash in Gdynia in 1959, and said that since then more than a dozen extraterrestrial biological entities, (EBEs), have been retrieved.

In February 1979, a disc crashed near the town of Zhigansk. It contained two dead aliens, who were transported to the biological facility at Moscow University for autopsy. Afterwards they were transported to the Odintsovo facility, along with the disc, and another craft which crashed the same year, near the town of Zhidansk.

Anfalov also made claims about many 'abductions', and indicated that the USSR had several alien 'guests' with whom they had made 'mutual agreements' similar to those which have allegedly been made in the West. There is no way of ascertaining the accuracy of these reports, and whether they are just State sponsored disinformation.

There is no doubt, that at the time of his many 'disclosures', Anfalov was concerned about his own safety. He mentioned the murder of Russian scientist and Ufologist Dr. A. Zolotov, and that Svetlana Petrova, who publicly made some astounding claims, barely escaped being murdered by an unknown individual and from being forced into a mental institution.

CHAPTER FIVE

UP INTO THE AIR

PART ONE

Italian researcher, Renato Vesco, published the book *'Intercept UFO'*, which is well worth reading. It details our own secret advances in aeronautics, from the early twentieth century to 1968. While it is very controversial and complex, it is recommended for any serious investigator.

He makes reference to the 'updraft' on many of the prototypes being tested by the leading nations. A classic example of this may have occurred in 2003, when Mrs. S and her husband were driving home for lunch. In the clear blue sky was a 'ball' of thick, heavy cloud.

A dull, metallic-type saucer descended from the cloud. It had a 'bump', top and bottom, and appeared to be oscillating or wobbling. As it passed over the top of their vehicle, they felt a 'prickling' sensation, and the back window disappeared with a loud 'pop'.

She stopped the car, and looked in amazement as they saw their back window disappear up into the sky and vanish. They unsuccessfully searched the surrounding fields and paddocks for days, and eventually had to seek a replacement. The rubber around the window was completely intact, and the windscreen fitter told them it was impossible for the glass to be removed in this way.

This kind of event was not without precedent. Fifty-five years before, in Oaklands, California, a young lad was on his early morning paper round. He took a shortcut through the rim of a gravel pit, and was startled when a large object flew up from the centre, and disappeared into the sky.

He said it 'seemed to pull the bike, which then disappeared, 'from under me'. He was almost knocked unconscious, and suffered several cuts and bruises. His bicycle was never found.

Another strange event occurred in Jacinto Arauz, Argentina, on 2nd August 2002. Rancher, Dorado, who was surveying his field, three miles out of town, heard a sound like a 'whirlwind', and looked up to see 'a green circle with three legs' hovering overhead, about five feet away.

He felt something similar to an electric shock, and fell to the ground. He was paralysed, and unable to reach his shotgun, which was on the ground beside him. His binoculars were in his right hand, and his cell-phone in the left. The phone was 'sucked up' from his hand, and he watched, helplessly, as it rose and disappeared.

It took him an hour to recover, and get back to his car. Upon his return home, he was suffering from 'severe shock', and his wife and neighbours took him to hospital.

Local newspaper, *'La Neuva Provincia'*, reported that the Deputy Sheriff investigated the incident. He unsuccessfully rang the cell-phone several times, only once hearing a breathing sound, and the phone company concluded it was either turned off, or out of range.

It's possible that some of the early cases of 'updrafts' may be attributable to our own 'prototypes. In October 1954, a circular object was seen floating slowly to the ground. It stayed there, motionless, for several minutes before finally taking off – straight up. It left a twenty feet diameter crater where it had landed, and the earth was torn out, as if by powerful suction.

An 'updraft' may also explain some incidents of cars being temporarily 'lifted' from the road, but not where people and entire vehicles have disappeared into a UFO. Do the mechanisms of certain unidentified objects also involve some form of magnetic component or a powerful 'suction' mechanism from underneath?

We must not dismiss the thought that some 'uplift' scenarios may represent part of 'teleportation' technology. The evidence of this is hard to come by, but one case, which comes to mind, was reported by Brazil's Irene Granchi.

In 1992, when discussing cases from the 1970s, she mentioned an unusual event that happened to Severino Netto, who lived in the south-side of Rio de Janeiro. He had gone to visit his girlfriend, who lived in Tijuca, on the north-side, and at 10.30p was waiting for his bus home.

A 'normal-looking' man came up to him, and asked the time. He was about 1.70m in height, clean-shaven, and wore a dark blue suit, with a turtle neck shirt of the same colour. Severno said his movements seemed totally human, as did his voice, which was 'deep-pitched'.

At first Severno was a little nervous, fearing he may be assaulted, as holdups were frequent in the area. He relaxed when the man took four or five steps, looked up at the sky, turned around, took another few steps and looked up again.

While Severno was keeping an eye out for his bus, he noticed a beam of light coming from about thirty metres overhead. It was yellowish-grey, and sixty centimetres wide. It came straight down towards the man, enfolding him in something like a 'power-net. Once it reached the man's body, and covered him, it turned reddish, and created the impression of a power or electric field.

At the same time, the 'man' was drawn up, his feet only just leaving the ground. Gradually, he started to disintegrate, starting with his sides, and only at the end, his feet, which were then lifted right into the air. The beam of light subsequently disappeared to some point 'not far away' in the sky.

This brought to mind, a letter I have, which was sent to New Zealand researcher, Fred Dickeson. In *'The Days of the Space Brothers'*, I detail George Adamski's 1959 tour of New Zealand. It was said that two of the 'brothers' quietly accompanied him, and used to slip into the back of the hall after he started his lecture.

One of the audience, a local group member, was vigilant in trying to identify the 'visitors', and one night he spotted a possible contender. He reached into his bag, pulled out his camera, and directed it to the suspected fellow sitting at the rear of the audience. Suddenly, the man started to disappear, from the feet up. The witness's photo clearly displayed only the upper half of the man's torso!

'Research of Australian Close Encounters', detailed an interesting report, which dates back to New Year's Day 1920, when we certainly had no comparable craft, or technology.

The informant detailed some incidents that occurred to her family; "My grandmother saw UFOs her whole life, and told me of this before she died, aged 77 in 1991."

Granny lived in a very isolated area, on a property owned by her father. Sometimes other relatives would stay with them, before travelling on.

When she was about six, her elders told her that there are flying saucers which will take some people – lifting the motionless victim off the ground and taking them inside an opening underneath. Older people had been taken from around the region, and nobody went out after sunset. One night, her grandmother's first cousin was still playing outside after dark.

Granny started yelling at her to come home because the 'flying saucers' would get her – but she didn't listen. Suddenly, out of nowhere, an object appeared overhead. The family screamed at her to run for the house, but it was too late.

As it started to lift her up from the ground the entire family, and other witnesses were running out, yelling and throwing things at the saucer, but it had no effect. She was taken inside the opening underneath, the 'door' closed, and she was never seen again.

In 1955, Dr. M. Jessup, of Michigan and Drake Universities, was an astronomer, mathematician and archaeologist, who also explored the jungles of Central America. In his 1955 book *'UFO'* he wrote of a case even earlier than Granny's experience. In 1890, on Christmas Eve, an Indiana family were gathered together at the Lerch farm on the outskirts of South Bend. Their guests included the local Methodist minister and his wife, a lawyer and several other friends and neighbours.

It was around 10pm when Mrs Lerch asked her twenty-year-old son, Oliver, to take a bucket and get some more water from the well across the yard. The young lad took two buckets, put on his cap, coat, and gloves, and trudged out into the snow.

He had only been gone for a few seconds, when the piano and carol singing were interrupted by his frantic cries for help. Everybody ran outside, but could not see Oliver. The minister held up a paraffin lantern, and in its flickering light they could see Oliver's footsteps in the deep snow. They extended for some distance towards the well before suddenly stopping.

The horrified witnesses could hear Oliver screaming, from above them; "They've got me! Help, help! It's got me!"

The light from the lantern did not extend into the pitch-black sky, and although they could not see Oliver, for the next five minutes they could hear his cries gradually becoming fainter and fainter.

Everybody searched franticly, checking the well, and even climbing ladders to the roof and up trees. Oliver's footprints stopped about 225 feet from the house, about half the distance to the well, beyond this the snow was undisturbed. Only one of Oliver's buckets was found, about fifteen feet from where his footsteps ended. There were no signs of animal tracks or a struggle.

The next day the search continued, and the police reluctantly came to the conclusion that Oliver had been seized, on his way to the well, and taken directly upwards. The facts of this case are contained in the South Bend police records, and are attested to by several witnesses.

Jessup also mentioned another case, which happened in the same area, and occurred about twenty-five years earlier, in the late summer of 1865.

Just after dark, several timber workers were sitting on the hotel porch, when they noticed a stranger, apparently drunk, muttering to himself, and staggering down the street. He had only gone about two hundred yards, when he suddenly began to shout; "Damn you, let me go!"

The men from the pub rushed out, as did some from Kelley's farm in the opposite direction. The stranger was nowhere to be seen, but his voice could be heard shouting from overhead. After a while, his voice became fainter and stopped.

The dust in the road, which was several inches thick, showed his footprints, which abruptly ended. Even experienced trackers could not locate the man. The local Indians had a legend about a giant bird that could carry off men and animals.

On Christmas Eve, 1903, in Szuhabaranka, then part of the Austrian-Hungarian Empire, a 'glistening ball' illuminated the whole remote mountain village. Before it eventually flew away, there was some movement around the object, and vague silhouettes were reported. The local Greek Orthodox priest told the local police and District Attorney how the villagers hid in his church. They prayed as they expected the end of the world to arrive.

At the same time, Petrovszky Ivanku, a simple woodcutter in the area, went outside to get some water from a nearby well. He was never seen again, and the authorities could not account for his disappearance.

Bob Pratt investigated a similar event in North-East Brazil, south-east of Santa-Cruz, in 1979. Late one evening, after visiting a neighbour, Francesca was walking home with her thirteen-year-old daughter, Josefa. They were about 200 metres from their home when a bright light appeared over the top of the hill.

As it came closer, it became bigger and brighter, and shot a beam of light towards them. Francesca was caught in the beam, and unable to move. She shouted to Josefa to run to the house, as quickly as she could.

As Francesca started to rise off the ground, Josefa grabbed her, but only managed to pull her down a little. Francesca continued to slowly rise, and she felt a strong 'wind' blowing around her, but there was no noise or dust.

She was hysterical, crying and praying to God for help. After being drawn about forty metres towards the object, the wind stopped and she was lowered, unhurt, back to the ground. The object swung back and forth in an arc for several seconds and then took off.

Francesca was trembling with fear, and her body was tingling all over. She was numb for a couple of days, and had severe headaches for a week. Other than that, she seemed to recover without any side-effects.

A similar occurrence happened in Manitoba, Canada, in late June 1967. This case was investigated by L.Chickoski and E.Barker from CAPRO.

This event was witnessed by Mrs Le Marqunda, her husband and three children, as well as four neighbours and two other children. It was 6pm, still summertime daylight, when they were all out in the garden. Mrs Le Marqunda had just gone inside, to the kitchen, and heard an unusual beeping noise. When she looked out of the window, she could see dirt and debris moving rapidly around the house in a circular pattern.

She raced outside to see her husband, who had just driven into the yard, along with the five children, all staring into the sky. Overhead was an object, described as being very large, and of an oblong or cubic shape. It was silently revolving in a counter-clockwise direction, and appeared to have alternating shiny aluminium and then black sides as it moved. There were no apparent openings or lights.

Her attention was distracted by a muffling sound, and she turned to see the thirteen-year-old boy, from across the road, pinning her eight-year-old daughter to the ground. At this time, the object moved away, at a 45 degree angle, dropping the debris in a yard across the street. It then levelled off, hovered and flew to the south-east.

The children were all frightened. Apparently the young girl had risen into the air, towards the object. As she was lifted upwards, her skirt, blouse and hair had also risen straight up her body. The thirteen-year-old boy had grabbed and saved her when she was a few feet off the ground. When she got back on her feet, she could remember nothing from after the 'wind' started.

Was this an inadvertent 'updraft' or an attempted abduction? We may never know.

These events have occurred all over the world, especially in South America. Carlos Diaz was walking home at 3am, having worked the late shift at his second job as a part-time waiter. He bought the early morning *'La Neuva Provincia'* newspaper, and caught a bus to his home in White, Bahia Blanca, Argentina.

He was walking to his house, only one hundred metres away, when suddenly his legs 'would not work'. He felt a current of air, violently rising him up, and then lost consciousness.

All he could remember was that he woke up in a silent, translucent sphere, about three metres in diameter, with no windows or doors bar one small opening. After about fifteen minutes, three beings approached him. They had human form, but their faces were smooth, with no sign of ears, nose or mouth. Their arms seemed to end in 'stumps' without any hands.

Two of them grabbed him, and seemed to be trying to pull out his hair. He fought back, and lost consciousness again.

He recovered with the sun, high in the sky, beaming down on him. He did not know where he was, and was taken to the nearby Central Railway Hospital in Buenos Aires. He was two hundred miles away from his home, and no-one believed his story until they saw his newspaper. That edition had still not been delivered from Bahia Blanca.

Bob Pratt also discussed another South American case from Brazil, which occurred in 1978, in Penalva, nearly two hundred kilometres south-west of São Luis.

On 24th March, Good Friday, sixteen-year-old Luis was gathering guava fruit in the forest when he heard a loud sound overhead. It resembled something like a car horn, and with some trepidation he looked up to see an incredible bright light above the trees. It hurt his eyes, and as he looked away, he fell on his back.

He couldn't move, and after a while felt himself rising into the air. As he rose, he could see a round object above the trees, and when he floated up level with the strange craft, he moved sideways into it through what appeared to be a window, and fell softly to the floor.

Inside were three small people, not more than one metre tall, wearing helmets and visors, who were moving around and talking in loud, non-human voices, which Luis did not understand. Even when the object made a rumbling sound and started to move, they didn't seem to be paying attention to him.

Luis remembered being taken to a strange field with long grass. There were no trees or wildlife, and he could not see the sky – only darkness. He floated out of the craft, and came to rest on what he thought was a flat stone or table.

The 'small beings' put a tube in his nose and something in his mouth. When he felt liquid going down his throat, he passed out, and remembered nothing more until he regained consciousness in São Luis hospital a week later.

After Luis went missing on Good Friday his frantic mother searched everywhere, but couldn't find him. Eighty-one hours later, on Easter Monday, a fisherman heard cries for help, and found Luis in the forest, dazed and unable to stand-up. He and a neighbour carried Luis through the forest, and to his home, and, at his mother's request, on to the local hospital.

Dr. Linda Macieira examined him, and said Luis was completely dumb and had muscle contractions like paralysis. Four of his teeth were broken, and still bleeding. His hair was missing, as if it had been burned off, but there were no marks, cuts, scratches or bruises to account for his paralysis. There were no drugs in his system, and doctors were at a loss. He went nine days without eating or drinking, and was eventually flown to a large hospital in São Luis.

Three days later, although still unable to talk, he recovered from his paralysis, and wrote down what had happened to him, complete with sketches, during his encounter with the UFO. When he could speak again, he told the same story over and over, without variation.

Many specialists examined him, and found him to be quite sane, although obviously badly frightened and traumatised.

Sometimes it is not just an updraft or magnetic force which captures an object, animal or person. Many times a beam of light will emanate from a craft, capture the desired quarry, and lift it into the ship.

Friends of mine, a married couple who live on a property in the Great Dividing Range, west of Sydney, took twenty years to confide a similar disturbing incident that also happened just after the turn of the Millennium.

They had gone to bed for the night, and their dogs were safely tucked up next to them or in the lounge. Suddenly they found themselves outside the front door, with the dogs beside and in front of them.

Across the valley, on a nearby hill, they could see their neighbour's house. The husband and wife, along with their two children were also standing outside. Above them was a huge saucer, which projected a beam of blue light and raised the entire family into the craft.

My friends and their dogs seemed to be paralysed – none of them could move, and the next thing they knew it was morning, and they were back in their respective beds. At least the family across the valley were returned, but they did not fare very well. The wife committed suicide, and the daughter, now a young woman, suffers from psychological problems.

Twenty years later, the experience is still as clear to my friends as if it happened yesterday, and they are still questioning was it a dream or real?

In his book *'UFOs Over Romania'*, Dan Farcas interviewed a relative, 'S.C.', who confided an extraordinary encounter in 1968.

At that time he was a student living in a small primitive rental apartment in Constanta. One winter night, before going to bed, he took a few steps out into the snowy courtyard, and was struck by a brilliant, blinding light coming from above.

He felt himself, unable to move, being raised higher and higher into the air. He could see all the adjoining courtyards, which were separated by tall fences, and noticed one neighbour had an old, but distinct, vintage car.

He found himself in a big, 'indirectly illuminated', room, and could hear three or four 'telepathic voices' which he only understood when he felt a 'twinge' in his head. He asked what they wanted, and the voices said that they knew he wanted to go to university. They instructed him to take an experiment by arranging some metallic squares on the floor. After completing the test, the voices advised him to apply for the 'arts' section of the college instead.

The next thing he remembered was lying face down in the freezing snow. He was several metres from where he had been previously standing, but there was no sign of any footprints. He went back inside where the fire had died out, indicating he had been gone for some time.

Thinking it must have been a dream, for the first time he climbed into the attic of the apartment house and looked down over the neighbouring courtyards. They were exactly as he remembered from his unusual experience. Further, for the first time, he saw the vintage car.

He eventually confided in his mother, who was sure he'd been kidnapped by the devil, and begged him not to tell anyone else. She explained that when S.C. was a baby, in the Danube Delta, she had hung him in a basket, from a tree branch, while she weeded the garden.

She had been regularly checking on him, until she saw a large hat-like object, resting on three legs, nearby. She went towards it, but a blast of light knocked her to the ground. When she recovered both the craft and her baby, S.C., were gone.

Despite a search, he could not be found, and everyone feared the worst. Three days later, S.C.'s grandfather was outside in the garden. It was 5am, and he was glad the grieving mother was getting some sleep. Suddenly he saw a 'fire' coming down from the sky, and the same craft as before landed. Before taking off again, three small 'black figures' put the basket and unharmed baby back where he had been taken from.

Hughenden- Central Queensland - 1956

My colleagues in VUFORS documented an occurrence which happened sixty years ago in late 1956. To observe her wish for anonymity, they called her 'Miss L', so I'll use the pseudonym 'Loretta'.

Loretta was only twelve years old when she lived on a farm near Hughenden. It was a fine day, and as she was walking across the flat open paddock, at about 4.30pm, she heard what sounded like 'the soft hum of a vacuum cleaner'.

"I felt some kind of force across my shoulders and down my back, and realised I was being lifted from the ground. As I tried to see what was above me, I must have fainted, and when I recovered, found myself in a large room. There were two men, with their backs to me, dressed in silver-white ski suits.

"They seemed to be operating a panel which faced a wall upon which was a screen showing what looked like a full colour outline of a galaxy. I looked around the room which was unfurnished - on one side was a three metre high arched doorway which led into a corridor. Along another wall were porthole type windows, which appeared to be made of dark, highly polished glass.

"The floor looked like thick frosted glass, and the colour of the whole room varied between light tan and mauve-white, except for one wall which was jet black. The floor, ceiling and walls seemed to be moulded together, as there were no apparent joins. The two men had not communicated with me at all, and as I was still looking around the room, I felt an enormous pressure on my head and neck, and lost consciousness again.

"The next thing I knew I was back on the farm, but in a different paddock. Hovering about six metres above me was a huge saucer shaped craft, about eighty metres in diameter. It moved slowly at first, with a bouncing movement, as if on a cushion of air. As I tried to get back to the farmhouse, a violent, ringing sound nearly deafened me, and I turned back to see the craft rapidly ascending towards a bank of clouds in the west."

When Loretta got back she realised two hours had elapsed since she first started across the paddock. She was a very shaken little twelve-year old, but there were no witnesses, and she didn't tell her family or anyone else. Later in life she was hesitant for fear of ridicule.

'IUR' Vol 16/4, told of another incident, which occurred in a rural area of Florida, on 3rd January 1979. Filberto Cardenas, a Cuban refugee, was with his friend, and his friend's wife and teenage daughter, as they drove home from a trip to some local farms. The car inexplicably stopped, and Cardenas and the driver got out to look under the bonnet.

Suddenly, they heard a buzzing sound, and a blinding light shot down in front of them. As the two women screamed in terror, Cardenas was lifted up and out of sight. The family fled to the local police station, where officers mounted an immediate search.

An hour and a half later, Cardenas was found sixteen miles away from where he had been raised into the sky. He was dazed and confused, with an abrasion, pains in his legs and vision problems. Investigators placed more importance on this initial event, as there were three independent witnesses.

Later hypnosis revealed a typical abduction, which British researcher, Gordon Creighton, commented on. Cardenas claimed a second, later abduction, along with his wife. He said that the alien beings have several bases in our seas, and amongst other things, they spoke of coming 'Earth changes', including devastation of the Californian coast and the return of Mexico City to an area of 'an ocean or lake of importance'. Creighton pointed out that Cardenas spoke very little English, had never been to California, and knew nothing of the prophecies of Edgar Cayce.

Sometime witnesses have been lifted up, or snatched from 'mid-air', in order to save their lives.

In 1979, the Yorkshire UFO Society investigated a report made by a British Rail worker, who, on 12th February, was on his way home, and walking along the tracks from Headingley in Leeds.

He saw a strange green light above him, but then had to move quickly to an adjacent track as a train came by. He wondered if someone, or something, had thought he was in danger, because suddenly the green 'thing' came low overhead and sucked him several feet up into the air.

He was gently put back down, unharmed, further on along the tracks. Looking up, he could see an oval object, with a misty vapour, moving away.

My friend and colleague Margaret Fry recounted the case of the Tite family, her friends for some years in Mid-Wales, which gave further insights into the *mind's* ability to see a projection, as distinct from the actual vision of our eyes.

John Tite was totally blind, had been for fourteen years, and relied on his wife – 'his devoted eyes'. She went out for the night, leaving him in their 'home' – a houseboat on the tow-path of the canal. His young daughter was asleep, when he realised that their houseboat was filling with smoke – it was on fire! He groped about for his little girl, and once in his arms, he made his way onto the deck. But where to from there?

He felt himself being gently lifted, and deposited with his daughter, outside the venue where his wife had gone. He claimed that during this experience he 'saw' a UFO. Margaret suggested that it was 'in his mind's eye'.

"No," he insisted; "I actually saw it. I saw the craft that rescued us. I did not know about UFOs. I am totally blind, but I saw it, and since then, when they are in the vicinity they show me symbols in the sky. I would like to know what these symbols signify."

Of course, given the difficulties of his blindness, there was no-one in rural Wales who could help.

One hot day in 1953, Fred Reagan took off in his Piper Cub plane, and quickly climbed to eight thousand feet. He saw what looked like a traditional flying saucer at the same altitude, and instead of taking evasive action, banked and headed towards it.

By the time he realised he was on a collision course, it was too late. He threw his plane into a tight, diving turn, but the unknown craft tore away his tail. As his plane plummeted towards the ground, Fred was thrown clear. He could feel himself falling, alongside his plane.

Suddenly the wind stopped rushing past him, and he was hovering, motionless above the farms and fields below. He said; "Far below I could see the wreckage of the plane, dropping away. But I floated there....like a human cloud, thousands of feet in the air.

"How long I couldn't tell. Time had stopped for everything but me....I was afraid to move lest I disturb the mysterious balance which held me there."

Fred sensed an invisible force, like a giant suction cup, and felt himself rising upward at an ever increasing speed. Looming above, his could see a monstrous, brilliant object, which 'swallowed him up'. He found himself suspended in a dark room, and through a round opening underneath could see the countryside thousands of feet below.

He looked around in the dim light, and screamed in terror when he saw three short 'alien' type figures moving below him. He thought he must have fainted, because the next thing he remembered he was lying on his back on a metal type 'bed' which was soft to the touch.

He felt stunned, but strangely calm, and didn't know how long he lay there before he heard a 'click', like a switch being turned on.

A sudden voice, speaking in an expressionless monotone said; "How do you do, man."

It continued, in perfect English, but hollow and muffled, as if coming through a loudspeaker; "Do not reply. Only I shall speak. We, from outside your planet, regret extremely the unavoidable circumstance which caused our vehicle to collide with yours. We are here only to observe your primitive....your civilisation.

"We do not wish our activities to interfere with man-living in any manner. We cannot replace your vehicle, but we have examined your body and assured ourselves of its undamaged condition. We have also corrected an abnormality in your body which we have found is most common in your species. It is called ....". Again there was hesitation, as though the speaker was groping for the word, ".....cancer. We offer this as slight reparation for the loss we have caused you.

"We shall return you to the surface of your planet. We caution you, for your own peace, not to reveal your experience with us. You will not be believed...Think of us in kindness." Fred heard a humming noise, and everything went dark.

Fred was found lying in a field, besides the wreckage of his aircraft. Whilst he had not been wearing a parachute, he was uninjured, with not even a bruise or a scratch. His plane, however, was totally demolished, and buried six feet into the ground.

He woke in a hospital bed, with a doctor and nurse and several men peering over him. When he told them what had happened, nobody believed him. It was just as his rescuers had predicted.

Fred's experience did not have a happy ending. The authorities committed him to a State Asylum for the Insane. The next year he died from a degeneration of his brain tissue 'due to an inexplicable exposure to extreme atomic radiation.'

British researcher, Gordon Creighton, related a second hand account received by Alberto Fenoglio of the Turin Centre. It is of particular interest because it also refers to an underground alien base.

Olaf Nielsen was a Swedish student of agriculture, and he told of his strange experience on the afternoon of August 25th 1960; *"I was walking near Halmstead, and the spot was lonely – on one side a wood and on the other side fields – an ideal place for one who has to study.*

"Suddenly I felt myself caught, as it were, in a dizziness, and sucked up into the air. Despite my terror, I had the presence of mind to note what was happening. At a height of about twenty metres from the ground was a flying saucer, and I was being drawn straight up into it. Finding myself in empty space like this, and carried off in such a manner, I lost consciousness.

"When I came round again, I found myself stretched out on a very soft couch, inside a small cabin. The cabin was of a pale green colour, and lit by a faint

diffused light that had no source. One would have said that the light came from the walls themselves.

"Suddenly, a door opened and a being came in. He was in every way similar to us, except that he was wearing an overall. He approached, smiled at me, and in my own language, begged my pardon for the way in which I had been carried off."

Olaf was the taken, very rapidly, to a subterranean 'Space Base'; *"It seemed, at first, as though I was out in the open, but instead I found that I was in a large, brightly lit cavern. In my curiosity, I asked the guide whether there were many of these bases on Earth. After a moment of hesitation, he replied that such bases had existed on the Earth for very many years past.*

"Some were in Central Asia, where thousands of years ago there used to be flourishing cities. Others, he said, are on the high plateau of the Pamirs, in Central Africa, and in Central America, where the space visitors had adapted, for their own purposes, secret pre-Incan cities."

Olaf was shown several saucers, and also an apparatus used to magnetically defend the entrance to the base, not from humans, but from 'the Dark Ones' – bellicose space beings who would like to conquer the Earth.

Olaf was not the only person to be lifted into the air by an unknown craft. There have been several cases reported in Australia.

Andrea Reynolds - Gundiah - QLD

4th October 2001

This case attracted some publicity at the time. I have still given this abductee and the other two witnesses pseudonyms, as they need to be able to get on with their own lives, free from harassment. Investigated by two other researchers, and the subject of TV coverage and an article in a prominent magazine, the case was contentious, but certain aspects indicate she was indeed telling the truth. Although some sceptics have suggested it was an elaborate hoax, I don't agree.

The basic facts are that Andrea was taken from Gundiah, 250km northwest of Brisbane at 11pm, and found, two and a half hours later, at 1.30am in McKay, 800km away. The aviation records show that there were no private jets that night, the only known possible way to make that journey within the proven time frame. Andrea, her husband Kevin and friend Paula were all intelligent enough to know that you do not involve the police if you are going to 'pull a stunt' – and Kevin and Paula's actions were all consistent with the circumstances as reported. Their characters were attested to by local townspeople, and they suffered considerable financial loss by having to close their business, due to the publicity.

Andrea and her husband, 'Kevin', along with their business partner 'Paula', were living in a caravan and annex on a property they were developing. At 11pm that night Kevin had gone to bed, and Andrea had fallen asleep on the couch, in front of the TV in their annex 'lounge-room'. Paula woke suddenly, and when she walked into the annex saw a rectangular beam of light being projected, through the open window, from a disc shaped object hovering outside. Suspended in the beam was a sleeping Andrea and a few items off the coffee table which had been beside her.

Paula fainted for a few moments, and when she recovered Andrea and the craft were gone. She screamed for Kevin, who came out to find the window screen torn and open, and the contents of the coffee table strewn on the floor underneath. At first Kevin did not believe Paula, but Andrea was nowhere to be found.

At 11.40pm Kevin called the very sceptical local police, who arrived about 1.10am, to investigate what they thought might have been foul play or murder. They investigated the torn fly-screen and one bush outside, which seemed to have been affected by heat. While they were still searching the property, they took a call Kevin received from a woman in McKay, nearly 800km away, saying Andrea was in hospital there.

Andrea later recounted her memory of the events. She could remember falling asleep on the couch, and the next thing she was lying on a bed with a thin sheet up to the top of her legs. She got up and cautiously inspected her surroundings. The room was semi-lit, with the light appearing to come from the ceiling and walls. The floor was a dull grey and it was devoid of any furniture except the bed. It looked like it was an internal area as there were no windows or 'control panels'.

She could not see or hear anybody, so she started screaming out asking where she was and why? A robotic voice told her to remain calm, and asked permission to enter the room, and her questions would be answered. It was such a strange monotone voice she asked what he looked like, and he said 'like a man – a humanoid'. He said he would release her if she would at least talk to him. She agreed and got a shock when the wall seemed to 'move away' and a six foot tall 'man-like' person entered the room.

He was wearing a grey 'bodysuit' of fine, smooth fabric unlike anything she had seen before, and a face-fitting mask which looked similar to the pictures people draw of aliens. Before she left he revealed part of his face, and he had blue eyes – similar to human!

He told her that he was a biologist from another planet far away, and he and a geologist companion were travelling through the galaxy, and hoping to gather information about Earth and its inhabitants along the way. They were keeping to the 'dark side' of our planet, and their scans had 'picked her up' when searching for organic specimens. They wanted to carry out experiments without being witnessed, and it was too late when they had already taken her on-board.

A small shorter version of him then inserted a metal probe into her thigh, and put two circular discs in her heels. (Later photographs were taken of triangular marks on her right thigh and marks on each heel.) She consented to this as he told her it was merely to monitor her bodily functions

She asked about where he came from, what were they like? He told her there were many like him throughout the galaxy, but their bodies are all genetically engineered. Their planet is sterile – everything is made of miniature computer chips – and air, food and water are all manufactured. He told her they don't eat and have no emotions.

(From an investigators point of view this made disturbing sense. Our own scientists have recently warned about the dangers of modern technology and robotics to the fate of mankind and our own 'humanity'. Could previous 'contactees' be right when they say these aliens – so similar to us – are seeking to discover the secret of our souls, spirituality and emotions – qualities they have 'lost'?)

Before she was returned to 'earth' he showed her his 'workstation' which comprised some chairs and a big screen which looked 'holographic'. He also assured her she would never see him again. She fell asleep on the bed before waking up in the bush near McKay.

Although reports have Andrea being located at 1.30am, it may have been earlier – making her 800km transit time even shorter. She had woken up 'in the middle of nowhere', feeling alone, disorientated and confused. She was on the ground, with trees around, and she stumbled through the bush for some time before coming to a road. She saw a petrol station in the distance, and walked to it.

At first she didn't know who or where she was. A passing female motorist took a somewhat distressed and dehydrated Andrea to McKay hospital, and then rang Kevin. At that stage Gundiah police contacted their counterparts in McKay, asking to be incorporated into the investigation. They went to the hospital, and later took her sworn statement at their police station.

Kevin and Paula both immediately went to McKay to be with Andrea. Over the next few days they moved to at least three different motels due to not only the publicity, but also a claim that they had experienced what could have been a 'men in black' encounter. They had been followed by a high powered, dark brown four-wheel truck, which frightened them.

They were also being contacted by well-meaning researchers, who were frustrated by Kevin's attempts to protect a very fragile Andrea. He supervised all interviews by both the media and investigators.

The most intriguing aspect of this entire incident is a detail I have not seen any discussion about. Andrea's captor looked human, but was wearing a mask to resemble a typical 'alien'. It therefore begs the question – are human looking extraterrestrials wearing masks to detract from their true identity – or are terrestrial MI-LAB operators masquerading as 'aliens'?

Many current debates are centred on human/military 'black-op' experimentations masquerading as extraterrestrial abductions. One interesting factor would suggest this encounter may not have been with someone terrestrial. The 'humanoid' indicated he was aware people were looking for her, - our own technology would have ensured Andrea was left close to home, as he intended – not nearly 800kms away.

Whilst the original investigators consider this affair to be an 'elaborate hoax', the QLD police refused a FOI request to release any documents pertaining to this incident. Andrea, Kevin and Paula found the publicity prevented them, at great personal loss, from continuing their vineyard project on the Gundiah property and returned, or more likely 'fled', to the UK. Perhaps they just wanted to get on with the rest of their lives.

Australian researchers were still trying to locate them overseas, although I don't know why when they had already publicly stated it was fraudulent! Since there is no 'proof' of any hoax, and only the evidence as presented, it is submitted that it up to our own individual subjective judgement to decide about this case.

This was not the first reported case of someone being levitated through a window – in Andrea's case it was only a mesh flyscreen. In a similar incident – reported by the *'Macleay Argus'* – it did not quite go as our 'visitors' planned.

On 8th April 1971, a man from Greenhill, (northwest of Kempsey NSW), had gone into his darkened kitchen to get a glass of water just after 10pm. As he tipped his head back to take a drink, he could see a strange face pressed against the window in front of the sink. It was like 'a small saucer', with features but no hair. He got a shock, but 'could not run' – instead he found himself suddenly 'drawn' head- first through the glass window as if he was 'sucked out by some unknown force.'

His wife heard the breaking glass and rushed into the kitchen to see her husband's hips and legs disappearing horizontally through the window – 'he was not struggling or thrashing about at all – just going through.' Later investigation showed it would have been almost impossible for him to achieve this alone, however I suspect he may have already been 'immobilised'.

His seven feet fall onto his back on the steps and the ground below should have caused more injuries than a couple of minor cuts to one hand and arm, however if a body is totally relaxed it suffers far less injury than one which is rigid on impact. His wife raced outside, and couldn't believe that instead of being at least stunned or injured, he jumped up and ran down the road very distressed. This leads me to believe that whatever induced state he was in, once he hit the ground the 'link' was broken. He could not remember much after he first saw the face at the window, and didn't recall going through the glass. He was found some distance away, crying and shaking, begging his wife not to leave him alone, as he was frightened.

Several Kempsey witnesses had reported unusual bright lights in the sky between 6.10pm and 6.30pm, and had seen an 'object come to ground' on a scrub covered reserve, just over a kilometre from our poor victim's residence. Whilst he did not previously believe in 'ghosts or men from space' the incident had terrified him so much he refused to live in the house again, and moved to Sydney, asking his wife to join him there.

British researcher, Philip Mantle, documented an interesting case from 1954.

Just before 11pm, on 13th May, Retired Naval Commander Horatio Penrose was driving along the main Burton-Buxton Road, towards Birmingham. As he neared the Hilton Gravel Works, near Burnaston, he saw a bright light ahead. Thinking it was an oncoming, speeding vehicle, he slowed down, then suddenly braked when the light halted over his black Vauxhall car.

He was thrown forward in the driving seat, hitting his head on the steering wheel. At first the Commander thought there had been an accident, but then he felt the car rising – 'as if it were being lifted through the air by something magnetised.' He noticed the metal roof of his precious car being distorted by the pull of whatever it was, and peered out the window, only seeing the intense light above.

Horatio must have lost consciousness, because the next thing he knew he was waking up in a bed in the Derbyshire Royal Infirmary, where the nurses told him he had received stitches to a cut on his forehead.

Although they thought he had just been involved in an accident, he remembered that after he looked out the window, his car was lowered to the other side of the road.

A man, in a one-piece suit, leaned in through the window and pulled him out into the air, and up into an opening underneath a large, brightly lit circular object which was hovering overhead.

He found himself in an illuminated room, and was laid on some form of 'medical examination' table. He looked around, and could see about five, normal looking men and women operating what appeared to be control mechanisms positioned around the walls.

These people who were wearing one-piece blue suits, were not very tall, more like the average height of Asians. Also they had slightly almond-shaped eyes, white skin and short, dark straight hair. One of the females, whom he thought to be young and attractive, came over and examined the injury to his forehead and other bumps and bruises. She spoke to him telepathically, and gave him an injection from a syringe containing green fluid.

The mind-to-mind communications continued, with the woman asking questions about his naval experiences, and in particular his work with radar. He, in turn, asked questions about the mechanics of their ship, and was told it involved magnetic fields. When he asked further questions about their craft, she avoided direct questions, but did make the strange comment; 'We are not born in the same manner as you'.

He then became drowsy, perhaps as a result of the injection, and regained consciousness back in the wreckage of his car, where a passing RAC patrolman found him.

Later, the police questioned him, as an unaccountable amount of blood was found in the car, but he did not mention the strange craft or his experience.

One case, from January 2005, had investigators wondering if 'alien abduction' was a convenient excuse for unfaithful husbands. When an Argentinean taxi driver failed to return home from his shift, his wife notified the local police, who instigated a search. They found his taxi, on a nearby road, with the door open, and no sign of the driver.

Fearing he had been a victim of bandits, they intensified their efforts, only to be told by the wife that her husband had telephoned home from Quilmes, many miles away from La Plata. He had apparently been struck by a 'blinding light', sucked up into the air from the roadside, then dumped in that town by 'the alien controllers of the UFO'.

The wife told the police that she was not very convinced by his explanation. He had used this excuse before, and after such absences, had the smell of alcohol on his breath, which he blamed on his alien abductors!

My colleague, Rex Gilroy, investigated a case where it seems that perhaps some cases do involve human abductors rather than alien culprits.

One weekend in July 1977, Hayden Squires had been camping in the remote Burragorang Valley, west of Sydney, Australia. He was sure there was a secret base in the area, and had basically been 'snooping around'.

At about 9.30pm he was woken by a distant 'boom', and walked out of his tent. A large, silvery-glowing, fifteen metres wide, flying saucer was hovering about sixty metres overhead. A wide, round opening in its underside was emitting a yellow searchlight type glow, which spread all around.

Hayden suddenly felt weightless, and was drawn up into the yellow light, and inside the craft. A sliding door closed beneath him, and he found himself in a kind of engine-room, full of silver metal piping and technical apparatus. There was a door in the side wall, and a male American voice told him to enter, and then to use a small lift which took him to a circular upper deck containing black covered metal chairs.

He sat down for a while, and then looked out the window, and could see the lights of Sydney and a couple of country towns below. The voice told him to resume his seat, as they were going to take him back to his campsite.

The voice warned him not to return to the area – next time he may not be so lucky. When he asked how come they had a flying saucer – did they build it in America – he got no answer, but heard what sounded like several men laughing from some other part of the craft.

Hayden was instructed to go back to the bottom of the ship, where he was bombarded with silvery light. He felt weightless again, and found himself in the same yellow glow and descending out of the round opening. About four feet above the ground, he landed with a thud, and the saucer zoomed off into the night.

CHAPTER SIX

UP INTO THE AIR

PART TWO

Sometimes, it's not just people and animals that UFOs take. Often, when entire cars are 'grabbed' by a UFO, often being lifted above the road, it seems like some magnetic forces are in play. Given the hypothesis that an alien pilot, or automatic craft control, has a level of experience, perhaps some of these cases are due to our own prototypes being erroneously or irresponsibly controlled.

In February 1996, Andres Landeira was having trouble driving his car up a steep hill in Spain, near the city of Lugo. Suddenly he realised that his car was rising into the air. In panic, he opened the door, only to see he was thirty feet above the ground – too high to jump out.

He forced his back into the driver's seat, and hung onto the steering wheel. He didn't know what has happening, but fully expected to be spirited off into the black sky. Perhaps his abductors changed their minds, because just as suddenly he was deposited, sideways, back onto the road, just ahead of his original position.

At the same time that night, several people had witnessed strange lights and luminous phenomena, and there had been an unexplained blackout.

Mundrabilla (WA), 20 January 1988 - (*The Knowles Incident*)

This event caused massive disagreements among UFO researchers, and since I respect the integrity of the research of all my colleagues, it is intended to relate the various conclusions as presented.

On the night of 20th January, the Knowles family, Faye and her three sons – Wayne, Pat and Sean, were on a 3,500 kilometre journey, from Perth, Western Australia, to Melbourne, Victoria, which entailed crossing the Nullarbor Plain, a very desolate desert area. At 1.10a.m. they had stopped at a Caiguna (WA) roadhouse to refuel and have a quick meal. While it may have no bearing on the case, Faye commented on seeing a "blond-haired lady" who smiled at Wayne, who also remarked on noticing a "blond lady" and a "bearded man."

It was a dark moonless night, with Sean driving, and not long after they had started off again, all experienced a period of confusion, disorientation and a mutual sense of fear.

After a while their awareness of their thoughts and surroundings returned to normal, and they recalled travelling down the Eyre Highway, at about 110kph. Soon after, they noticed a curved-shaped light pacing the car from a distance. Sometime later, they encountered what they thought was the same light obstructing the centre of the road. It was extremely bright, shaped like an egg sitting in an eggcup – white with a yellow core, and a brighter light at top and bottom. It was bouncing on the road, backwards and forwards, and coming towards them. Sean swerved to the right to avoid it, and nearly collided with an oncoming car and caravan as he went back to the left-hand side of the highway.

The family stated that the object pursued them down the highway for the next hour and a half, despite Sean's attempts at evasive action. A truck driver, travelling west, in the opposite direction, later reported to Eucla (WA) police that he had seen a car, travelling east, being followed by a light.

The light had been some distance behind, just over a kilometre, when suddenly without warning it jumped on top of their vehicle. Everything, including the car, seemed to slow down – and yet the instruments indicated that they were travelling at 200kph (something not possible on the ground). The car was filled with an extremely bright light, which at first made them think it was on fire. The vehicle appeared to be vibrating with a combination of three sounds – hissing, whirring and humming, and when Faye touched the inside of the roof, she could feel these vibrations.

Pat opened a window a little way, and the inside of the car was darkened by a fog of black dust which smelt like burnt Bakelite. Breathing became difficult in the foul, strong choking atmosphere, and the vehicle, dogs and family were covered with a fine grey-black dust.

Everyone independently reported a feeling of pressure or force, and their voices assuming a robotic quality. (Some reports say "deeper and in slow motion", which equates with other similar incidents.) Wayne's hair was standing on end, and Pat said he saw Sean slumped over the steering wheel, as if unconscious – head down and arms and hands hanging loose at his side. Faye partially opened her rear window, and as more dust 'sshhhed' in, she stuck her head out and placed her hand on the roof. She saw and felt something round, black and spongy – warm to the touch - which she thought was some form of "suction thing" trying to lift the car up.

"Oh my God!" she shouted, "It's on top of the roof. I'm burnt, I've touched it!" Almost immediately her hand began to redden and swell-up and has ached ever since. Pat said that as soon as Faye touched the roof, and pulled back her hand, the car was dropped to the road, and the right-hand rear tyre burst with a bang.

It was about 3.55 a.m. when they came to a halt at right angles to the road, fifty kilometres before Mundrabilla Roadhouse (and 210 km from Caiguna). The bright white, glowing UFO was up the road and at a very low altitude of about thirty metres. After the family fled the car, and took shelter in some low bush, 180 metres to the south, they could see the object had a spotlight which appeared to be searching the terrain below. Another truck driver had witnessed the car, at the side of the road, but he did not stop fearing danger from strangers in such a deserted place.

Just before twilight the UFO mysteriously disappeared, and at 4.15 a.m. the family returned to the car, changed the tyre, and travelled in great haste to Mundrabilla (WA). They were still in a state of shock when they told the station owners and three truck drivers (one of whom had seen an unusual yellow-white light in his rear-vision mirror) what had happened. One driver said Faye was hysterical, the boys were terrified and the dogs still cowering.

At the beginning of the entire incident the two dogs had been really crazy, jumping around the car and barking. Due to all the confusion and blank periods, the family cannot be sure when the change occurred, but later they were "quiet, stiff, cowering and frightened." Later examinations showed both dogs to be covered with black dust, and they subsequently suffered a lot of hair loss, which was similar to that caused by radiation; - "Blood haematology, coagulation and immunology showed biochemistry abnormality."

They then headed towards Ceduna (SA) and later the Victorian border, where the subsequent police and researchers' interviews and the media frenzy began. The newspapers, anxious to go to press as soon as possible, often got the details wrong. There were so many experts giving their points of view, often without the benefit of all the facts. Several varying theories came from sceptics – dry lightning or thunderstorm, ball lightning, meteorite, Jupiter, and a distorted view of the rising sun! (One 'expert' even altered the time of the incident to fit his theory!)

Hang-on fellows, you can't all be right! In fact, there was such a concerted effort to discredit the Knowles, the poor family went into hiding. I began to wonder what it was these 'experts' were trying to cover-up.

Several investigators have researched this incident in some detail, and a full account of their conclusions can be found in my book *'Contact Down Under'*.

The October 1988 edition of the *'TUFOIC Newsletter'* detailed a second, almost simultaneous event. A Tasmanian man and his girlfriend were on holiday and travelling the 73 kilometres from Penong (SA) to Ceduna (SA) on the Eyre Highway on the night of 20-21st January; "It was about 2.40 a.m. when I heard a loud thump coming from above the vehicle. I couldn't believe it was the gas bottle on top of the car – it was screwed down, and hadn't come off in 450,000 miles - but there was stuff coming off that roof I still haven't found.

"Then we saw a series of flashing lights in the sky, which lasted about fifteen minutes. They looked like a row of bright white steady beams, covering a wide area of the sky, and coming towards earth. I don't know what they were, but it was funny that the wind picked up at that time. As it buffeted the car, things were flying off the roof. It moved the vehicle about and across the road. During this period the car would not go over seventy kph."

What was interesting about this report was a forty-five -minute time anomaly. The witness said that as soon as the light beams finally disappeared the car regained power, and the one-hour wind-buffeting stopped. He said originally he only saw the lights for fifteen minutes.

After this incident, many people coming into the Mundrabilla motel and roadhouse started recounting their own experiences. Alan Stewart, a 53 year-old, WA Main Road Department foreman, said he had encountered similar objects on four occasions, one resulting in him being hospitalised.

In March 1982, Francis Collins and Maggie Yeend were driving in their Combi-van to Esperance. About three miles past Munglinup, a silent object, about the size of a small helicopter, with red, white and yellow lights underneath, hovered about twenty metres above and beside their vehicle. When a truck approached, it sped away, spraying some kind of mist from behind.

It returned and accompanied them all the way to Esperance, where it hovered over the Bay. They woke up the local policeman, Constable Gordon, who was asleep in his own home. He came out and also saw the UFO, which later disappeared, and he said it was definitely a star or the moon.

'CUFOS', in the US, discussed a sighting which lends credence to my belief that sometimes vehicles are inadvertently lifted off the ground due to a magnetic force under a saucer-type craft, be it ours or extraterrestrial.

On 10th April 1967, a man in Jonestown, Pennsylvania, had trouble starting his car, but after he got underway, he had only travelled half a mile before his vehicle started to splutter, his headlights went out and the engine stopped. Suddenly, a huge round UFO, with pale white lights around the edge, moved over his car.

It then tilted, and flashing a blue light, moved away, at high speed, to the north-west. As the craft departed, his car was picked up off the ground and moved about four feet. Later, his car's motor and headlights came back on by themselves.

Again, on 25th January 1969, in Marcellus, New York, a couple were driving late at night, when they saw a huge, brightly lit 'cone-shaped' object hovering over a farm about a quarter of a mile away. Their car lights went off, as did the lights outside the farmhouse.

The object spun around and stopped three times, and simultaneously, each time, the front end of the couple's car rose three feet off the road. The UFO gave off a light beam, tilted up and rose to the north-west. After it left, they were able to restart their vehicle.

Perhaps 1969 was the year for testing out new prototypes. *'FSR Case Histories'* documented a case reported in the Rio de Janeiro newspaper *'O Journal'*. In July of that year, four travellers, from Santa Catarina in Brazil, were startled to see a low-flying saucer-shaped object which shone a beam of light onto their Kombi station-wagon. The men were even more concerned when the engine and headlights failed.

Suddenly, their car was lifted a great height off the road. After a 'marvellous but terrifying trip' they were set down some distance ahead. The UFO, looked like two basins face-to-face, and was shooting forth an intense beam of light, which was changing colours. It then turned its attention to a nearby truck, whose engine and lights also failed after it hovered overhead.

At the end of the following November another case was reported by *'UFOLOG No.68'*. In Quincy, Illinois, three people driving along the highway saw an object, shaped like a rounded triangle. As it came down low, and very close to their car, the vehicle was lifted ten feet above the road. The lights and motor continued running, but they did not gain control of the steering until after the object had left the area.

The *'UFO Register'* reported that just over three years later, on 16th January 1973, in North Carolina, two witnesses noticed a domed, metallic craft following their car. Suddenly they felt weightless, and their vehicle was raised off the road. They were also unable to control the car until after the object departed.

Similar cases were also happening to the north, in Canada. On 14th May 1971, Blackfoot Indian, Wilton Raw Eater, and his wife were driving home near Geichen, Alberta. During the day he was the driver of the local Reservation school bus, and he and his wife were considered to be reliable witnesses.

It was dark, and just as they reached the top of a hill, a brilliant light hit the car. Wilton's wife was startled – the car was now off the ground! He kept trying to steer it for the next quarter-of-a-mile before it hit the ground again, and the 'light' eventually moved away. They returned to their own home and children, then fled to his brother's house, where they managed to calm down.

Launceston, Tasmania, 14th December 1987

About six weeks before the Knowles encounter, on December 14th 1987, sometime after 9.30 p.m., an executive was driving home from an isolated area thirty kilometres from Launceston. Mr. A, who worked for a car dealership, was driving his employer's expensive Mercedes car. Two miles before the junction with the main road, he noticed some lights behind, which he assumed were from a helicopter or plane. About a kilometre further on, the lights passed overhead, and as his car lights and motor all stopped. A mass of light landed, blocking the road, about fifteen metres ahead.

He got out of the car. The lights were so brilliant, it was hard to distinguish the object above and behind them. He thought it was a grey colour cigar-shape, about five to six metres wide and two metres high. He ran and took cover behind some bushes, so scared, he vomited. The situation worsened when he saw his employer's car being dragged about ten metres down the road towards the object.

He thought he was only in hiding for a few minutes, however, subsequent investigation into the timeline indicate there may be an unaccounted period for up to two hours. A man in another vehicle, whose lights had also failed, pulled up behind him, and left his motor running. Mr. A ventured out and explained what was happening.

They heard a high-pitched whining sound and the object rose into the sky and curved off, disappearing to the south. There were rubber marks on the road where the car had been dragged, and the bitumen had melted – -some of it splashed on the front. While TUFOIC said there was no soot, Mr. A told a VUFORS investigator that there was a "sooty sort of carbon" covering the car, which also needed electrical repairs before it was sold. When he got home it was midnight – he should have arrived about 10 p.m. The incident was also thoroughly investigated by Keith Roberts of TUFOIC.

Kununarra, West Australia

Wayne Trembath of the *'Northern Star'* reported that a man returning to Kununurra from Derby, had parked his landrover-ute next to the old Mary River crossing to have a short sleep. He had rolled his vehicle earlier at a washaway near Halls Creek, and was still feeling a little shaken up. He was woken by lights flashing and a strong wind rocking his vehicle. Thinking a storm was coming, he wound the window down to discover the lights were only around his vehicle, which was illuminated as bright as daylight.

As he was sitting there he had the sensation he was being lifted up, and put his hands down to find a space between himself and the seat. He didn't fall back down until the lights and wind stopped. He drove straight to Halls Creek, and stayed under the street lamp in front of the police station for the rest of the night.

 This was not the only case reported from the deserted outback of Western Australia. In his book *'Mysterious Australia'* Rex Gilroy detailed a report from

Andy Quirk and his girlfriend Sandra. One night, in February 1979, they were in their four-wheel drive Land Rover, travelling towards Derby.
Suddenly an ionised blue glow, accompanied by a high pitched humming sound surrounded them. Andy lost control of the vehicle, which rose over two feet above the road. He panicked, and Sandra was screaming.

As the glow and noise faded, the Land Rover hit the ground with a thud, and they could see, high in the sky, a dark object, flying at great speed, off to the south.

Coonabarrabran, NSW

In our book *The Gosford Files*' we published the case of Jack Ulster, a country farmer who had a memorable experience just before moving to the New South Wales Central Coast in 1988:

He was returning home, along a dark tarmac road at about 8 p.m. His utility truck was suddenly flooded with brilliant white light, and he pulled over and looked up. There was a huge object, no more than eight or nine feet overhead. The dark, round underside was about six feet in diameter. A large round white light in the middle, shone down upon him and the road below.

"I could hear a faint whirring sound, and felt a sense of awe, rather than fear. There was some kind of intangible, almost benevolent quality about it. I stretched my hand out to touch it, but before I could reach it, the craft rose slightly and glided a few feet backwards. I could see it much more clearly – a large black saucer shape, no windows or lights except for the searchlight on the bottom."

After a few minutes it moved smoothly and quietly back down the road, and Jack got back in the car and continued his trip home. He had only travelled a short distance when his vehicle was flooded with white light again. The whole area was illuminated, and he realised he was no longer on the road or in control of

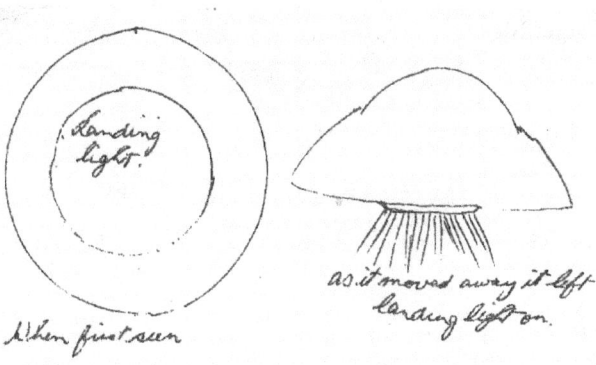

his little truck. Out of the windscreen and side windows he could see he was now at treetop level.

"I travelled mid-air for several hundred metres. I wasn't really scared, for some reason I trusted them, whoever they were, but I did wonder what was going to happen. I was put back on the road again, and the craft departed to the south. When I got home I just wandered around, looking at the sky, thinking if it was all real. Could I have just imagined it?"

Jack had not imagined it. A neighbour had been driving along in the opposite direction, and passed under the bright white light with Jack's vehicle hanging from it. He rushed home to tell his sceptical wife; "It's a big one and it's got Jack!" He had wondered what to do at the time – if his wife didn't believe him, the police certainly would not.

Blue Mountains, NSW

Rex Gilroy reported several similar incidents in the Blue Mountains. The first happened on 15th June 1978 when a couple were driving along Tablelands Rd, in Wentworth Falls. A "green glowing saucer" appeared from nowhere, hovering overhead. It was emitting some form of force field which lifted their car about four feet off the road then dropped them again. This happened three times in succession before it zoomed off over the valley.

The second incident was at about 2 a.m. one morning in June 2000. A car containing four people driving from Bell to Bilpin was surrounded by an ionised blue glow.

As the terrified occupants tried to speed away they felt the car being lifted at least two feet off the road. After being carried for some few hundred feet, the glow vanished and the vehicle hit the road.

North Ballarat, Victoria

'The Daily Mirror', of 22nd January 1988, noted an incident which occurred the same day pilot Frederick Valentich, and his plane, went missing over the Bass Strait.

Evonne Hall, a 44-year-old farmer's wife, was driving along a country road with her two children, seven-year-old Jenny and David, aged four. A cigar-shaped object, about half the size of a single-engine light aircraft, hovered over her car. It made a loud whirring noise, and she felt it was actually on her car, which was lifted at least a metre off the road then dropped with a thud. The craft disappeared, and Evonne was left with an injured back.

Black Creek, NSW

'People' magazine published an interview with a motorist from Yass, who was travelling from Gulgong to Gunning on 13th June, 1993. He had stopped just before dark, at Black Creek, to have his sandwiches and coffee. As he drove on again, his glasses seemed to be covered with some kind of substance, and he stopped to clean them so he could see the road ahead.

"As I sat there alone on that desert road, I heard a sound like wire scratching against metal. And then I felt something grip the rear of the car and lift it up. I could see nothing through the rear vision window, but this invisible force, whatever it was, lifted the car's rear four times before dropping it back onto the road."

He drove away as fast as possible, still shivering as he felt he was being observed. When the road curved to the right he could see a small, bright, brilliant-green object hovering only about forty-five centimetres off the ground. He could not see anything else in the darkness, and as he kept driving it kept pace with him to the left of his car; "It seemed to be relating closely to me, and vanished after a few kilometres. I'm sure it had something to do with my car being lifted from the ground."

Similar car-lifts

Investigator, Marc Davenport, discussed a couple of incidents, where some magnetic force may have affected vehicles.

In January 1961, Adolfo Pisani was travelling on the Andean Highway, between La Victoria and El Vigia, Venezuela. He had pulled over to the side of the road, to let a truck pass, when he saw something strange streak down out of the sky, and come close to the hood of the truck.

It was a brilliant blue disc, which looked like polished steel. As it turned upwards, and left at incredible speed, the truck rose a few feet into the air, and overturned, landing on its hood.

Another truck met a similar fate in Herman, Minnesota. On December 20th 1965, Edward Bruns was driving a pickup truck at 11.45pm. Before he reached his farm he encountered a bright, lighted UFO hovering above the road ahead.

The truck's lights and engine failed, and as the UFO started to ascend, his truck rose with it. Edward and his vehicle ended up in a ditch, on the other side of the road!

In July 1957, David Ellis was riding his motorbike along the A227 in Kent, England, when he was suddenly sucked up into the air, and thrown into a nearby field, fracturing his collarbone. He watched his bike follow him and land a few feet away, and his lunch-box, which had been strapped on the rear, ended up in a tree, hundreds of yards away on the other side of the road.

Why did investigators suspect that a UFO was responsible? When David recovered, he realised he was lying on the edge of a seventy-foot crop circle!

US researcher, Richard Hall, discussed a case which occurred in Argentina on 23rd September 1978. Carlos Acevedo and Miguel Moya, both from Chile, had been participating in a road rally. Due to car problems, they had dropped out of the race, but were completing the last leg in their own time.

At about 3am, they were thirty kilometres north of the Rio Negro River, when a very bright yellow light appeared in the rear vision mirror. Thinking it was another car, approaching at high speed, they pulled over to the right to let it pass.

Suddenly their car was filled with a blinding light, and the car was ascending into the air, totally out of Acevedo's control. They were both terrified, and lost all concept of time until they felt a bump when the vehicle returned to earth. The light diminished, and they found themselves on an embankment on the other side of the road.

When they reached Pedro Lura, in Buenos Aires Province, they stopped at a service station to discover the odometer showed only half the distance they had covered, and the reserve petrol tank, which they had not used, was completely empty. The service station attendant reported also seeing the yellow light from a distance.

It is not known whether the incidents of cars being lifted off the road are deliberate, or an accident due to some unknown magnetic or similar force. Although sceptics doubt that this has in fact occurred, there are many cases documented in both Australia and other countries. Some indicate it may not have been an intentional act, with the vehicle accidentally being caught beneath a craft – on other occasions the capture may well have been intended.

One disturbing encounter, which was less likely to be one of our own prototypes, happened in Kurrajong, at the base of the Blue Mountains, one September night in 1986. Leticia Martin was driving along Richmond Road towards Kurrajong when a blue glow totally enveloped her car, and her engine and lights died. She felt as if the car had been lifted off the road, and experienced a feeling of weightlessness.

"Suddenly I felt the car come to rest, and the blue glow faded away. I was terrified, and opened the door to find myself in a paddock, which I later discovered was on the outskirts of Penrith, miles away from Kurrajong. About fifty feet ahead of me was a large, pulsating, yellow, glowing egg-shaped craft. A round opening appeared and I could see a pink glow, but nothing else.

"I was dumbfounded at first, but regained my senses and was about to run for help to a nearby house, when I felt my arms being held by some invisible force, drawing me towards that opening. When I was only a few feet away I tried with all my might to break free, but felt magnetised, drawn inside. The opening vanished behind me. In my terrified state I found my whole body frozen of movement as the feeling of unseen fingers prodded and pressed into my body.

"I must have blacked out, and when I came to I was lying on the ground, and the family came out of the house nearby. I ran over, crying and sobbing, and asked if they had seen what had just happened. The couple could not understand what I was raving about. I was on their property, and they wanted to know how I had driven my car into their paddock, when it was all locked and fenced off?

"I told them what had happened, but they had been watching through the window, and said all they saw was me leaping out of the car, and making funny movements before standing still and collapsing on the ground. I was so embarrassed; they were laughing at me. I got back into the car, and after one of the sons opened a side driveway gate, I was off as quickly as possible."

Looking for similar cases, I found one which occurred in September 1973, when a man was returning from a late night dance in Northamptonshire, England. At 2am he reached the village of Little Houghton, and one minute he was passing the local church, and the next he was on foot, sixteen miles away near Bedford. All he could remember of the previous night, was seeing a fuzzy white light heading towards his windscreen.

It was daylight, there was no sign of his car, and despite the weather being dry, he was dripping wet. He called a friend, who picked him up and together they retraced the route back to Little Houghton. After travelling for five miles, they spotted his vehicle in a field near Turvey.

The gate to the muddy field was bolted, and there were no signs of tyre tracks to show how it had got there. The car was locked, but undamaged, and the witness found the keys in his pocket. Due to the mud, it could not be driven out, and the farmer had to use a tractor to tow it back to the road.

Jenny Randles mentioned a case from Hungary, in 1992, when a woman driving late at night also saw a fuzzy, white light coming towards her windscreen. The next thing she remembered was when, hours later, she was scrambling away from her car, looking for help.

Someone took her to hospital for minor injuries, including a 'red rash' on her exposed flesh. Later the police recovered her car from a field, which was covered in day old snow, and well away from any road. There were no tyre marks indicating how it could possibly have been driven there.

Again, the car was undamaged, except for the door handle, which was 'welded' shut, as if by some localised heat, which had left no other traces.

At 10.30pm, on 28th July 1994, three men were returning home from working late, when, near Gravesend in Kent, they saw a bright light on the highway ahead. Suddenly their Bedford van left the road, and they seemed to have 'blanked out' for ninety minutes. After recovering sufficiently, they realised that they were in the middle of wheat field.

They were still dazed and confused when local man David Stanton, who was walking his dog, passed by. He called the Gravesend local police, who arrived at 12.35 am. They were puzzled, as there were no signs of entry to the field, which also had securely locked gates. Further, there were no skid marks on the road, or tracks leading up to the upright vehicle, sitting in the centre of the ripened wheat.

All three men were severely traumatised, and later found 'scoop marks' on the inside of both legs. One suffered severe depression and panic attacks, later diagnosed as post traumatic stress disorder. His two workmates retreated into anonymity, and refused to discuss the matter any further.

In 1970 the *'Flying Saucer Review'* detailed several similar cases. A couple of years earlier, a Brazilian couple, Marcilo Ferraz and his wife, were driving south from San Paulo, when, somewhere near the Uruguay border, they also encountered a 'white cloud' on the road.

They 'woke up' in Mexico, suffering severe traumatic shock, and a few weeks later, Marcilo was told he had developed a brain tumour. Shortly after he shot himself. When investigators approached the Brazilian Air Force for further details, they were told the case was authentic, but could not be discussed or publicised as it fell within the scope of National Security and was classified as 'top secret'

In May 1979, the *'La Nueva Espana'* newspaper published this report, noting that although there had been slightly differing accounts received, that night a large white, red and yellow 'ball' had been seen just yards above the Spanish highway where the couple had been driving.

The husband and wife were travelling, in their new car, to Andalusia in Southern Spain, when they suddenly drove through an unusual cloud on the highway. He was not familiar with the route, but lost track of where they were, and felt it was not the highway to Seville. Perhaps they had taken a wrong turn.

Eventually, they found a man, who looked like a peasant, sitting under a tree at the side of the road. They stopped to ask directions, but the fellow didn't have any idea what they were talking about. When asked exactly where they were, an astonishing reply was received – "Forty-five miles from Santiago de Chile!'

The couple were confused and terrified, and sure he was mistaken, drove on until they reached a town, and headed for the police station. They were indeed in Santiago de Chile, and at first their story was not believed. Government officials arrived, and told them similar events had also happened in the area recently.

They were also frantic about their children, still in Spain, and they were given two tickets to return home, however Chilean authorities kept the car for further inspection. It is not known if it was ever returned. The couple, to their credit, never sought publicity, and refused to have their names published.

It seems our alien visitors have a better degree of respect for horses, and leave them undamaged when 'snatching' their riders.

In 1979, the SBEDV group from Brazil, told of a farmhand, Afrãnio Josê Pena, from Cardoso Moreira, north of Rio de Janeiro, an area known for UFO activity.

One night, whilst riding his horse home, he saw a light, which was approaching fast. He noticed a sudden 'loss of strength', and losing his grip on the horse, was lifted into the air. Just as suddenly, he was gently put down on the ground on the other side of the road.

His horse trotted over, and bent his head down to him, but Afrãnio was unable to get up. He shouted for help, and a neighbour came and took him to his own house, where they waited for Afrãnio's brother to take him home.

Afrãnio couldn't sleep that night, and some red specks temporarily appeared on his skin. For the next three days the horse wouldn't move around, and spent most of the time lying on the ground.

In another case from the State of Goiás, Brazil, researchers Dr Buhler and Wayner Montiero, reported on an additional horse-rider 'abduction' from Fazenda Cerradinho.

On 20th April 1969, several people in the town had been talking about mysterious lights in the sky. That night, Dolor Roque was riding into town, to buy some medicine from the pharmacy, when he also saw some unexplained lights.

The next thing he knew, it was dawn, and he found himself, minus his horse, on top of some rocks on the banks of the Paranaiba river, nearly four hundred kilometres away. He staggered off, not knowing where he was, and a passer-by, with a horse and cart, took him to the nearest long distance bus station.

When he eventually got home, his family were very relieved. All they knew was that his unharmed, riderless horse had made its own way home.

In his book, *'UFO Dreaming'*, Rex Gilroy described two incidents in the Moree area of north-western New South Wales.

In 1986, at about 11pm two aboriginal boys were out in their truck, heading towards their favourite fishing spot on the Gwydir River. A large, 50ft, yellow-glowing 'saucer-type' craft, appeared overhead, 'enveloping' their vehicle.

Tom Coleman said; "We tried to drive away, but the truck just left the ground, and was hovering some feet above the dirt track. We seemed to be 'drifting along' and my mate Joe was panicking."

Suddenly the saucer let go of its grip on their vehicle, and the truck came back down to earth with a crash. They watched, still petrified, as the craft moved silently away.

That same year, two other aboriginal men, in the same district, were not so lucky. They were camped near the banks of the river, when a large, 60ft saucer-shaped craft, descended from the sky and hovered over their car, which was parked about one hundred feet away.

A blinding beam of white light shot out from beneath the craft, and 'sucked–up' their vehicle into the saucer, which then zoomed off at increasing speed, and disappeared over the bushland.

One witness, from the US Lake of the Ozarks, told of a contactee, who was sure he'd been abducted, but couldn't remember the details. Was he just imagining things?

One night he was in his boat, under the bridge near a railway embankment. The next thing he was in an unknown area, of stump filled water, some distance away. He was puzzled for a while, even doubting his own sanity, when he remembered he had GPS equipment on board.

He checked his trail from that fishing trip, and found his boat had gone over the railway embankment and travelled back to the new spot, in a rapidly moving, parabolic curve. Somehow, the boat had to be travelling through the air!

Whilst most vehicles may have been lifted only a short distance off the road, there are several cases where an entire car, boat or even a helicopter have ended up inside a spaceship.

THE 1954 MOON FILM

Researcher Mike Farrell brought this case to my attention. Part of the SBS series, *'Eat Carpet',* featured a French production about Tibor Nagy, a Hungarian immigrant to the United States. He settled in Massachusetts in 1941, but could speak very little English

At 10.15 am, 15th April 1954, he was driving along a rural, deserted highway with his wife in the front seat, and twelve year old daughter in the back. Tibor said; "We were all alone on the road, when a huge shadow stopped right above us, and brought our car to a standstill....Nothing would work...My wife screamed! My daughter started crying, and I told them not to be afraid. It seemed like 'the night fell around us'.

"I don't remember how much time later....I opened my eyes and we were still in the car, but it was 'vibrating gently' and in a large white room. I got out and right in front of me, I saw the Moon coming at me. So I took out my camera, which I always took with me when we go out to visit, and I filmed. I was shaking with fear. Good God, I was frightened!

"At the same moment I was filming, my daughter woke up, and I had to explain to her that I believed we had been picked up by a flying craft. Then a man stepped into the room. He seemed like us, but he was wearing a helmet on his head, and I couldn't see his face.

"He didn't say anything – but we 'understood' that we need not be afraid. I could film whatever I saw, but not the inside of the ship. I remember perfectly saying; "yes sir,"...and my daughter yelling; "we're higher than the Moon". I watched and filmed until I ran out of film. Then I felt like we were 'falling'.

"When I opened my eyes, my wife and daughter were now both in the back seat of the car. We were a few meters away from a road 'we didn't know', which turned out to be some miles away from where we were taken. I turned to my wife and daughter, saying that God wants to test us – be brave!"

Three weeks later, on 6th May, Tibor was called before Senator Lawley's Committee of Inquiry, but he could only testify in Hungarian, and wasn't believed. The results of a second hearing, held a few weeks later, remain secret.

Tibor didn't fare very well. He was ridiculed by the press and the public, and became obsessed with wanting to see the 'Visitors' again, to get proof that he was not a liar. Within a few years his wife died. His daughter moved to Canada to get married, and never saw him again.

What is astounding is that Tibor's film of the Moon's surface, taken fifteen years before we first set foot on our closest neighbour, was very similar to those taken by NASA's fly-overs and landings. As the camera reaches the horizon, you can see the blackness of space and the Earth rising beyond.

Two of my Welsh colleagues, Peter Paget and Margaret Fry both investigated this case, which was dubbed 'The Winchester Mystery'.

At 8.50pm on 14th November 1976, Joyce Bowles and her friend Ted Pratt were driving in her white Mini Club-Man car from Winchester to Chilcomb. As they turned into a narrow lane of the lonely countryside, they noticed an orange glow in the sky. Although she was only doing 25mph, her car began to shudder and felt as if it was being lifted off the ground. She lost control, and ended up in a ditch.

Hovering in front of them, about one foot above the ground, they could see a cigar shaped object, emitting several jets of vapour. It was about sixteen feet long, with a forward cockpit and illuminated windows, through which they could see three figures. They looked perfectly human, and were wearing silver jumpsuits with polo necks.

Some kind of hatch opened, and one of the crew stepped out and walked over to Joyce and Ted. He looked to be about forty-five years old, and just over six feet tall. He had long fair hair, and side-burns which extended into a 'Van-Dyke' beard. His skin was very pale, and his eyes 'pink'.

He rested his left arm on the roof of the car, and stared in at the occupants. Ted said his penetrating gaze left him with a sense of calm and he wanted to get out and talk to him. Joyce, who claimed she could hear a high-pitch whistling sound, became hysterical. Whilst Ted was trying to reassure her, the stranger moved around to the back of the car, and when they looked again, both he and the craft had disappeared.

Joyce was left shaken by the incident, but six weeks later had regained her composure and put the incident behind her. At 6.45pm on 30th December, she and Ted had gone out to get petrol and were travelling home again, when they saw another orange light in the sky. There was a high pitched whistle, the same as Joyce had heard before, and the car started to rock violently.

The next thing they remembered was standing in a dome-shaped chamber, about fourteen feet high, and beside them, also in the chamber, was Joyce's Mini car.

The same 'alien', whom they had seen before, was there along with two other younger men, who were clean-shaven. They all wore identical silver jump-suits, but had no helmets, indicating that they could breathe in our atmosphere. Joyce had the opportunity to observe the leader more closely, and noted that his nose was thin, and his skin flawless. His eyes were the only feature which indicated he may not be 'of this Earth'. The pupils, which had been overly large in the darkness, had now almost disappeared under normal lighting.

For a while the men spoke to each other in a strange Oriental sounding language, which Joyce did not understand. Then the older man, who appeared to be the leader, spoke to Joyce and Ted in accented, broken English.

He asked Ted to step forward towards a red and black rotating central column, which had symbols, similar to those used in astrology, around it. The walls of the chamber were covered with curious charts of circles and lines, and to the side of the central column was another crew member operating a console with numerous multi-coloured flashing lights.

Ted returned to Joyce's side, and asked the leader why they had taken them and the Mini. He said they had marked the car, and would return some time in the future. Joyce said that he conveyed some information to Ted, most of which he didn't understand.

He then said; "We are not hostile towards you. You must tell the world."

The next thing she remembered was being back in the car, with a beam of bright white light shining through the rear window, and out the windscreen. She and Ted were parked on the other side of Winchester, some distance from where they had been taken. It was now dark, and 8.15pm.

The visitors did indeed return. On 7th March, Joyce was driving her friend Ann Stickland to visit some people in Hampshire. Suddenly, at about 10.15am, her car slowed and came to a halt. They both got out of the Mini to see what was wrong, and could see a large glaring light, as bright as the sun, coming from a large oval object on the ground nearby.

A man stepped out of the craft, walked towards Joyce, and took both her hands in his. She said his hands were warm, like any human being. He was about six feet tall with long sandy hair, and dressed in a one piece shiny suit, and although his beard had grown longer, was sure he was the same person she had encountered some months before.

Ann said he appeared to be speaking to Joyce in broken English, but she could not hear what he said. He had just stared at her, and she found herself unable to move until he raised his arm while returning to his craft. Joyce later said he had given her a message, which she understood, but will not divulge.

After the craft left, whistling and humming as it gathered speed, they decided to abort their trip and return to Winchester.

There was a final encounter in May 1977, when she and Ted were together in the car again. This time two of the same ufonauts conveyed more messages, some of which expressed their concern over nuclear activity on Earth.

By this time Joyce was becoming traumatised in more than one way. The man had said to her – "You are one of us", giving her the mistaken belief that they would take her away permanently. Also, she had received too much attention and harassment from UFO investigators and the media, and just wanted to avoid any more publicity.

Barry Richards wrote of another incident, which occurred in a small mountain town in West Virginia.

On the night of the 3rd February 1977, Sandra Cashell, a mother of three, was driving to the nearest drug store, fifteen miles away, to get some medicine for her four-year-old daughter, who had a fever. It was cold and snowing, with icy roads to navigate.

She was climbing a steep hill, and as her radio became static, she saw an orange ball of light, which shot out of the sky and in front of her vehicle. Despite having the heater on, she was suddenly so cold, she felt paralysed, and couldn't move her arms or legs.

She looked out of the windscreen again, and the orange ball in front of her now appeared to be a physical dome-shaped craft. It was resting on a tripod, or landing gear, and had a row of brightly lit portholes. Suddenly, the air was filled with a strange, high-pitch hum, and the station wagon began to vibrate. It was being lifted off the road, apparently caught in a powerful beam of white light.

Her car was floated through a hatch at the side of the disc, and it was at that stage she must have passed-out. When she recovered, she was no longer in her station wagon. It was dark all around, and she felt as if she was lying, still paralysed, on a table. A blinding blue light filled the 'compartment' she was being held in, and a figure stepped out of the shadows. She was terrified, expecting a monster of some kind. Instead, she saw a man, wearing a tight-fitting, one piece jumpsuit, who looked quite human, except for a slightly high forehead, and ears which 'stuck-up' a bit further out of the side of his head.

She knew he wanted to talk to her, but he didn't speak. Instead all communication seemed to be an exchange of thoughts. He identified himself as the 'Leader', and explained that he was from another dimension, and that his people were worried about our use of nuclear power for other than peaceful purposes.

He said that they had chosen her for contact, because she was humble and open-minded enough to treat her experience with a certain amount of respect. In the past, several contactees had tried to profit from the experience, and in the process, misused any information given to them. They had also met secretly with the governments of the United States, Canada, England, Russia and India, but no nation was willing to be the first to admit they had been contacted by beings in flying saucers.

Sandra was still agitated, wondering if she would ever get home, and the man released the braces which had been holding her down on the table. She stood up, and feeling a little less uneasy, asked him what did his world look like? He flicked a few switches, and a large screen on the wall lit up.

She saw a large metropolis, with people walking around. He said no-one was poor, everything was free, they were all vegetarians, and there was no sickness. He said many people had entered his world, and chosen not to leave. He said there were 'windows' such as in the Bermuda Triangle, and a certain town in England, where planes, ships and people vanish because of some sort of magnetic flux which 'zips' them away.

He also mentioned other places, inhabited by 'evil beings', and said that, whenever possible, they stay out of their lanes of travel. He hoped that in the not-so-distant future, our two worlds would join as one – after all 'we are but part of the whole'.

Before returning Sandra and her car to the road, the man advised her not to try and report her experience to the newspapers, radio or television, as they would ridicule her. If she wished she could contact one of the larger UFO organisations, and they would do their best to see that the information she was given was passed on.

The following year, on 23rd September, businessman Alejandro Hernandex was driving, with his thirteen year-old son, in southern Chile. They were terrified when a huge saucer hovered overhead and 'swallowed' their car inside. Alejandro said five bulky figures 'stuffed his son in a box', while a sixth 'interviewed' him in a metallic voice. A report a little difficult to accept - however witnesses saw the car descend back to the road with a very frightened father and son inside.

The *'MUFON Journal'* January 1982, documented the 1980, August 22nd, East Texas case of 'Megan Elliot', who was driving home in the early hours of the morning. She had her 18 month old baby, Renee, in the car with her, when the radio became garbled, and she could hear a loud electrical noise. Her lights dimmed, and she felt the car being lifted off the road.

As she rose into the air, she could see the tops of the pine trees being blown around, as if by some windstorm. Her vehicle suddenly entered the bottom of a flat metal object overhead, and she found herself in a brightly lit circular room. A 'voice' told her to get out of the car, and when she refused, a small humanoid figure approached, and removed the locked door of the car.

She and Renee were taken by the being, and clamped down on tables, where they were probed with various devices. Two other creatures participated in the examination. They all had large heads, oval eyes, broad flat noses, small slit-like mouths and thumbless four fingered hands. She did not notice any body hair, eyebrows or lashes.

Afterwards, they were given some various coloured and shaped pellets to take, before being returned to the car, and lowered back down to the road. Megan found herself only five miles from home, and twenty-five miles away from where the aliens had picked her up.

There have been pilots who have also complained of the effect of a mysterious 'updraft' associated with UFOs.

The *'APRO Bulletin'*, detailed a disturbing 1973 report from Captain Lawrence Coyne, an experienced army helicopter pilot from Ohio. On the night of October 18th, he and three other crewmen, Lieutenant Arrigo Jezzi, Sergeant John Healey and Sergeant Robert Yanacsek, were cruising at an altitude of 2,500 ft, near Mansfield, when they spotted an unusual craft pacing them.

At first it was a bright light, but when it became closer they could see a grey, metallic-looking hull, about sixty feet long, with a centre dome. There was no noise or turbulence, and no sign of any intake openings, portholes or markings. The leading edge glowed red, a short distance back from the nose, and a green light, at the rear, reflected on the hull. This light swivelled like a spotlight, completely flooding the helicopter's canopy. At this time the chopper's radio stopped functioning.

By then, the strange craft had reduced its speed, and was hovering directly overhead, within five hundred feet, and dangerously close. Fearing a collision, Coyne had grabbed the controls from Jezzi, and took evasive action, throwing the helicopter into a dive. The UFO then turned to the right and sped off to the north.

When Coyne pulled out of his dive, what amazed the crew was that when the object swooped in over the helicopter, they were at 1,500 ft and still descending. When they levelled off, they were at an altitude of 3,800 ft, and in a vertical ascent, something that was impossible for the helicopter to do under its own power. Further, despite their 1,000 feet per minute climb, the army's UH-1H helicopter's cyclic and collective controls were still in the 'full-down' position. The magnetic compass was spinning out of control, and later had to be replaced.

Witnesses on the ground had also seen the near collision and a green beam of light. A woman and four children pulled up in their car, and two of the kids, despite their mother's protestations, jumped out. Initially when she saw the helicopter hurtling towards the ground, she was terrified it would hit them.

Although she was preoccupied with getting her children back into the car, she was sure she saw the two objects 'converge' and then the helicopter flying higher, and the UFO going into the distance.

Coyne and the other witnesses made a report to the Army and the news media. In January 1974, Dr. Hynek interviewed the crew at length. All recalled being very scared, and Coyne commented; "It was like looking into another world!"

CHAPTER SEVEN

ALIENS AMONG US

There have been, and still are, cases of extraterrestrials living, incognito, in society.

There were many incidents in Italy in late 1962, early 1963, and the following years. The 'Amicizia', (Friendship), was the name used for a very secretive forty year interaction between normal citizens and humanoid and other friendly aliens. To the best of investigators' knowledge, it began in 1956, however some evidence indicates that it might have been occurring much earlier. There is evidence of similar groups in Switzerland and other neighbouring areas, where the same terminology was used; 'Amitie' in France and 'Freundschaft' in Germany and Austria.

In Australia, we have many migrants from Europe, who arrived in the decades after World War II. Colleagues and acquaintances who came from Northern Italy, Switzerland, Austria, Germany, France and Northern Siberia told me of some of their parents and older relatives who had been involved with the 'Friendship Groups'.

(Given the still centralised area of these particular groups I have wondered how long they were actually there, and about any possible connection, good or bad, with the Third Reich who were the occupying force, during World War II.)

The visitors had their bases in a variety of hidden subterranean locations, some under mountains, others below existing buildings, or even under the sea.

Anthony Huneeus, a leading researcher in Chile, claimed that at one time, the Amicizia had established a base on an island off the country's south coast. This was divulged to the public during a TV program, when a well-known radio broadcaster claimed the aliens on the island had healed him of a terminal illness.

Naturally, the military sat up and took notice. There were hundreds of small islands off the coast, and the Chilean Navy's investigations led them to a small island where a mysterious ship, the *'Mytilus'*, which was not registered in accordance with Chilean law, used to ferry people back and forth. Of course, by the time the Navy got there, they found no evidence of a base.

Umberto Visani investigated and documented the Amicizia, saying that their interaction did not just involve a small group of individuals, but specifically chosen people of varying walks in life, from professionals to students and housewives. Politicians, university professors, company presidents, military officers, engineers, journalists and many others, were all reputed to be part of this clandestine interaction. Further, there was ample evidence at the time, including recordings, photos and videos. The level of contact went from single encounters to deep participation lasting over forty years.

In 2009 Professor Stefano Breccia, a retired expert in artificial intelligence and computer sciences, who was apparently also involved, wrote a book, *'Mass Contacts',* which detailed the accounts of Bruno Sammaciccia, a Catholic scholar, and the leader of the Italian group. Sammaciccia was a prominent Italian theologian and psychologist, and he entrusted his notes to Breccia, to be published after his death in 2003. Other books and articles have also surfaced, but usually not until after the supposed 'departure' of the visitors and the demise of the witnesses.

One observation, which sounded familiar to me, was that Breccia claimed one of the Visitors told him, in 1967, that there was another star, as yet undiscovered, fairly close to our Solar System. (It reminded me of what the 'Khan' had told Ruth, and the multiple reports over the last few years, that there was a large body near the Solar System which some considered may be a brown dwarf binary companion to our Sun – detailed in *'UFOs Now and Then'*).

Breccia said that the Italians had nicknamed the 'Amicizia' visitors the 'W56' due to their first contact in 1956. Some of these beings were much shorter or taller than their human counterparts, and far different in physical appearance. Others were essentially the same as us. Together, they comprised a 'joint task force', collectively known as the 'Akrij'.

Bruno Sammaciccia, and three friends, were in a pub in Pescara when they experienced an inexplicable urge to go to the castle on a nearby hill. After arriving, they heard a calm but 'imperious' voice telling them to 'stand still', as 'one of them' was about to arrive.

From the side of the castle two 'beings' appeared, one very tall and the other much shorter. Except for their respective heights, they looked quite human. During several meetings, Bruno and his friends were told that these aliens had been visiting Earth for centuries, and had several bases on our planet.

They also mentioned an ongoing war against a hostile race, the 'CTR', who presented a threat, and were responsible for human abductions and cattle mutilations.

Bruno said the visitors varied in appearance, but those who looked human, had either blond or black hair, with greyish-blue or black eyes. They were slim, with strong bodies, and often sported a beard. Unlike some of their colleagues, who were very short or tall, it was relatively easy for them to integrate and live incognito in society. It seems that they had been here for a long time, and a few are still among us. He claimed that they are so closely related to us genetically that they can, and probably have interbred.

Bruno made mention of radio contacts with the 'W56', who were able to 'hide their radio signals and transmit their own messages'. This supports the evidence of other ham radio operators, around the globe, who were surreptitiously communicating with the 'space people'.

Most of the craft seen in the skies were primarily used for observation, rather than transportation. The 'Akrij' who mingled in society adopted assumed identities and used normal earth vehicles such as cars, trucks and sometimes small planes. Like us, they believed in God, a Supreme Being, and were, in some ways, so genetically related to us that, as I've said, they even interbred with humans.

As a result, they were often imbedded in everyday life, and engaged in worldly professions. Stefano Breccia mentioned how one was a university researcher, another a textile company manager, and a third a senior manager of a large German telecommunications corporation. Their true identities were strictly secret, and never divulged. Contactee, Daniel Fry, mentioned another one who was also a company director.

Sammaciccia and other local people continued to assist the 'Akrij' in their mission to monitor Earth and spread their message. They also said the 'visitors' mentioned countless other worlds, almost all of which are inhabited by human-like beings.

Often their human 'friends' purchased items for the 'visitors', however the 'Akrij' in hiding, did not seem to use our currency, and repaid their helpers with platinum or gold ingots, which were sometimes difficult to exchange.

(This reminded me of the report from Mt. Shasta in the US, where unusual beings, living deep in the mountains, would visit the local market and pay with gold ingots. Also Daniel Fry, who was asked by Alan, an alien, to help him infiltrate earth society, was offered ingots of gold to help pay any expenses. In the US, there are many legal requirements for selling gold, and Fry had to request an alternative method of payment.)

Why were they here? Australian ufologist, Warren Aston, British researcher Timothy Good, and other investigators have extensively researched the Amicizia. Warren published the following letter, written in 1967, by Franco Saiji, a magistrate from Turin, Italy, to Count Gian Luigi Zoccoli of Bologna, where he described his experiences with his Akrij friends;

'We are dwarfs with respect to their values! We cannot hope to receive easily from them what we are meant to achieve, day after day, as centuries go by...We have to dig our own road. This is the purpose of life and human evolution. Man has a divine destiny!

'Only one thing is possible to those who have confronted this new reality...to witness that elsewhere the purpose of life and the Universe has been understood. The dreadful questions that have always tormented us about existence have been answered. But the right road is different from the one we are now on, and we must change now, before it is too late.'

Warren wrote a very persuasive comment regarding this letter; *'The pathos in Saiji's letter is an eloquent commentary on humanity's common destiny. It echoes the underlying conclusion of all the genuine contactees: we are meant for much more, a future in a universe of limitless possibilities.'*

In 1963 Gordon Creighton reported upon Italian aerospace journalist Bruno Ghibaudi's collection of photographs of saucers, and his account of contact with their occupants.

Ghibaudi had not really given the subject much thought, until in 1961, his bosses asked him to prepare a TV programme about people who claimed they had seen flying saucers.

He was aware of accounts of sighting and contact reports from other parts of the world, but as he travelled around Italy, was astounded at the number of cases being related by people from his own country.

He said his job was not easy. Many people who had previously taken pictures, or related their experiences, regretted being outspoken. Some had lost their jobs, others subjected to ridicule, and a few had endured hours of intensive questioning by 'officialdom'.

Suddenly, his TV producers told him the documentary was cancelled. By this time Ghibaudi was fascinated, and conducted further investigations on his own initiative. After a while, he was recognised as one of Italy's leading experts.

One breakthrough occurred in the summer of 1961, when he was invited to meet some of the 'Space People'. He has always refused to divulge the location of the house where the rendezvous took place, or the name of the 'go-between' who issued the invitation.

Along with other witnesses, he learned much about the Space Brothers, and their reasons for visiting our planet. He said that some of them are so much like us in appearance, many have infiltrated our society and live, incognito, among us now. If they ever wish to identify themselves, it is usually by gesture or telepathy, or sometimes in the language of the people they meet.

Ghibaudi states emphatically, that they are only men like us, and not omnipotent deities. They are however, thousands of years ahead in science and technology, not to mention morality. They have an 'exact estimate of our natures and the level that we have reached'. While their intentions are benevolent, we must not rely upon them to get us out of our difficulties.

There are cosmic laws which prevent the more evolved races from interfering, beyond certain limits, in the evolution and development of the more backward races. For every race must be the maker of its own progress, paying the price for it with its sacrifices, failures and victories.

One of the principal reasons for their coming is to prevent nuclear disaster, however they are not infallible, and their efforts and concern might not suffice in preventing catastrophe if something went wrong, or some accident nullified their plans to avert the worst. While they are capable of destroying such weapons, mankind would still retain the ability and intention to build fresh nuclear devices. For this reason, extraterrestrials are working in a more subtle manner to influence the minds of men.

In 1954, UFOs were certainly also being seen over Italy. On 27th October, a football game between Pistoia and Florence came to a sudden halt when the referee, players and ten thousand spectators stared at two mysterious spherical objects passing over the stadium. Reports described how they passed over Florence three times, and discharged 'hairy filaments' similar to 'angel hair'.

The 1962 *'Flying Saucer Review'* published an article from the Italian Magazine, *'Domenica della Sera'*, (translated by Gordon Creighton), where Italian engineer, Luciano Galli, said that one July, in the late 1950s, he met extraterrestrials who took him for a ride in their craft. In keeping with most of the witnesses at the time, Galli had conscious memory of the event. The use of hypnosis didn't occur until decades later.

Galli was a modest man, and head of a small workshop. He was walking back to work from lunch, and when he reached the blind alley where his business was located, a dark coloured car pulled up in front of him. A tall, dark man, with a friendly face, normal features, a moustache and very dark eyes, got out and offered him a lift. He had seen this man, who wore a business suit and spoke perfect Italian, several times around the town. Once, when he tried to speak to him he suddenly disappeared. Galli described him as having 'a face like an angel in plain clothes'.

There was another man in the car, who never spoke, and after Galli got in, they travelled fifty-seven kilometres from Bolgna to the Croara Ridge, where there was a shining grey flying saucer hovering about six feet off the ground. They all entered the ship via a metal cylinder, which 'came out'. Once aboard he could see what he described as a pilot's cabin with instruments and panels all around.

They seemed to be flying through space until they arrived at what Galli described as a giant dirigible, at least six hundred metres in length. (I assume this was a 'mother ship'.) At one end were six openings – each one divided into six smaller 'cubicles' – out of which small flying discs were seen coming and going. Once inside the large craft, Galli could see about four to five hundred men and women, all very friendly and good-looking, walking around or standing in the hangers. They all wore overalls of some silky or shining plastic material.

"This is one of our spaceships", his companion said, and proceeded to give him a brief tour of some of their amenities. Afterwards his companion took him back to their original 'transport' disc, and they returned to the same spot on Croara Ridge. The entire trip had taken just over three hours.

Some researchers tried to discredit this report, as he claimed the visitors told him that they came from Venus. Considering many other contactees were, for some reason, told this falsehood, it appears that the Space Brothers were deliberately misleading us.

New Zealand '*Xenolog*', Number 107, details a 1952 report from near Mt. Etna, in Sicily, Italy. The witness, Eugenio Siragusa, was waiting for a bus, early one morning in Martyr's Square, Catania, when a white, mercury-coloured, luminous object appeared in the sky. As it zig-zagged and rapidly descended towards him, he could see it resembled a spinning-top.

When it hovered overhead, a brilliant 'ray' left the object, and "completely pierced me!" At that moment, his fears turned to 'indescribable serenity'. The 'ray' shrank back into the craft, which then moved left and right in an arc across the sky before disappearing. For the next ten years, his personality changed and he developed extrasensory perceptions, and telepathy;

'When I pulled myself together, I rapidly discovered, more and more, that something extraordinary had happened to me...Ever since then an inner voice began to instruct me on geology and cosmology. It opened my mind to the mysteries of Creation and of my former lives. This re-dimension of my existence was possible thanks to continued ESP, contacts which were established between certain extraterrestrials and myself. This extra-sensory perception was continually developing within me. It lasted eleven long years before I could actually physically meet my extraterrestrial instructors.'

One night, in April 1962, he felt compelled to go back to nearby Mount Etna. As he was driving up towards Mount Manfre, it felt as if his car was being guided up the mountain by some superior force. He stopped his car at the side of the road, and as he walked along the path he saw two silhouettes on top of the isolated hill. They were two, well-built men, about 5'4", with long blonde hair and 'soft' features. They wore silver space-suits, with gold armlets around their wrists and ankles, a luminous belt and a strange metallic chest-plate.

At first, he was terrified, but one directed a green beam toward him, from an object he had in his hand. Immediately he felt a sense of calm, and the men spoke to him in Italian, saying: "We have been waiting for you. Record in your memory what we are going to tell you."

He was given a message to pass on to our leaders, similar to what other contactees of the day had been told: We must stop our warlike tendencies, and nuclear weapons, (especially the Hydrogen Bomb), and practice justice, freedom, love and fraternity to all. They mentioned being part of an 'Intergalactic Confederation', and said the 'Cosmic Counsel' condemns the people of Earth for their inhuman behaviour. Eugene heeded the message and dedicated the rest of his life to furthering their aims.

On September 4th, he met two other beings, who were much taller, but dressed the same as his previous contacts. This time he got a much better view of their saucer, which was an 'enormous spinning top' with a diameter of about twenty-five meters.

He had several other meetings with his mentors, who reiterated their messages, alluding to us ignoring their previous missionaries.

'A highly evolved humanity send you astronauts and missionaries from a distance of several light years to enlighten you on the nature of your existence, but instead of being thankful for their efforts, you ignore them and mock all the teachings they bring you; know that an evolution that has failed is a planetary catastrophe, and this will be the consequences of your acts!

'In a past life, every one of you has worked towards the establishment of the civilisation which exists today; you have all collaborated in participating in the development of humanity.

'Understand that you are preparing yourselves today! As tutors of your kind, we can do nothing else but condemn your acts; know this, you are rigorously supervised by a superior race, who will never permit you to come to the disaster of a 'nuclear war'.'

Siragusa's mission was to quietly spread their message by recruiting other contactees. They avoided the publicity of lectures or public meetings, and carried out their mission quietly and effectively.

There is a curious and unusual twist to the ending of this case. On July 4th 1978, Eugenio Siragusa died. At 10.30pm that same night, Italian Naval Officer Maurizio Esposito, along with two Italian Air Force sergeants, Attilio Salvatore and Franco Padellero, were walking near Mt. Etna.

They noticed three red lights in the sky, and when one broke off from the rest, they jumped into Salvatore's car, and headed to the spot where the object had seemed to land.

They found a saucer, resting on the slope below the road. Standing next to it were five very tall, human type beings, with blond hair and 'beautiful' features. They were wearing what appeared to be black, tight fitting 'flight suits'. They climbed up the slope until they were only about ten to fifteen feet away from the witnesses, then smiled and nodded before making their way back down to the disc.

Esposito and his companions could not move, as if immobilised by some unknown force. They felt so disorientated that they didn't wait for the craft to leave, and sped off back down the road. Were Siragusa's space friends bidding a final farewell?

It was suggested that after the US rejected their offer for help in 1954, these aliens, (who were in opposition to another more hostile race – the *'contrari'* or 'CTR' – who were also visiting Earth), decided to convey their message of peace and morality to the general public.

In my book *'The Days of the Space Brothers'*, I discuss a New Zealand contactee – Mr.X. – who had a long-term contact with human-looking 'visitors'. On 17th February 1963, he received the following disturbing note.

'We are sorely troubled at the trend of events in our sphere of influence. Rebellion has been threatening among certain cosmic entities which are even now moving in the direction of your location. We are doing our best to divert their direction of travel. If they come too close to your place in space, their influence will be tragic for your present uneasy peace, as past wars will be nothing to what this will cause if they succeed.

'We have been too busy with this cosmic trouble to communicate with you, but give this as a kindly warning that trouble may come your way. We hope to be strong enough to stop it. May the good Lord help us.'

'God bless you and all who look for truth.'

'Your two friends'

(I wonder if it related to the less than pleasant aliens, of different appearance, who later abducted and mistreated innocent victims? Were they referring to the 'Greys', or CTRs which the 'Amicizia' spoke about?)

The references to the CTRs also became much more meaningful in later years, when hapless victims reported unpleasant abductions by the 'greys' with skinny bodies, large heads, black wrap-around eyes, and no visible reproductive organs. One of the W56 told Stefano Breccia that; "The CTRs are the result of a W56 experiment that has run out of control. They are robots, in the full sense of the word, even if centuries ago they began as a biological reproduction with no soul or emotions."

He added that it would be difficult for us to discriminate between a natural being and a biological robot, and these entities are trying to understand how to bridge the difference between them and us. This certainly would explain the behaviour of the 'greys', and makes sense of their interest in genetics, and human and animal reproductive and biological material.

Umberto Visani also reported that in 1978 the CTRs attacked and destroyed most of the W56 bases, including ones under the Adriatic. The largest, which was the scene of a heated battle, was at a depth of twelve miles from the surface, and extended from the centre of the Adriatic to the centre of Italy. At the time, massive explosions, of unknown origin, were reported from off the Italian coast.

Bruno Ghibaudi had said that there are other reasons for the Space Brothers visiting and sometimes revealing themselves, but he was forbidden to speak of them. (The alleged conflict with the CTRs undoubtedly being one, I would assume).

Obviously, there were extraterrestrial bases under the sea, sometimes deep beneath our oceans, however it was not common practice for the visitors to divulge their actual locations, or to take anyone there. In recent years, the Earth's major powers would be more capable of detecting any suspicious underwater activity.

(One exception was Orlando Ferraudi, whom I mention in *'UFOs Now and Then'*. Orlando was flown from Beunos Aires in Argentina to an undersea base in the Caribbean.)

(There have been many accounts of suspected bases, bordering the South American continent, under the Pacific and Atlantic Oceans. Multiple reports have come from Venezuela, Argentina, Chile and Brazil. Puerto Rico, a US Protectorate in the Caribbean, which has many military bases and 'prohibited weapons testing areas', is rife with rumours of a nearby undersea base.

For more than 120 years, reports of strange aerial craft, emerging from the water, have been received from all over the world. The witnesses are often military personnel.

In 1945, when the US Army Transport 'Delarof' was heading back to Seattle from Alaska, a large round object, about two hundred feet in diameter, emerged from the sea, circled the ship two or three times and then sped off.)

After losing the battle with the CTRs, many of the Akrij fled, and most had departed Earth by 1986. They promised that they would return, but we don't really know when. Some have remained integrated in our society, and maintain smaller bases elsewhere on the planet. Since then, reports of flying saucers with beautiful blond haired emissaries have been almost non-existent.

NOT JUST ITALY

Respected British researcher, John Spencer, investigated the possibility of the same, or similar group operating, simultaneously, in Scandinavia and other parts of the world.

Sten, his witness, had his first contact in 1954, when a ten metre diameter, green-yellow sphere descended from the sky, and hovered one hundred and fifty metres overhead. It remained there for about five minutes before zooming back into the sky.

About a year later, Sten and a friend were playing badminton in the same area, when they saw a large metallic cigar shaped object, without windows or wings. It was two to three times the length of a normal aeroplane, and moved silently across the sky, about one kilometre away.

After that, Sten developed a passing interest in UFOs, and in 1963, along with his girlfriend and parents, he observed a classic flying saucer in the sky near his home.

Later that year, when he was waiting for a tram in Stockholm, a girl nearby suddenly stared at him. Her eyes seemed to emit some form of powerful ray, and at that moment, he received a telepathic message, informing him that she was an extraterrestrial. Her mission was to initiate contact with him.

Sten was confused, but too shy to speak to her. They both got on the tram, and she alighted after a couple of stops, giving him a smile as she left.

One night, in 1964, Sten was walking near a gas plant, when he noticed a 'small' cigar-shaped object, partly over and partly under the clouds. He was startled to suddenly hear a male voice, clearly in his head, saying, in perfect Swedish; "Sten Lingren, we are going to contact you in the future."

The voice was almost metallic, with a little reverberation. He was later told this was a communication, created by an electronic beam from the ship, which modulated the hearing nerve in his ear.

The craft departed, and it wasn't until much later that Sten was contacted by a woman he has called 'Bea'.

She explained that she was connected with a group of cosmic visitors who were here. She imparted a lot of information to Sten, much of which he would not disclose. When he asked Bea if she was one of the 'visitors', she would not answer. Sten felt, due to his own observations, that she was an extraterrestrial, and later learned that in fact she was one of the Cosmic Brotherhood. (She later told him that they had a network of physical beings stationed in different countries on this planet, with most participants staying for about thirty years. Bea herself, left in 1980.)

In 1965 the first 'contact' was made by Sten's friend Daniel, who was alone at a lake near Nävsijön, a remote nature reserve one hundred and fifty miles from Stockholm.

A big craft came down, about two hundred metres in diameter, and hovered above the swamp. A ramp came out, and a 'being' emerged and walked towards Daniel, stopping about two metres away.

He was not sure if this was a person or a robot. It was well built, over six feet tall, and wearing a helmet. Originally he could see two human eyes staring at him, but suddenly, with an electronic noise, a shield was lowered over the face.

Daniel also noticed it was wearing a belt with flashing lights around it. Nothing was said, and after a few communications using hand gestures, the being returned to the craft which 'took off'.

Daniel was left very shaken, but a few weeks later he was contacted again. This time there were two men, and they had several meetings. On the second occasion one of the visitors removed his helmet. Conversations were verbal, at first in English, and later Swedish.

Sten had then become involved with Crister, another contactee, and they advised that their contacts were part of a group called the Cosmic Brotherhood, who were outer-space people working on Earth. They said they were the same beings who had been in contact with George Adamski, Howard Menger and Daniel Fry.

Besides having people stationed in Sweden, they had others working in Denmark, Finland and Norway with their main communications and transport based in England. Globally, different 'groups' are allocated to other parts of the planet, each given varying missions and projects. They also told Sten and Crister that every person has a unique, specified frequency which can help them locate anyone on the planet.

Sten saw his mission as being the promotion of the Cosmic Brothers, and in order to do this, he and Crister started a UFO research organisation, and liaised as much as possible with the media and television outlets.

He said; "When you get in contact, you get a responsibility inside you, and it causes you to act. First you understand yourself and your connection with them. Then you understand the Earth people and the problems the Earth has. When you can see both the Earth situation, and their society, then you think the people here are completely mad.

"Then you feel compassion for the Earth people, which leads to an inner consciousness and a desire to try to help in some way. What I try to do is to communicate my experience to people here in Sweden and that the Cosmic Brotherhood exists. If I can focus on their message, perhaps we can lift mankind up in some way."

Sten and his colleagues gave a slightly sceptical John Spencer multiple examples of their success with Swedish newspapers and television producers.

This would not have been possible without the assistance of the Cosmic Brotherhood.

There are other cases of the 'visitors' asking humans to assist them with their mission on Earth. Rueben Stone wrote about Brazilian policeman, Jose Antonio, One sunny afternoon in May 1969, he was fishing in a lake in Minas Gerais. An upright cylindrical craft, and two four-feet-tall creatures, paralysed him with a beam of light. He was promptly taken inside the craft, and tied up with a helmet being put on his head.

The craft took off, and he did not know how long they travelled before they landed at an unknown place. Jose was then blindfolded, and taken to a brilliantly lit room, where he saw the bodies of four other humans. About fifteen other 'little guys' were there, and during an 'interrogation', they examined his fishing gear, and by means of drawings and sign language suggested that he be 'their guide among men'. (Obviously this species of alien were not able to communicate telepathically with Jose.)

It must have been with some trepidation that he refused, however they blindfolded him again, and returned him to Brazil. Once on the ground he collapsed, and found himself near Vitoria, in Espirito Santo, two hundred miles away from where he had been fishing. Whilst he thought the experience had only lasted a few hours, four and a half days had elapsed between his initial abduction and subsequent return.

French researcher Leo Noury has discussed the very controversial Ummo case, which also involved aliens living in Europe. These 'visitors' concentrated on interacting with people from the scientific community, rather than contacting members of the general public.

The first known occurrence was in Madrid, during the 1960s, when a young dactylographer advertised for work, and two 'Danish' doctors asked him to type some scientific articles. They were both tall and blond, and no different to any other human beings. One day they asked him to type a paper on their 'home world', the planet Ummo, fourteen light years away. He thought they were pulling his leg until one pulled a small transparent ball from his pocket. It started to levitate, and in it was a recording of all the scenes from the dactylographer's home the night before. They advised this was just a sample of their technology.

The Ummites claimed that they had arrived here in 1950, and for nearly forty years, about twenty people in Spain, together with many others from France, East Germany, Argentina and a number of other countries, had been receiving typewritten reports, on technical matters, from the Ummites.

Enrique Novoa, a civil engineer, claimed he had several lengthy telephone conversations with them, although the answers to his queries were so thorough and precise, he wondered if he was talking to a computer.

Strangely enough, French physicist Jean Pierre Petit claimed that part of his work on MHD propulsion systems was made possible through the Ummo letters.

This entire episode was debunked as a hoax by some researchers, but others firmly believed it to be genuine. Although French researcher Jacques Vallee firmly believed the Ummo affair to have originated from some Earthly conspiracy, he was not able to positively identify the source. Forty years is rather a long time to perpetrate a hoax!

If aliens were already present on Earth, then there would be no way to know of their clandestine lives, hidden locations or possible secret bases. Timothy Good wrote about one witness, Joelle, whom he knew well. She claimed contact with two Visitors, Mark and Val, she had met in 1963, when their craft landed in the Derbyshire Peak District. For well over a year she maintained contact with them at several places in England, and entertained them in her flat on at least two occasions.

Joelle claimed they were physical beings who looked totally human and fair-skinned, with perfect teeth, although she noticed that there was a dark-skinned man who was part of the group. They spoke their own language together, but could also use mental communication between minds, and advised they usually employed telepathy to influence people, and on odd occasions interfered directly. They did not say from where they originated, but admitted that on two occasions in the past, their people had genetically interfered with us.

Whilst they did not discuss their reasons for coming, they met, a couple of times a year, with scientists they were liaising with on a highly secret project. They suggested that we need to evolve psychologically and spiritually, and remarked; "What a beautiful planet. Such a pity you're destroying it." They also referred to other extraterrestrials also coming here, which were 'not so well disposed towards us'.

They had told her that their 'people' had established communications with scientists, and had facilities in several countries including South America, Australia and the Soviet Union. She also claimed they said that they had been liaising in secret with a team of scientists from several nations, and some of them had worked at their bases.

During their discussions Mark mentioned to Joelle that they had bases on two unspecified moons around Jupiter. (Upon reflection, this made me consider there may be other similar bases 'out there'. Since we are on an outer arm of the Milky Way, perhaps our Solar System has some significance – a military outpost in the Galaxy? Was there more than one extraterrestrial race anxious to have a presence? No wonder the aliens were getting fidgety about our own ventures into space!)

In 1967, three years after her last contact with Mark and Val, Joelle received a visit from two people from the Home Office in London. They were enquiring about the disappearance of some scientists who were mutual acquaintances. While they seemed to be reasonably knowledgeable about everything, they actually seemed pleased when she refused to answer certain questions.

In later years the presence of humanoid aliens has become much more secretive. They have to avoid contact or detection from our own government or military, let alone the more threatening CTRs or other alien races. However, the extraterrestrial/human interaction on Earth, still continues today, often in the most unlikely places.

In 1999, my friend Glennys McKay took some colleagues into the vast Australian 'Outback' to meet with some of the indigenous aboriginals. There she was told that the lights the white man called 'Min-Min' lights were in fact the lights of the vehicles the aliens travel in. On another occasion, the residents of a remote aboriginal settlement told of visits from extraterrestrials, who often stayed there with them.

Timothy Good, in his book *'Unearthly Disclosure'* writes about 'Carmina', a professional woman from Puerto Rico, who was working late one night in her 16th floor San Juan office.

The building was closed, however a strange man knocked on the door, and said he just wanted to talk to her. He was about 38 years old, over six feet tall and slim, clean-shaven with a sun-tanned skin and light brown hair. He was smartly dressed and spoke both English and Spanish. What really intrigued her were his beautiful, large lilac coloured eyes.

He had a message for her daughter, who was a television reporter, and this was the only way he could communicate without being detected by intelligence agents.

The information he wanted her to relay, was that she should not give up on her investigations into the alien phenomena at El Yunque, where there was a big base and military operations, which were investigating people from another planet who lived there. He wanted Carmina's daughter to get the information out to the public.

He was vague about himself, except to say he was part of a team which worked at the Arecibo Observatory. Any other personal questions he avoided answering, saying he had only come to give her some information.

Carmina had a feeling that he was in fact an alien, collaborating with the US government. He knew everything about her, her ex-husband, where she lived and more. When she mentioned that she was having problems with her computer, he walked over to the desk, and without touching it, rectified the problem by merely blinking.

When he left, she didn't see which way he went, and he didn't take one of the six elevators. The cleaner in the hall didn't see him either. He didn't use the stairway, outside her door, and he would have needed security to let him out. There was tight security after hours in the building, with guards in the lobby and on every floor. Nobody saw her visitor except for the female guard on the 16th level, who only saw him enter her office.

Timothy Good also mentioned 'resident aliens', and said a senior reporter, whom he trusted but would not name, was ex-military with a lot of contacts. He passed on the following information; A high ranking officer, who also had to remain anonymous, said that aliens had been coming to Earth for a very long time.

After World War II they established permanent bases in Britain, Australia, the USA, Russia, the Caribbean and the Pacific Ocean. He also confirmed that six alien craft had crashed, and had been recovered, along with bodies, by the US military.

Some reports indicate that besides masquerading as normal members of the community, the visitors still have discreet settlements in various countries, usually hidden by or close to mountain ranges or outcrops. Apparently, some humans have gone to live with them there, either retreating from everyday life, or helping the visitors with their earthly mission.

In his book, *'Unearthly Disclosure'*, Timothy Good gives a very detailed account of the experiences of Enrique Castillo in South America. I have not been thoroughly convinced as to the accuracy of all his reported contacts, but given evidence from other unconnected witnesses, this one really grabbed my attention.

In December 1974, Enrique had a humanoid-alien contact, Cyril, who took him on board a space ship to visit a 'base' in what he called the 'Vortex of the Andes'. They entered the valley facility through a tunnel in the mountain, and the people who welcomed him were not aliens, just normal humans. Castillo was told that contactees from nineteen different countries would be joining him soon.

Castillo said; *"I thought I was going to see a city of the future, but the buildings were wooden, sort of 'Canadian type' cabins, with smooth and well-cut, but rustic, beams and boards. The great rectangular cabin had two rows of bedrooms, on both sides of the central passageway.*

"At the moment there are 318 people here, who for many years...even entire families...have been contacted and brought here voluntarily. Here they live, work, study and learn. They are instructed about the great events that humanity

will experience....Many of them will be trained to help when the moment arrives.

"Nobody will know who instructed them, and besides, nobody would believe them, it could even be dangerous for them. This place, at about 3,200 metres above sea level, is located between two great mountains that give natural protection against blizzards and frosts, and is known as Alto Peru. (Peru Highlands).

Castillo saw cultivated fields of a large variety of fruits and vegetables, and also noted that all their eating utensils were made of wood. This base was entirely self-sufficient, and was camouflaged by a magnetic shield.

He said that some contactees were given different kinds of information and instructions; *"They would act in a different way than us, penetrating at the executive level and very discreetly passing information, suggesting the possibility that we were being infiltrated by two different extraterrestrial societies, one dedicated to corruption, manipulation and domination, and the other one with the intention of helping, but while acting very discreetly."*

Timothy Good discussed a similar case in his book *'Alien Base'*. In 1962, Ludwig Pallmann, a German businessman, met an unusual companion during a lengthy train journey in India.

Although he appeared to be totally human, Pallmann noted that when the stranger, Satu Ra, spoke, his voice did not seem to come from his mouth, but rather a small 'speaking device' clipped to his chest.

During the trip, Satu showed concern for the more impoverished passengers in third class compartments, and gave several of them an unknown tablet to take. When Pallman asked him where he came from; "Cotosoti;" was the reply, later qualified with the explanation it was on 'Itibi Ra II'.

When Pallmann queried where 'Itibi Ra' was, Satu merely pointed to the eastern sky, leaving Pallmann wondering whether he meant another planet, or some mystical Shangri-la.

Pallmann kept contact with Satu Ra, and later met his sister, Xiti, whose verbal communications were similar to her brother's - his from the 'gadget' on his chest, and hers from a brooch she was wearing. They confirmed that they were from another planet, and both were currently involved with humanitarian work in the poorer parts of India.

A few years later, Pallmann was involved with the installation of milling equipment and pulverizing plants in South America. An Austrian tour guide spoke of an unusual settlement in a remote jungle area, where there were 'white folk turned native'. He had been taken ill, and they cured him with fruit juice and an unfamiliar tablet.

In early 1967, Pallmann was taken to hospital, and scheduled for a kidney operation. During the night, whilst in severe pain, he felt a hand clasping his, and turned to see Xiti beside his bed. She gave him a tablet to take, and before long he was pain and fever free. The doctors were amazed at his spontaneous recovery, and he discharged himself a couple of days later, and checked into the Savoy Hotel in Lima.

Xiti met him there, and during the next few days she told him of her people, the 'Itibi Ryans', their culture and home planet. She then invited him to meet her brother again, and on 17th February 1967, they travelled to Huancayo, a town high in the Andes Mountains.

Satu Ra met them at the station, and after taking a taxi part the way to the settlement, all three sat down beside a peaceful lake, and watched the sun go down. Suddenly a 'flying saucer' descended and scooped them up and into an opening beneath its circular surface.

During his stay on the ship, he was shown images of their home planet, in a solar system closer to the centre of the galaxy. Their technology was so advanced that he could interact with these people from the craft. He learned of their culture and society, which was similar to ours. They had marriages and children, however their unions were not life-long, and early divorce was common.

Satu told him that they had come here in 1946, and established several plantations in South America, for the research and hybridization of various plants and fruits required for their diet. Were these also secret extraterrestrial 'retreats'? There were three craft at their base, two were unmanned supply craft, and the other carried a crew.

Pallmann was confined to the space ship, and was told this was for quarantine reasons, however he noticed that the local South American Indian peasants mixed freely with the Itibi Ryans, and were employed to work on their plantations.

Three days later, Pallmann accepted their offer to travel on to Colombia, where they landed on a delta swamp on the banks of the Magdalena River. Two speed boats took them on an hour's trip to Barranquilla, where they purchased fruit from local street stalls.

On 26th February, Satu informed Pallmann that his people had received orders to evacuate their plantations in South America, and he was taken back by spacecraft to the Peruvian highland lake where he had been originally picked up.

Two years later Pallmann bought a lakeside property in El Salvador, and met a very forlorn Satu, who told him his sister had been killed in a spacecraft disaster when visiting another planet.

Pallmann seemed to disappear after moving around Peru in 1968, and despite attempts by researcher Wendelle Stevens to locate him, he was still unsuccessful after ten years of searching.

In my book *'Contact Down Under'*, I discuss the ongoing experiences of Patty, and her family and friends from New Zealand. Patty was also taken to a similar place to that described by Castillo.

Patty's experiences lasted many years, and having moved to Australia, after a short break, in about 2009 the 'contacts' resumed.

She explained; "It was another really windy one night, I had gone to bed, but something drew me outside in my pyjamas. Next thing I was on a little craft with windows all around. I was taken to a place with a lake, pine trees and snow-capped mountains behind. There was a group of about ten of us, all in our pyjamas. We got out and it was like stepping into an old 'cowboy movie'. It was a deserted community settlement, like an old mining town, deep in a pine forest. It was like an old town out of a 'cowboy movie' and we were being shown a 'shop' and log cabins with handmade benches and kitchens. There were even fires burning in the fireplaces, as if it was ready to move into. I somehow felt this is where we would be brought as a refuge' sometime in the future."

It seemed Patty's 'Friend', (who was a 'humanoid visitor), felt the necessity to impress upon her the existence and location of the 'Safe Haven'. There were other aliens there, but they communicated telepathically, and got the impression they were also showing us some kind of 'refuge' for times to come. I still feel physically shaken when I talk about this."

(Again Patty's recall and testimony had astounded me. She had no way of knowing that other experiencers had described being taken to the same or similar places with log cabins.)

Although this 'trip' was consciously recalled, some of her subsequent second visit to the 'Refuge' was retrieved via hypnosis.

"In late summer 2011, I was camping with my then boyfriend David. We were in the vicinity of Whyalla in South Australia, close to a beach. It was an eerie sort of place – I think there was an Army Base nearby.

"I was walking around the remote campsite, just admiring the night sky, which, in Australia, can be magnificent away from the major cities. The moon was just so bright, almost like daylight. As I looked inland, I could see six craft hovering and moving over a mountain.

"I was terrified, and raced back to the tent, waking my dog and David. I told him I didn't feel safe, and we had to leave **now.** He wanted to pack up our camping gear, but I told him something was wrong, and to just leave it. The Australian 'outback' can be a dangerous place to be alone, so he didn't argue. We threw some bedding in the back of my ute, and drove for about thirty minutes back along the main road towards Whyalla. We stopped a few kilometres out of town, and slept at the side of the road, with the dog in the front, while we squeezed into the back seat."

The next thing Patty knew was waking to find the vehicle surrounded in blue light. She felt scared, but got out of the ute to investigate. As she stood there, the blue light shrank around her, and she found herself being lifted up to the familiar 'porthole' beneath a craft.

"It seemed to be the same 'ship' as before, and I was all alone in the large, octagonal room with black shiny walls. I felt more relaxed when I saw my

'Friend' coming towards me, and he put out his hand and told me we were going somewhere special. A few other men and women joined us, and I'll never forget an older man who looked really scared.

"The 'little ones' arrived, and each took one of us by the hand and led us back to the 'porthole'. My 'Friend' didn't appear to be coming, but did join us later. The floor was open, and below I could see a smaller ship. It was round, and although bigger than a car or truck, not very large. Much, much further down I could see my own ute on the roadside."

The little disc moved up and underneath them, and connected to their porthole via a hole in the top. Each of the humans, with their little 'companion', had to go backwards down a ladder into the smaller craft.

After a short while they noticed daylight streaming through the windows, and they could see they were approaching a big lake with pine trees all around. They landed slowly and smoothly upon the water, and after the door opened, her 'Friend' exited first saying 'Come on everybody'. She followed, with the 'little one' holding her hand, and they all walked up a small boardwalk/jetty towards the land.

"As we walked up a medium width path, I could see the blue sky, and a few clouds. I could smell the fresh fragrance of all the old pine trees, and looked back down at the lake and our craft. There were no houses visible around the shore, but further up we came to a log cabin.

"The building was obviously new, with beautiful polished wood fittings, but had been constructed in an 'old-fashioned' way. It was quite big - two-storey - with furniture, china, cutlery and everything one could possibly want. My 'Friend' told us there were a few of these structures, and it will be a haven when the world gets bad."

Patty commented that everybody seemed more relaxed, and started looking around and checking out the bathroom, and the rooms upstairs. The elderly man, who said his name was Bob, started talking to Patty. He was from America, and had been contacted for a long time also, but this was his first visit to one of her 'Friend's' retreat.

"We were led outside, and then further up the path, where I could see lots more cabins scattered around. This seemed to be the same, or a similar place, I'd been brought to before. We were given ten minutes to explore, and I walked up to what looked like a row of shops. It looked like they had been older buildings, in the process of being renovated. Most were empty, but I could see what looked like cans and bags of rice through the window of one."

Bob walked over to join her, and he seemed to feel more secure chatting to her as they walked back. The other people were returning, asking so many questions at once. Patty found it all rather overwhelming, but her 'Friend' seemed to be coping.

"They were all different people from different countries, with different accents. There was a German lady, who didn't speak English, so my 'Friend' was communicating with her separately by telepathy. She seemed to understand – perhaps he spoke German."

Her 'Friend' explained again that this was a sanctuary he wanted to share with them, and they would continue to visit more than once. At that stage, Patty had forgotten her previous trip. This time more details were imparted. There were humans involved, and the project/community had been set up by people who had mainly previously been in the Air Force or worked for the Government. There was a garden further up, obviously to enable self-sufficiency.

As they were all ushered in a line back down the path, they were joined by their 'little guides' who took them back along the jetty to the disc.

"I could still smell the pine trees, and didn't want to leave. Bob and I sat together for the return trip, and as we rose from the surface, I could see the small village from a height. It was surrounded by forest, and I wondered if it was in the middle of a national park or something."

She felt a strange feeling of movement, and saw the darkness return outside the windows. Soon they reached the larger ship and re-entered the same way they had left. Her 'Friend' asked them all what they felt and thought, and since everyone was much more relaxed they were all 'talking over one another' at once.

For many years, our spy satellites have been able to photograph anywhere in the world, regardless of the weather. Be it day or night, they can zoom in on any area and transmit thousands of images. This recent technology would have prevented any obvious alien presence, and forced them to find undetectable locations and adopt more covert measures.

Given the extraterrestrials' obvious superior technology, it is certainly possible, and indeed logical, that the best hidden location for a facility would also be under our oceans. This would certainly account for the multiple reports of unidentified objects flying out of the water, especially in the South Pacific. There have also been reports of craft shooting out of the Arctic waters before taking to the sky.

During their interaction with humans, the 'visitors' did not seem to mention the Antarctic, the most logical place of all, as being the location of one of their bases. Strangely, even today, investigators have reported stiff resistance when pursuing this line of inquiry.

Up until recent times, and the advent of widespread satellite surveillance technology, this part of the world was safe from spying eyes, and very few human intrusions.

One enduring mystery is the Piri-Reis map, made before modern Europeans explored Antarctica, yet detailing the sub-glacial geography, including mountains and rivers, of the continent. How and when this information was first obtained remains unknown. In 1513, Ottoman Admiral Piri Reis had the map compiled from fifteen different documents, some very old and dating back nearly two thousand years. Another 1531 map, owned by Orontus Finaeus contained similar details. Most experts claim the only way these charts could have been compiled is from the air.

Modern exploration of the Antarctica did not begin until the nineteenth century, and no really accurate mapping was completed until 1951, the International Geophysical Year. It has only been in the last few years, due to the Radarsat I satellite, that we have verified the accuracy of these ancient maps.

After World War II, the British had sufficient intelligence reports to indicate that many Nazis may have also fled there in submarines, and had a large underground base with advance technology. We can only speculate that they already suspected these were more alien than human facilities. They wanted to investigate this ahead of both the US and Russia. The British already had a well established base at Maudheim, 200 miles away from the suspected Nazi or alien position, and it was from there they launched an expedition in 1945. The entire team perished, but not before they sent radio messages about Nazis, strange men and 'tunnels'.

The British military and security agencies closely monitored this activity during and after the War, with secret military bases of their own established on the Antarctic continent itself, as well as the nearby Deception and Wiencke Islands. The codename for their covert presence was Operation Taberlan, and in 1946, using their 'sovereignty' of the Falkland Island Dependency, declared themselves the legitimate 'owners' of territory in the Antarctic, including parts which Chile and Argentina could also legally claim.

The next summer they sent another expedition, which allegedly found a massive network consisting of a self-sufficient base, with tunnels and caverns, which they partially detonated after considerable loss of life.

Later, in 1946/7 during the following Antarctic summer, US Admiral Byrd, who had made aerial surveys some years before, conducted 'Operation High-Jump', to purportedly investigate possible sites for bases, as there were huge mineral/ore deposits in this vast unexplored continent. The four participating military groups were collectively referred to as 'Task Force 68' participating in 'The United States Navy Antarctic Developments Program'. (It has always been believed that it was in fact to eradicate the remaining Nazis or aliens, and if the reports are accurate, Admiral Byrd spoke of well documented German activity there before, during and after the War. I consider this was a 'cover story' and he already suspected the alien presence.)

Comments were made at the time, that due to the large numbers of US military personnel (several thousand), and the nature of the equipment, both ships and air-power, it looked more like an assault team than a survey mission. It comprised the flagship aircraft carrier USS *Philippine Sea*, with many planes, the destroyers USS *Brownson* and USS *Henderson*, the *Sennet* submarine, two tankers, the *Canisteo* and *Capacon*, and the supply ships *Merrick* and *Yancey*. In addition there were two icebreakers, the *Burton Island* and *Northwind*, plus seaplanes and helicopters. (Hardly necessary for a few penguins, seals and whales!)

They commenced building a headquarters and made many reconnaissance flights, recording over ten mountain ranges. 'Operation High-Jump', which was planned to last for several months, ended prematurely after forty days in a strategic retreat. The US contingent met with stiff resistance, and engaged in several battles, suffering many casualties. There were reports of 'ray-type' weapons and Byrd described 'flying objects that could go from Pole to Pole at incredible speeds.' A Chilean newspaper is reported to have stated, at the time, Admiral Byrd had advised that the US had to initiate immediate defence measures against hostile forces threatening from the Arctic or Antarctic! He is also quoted as saying this resulted from his personal knowledge gathered at both the North and South Poles! Of course, once he returned to the US, the matter was conveniently 'covered-up'.

Personally, I believe this was indicative of a covert, advanced alien presence. What type of alien, and if they were indeed the ones connected to the Third Reich, would be a matter of conjecture. The Nazis did not have the ability or technology, at the time, to construct any kind of meaningful, permanent underground base in such a hostile environment. If they had possessed the craft documented by Admiral Byrd, Germany would have been winning the War.

The British did not return to the Antarctic until 1948/9. It is rumoured that the 'hostile forces' were later eliminated by several 'large explosions'! The truth of what happened will probably never be known.

In the 1950s, following World War II, the major powers agreed to co-operate in their activities on this icy continent. In 1957 the Americans, along with scientific representatives from sixty-seven countries, officially returned to the Antarctic as part of the International Geophysical Year. Eventually many 'stations' were established on the continent.

On 3rd July 1965, a giant lens-shape solid flying object was seen, tracked and photographed over the Argentine Scientific Naval Base on Deception Island off the Antarctic coast. Lt. Daniel Perisse watched as it alternatively hovered for up to twenty minutes at a time, then accelerated and manoeuvred at tremendous speeds. Its colour changed from red/yellow to green and orange and caused strong interference with variometers, used to measure the Earth's magnetic field. It interfered with other electromagnetic instruments and the Magnetograph tapes showed unusual registrations.

Similar reports were received from the British Base, and a Chilean naval transport ship, the 'Punta Mendanos' - whose compass needles pointed directly to the object, which was over a mile away, indicated an unusually strong magnetic power was radiating from it. Altogether the craft was sighted by thirty-one people, and none of these many witnesses believed the object was of terrestrial manufacture. Recently Russian scientists have theorised that electromagnetically operated extraterrestrial vehicles would take advantage of the streams of magnetic energy which is at its greatest at the North and South Poles. It was the detection of these forces which was one of the tasks Admiral Byrd was supposed to undertake.

In 1976 it was reported that years before a Brazilian scientist, Dr.Rubens Villela, who was on an icebreaker in Admiralty Bay, saw a strange object, which looked like a 'silver bullet', come shooting out of what must have been 40ft of sea ice. It flew off, high into the air, and huge chunks of ice 'came hurtling down'. The water inside the large gap left in the ice appeared to be boiling, with steam all around.

This was only one of many occurrences reported from the Antarctic. Villela later said; *"Many of the incidents are reported by highly qualified people, who work in observatories and scientific facilities equipped with some of the most advanced scientific resources available for detecting geophysical phenomena.....Furthermore, I have had access to UFO reports from other nations' Antarctic programmes which are unknown to the public. These reports suggest the phenomenon is very real."*

From time to time there were more reports of ice-free regions and lakes, and in 1977 scientists from the Scott Polar Research Institute discovered seventeen lakes under the Antarctic Ice. British investigator, the late Graham Birdsall, attempted to undertake a research project into current activity in the Antarctic, and was met with a fear to speak by some who knew the details.

In *'Contact Down Under'*, I discussed the 1979 case of a New Zealand airliner, which crashed into Mt. Erebus in the Antarctic. Some ham radio operators claimed that they had picked up transmissions from the doomed aircraft, saying they were being 'buzzed' by a UFO. As I pointed out in the book, it may have been trying to warn them they were on the wrong course – we will never know.

What of the Antarctic today? In 2015 Linda Moulton Howe published information from a retired US Flight Engineer who was stationed in the Antarctic during the summer months, in 1995/6. On several occasions during those years he saw silver aerial discs darting around over the Transantarctic Mountains. There was one area which was designated a 'no fly' zone, which they were told was an 'air sampling' area. Once, when traversing it for a medical emergency, they saw a very large hole, like an entrance, going down into the ice. The debriefing they received indicated a lot more than an 'air sampling area'.

They were told 'they had never seen it', and never to talk about it. After their flights they would have a few beers at a club, where they heard some of the scientists not only talking about guys at the South Pole working with 'strange looking men', but also confirming a future trip to the 'air sampling area' (ie. big hole in the ice!) 'to meet-up with those ETs that were there.'

Is there an alien base at the South Pole? We have to ask where did the unusual craft, seen over the last years originate? Were they ours or 'theirs'? More recently there have been reports of covert visits to the Antarctic by some of the world's most influential leaders. Why?

CHAPTER EIGHT

ALIEN ENCOUNTERS

PART ONE

In the days following World War II, official investigations of UFO activity did not mention much about the alien occupants of strange craft.

At an AAAS symposium in 1966, Dr. Alan Hynek, head of the US Air Force 'Project Blue Book', said the following; *'I would be neither a good reporter nor a good scientist were I deliberately to reject data. There are now on record some 1,500 reports of close encounters, about half of which involve reported craft occupants. Reports of occupants have been with us for years but there are only a few in the Air Force files: generally Project Blue Book personnel summarily and without investigation, consigned such reports to the 'psychological' or crackpot category.'*

Royalty have always shared a secret awareness in UFOs and aliens. I knew about Britain's Prince Phillip and Lord Mountbatten's interest, and had heard about Adamski meeting with Queen Juliana of the Netherlands. Until now, I did not know about the following incident.

In 1946 President Truman received a visit from the Swedish Ambassador with a letter from King Gustavus V.

This is the essential part of it; *'In 1941 we were notified that scientists of your country were working on the elaboration of a weapon which a certain part of the world regarded as too dangerous to be permitted. But, a year later, after a fantastic meeting in the Parliamentary Palace, with three strange beings, who appeared out of nowhere, we could no longer harbour any doubts regarding the existence of 'someone else' on Earth. Of beings who are unknown to us, and yet are as terrestrial as we are.*

'This, no doubt, will surprise you, Mr President, but please imagine our situation, face to face with these strange, yellow, thin creatures little more than 1.20 metres in height, speaking in a monotonous voice, without gestures, - as though projected upon one of the walls of the audience chamber – and with big

eyes and with a certain note of urgency in their insistence that, once and for all time, concord must be established among all mankind.

'They were with us little more than ten minutes and, in perfect English, gave an astonishing testimony that has obliged my Government to change all of its security measures. This testimony I now place before you, in view of the evidence that the 'atomic danger' based on the construction of nuclear weapons is already a reality. May you therefore now know how to proceed as reason and commonsense recommend.'

The next part of the letter is obviously part of the message from the aliens;

'.........Now, at a time when evolution has slowly endowed the humans with a good intelligence, you are preparing to fall into the same trap as the original race did. You have taken the first step towards the mass-manufacture of the atomic bomb, a weapon whose dangerousness is without limit, and which will serve to establish terroristic governments that will plunge the world into total disaster – a disaster that involves us too, because it is never possible to know what the results will be in a war fought with nuclear weapons.

'We are not prepared to permit it, and therefore we are warning the world now, via its most important countries...In return for that., we are prepared to reveal to you the secrets for attaining control of magnetic energy...'

Researcher, Freixedo, then went on to write; *'(I omit here one paranormal 'detail' which accompanied the presentation of this document, so as not to make the episode appear even more 'implausible', but knowing – as I do – certain other similar 'details' in the field of Ufology, it is my belief that this paranormal episode did take place.)'*

I am not about to enter into the debate about retrieved saucers or aliens we may have captured or have as our 'guests'. There are countless books, articles and documentaries about this topic. One lesser known report came from George Filer III, when he was based at McGuire Air Force Base in New Jersey, USA.

On 18th January 1978, George arrived at 4am to be told that UFOs had been flying over the base all night, and one had landed or crashed at neighbouring Fort Dix. Later reports confirmed that about twelve bluish-green lights had been seen in formation above the base.

An Army MP at Fort Dix reported that a UFO had been hovering close to his vehicle when, 'out of nowhere', a 'thing' – a 'being' – appeared right in front of his vehicle. It was four feet tall, greyish-brown in colour, with a huge head, long arms and a slender body.'

The soldier panicked, and fired five shots into the 'creature' and one more into the object floating above him. The wounded entity fled, and the UFO joined the others hovering overhead. Two more soldiers and a State Trooper joined him in the search for the wounded intruder, and when they reached the inactive McGuire runway, 'their headlights revealed, about fifty feet ahead, a motionless figure lying prone on the cold concrete.'

Researchers Leonard Stringfield and Richard Hall, who also investigated this case, said one of the security police officers commented that there was a strong scent of ammonia, and described the entity as 'a smelly, slimy creature that appeared to have an almost snakelike texture.'

George Filer was told that a C-141, from Wright Patterson Base, Ohio, was on its way to pick up the alien's body. When he asked what country the intruder was from his commander replied; "No, not a foreigner – an alien from outer space."

Within thirty minutes, a heavily armed recovery team, with no identifying insignia, arrived. They sprayed something on the corpse, put it into a crate, and flew off with it in their plane. George had a lot of questions but no answers. As normally happens in these cases, all witnesses were debriefed, sworn to secrecy, and within days retired or transferred to various other bases.

It was this and other incidents which prompted Filer's lifelong interest in UFOs, and led him to become a serious investigator in his own right and also a member of MUFON and their New Jersey State Director.

There have been other occasions when aliens have been unjustly killed by humans. In 1980, in Puerto Rico, teenager Jose Zayas was with a group of friends exploring the caves of Tetas de Cayey. They came across some 'small humanoids', and when Jose thought one was going to attack him, he battered it to death with a stick.

Its head was stoved in, and for a while, the body was kept as a trophy. The local undertaker preserved it in formaldehyde, and it was later examined by Professor Calixto Perez. He said some officers arrived, saying they were from

NASA, immediately photographing and seizing the remains. When subsequent inquiries were made, it was claimed the body had been 'lost' by US officials.

VIRGINIA

Researcher, Rufus Drake, a US pilot and Air Force veteran, spent many years trying to discover whether the government had any crashed saucers in its possession, and interviewed over a hundred potential witnesses.

One interesting case was related by retired Lt. Col. William Anderson. In the summer of 1952, he was piloting an F-94 when he was asked to divert to a remote swamp in a Virginia tidewater region, where there had been reports of a crash.

Anderson said; *"When I arrived, I circled overhead at 1,000 feet, and looked down at a saucer-shaped craft which had burrowed into a mud flat and partially disintegrated. It had knocked over several trees on its way in. There were signs of activity around the wreck, impressions in the mud, and apparent scorch marks.*

'I was told that the area was being sealed off, and that teams were en route by helicopter. Yet according to the radio traffic, rescue teams had not arrived yet. Low on fuel, I was also told that they didn't need my help, after all.'

Drake spoke to another Air Force officer, who remembered the flurry of activity, and helicopters 'coming and going'. Apparently the helicopters retrieved the saucer only to find that its crew had been pulled out, by an identical saucer seen on radar at the crash site before any aircraft arrived. The saucer was taken to a guarded hanger at Andrews Air Force Base, and ground crews scoured the crash site for days, recovering debris and detecting signs of radioactivity.

HAWAII/CALIFORNIA

An unusual report starts in June 1973, when a US destroyer was sailing from California to Hawaii. A strange craft had flown over the ship, and it crashed into the sea after being targeted by a missile. The UFO was later recovered, from a depth of 350 feet, by the 'Glomar Explorer'. It was then shipped to Honolulu and taken from there to a naval base in Chicago.

Three months later a navy seaman, on guard duty outside a building at the Chicago Great Lakes Naval Base, was told not to let anyone inside, as it contained highly top secret material.

A courier arrived with documentation which required a receipt, and the guard went inside to get a signature. He was escorted down a corridor and entered a large warehouse area. Once inside, he saw a very unusual craft, about thirty-five feet wide, and twelve to fifteen feet high at its thickest part. There were no windows or seams, but it had a flange running along the topside.

After getting the signature, the seaman was escorted out, and warned to never say anything to anyone about what he had seen.

ALIEN PHYSIOLOGY

What should an alien look like? Soviet Dr. Yuri Rall summed it up nicely in a 1961 article in the government newspaper *'Izvestia'*.

He said biological factors had persuaded him that the inhabitants of other planets did not take the forms which science fiction authors had imagined.

'An intelligent inhabitant of remote planets is sure to have a highly organised nervous system (comparable to the human brain) and a skull to protect it against accidental damage. Since there is a force of gravitation on any planet, the brain must be located in a special part of the body, free from excessive strain.

'Another surmise is that intelligent beings on other planets must move in space, and consequently must have symmetrical limbs and organs of sense. The law of unity of physiological functions and the most economical adaption to environment must inevitably lead to a similarity in principle of higher organisms in the universe.'

A DIFFERENT PHYSIOLOGY?

While dogs basically have the same physiology, they come in a very wide variety of size and appearance, yet they can still breed, and produce mixed progeny. They are all genetically compatible. Why should it be so different with humans and some of the visitors who are more comparable to us than some dogs are to each other?

Before the 1970s, many of the extraterrestrials reported, looked human and were friendly, often imparting warnings about our use of nuclear weapons, and lack of care for the environment. I wrote about these particular 'visitors' in *'The Days of the Space Brothers'*, and many, but not all, were very good looking, with blond hair. Due to their similarity to Scandinavian people, they were referred to as the 'Nordics'.

In the Portuguese *'OVNI Documento'*, South American editor Irene Granchi published a report of an incident which happened on 16th May 1979. Arlindo, a thirty-two-year old farmer, had walked with two companions, to a remote corner of his farm, about five kilometres away.

He left his friends outside the thick forest, and went on ahead to a clearing in the trees. He saw three small objects, each only a few feet long, land and then take off again, making a hissing noise as they vanished. He took out his camera, but only managed to get a couple of shots.

He was about to return to his friends, when a fourth, much larger object landed. It was a long, oval shaped craft, about twelve metres long. He put his cap and satchel on the ground, and as he attempted to take another photo, a big flash of light came from the object.

He attempted to run away, but found himself immobilised by some strange force. Suddenly, two uniformed people, with transparent head coverings, grabbed his arms from behind, and turned him back towards the craft. He begged them to let him go, but they answered in Portuguese saying that they were all the brethren of God, and would do him no harm. They only needed him on their craft for a short time.

A third person met him at the craft, and showed him into a 'hall', where two others were seated. Several of the beings, who all looked human, started to converse with each other in a different language, which he did not understand. He was then ushered into a smaller room, by a girl with long hair who showed him screens of astronomical bodies, as if explaining how they had reached Earth.

Although she spoke Portuguese, Arlindo could not grasp the meaning of what she was trying to explain. Further, it seemed as if her voice was coming from somewhere else in the room. The 'people' let him off the craft, and told him not to watch as they took off, as it would hurt his eyes.

He went back to his friends, and when they returned to the site, there was scorched grass inside a circle where the large object had landed. There was no sign of his cap or satchel, and a later search, a few weeks later, failed to locate them. It was only when investigators went out after two months, that the cap and satchel were found, exactly where Arlindo had left them. The satchel's contents were missing, and the outside material showed signs and sketches which they assumed must have been made by the visitors.

While the 'Nordic' humanoids look similar to humans, there may be some differences.

Jean Sider, a veteran French UFO investigator, detailed a case from Amiens in 1932, when an unconscious car accident victim was taken to a local hospital. The attending doctor, Victor Pauchet, was considering a transfusion when he discovered her blood was not any recognisable human type, and furthermore a bluish colour. While officially the patient had been admitted as an Englishwoman called 'Smith', the hospital's reaction to her abnormal blood was to place her in a guarded locked room with barred windows. When the police arrived later the woman had disappeared from the locked room, and the crashed vehicle had also vanished.

Some Europeans refer to nobility as 'blue bloods'. Is there more to this saying than we realise? It has been explained that human, and other mammalian and terrestrial blood is red due to a cocktail of iron-containing pigments such as hemo-globins, chlorocruorins, and hemerythrins. Crabs, and certain other organisms, have blood in which the oxygen carrier is hemocyanin, a copper-containing pigment which is blue.

Researcher, Timothy Good, discussed another incident, which happened over forty years later. A Dr Leopoldo Diaz told of this incident during a 1978 interview on Radio WOAI in San Antonio, Texas. In 1976, when he was head of surgery in a major hospital in Guadalajara, Mexico, a man came in and requested an examination because he had been travelling extensively.

The man was about five feet two inches tall, with very white skin, a small tuft of black hair on his head, and violet eyes. He appeared to be normal in every way, and it was only when he explained who he really was that the doctor realised the 'man' was not 'human'.

His patient advised he was not from this planet. In fact he was only one of many who were here, intermingling because we had serious problems on Earth. He had visited the doctor because he wanted someone respected and influential to pass on a message. Their efforts to convince government scientists and officials had not been very successful.

He advised that many people from his planet were living undetected among us, trying to help us avert catastrophe. He and the doctor had a long discussion about the Earth's future, religion and other matters. After he left, Diaz was so impressed, and concerned about our future, he flew to New York in an unsuccessful attempt to have a United Nations delegation initiate an investigation.

THE 'LITTLE' GUYS

It wasn't just the aliens who looked totally human that appeared in doctors' offices. The 19th August, 1967, Venezuelan evening newspaper, *'El Mondo'*, detailed the case of a stranger entering the Caracas surgery of Dr Sanchez Vegas.

He appeared to be about four feet tall, and had a strange way of moving and talking. Relatively human in appearance, he was wearing a silver-coloured suit, which covered him from neck to feet. He asked for a physical examination, and explained that Dr. Vegas should not be alarmed by his high temperature as he did not come from Earth.

He spoke perfect Spanish, and in answer to a question about his ability to speak the language, he said that his people learned languages with the use of instruments. The creature could not comprehend Vegas' question about his age, and said he did not know about parents since the system of reproduction used in his civilisation was considerably different from that of Earth.

He talked about the way of life and advances of science and technology on his home planet, and the eradication of those diseases which still affect Terrestrials. He spoke of the causes of war and bellicose behaviour which no longer existed on his world.

He stated that his current mission was to take a number of scientists from here to his home planet, so they could be 'brought up-to-date' with the advances they had made.

He also claimed that he had arrived in a ship about the size of the doctor's examining room, and that it was parked outside near the building. During the interview, the creature said that where he came from there were no wars or disease. Vegas was puzzled about how the visitor had got into his office; he replied that he didn't need doors to enter a building.

The little man warned Dr. Vegas concerning a fissure in the Earth's crust, under Caracas, which had filled with water and would eventually result in a disastrous earthquake.

Probably the most interesting physical features of the strange little being were the following, which Dr. Vegas swore he found during the physical examination. He had a misshapen bald head and no ear orifices. His heart made noises like a human foetus, his eyes were completely round, with enormous eyebrows, and the trunk of his body was extremely long. He had ten teeth – five above and five below – which were arranged with one in the middle and two on each side. The ones in the middle were 'double', much like the two front teeth of a rodent.'

Vegas was a physician of good standing and reputation, but two days after had a 'supposed' heart attack, and was kept incommunicado in hospital for several days. Information filtered out via his brother, Julio, who was also a doctor, and Father Gonzales, a Dominican priest. His family protested his incarceration, suspecting that his medical colleagues did not want Vegas' claims discrediting them. (Dr Vegas had not intended to publically discuss the event; it had leaked out by accident when he confided in a couple of trusted colleagues.) He eventually amended his statement to say that maybe the little man was not extraterrestrial after all.

Pedro Riera, a youth who lived nearby, said he also saw the strange visitor. His description, which tallied with that given by Dr. Vegas, was of a being of small stature, with a large head, agile movements, and dressed in a strange suit which seemed to be made of flexible cloth of metallic appearance.

He had seen the little man inside his apartment building, and tried to grab him by his clothes. The 'being' escaped through a window, and went towards his 'space-ship' which was parked at the side of the road.

The police were very interested in the case, and searched for any traces the visitor may have left. Further possible corroboration of his account was the testimony of four other people who saw a strange disc-shaped object parked outside a nearby building. Although no occupant was seen, it remained there for several hours.

Not all of these 'little aliens' had identical features, however a good anatomical description of one these species was given by a Brazilian medical team in 1996. Timothy Good discussed an interview on the *'Brazilian Roswell'* documentary, directed by Bruce Burgess, where Dr. Roger Leir spoke at some length with medical personnel from the Hospital Humanitas where an injured alien had been brought for treatment.

The incident began on 13th January 1996, when a saucer crashed near Varginha. A week later, on 20th January, after another saucer seemed to be in difficulties, a number of strange creatures were seen wandering about various parts of the town. The army and local authorities killed one and captured the other which was injured and taken to hospital.

It was taken into a sterilized operating theatre, with armed guards on the doors. The doctor said; *"When I first saw the face of the individual lying there I was in a state of shock. It was far from a human face. The eyes were large and red, and staring at the ceiling with a blank stare. We were all dumbfounded.*

"One of the military officers, of high rank, told us the victim on the table had suffered a fractured leg, and we were to fix it. I asked him for some details regarding the patient, and was told I was not to ask questions but only to perform the requested task. He also told us to do the best job we could and to solve any problems that might arise, no matter what the nature...Any questions or requests would be relayed through the military personnel on the other side of the operating room doors.

"......The being was less than five feet tall. It was bi-pedal with two arms. The colour of the skin was dark brown, which appeared rather shiny; like it was oily or wet, but in fact the skin was dry, and looked reticulated, like large scales, but

when you touched it, the demarcations of scales were not present. It was smooth to the touch.

"The head was large, much too large for the size of the individual. There were three bony protuberances on top of the head, one in each parietal area, and one central. They extended from the frontal to the occipital positions, like ridges. There was no hair present either on the head or the rest of the body. The head was also larger in its upper portion than lower toward the jaw area.

"The eyes were large, slightly upturned toward the lateral aspects, oriental-looking. They were red in colour, and looked like two glimmering pools of liquid, For some reason, all of us did not want to look into this creature's eyes, and refrained from doing so.

"There was a very small remnant of a mouth, and two little openings, with a slight ridge, where the nose should have been. There were no noted ears, only small openings that looked like vestigial ear canals. The neck was narrow, and appeared it would not have enough muscular strength to support such a large head.

"The upper portion of the torso was slight of build, with an obvious ribcage. There were no noted breasts, areola or nipples. The abdomen was similar to that of a human, with the absence of a navel. (No genitalia were detected.)

"The upper thigh portions were muscular, and out of proportion to the rest of the torso. This was totally different from the arms, which were thin and emaciated. The hand ended in four fingers with no thumb. The fingers were strange, and different from human fingers. The creature was able to move each of his fingers, so that they could articulate with each other, and by doing so, was able to probably perform all the things we could with the use of our thumbs. We were not able to tell whether these fingers were multi-jointed, or if for some reason the bones were flexible, enabling the fingers to perform their desired functions.

"The upper leg and thighs ended in what appeared to be similar to a human knee joint, with oversize patella. The lower portions of the legs were also similar to that of a human. The entire lower extremities were heavily endowed with muscles. It crossed my mind that wherever this creature had come from, the gravity might have been much more than here on Earth.

"The foot was narrow and fleshy, with three short fleshy toes that looked more like pads than toes. There were no visible toenails or fingernails. There was an additional appendage that hung down from the medial side of the foot. This vestigial appendage was elongated like a finger, and ended in what appeared to be a claw about three quarters of an inch long. Later, we found that when the being walked, it would move this appendage so it would become parallel to the rest of the foot. This enabled it to ambulate in a normal human-like manner."

They found that the creature's blood was red, of a similar cellular structure to that of humans, however, its bones were stronger than ours. The being was apparently awake while the doctors set the fractured leg, but it lay still, and did not scream or show any signs of pain. The medical staff tried to communicate, but did not receive any kind of answer.

After they had completed the treatment, a strange green 'gas' seemed to emanate from the patient, and most of the staff ran out of the room. But the doctor stayed and moved closer to the operating table.

"Without consciously realising it, my gaze caught the eyes of the being. His eyes were glowing red, and appeared as two swirling pools of liquid. They were pulling, pulling me deeper and deeper. All at once, giant portions of information came pounding into my head. They were like 'thought-grams' – large blocks of information, over and over again, like someone hitting me over the head with a hammer. I was becoming dizzy, and slightly nauseated.

"....He downloaded a tremendous amount of information into my head......Essentially, he told me his race felt very sorry for the human beings for basically two reasons. The first is that all humans have the potential and abilities to perform the very same things his race could do........and that we did not seem to realise that we were spiritual beings, only living in a temporary shell, and we were totally disconnected from our spiritual self."

The creature, seemed to recover very quickly, and only stayed in the hospital for twenty-four hours. It was then taken out the back door by the military, who later claimed that the being was only a 'mentally handicapped dwarf'. They confiscated all records, X-rays, laboratory data and materials used.

This report also interested me because I have encountered several contactees who claim vast amounts of information have been 'downloaded' into their brains.

There have been many reports, both now and in the past, of these 'little men', of varying descriptions, visiting our Earth. Just because they do not look like Earth humans, does not mean they are not biological beings, just like us. Our planet has both pygmies and people well over six feet tall. As I have already said, when we look at the differences between the many canine varieties and breeds, we must remember that they are all basically dogs. Many of our planet's species are now extinct, and these 'little guys' may well have naturally evolved in the environment of their own home planet.

Many American Indian legends make reference to 'Little People' living in remote caves and mountains, and Chinese historians are still researching the 'Dropa', small aliens who crashed and lived out their days on Earth.

Dr Widman, from the US Wayne State University, School of Medicine, Detroit, specialised in genetic research, and claimed that chimpanzees are in fact members of the human family, and are as similar to one another as horses are to donkeys. Also, genes active in the brain showed much more accumulated change in humans than in chimps – suggesting that those genes played a special role in human evolution.

Most Homo Sapiens only use about ten percent of their actual superb brain capacity, but as distinct from lesser species, some have shown a propensity to genius.

Are these 'little guys' a natural result of evolution, or are they specially engineered hybrids? They do not always appear to have a high intelligence, however they have apparently developed exceptional telepathic abilities, and at times they can also speak. When in the company of taller, human-like companions, they seem to play a subservient role.

A classic case, from Arizona, in 1975, was when Travis Walton, who after being hit by a light beam from a saucer, woke to find himself in a room with three little beings, dressed in overalls. Their features resembled those described by so many other witnesses.

They hurriedly left the room, and soon after a man came through the doorway. He was six feet two inches tall, clean shaven, with blond hair, a dark complexion, and golden hazel-coloured eyes. His blue one-piece suit and helmet made Walton initially assume he was totally human, and probably from NASA or the Air Force.

He was taken to another area, where there were also two more men and a woman, similar in appearance, but without helmets. Eventually he was returned to Earth, five days later.

Timothy Good asked Walton if there was some kind of liaison between human-type aliens and those who look like 'nothing on Earth'. Were they biological robots?

Walton said; *"Who was co-operating with whom? I saw nothing to indicate the answer to that question. In fact, I never saw the two types together in one place at the same time. There was nothing to indicate that one type was the bred-up slave of the other. Further, there was nothing that would indicate friendly co-operation either. ....But then again, the aliens and the human type might have been co-operating with each other in my abduction from the very start. There might exist an interaction and co-operation of all intelligent life-forms in space..."*

Jader Pereira, researched a case from Viamâo, in southern Brazil, which occurred on a plantation in early January 1968.

Five witnesses saw a ten-metre-wide disc, with a round hat-shaped cupola, hovering two metres above the ground. It had a metallic gleam, and emitted a reddish light, which made their eyes burn.

At first, two people could be seen beside the craft. They were both about six feet tall, bare footed and wearing white overalls. They had long hair, reaching their shoulders, and the two female witnesses said that they 'looked like Saints'.

Then three smaller beings appeared. They were about four-and-a-half feet tall, and wearing chestnut-brown coloured overalls. Their hair was also long, and they also appeared to be 'of the white race'.

These 'little guys' never seemed to move away from underneath the disc, however the taller beings went towards a wire fence and gate, before retracing their steps back to the craft. After a second attempt, the third time they opened the gate and walked towards the house.

By this time the plantation owner and his manager had taken up positions under two palm trees, both lying on the ground so as not to be seen. The manager was armed, but his employer stopped him from firing. Their five watch-dogs were unusually quiet, and the wife, who with her young son and daughter, had taken refuge in their home, became frightened, and opened the door, calling out to her husband to come inside.

The two beings hesitated, and halted several times, before returning to their craft. Along with the three 'little guys', they entered the object, which, with a slight rotary movement, rose up vertically and departed.

Much has been written about the UFO crashes and 'little aliens' at Roswell, and other nearby places in July 1947. I don't intend to rehash the events here, but several interesting reports have surfaced, which tend to lend further credibility to the many testimonies.

Len Stringfield wrote about Norma Gardner who was dying of cancer in 1959. When her 'home help', Charles Wilhem, was visiting, she made some startling statements regarding her 1955 employment as a civilian at Wright Patterson Air Force Base in the USA. Her job was to catalogue over one thousand items retrieved from UFO landings, and included the interior parts from a crashed disc, which had been brought to the base some years earlier. Everything had been meticulously photographed and logged.

She claimed to have seen two round, saucer-shaped discs in a hanger, and the removal of humanoid bodies. She had to write up the reports on some of them, who were autopsied. They were about four-and-a-half feet tall, with large heads and black eyes.

She treated her breach of security as a 'death-bed' confession. *"Uncle Sam can't do anything to me when I'm in my grave!"*

In 1994, Gordon Creighton published an interesting article detailing part of an initial *'Memorandum'* from Admiral Hillenkoetter to Eisenhower when he became US President in 1953.

'There then followed accounts of hundred of UFO sighting reports. On the basis of these, various military agencies, independently, have attempted, with national security in mind, to verify the nature and intentions of these objects. Eyewitnesses were interviewed and there were various attempts – unsuccessful

– by our own aircraft, to pursue these objects. The reaction of the public, on some occasions, was well-nigh hysterical.

'Despite these efforts, we were unable to learn much about the objects until a rancher reported that one of them had exploded in a remote region of New Mexico.

'On July 7th 1947, a secret operation was commenced to recover the debris of this apparatus with a view to making a scientific study of it. During the course of this operation, aerial reconnaissance of the region revealed that four beings, resembling humans, had apparently been ejected from the machine moments before it exploded. They were lying on the ground, some two miles away to the east of the spot where the debris of the machine lay. The four beings were dead, and badly decomposed.

'An analytical study of the affair, arranged by General Twining and Dr. Vannevar Bush, under the direct orders of the President, resulted in a preliminary estimate (September19-1947) that the disc was probably a short-range reconnaissance craft. This conclusion was based upon the fact that the disc was of small dimensions and apparently carried no food. An analysis of the four corpses was made by Dr. Bronk'.

As advised, the four small bodies were analysed by Dr. Bronk and his US team. The provisional assessment of this group (November 30, 1947) was that although the creatures resembled humans, the evolutionary and biological factors resulting in their development were apparently very different from those of Homo Sapiens.

'As it is virtually certain that these craft come from no country on Earth, we have had much discussion as to their point of origin and as how they could reach us. Mars is a possibility, though some scientists, particularly Dr. Menzel, considers that they are beings coming from another solar system.'

(This part of the report is especially interesting, as publicly Dr. Menzel always debunked and ridiculed every UFO report.)

'Among the wreckage of the craft there were many items bearing writing. All attempts to decipher them have been fruitless. Equally fruitless have been the efforts made to ascertain the method of propulsion and the nature of their power source. This was even more difficult inasmuch the craft has – alas – no propellers, no propulsion tubes or exhaust or other conventional fittings for *steering or driving the craft, and likewise there is total absence of metallic wiring, vacuum tubes or recognisable electronic components.*

'Since the motives and intentions of these visitors are still unknown, National Security is still involved in the entire affair. Moreover, since the activity of these craft has increased greatly since last May, and throughout the whole autumn of this year, it is believed that this indicates that there will soon be fresh happenings.

'For these reasons, as well as due to considerations of international and also a technical nature, and the need to avoid at all costs, a general panic, the Majestic-12 Group are of the unanimous opinion that the strictest security precautions (ie. absolute secrecy) must continue, without interruption, throughout the next Presidential administration. At the same time the 'Contingency Plan' (MJ-1949-04P78 Top Secret) must always be held in readiness for the case in which the necessity for issuing a communiqué to the public might arise.'

Further confirmation of these incidents has, over the years, surfaced from many sources. One of them was the actor, Gordon MacRae, who appeared on a TV show, six months before his death in 1968. He mentioned that he had been a security sergeant at Wright-Patterson Air Force Base in July 1947.

He was ordered to stand watch over a large tarpaulin covered pallet, which had been brought in under tight security. Under no circumstances was the tarpaulin to be removed. He and his fellow guards were curious, and when no-one was looking, they took a peep. Laid out, underneath, were four small humanoid creatures.

Both Stanton Friedman and John Carpenter investigated a separate incident which occurred on 5th July 1947. Gerald Anderson, a former police chief and County Deputy Sheriff, was only a young lad when his uncle drove his family into the desert 150 miles east of Roswell. They were going to fossick for moss agate, but found far more than they expected when they rounded the corner of a dry creek bed.

Stuck on the side of a ridge was a silver disc. It had a gash in the side, as if it had been crushed in. Anderson later thought that the contours of the vehicle would fit the gash perfectly. He speculated that maybe two of these discs had a mid-air collision, with one falling at Roswell, and the other crash landing where they found it. (In hindsight, this makes sense. Later reports state that a high-powered government radar, which had been set-up nearby, interfered with the controlling mechanisms of the saucers.)

There were four bodies on the ground, shaded by the wreckage from the hot sun. Two were lifeless, one apparently injured, and a fourth obviously terrified. A professor, Dr. Buskirk and his five college students arrived, curious to discover what they had seen crash from the sky the night before.

While Buskirk was trying, unsuccessfully, to communicate with the frightened alien, another witness, civil engineer Barney Barnett, arrived in his pick-up truck. Anderson had telepathically sensed the creature's terror, and felt great empathy. Just as it seemed to calm down, the alien 'went crazy' at the sight of a contingent of armed soldiers that suddenly arrived.

The civilians were manhandled, told it was a secret military aircraft, and threatened if they ever divulged anything about it. After they had been ushered back up the hilltop, the witnesses saw more military arrive, including trucks and planes which landed on the blocked-off road. Whilst Anderson and the others were pressured into silence, they all knew what they saw was not a crashed weather balloon.

This was not the first case of one of these little beings expressing fear. In *The Gosford Files* I discuss an unusual report I received from some 'no-nonsense' male witnesses.

About 2am one night in December 1988, Carter Robb and his mate were fishing from the rocks under the Woy Woy bridge on the Central Coast of NSW Australia.

They were talking to a couple of other fishermen when they heard a weird screaming sound coming from behind. At first they ignored the noise and kept fishing, but the cries got louder and more desperate. They also noticed the sound was moving away and back, as if the source was running extremely fast up and down the nearby rocks.

The two other men went to investigate, but the noise stopped as soon as they started walking around with torches. About ten minutes later, the screams started again, and they all put down their rods and started looking.

As they moved around the rocks the noise subsided to something like a 'small pitch grumble'. They quietly crept towards the area of the noise, and turned on their flashlights.

"I saw something totally inexplicable," said Carter. "It frightened the life out of me and the other guys. It was a little being, with a fairly big head, and big black eyes, but I never noticed a nose or mouth. It was probably only two or three feet tall. It was hard to say, as in an effort to get away from us, it tried to crouch down in a small space between the rocks."

If the little fellow was frightened, so were the fishermen, who fled. Thinking that they wouldn't be believed, they didn't tell the police. Carter drew me a sketch, which was clearly one of the smaller 'visitors'. Obviously, although unable to talk, it could articulate its fear quite loudly.

There are very similar details in many reports of actual aliens or their bodies being retrieved. There has been much written about corpses seen at crashes in New Mexico and surrounding areas, however Leonard Stringfield documented several lesser known cases of alien bodies being found or autopsied. In nearly all the reports of saucer crashes, the pilots or crew are these little entities.

One hospital physician, who had to remain anonymous, performed an autopsy on an alien being in the early 1950s. He said it was four feet three inches tall, with a pear-shaped head – oversize by human standards - and X-rays revealed a bone structure and mobile grayish skin.

The eyes were Mongoloid in appearance, slanted upwards, and recessed into the head, which had no hair follicles or outer earlobes. There were no visible eyelids, and the mouth seemed to be a wrinkle-like fold, with no teeth or lips – just a slit that opened into a two inch oral cavity.

Researcher Leonard Stringfield spoke of several other cases being reported by former military personnel, involving alien bodies, of a similar description, in 1953, 1966, 1973 and 1978. After speaking to Stringfield, most witnesses refused to say anything else, as if scared of the repercussions.

He also discussed an incident from Kentucky in March 1987, where a retired doctor found the skeletal remains of two 'alien humanoids' on his farm. They were lying next to a burned out circle, about four feet in diameter. He felt that the bodies had been exposed for less than one hundred days, and there was some evidence of the corpses being mauled by predators.

He was surprised that the bones were not of animal origin. They were bipedal, about four feet tall, with a large skull, cat-like jaw, barrel-like rib cage and long arms with three fingers.

He called the local sheriff, who in turn notified the Air Force. The next morning three helicopters and uniformed personnel arrived. They removed the bones, tested and removed the soil, and filled in the excavated areas.

He was obliged to attend a military base for further interrogation, where he was shown photos of other alien corpses. He declined any further interviews with investigators, saying the Air Force had 'put the fear of God in him'.

Ufologist Isabel Davis interviewed a doctor who claimed that in the early fifties she was taken to 'a highly secure facility' to study portions of 'human-like' bodies. She was told nothing about them, and was asked to write down her conclusions. She said they came from no earthly species, and before she left was instructed to never discuss the matter with anyone.

Researcher, Enrique Vicente, unearthed some Polish newspapers that reported dockworkers seeing a bright object crashing into the harbour at Gdynia. It happened on 21st May 1959, and the Polish Navy investigated, but made no comment.

Several days later, some guards found a strange creature crawling along the beach. It was wearing an unusual 'uniform' made of very resistant metal, and taken to the University Hospital, where it was isolated, and closely examined.

Apparently 'male', he was found to have different organs and blood system from ours, and an 'abnormal' number of fingers and toes. He survived for several days, until a 'bracelet' around his arm was removed. The remains were taken to the Soviet Union for further investigation.

In his book *'Earth – An Alien Enterprise'*, Timothy Good interviewed 'Thomas', who was with the RAF between 1955 and 1957. He was posted to West Zoyland, and seconded to Fleet Air Arm 'special duties', which involved caring for two little 'aliens' who had been moved, along with their craft, from the US to the UK. The authorities were never able to open their small disc, in which they had activated a self-destruct device.

One of the captives was male, and the other female. They had a greyish complexion, and were very thin, with large oval heads and big dark eyes. Although their 'guests' occasionally spoke audibly, during his time attending to the two 'beings', Thomas was able to 'feel' their thoughts.

He discovered that they were able to convey a sense of both humour and sadness, and their purpose for visiting Earth was concern for our future, which could be catastrophic due to war, overpopulation and pollution. They also needed gold, and later silver, as part of their craft's propulsion system.

Thomas and his colleagues grew very fond of the 'visitors', and did not pay much attention to any of their mention of only staying for a short time. One warm night in 1957, there was a commotion outside, where multiple glowing spheres of light were hovering. The two little beings said; "Do not be concerned – we are passing messages to our people. You can inform your seniors later."

After a while, the hubbub had not subsided, and Thomas and his two RAF colleagues went outside to see an enormous black triangular object, silently pulsating about fifty feet above the ground.

The next day the two aliens at first seemed unresponsive, and then indicated that they would soon be leaving. Thomas and the five other servicemen did not take too much notice when their guests said 'goodbye' and thanked them for their care.

Later, when Thomas and his colleagues were having lunch in his office, three duty officers came running in. They said they had all experienced a sudden pain in the head. They saw the aliens clasping hands, and suddenly fade and 'disappear into thin air'.

In his book *'Disclosure'*, Dr. Steven Greer interviewed Don Phillips from Skunkworks. He spoke of the 'little humanoids', which were short, but very intelligent – like 'super intelligent children'. They were apparently assisting US human engineers in building a 'trainer' for us to learn how to fly their craft.

Greer also interviewed Capt. Bill Uhouse, who in the late fifties, was seconded to work on a 'disc' flight simulator, and later a craft. He alluded to some captured aliens, who were tasked with working with astrophysicists and scientists. Although they could actually speak and converse, only one would talk to any of their human counterparts.

Uhouse claimed he attended a meeting with one of the aliens, whom it was difficult to communicate with. Basically, they only gave scientific and engineering advice when we couldn't figure out some of the problems.

These smaller 'entities' are apparently living, sentient beings, not human but neither animal - perhaps a species which does not exist on Earth. They seem to have a subservient, 'worker' role, and are often seen gathering 'specimens' near their landed craft. Often, when disturbed, they will scamper, like 'scared rabbits', back to their ship.

They have been seen in many parts of the world. One case occurred in Taupignac, France, on October 11th 1954. Three men stopped their car when they saw two unusual objects in the sky ahead. One silently landed nearby, and the men moved closer to get a better look.

It was about eighteen feet in diameter, and emitting a red-yellow light. There were four small humanoids, each about three feet high, performing some kind of 'work' on the craft, but when the curious fellows got within forty-five feet of the saucer, the little beings hurriedly got back on board. The craft emitted a dazzling display of multicoloured light, and departed vertically at great speed.

Jean Fumoux wrote of an incident which occurred near Figueras, Spain in October 1958. Senor Angelu, a forty-year-old businessman, was riding his motor-bike one evening, when he saw a craft falling from the sky. It appeared to crash into the forest, and he raced to the area, thinking he may be able to help.

When he arrived at the scene he saw a 'classic' saucer, standing on legs, with a transparent 'cockpit' on top. It was about eight metres in diameter, and he could see a figure inside the 'cockpit', with two more 'beings' on the ground outside. They were all human in appearance, but only about one metre tall, with overly large heads.

They were moving around, gathering something up off the ground, and Angelu watched them for about fifteen minutes, before they rejoined the ship, which rose and was quickly out of sight.

Many of these smaller aliens seem to be armed with a small 'torch-like' gun, which can be aimed and fired at an opponent or threat, rendering them temporarily paralysed. However, it seems as if these 'beams' must have a direct line of fire, with no objects in between, for their 'weapon' to be effective.

In 1979, Dr. Richard Niemtzow, a Houston physician and part of a UFO scientific study group, investigated these 'weapons'.

'It is a very selective and very calculated paralysis which is well defined throughout the history of UFOs. It seems to affect any nerve which is not vital to the person staying alive. We don't understand how it is done.....Without exception the paralysis strikes both the brave and the fearful.

'As a medical doctor I can say, without contradiction, that earthly medical science cannot do this. Only a very advanced civilization or an advanced technology, beyond our present knowledge, could do something like this.'

Irene Granchi investigated a case which occurred on August 11th 1971, in the Gavea district of Brazil. Just after midnight, Amanda was sitting in a 'patio room', next to an open window, having a cigarette while her husband, Francisco was asleep in the bedroom.

A large, metallic, elliptical-shaped craft, bigger than a Boeing plane, came out from behind a cloud. It moved towards the nearby P.U.C. University, and hovered over the science building on the campus. Amanda could now see that the UFO was a silvery-metallic colour, with an orange, phosphorescent band, containing oval shape portholes, going across it. She was sure she could see shadowy figures inside. Two smaller objects, exact replicas of the parent ship, came out from underneath, and started oscillating in flight around the larger one.

The large craft began emitting a broad beam of blue light, in a rational, methodical manner, directly through the window and onto Amanda. It was so dazzling, she turned her face away. Each time she did this, it 'switched off', only to come on again when she looked back.

She tried to call out to her husband, but whenever the light was directed at her, she could not make a sound. Every time the light was 'switched off' her voice returned. This sequence of events happened about five times over a ten minute period. When she eventually woke her husband, the two smaller craft returned to the large UFO, and all Francisco saw was the big metallic disc slowly moving backwards and forwards before taking off at incredible speed to the northeast.

It was interesting that the 'beam' came through the window, onto Amanda's face, apparently paralysing her vocal chords, but not the rest of her body.

Although most of the reports received have mainly occurred after World War II, it seems that these 'little guys', with their 'stun guns' had possibly been around much earlier.

In 1969, my old Sydney research group, UFOIC, unearthed the following 1893 case from Central NSW; *'A farmer claimed that a saucer-shaped object landed in one of his paddocks. As the farmer approached the object, a man in strange clothing emerged from it. The farmer walked towards the man, who shone some kind of 'torch' at him, throwing him to the ground and stunning him. When he came to, the man and the object had gone. The hand where the 'torch beam' had hit him was paralysed for life.'*

Researcher Jenny Randles told of one victim of this attack, Italian Professor Rapuzzi Johannis, a geologist and author, who was on a 1947 field trip in the Alps, at Carnico del Col Gentile near Villa Santina on the Austrian/Italian border.

On 14th August, he was half way up the mountain when he saw a red, polished metallic, lens-shaped object which seemed to be partially embedded in the rocky slope. While he was analysing the origin of this strange craft, he noticed two 'boys' coming out of a nearby wooded area.

He called out to them, but as he approached, realised that they were not children, but two strange 'beings'. They had large heads, long straight noses, a 'slit' for a mouth, and eyes that really 'stood out'. They had no eyebrows or eye-lashes, and were wearing blue, close-fitting garments, with dark skull caps.

They stared at each other, and the professor, trying to indicate a greeting, shouted – "Who are you?" – and raised his pick. This was obviously misunderstood by the pair of 'visitors'. One placed its hand on its belt, and a flash of light hit Johannis on the arm.

He was rendered almost senseless and thrown to the ground. At the same time his pick flew through the air, and landed about six feet away. The beings walked over and picked it up, before going back to their craft and 'vanishing'.

Moments later there was a small 'implosion' and rock-slide, which sent Johannis rolling down the slope. The strange craft and its occupants had simply 'disappeared'. He hobbled back to the village of Raveo, and at that time didn't tell anybody what had really happened.

On 24th April 1950, Bruno Facchini was putting up some fairy lights in his Italian country home near Varese. He saw some more lights outside – not his – so he opened the door to see a thirty feet, metallic, rounded object, beside a telegraph pole, about 100 feet away. On the side he could see an opening, and glimpsed some dials, and what looked like controls or cylinders.

Standing around the craft were four humanoids, each about five feet tall and wearing gray, tight fitting overalls and helmets with transparent face masks. They all had tools, and seemed to be trying to adjust something on their craft. Bruno wondered if they might need some help, but as soon as he stepped out of the front door they turned towards him and started chattering in a strange language.

One being pointed a 'tube-like' object at him, and a beam of bluish light struck Bruno in the chest, hurling him backwards onto the ground. The beings quickly went back into the opening, the door closed, and the craft began to hum, rose steadily and flew off at high speed.

Gordon Creighton translated a case from the French Côte d'Azur, in Spring 1954. A man came across a landed UFO, but before he could study it, two entities standing nearby, fired a torch-like instrument which paralysed him. They came over, stared at him, then gestured to follow them. He was still immobilized, and the entities entered the UFO as he lost consciousness. He recovered some time later, to see the craft departing.

These 'little beings', with their paralysing 'weapons', have been reported from all over the world. In 1971, people from Swedish Lapland, a remote, frozen area, close to the Finnish border, in the Arctic Circle, had nicknamed them the 'lightning men'. Several witnesses had described four feet tall entities who aimed strange, strong beams of light at anyone who tried to approach them.

In 1974, one Belgian businessman had a very lucky escape. On 7th January he was travelling down a deserted border road near Warneton, when his car's electrical system failed. He came to a halt, and got out to rectify the problem. He saw a domed craft on the road ahead, and two beings, about four-and-a-half feet tall, got out and came towards him.

They had pear-shaped heads, large eyes, small noses, narrow mouths and long arms. Without warning, one pointed a tube-shaped instrument at him. He heard a high-pitched noise, and felt a shock at the base of his skull, causing him to collapse. Suddenly, another car came down the road, and the 'little guys' ran back to their craft and took off.

The second driver who had seen the craft zoom away, stopped to help the businessman, who was still temporarily paralysed, and with some friends who lived nearby, searched the area. They found nothing, and the businessman, thinking no-one would believe him, did not talk about it for some years.

CHAPTER NINE

ALIEN ENCOUNTERS

PART TWO

Trying to capture one of these 'little fellows' is not a good idea. Early in the morning of 28th November 1954, two grocery employees were in their panel van, making deliveries in Caracas, Venezuela.

They had to slam on their brakes when they turned a corner to find their way blocked by a ten feet spherical shaped craft hovering just above the middle of the street. As soon as they jumped out to investigate, a little man, the size of a dwarf, confronted them.

Gustavo Gonzales thought it might be a good idea to capture this unusual being – he could grab it and throw it into their van. It was not such a good idea! When he made a move, the 'being' proved to be much stronger than he thought. One push knocked Gonzales fifteen feet to the ground.

His comrade, Jose Ponce, was watching the struggle, when he saw two more 'creatures' coming out of the bushes, with chunks of earth in their hands. Ponce took fright, and retreated into a nearby traffic inspector's office.

The two little men jumped back into the craft through an opening in the side, but Gonzeles and the other being were still grappling, until Gonzales made the mistake of trying to stab his opponent. The other two little guys came back out of the craft, and aimed a tube-like device at Gonzales. A blinding light temporarily paralysed him, giving the creatures time to jump back into their craft, and quickly take-off straight into the sky.

It seems the French population, having survived occupation and resistance during World War II, were not afraid to take on a diminutive alien.

In the 1969 G.E.P. journal *Phénomènes Spatiaux',* Joël Mesnard detailed an account by French baker, Germain Tichit, which happened in mid-1960.

It was 2am in the morning, when he was preparing the dough. Suddenly he heard an unusual noise, and coloured lights, of every description, shone through the bakery window.

He looked up the hill, and there on the old fairground, just below the church, was an enormous object standing on the ground. It was like a transparent upper half joined together with a different lower half, and was about fifteen metres wide and five metres high. On the upper portion, which seemed to be rotating, were four rows of fixed luminous tubes, each of a different colour.

He heard another, 'metallic', noise, and a small step-ladder was lowered from the right-hand side. A creature of humanoid appearance, but very small stature, descended and started walking down the hill.

At this time, Germain could feel a warm, pungent wind coming from the machine, which he thought was rotating in an anti-clockwise direction. Germain had heard what he had assumed to be fanciful tales of 'flying saucers', and decided to approach the 'little chap' with the intent of capturing him.

He described the 'creature' as a handsome dwarf, well proportioned, wearing little boots, tight fitting trousers, a buttoned-up greyish-green jacket, and a helmet of the same colour. He was wearing a belt, with four 'pouches' attached, and what looked like a 'scabbard' on his right-hand side.

As soon as the being noticed the fast approaching baker, he pointed a long tube, 'like a fireman's torch', at him. It emitted an intense beam of light, which struck Germain on the chest and head. He found it very difficult to breathe, and while he was still staggering forward, the little man went back to the saucer and up the ladder.

With another metallic noise, the ladder vanished into the craft, which immediately rose to a height of about thirty metres and shot horizontally away at great speed to the south.

Claude Raffy, another French researcher, wrote about an interview he had with an eighty-two years old lady, who was quite intelligent and lucid. In fact, she didn't look her age, drove at some speed around the countryside, and had a husband much younger than herself. Quite a feisty no-nonsense woman! She told of an incident which happened in mid-February 1956.

She was a forty-one years old business woman at the time, and was driving along the road from her parents' home, at Choisy-le-Roi, to Fresn, just south of Paris. At about 9.30pm she noticed a bright, white, shining phosphorescent object hovering just above the ground. It was over an area of vacant land.

As she pulled up, she could hear a slight hissing sound, and noticed a small person, about one and a half metres tall, moving about near it. The thought of flying saucers came into her mind – there had been talk of them in the newspapers.

"I got the sudden idea that maybe if I could grab an occupant, and take him to the newspapers, what a fine thing that would be for me! The little chap appeared to be small and thin – he would not be hard to carry!

"So, there and then, I opened my boot and got it ready to put my precious captive into it. By now, around the machine, there were eight of them, engrossed at looking at something or other on the ground."

The object itself had the shape of a 'flattened pumpkin', with luminous facets she thought may be windows. She could see two more beings inside the machine, and the others still seemed to be concentrating on the waste area around them. When they saw her approaching, without any signs of fear, they were 'off', like scampering rabbits, into the opening at the base of the craft.

"The last one of them – the one I was aiming to grab – turned around and fixed his big back eyes on me, intensely, as if wanting to say something. Just as I thought I was going to get him, a beam of light shot out from one of the windows on the upper part of the machine. It engulfed me, paralysing me on the spot. I couldn't move anything except my eyes."

It was only then, for the first time, she began to feel scared. She was not sure how long this lasted for, but once they had all disappeared into the craft, the light surrounding her started to fade, and she was able to back away and stumble back to her car.

She got in, but was unable to drive away. For the second time she felt unable to move. After a while there was a 'scraping sound' – like a door closing. Later, the 'hissing noise' increased in intensity, and the craft slowly rose to treetop height. It stopped, momentarily, then took off at 'top speed'.

"To start with, the entire craft turned orange, and then passed to red as its speed increased. Immediately I was able to start the car, and didn't even stop to see in which direction the machine had gone.

"Panic had now caught up with me, and I decided to turn back and return to my parents in Choisy. When I arrived there, still gasping, I poured out the whole story. My father told me not to tell anyone about it. I had my job to think of. Everybody would laugh, and the police would question and harass me."

She said after that she felt 'different'. She had dreams and premonitions which would come to pass, but there seemed to be no indication of an abduction or 'forgotten memories'.

She described the beings as being humanoid in shape, but slim, with heads proportionally bigger than ours. They had large protuberant black eyes, nostril holes and a slit for a mouth. They were clad in greyish-blue tightly fitting one-piece combination garments.

She confirmed the description of the craft as being circular, and flattened on top and below. The central parts were luminous and white – not glaring – and the rest of the machine a 'metallic grey'. Her estimates of size were a bit vague.

Because Granny could not recall the exact date in 1956, Claude Raffy searched the records and data for occurrences at Orly Airport, which was not far away from her encounter. On 19th February 1956, radar operators detected the presence of a flying object, twice the size of the largest aircraft of the time, which came down slowly, remained stationary, and later departed suddenly at a fantastic speed. The radar operator reported that it was behaving in a fashion totally different from anything he knew of.

The pilot of a *Dakota* reported that he could see the object for over thirty seconds. It was enormous, lit up with red luminescence, no navigation lights and a hazy outline.

In *'Contact Down Under'*, I discuss another experience where a human-type being seems to be in charge of these 'little guys'.

My witness, Jane, gave a very detailed description of three different types of alien she saw during her experience: When she entered the craft, one being was walking ahead of her. "He was about five foot, two inches tall, and gold in colour, with a long neck and square shoulders. While his legs were short, with square-back funny heels, his body and arms were long. His arms didn't appear to have joints, and he had four long fingers which had pads on the ends. The spinal cord looked more like deep indents running down his back." He later examined Jane, and was apparently "the doctor." She noticed he had a large, pear-shaped head with a lot of wrinkles and almond-shaped eyes.

"There were four little grey guys, about three feet tall, with big brown-black cat-like eyes, which were mirror-like, almost glassy, with no white or pupils. There was an extra flap of skin over the eyes, and they had no ears, just dents. They had small noses and well-shaped mouths, and they walked very strangely, with small steps like rubber men. When I was lying on the table, one looked into my face and he had a very funny smell..

"One was thin, six feet tall, but human in appearance. He was wearing a tightly fitting greeny-gold coloured suit which also covered his feet. On his shoulders were metal badges with something like a bird or animal on the end of it." (Several abductee reports mention the same type and colour apparel, and Penny from Roma, (see *'Contact Down* Under'), described a similar insignia.)

"He had white skin and small features," she said, "although his ears looked a little different to ours. His face was perfectly shaped, long black hair to his shoulders, the most beautiful being I have ever seen. His eyes were slightly larger than mine, no whites, just unusually blue, almost violet. I liked him from the moment I saw him; the next best thing to seeing an angel. He seemed to be in charge. Throughout my examination he was there, standing behind me."

In *'The Alien Gene'*, my witness, Patty, was in contact with humanoid aliens who were living incognito among the New Zealand local population whilst involved with a secret government project.

Under hypnosis Patty recalled a childhood event from Waiheke Island when she woke up in bed on night. There was a blue light coming through the closed window, she had seen this light before, and got up to look through the curtains. The whole house was surrounded in a brilliant blue light. She couldn't believe it, but was not worried as her 'Friend' was coming with several of his small companions.

She saw him appear through the blue light, and then he came through her window into the room, which was flooded in blue. He was accompanied by six or seven 'little people' – small with medium size, oval-shape heads, creamy/brown skin and big black eyes, like dark mirrors. They were not much taller than Patty, and had long, skinny arms with four fingers, but no thumb, on each hand. Her 'Friend' was much, much taller, and they were all wearing a similar, neck high full-body suit, which was a blue-grey shiny material, like a wet suit, with a red triangular motif on the right hand side.

Once in the room, her 'Friend' bent down to her and put out both his hands. He looked down and she placed her hands just above his, without actually touching. "He spoke to me, but his mouth didn't actually move. I felt good, and wasn't worried, when he explained we would always be friends, and not to be afraid.

"I knew that sometimes they took me up into the space ship above the house, and this time I was going there to play with the 'little people'. The small ones stepped into the blue light, which covered the roof of the whole house, followed by me and my 'Friend'. I felt good and relaxed as it shrank, like a spotlight, as we went up.

Patty's next memory was of being on board the craft. "The 'little people' were around me, running around and chasing each other, playing tag or something like that. I had seen them before, they were always there."

These 'little guys' definitely seem to express some emotion. Besides a playful nature, and as I have said before, the ability to express fear, there have been occasions when they have been reported to have a sense of humour.

The Lorenzen's, in their book *'Encounters with UFO Occupants'*, detailed an incident from Brazil on 7th February 1969. It was 7am when Tiago Machado heard people shouting and looking up into the sky near his Sao Paulo home. He looked through the window, and saw a basin-shaped, lighted blue object in the sky. Grabbing his binoculars, he raced outside, and made his way through a heavily vegetated area to where he thought the object had landed.

He was first to arrive on the scene, and stopped about ten metres away from an 'aluminium' disc. A 'lid' opened on the top, and two smallish men came out. He could see another two inside a glass enclosed cabin. They were wearing helmets and silvery-coloured clothing, including gloves and boots.

The creatures seemed to be afraid of his binoculars, so he took them off and laid them on the ground. Tiago felt very nervous, and when he lit a cigarette, the beings began to laugh. He put the cigarette packet on the ground, and pushed it over to them with his foot. One stretched out his hand, and the packet floated up into his palm. With a quick flick of the wrist, it completely disappeared.

They then started conversing with him by using gestures and sign language, but before long other witnesses arrived on the scene. The two small beings floated back up into the open hatch, and the last one pointed a 'pipe-shaped contraption' at Tiago. A bluish-red ray hit his legs, and he fell to the ground as the disc rose into the air, and disappeared at high speed.

Coral Lorenzen researched a 1954 case from Pennsylvania, where a widow and two farmhands were managing her deceased husband's farm.

One morning she went out on the porch, and was annoyed when she saw what looked like four 'children' pulling up her vegetables near the fence. She yelled at them, and went into the house to grab a broom.

When she came back out, there were six 'children' gathering up the vegetables, some of which had fallen on the ground. She started down the steps, but then stopped. All the 'brats' were wearing funny gray uniforms with 'Buck Rogers' space helmets on their heads, and toy pistols hanging from big belts!

She hesitated for a moment, and the 'children' pulled some flowers up by the roots, then, one at a time, leapt over the fence with their arms full of their ill-gotten gains. They disappeared into the woods, and a few moments later she heard a humming sound which rose to a crescendo.

The next morning, her female 'house-help', went out early to collect eggs from the hen boxes, at the side of a large barn. There was a low mist hanging over the building, and a high pitched whining sound could be heard approaching from above. The noise got louder and louder, until it seemed to be directly overhead.

The widow rushed out, and both women saw a twenty feet diameter saucer descend through the mist. It had a low-domed 'roof', with an open cockpit, where two of the helmeted 'children' were seated. The 'little people' waved cheerily, and the 'home-help' was so frightened she dropped the basket of eggs. The noise rose in pitch, and the saucer whooshed back up into the mist.

These 'little guys' are often seen collecting plants, soil and rocks -why? Although some have explained that they were needed for their own planet, I have often wondered if, being the 'workers', they were responsible for growing the food and other plants seen in the gardens of the more 'Earthly' secret alien 'retreats' reported by some contactees.

In the early days, perhaps when it was safer for them to be seen, 'Nordic' type beings were sometimes seen also collecting plant specimens.

In December 1954, Brazilian farmer Olmiro de Costa was working on his farm when he heard a sound, and noticed the animals in the next field running in different directions.

He saw a cream 'hat-shaped' object hovering just above the ground. One man was inside, looking out the 'doorway, and another outside examining his fence. They were medium height, with broad shoulders, pale skin, long blonde hair and slanted eyes. A third man approached Costa, raised his hand, and gave the farmer his hoe, which he had dropped in fright.

The two men gestured to Costa to stay where he was, and after uprooting a few plants, they returned to their ship, which rose to a height of thirty feet before accelerating and shooting off to the west.

Two days later, at 5pm, Pedro Morais, who lived two miles away, heard his chickens squawking. When he went to look, he saw an object which looked like an enormous polished brass kettle, with a 'hood' on the top. It was hovering just above the ground, and two 'men' were in a nearby cultivated field.

Morais moved towards them, intent on registering his displeasure. The intruders ran towards their craft, motioning him to stop. Before they jumped back into their saucer, and took off in great haste, they uprooted a tobacco plant to take with them.

By 1964, it seems the 'Nordics' were staying in their bases, and the 'little guys' were tasked with going out to collect plants and other specimens.

On April 24th, Gary Wilcox was working on his 300-acre farm in Newark Valley, New York. The *'Flying Saucer Review'* wrote about how a strange object suddenly hovered off the ground about 150 feet away from him. It was about twenty feet long, fourteen feet wide, and four feet thick.

Two human-like figures, both about four feet tall, and covered in silvery one-piece suits, came out of the bottom of the craft. They were carrying trays containing specimens of soil and sod.

One stepped forward and spoke with a deep voice, telling Wilcox not to be afraid, as they had 'talked with people before'. They asked him a lot of questions about soil, crops, fertilizer, and agriculture in general. They also wanted a sample of the manure he had been spreading.

They told him a very improbable story about having come from Mars, and also volunteered a great deal of information about space and other subjects, most of which he did not understand. Before they departed, Wilcox promised to leave a bag of fertilizer out for them, which he later left in the field. Although he didn't see the little men again, the next day the fertilizer had 'gone'.

Obviously, it was only particular specimens that the 'little guys' were collecting. On 3rd August 1967, on the outskirts of Caracas, Venezuela, Mr. and Mrs. D.S. were scared of recent earthquakes, and sleeping in the car outside their house.

They were woken by a bright light which flooded their home, and the greenhouses in their neighbour's yard. It was a strange craft, hovering over a palm tree. It looked like two saucers placed together, about thirty feet in diameter and glowing luminous white.

Part of the bottom opened up, and a 'light', descended to the ground. Out of a 'door' stepped a small man wearing luminous, silvery clothes. He bent over and picked up some rocks, which he was obviously examining. He looked up, and seemed to be talking to the craft overhead. After a short while he dropped the rocks and re-entered the 'light' which moved back into the bottom of the object. The 'door' closed, there was a slight humming noise, a rush of air, and the craft flew off.

Nearly eight years later, at the beginning of January 1975, another New Yorker had a similar experience with 'little people' gathering soil. Bud Hopkins investigated this incident, which occurred when George O'Barski was travelling home from Manhattan to New Jersey. He was passing North Hudson Park when he noticed static on his radio. At the same time a brilliantly lit object passed his car, and hovered ten feet above a playing field.

It was a thirty-feet-long craft, with evenly spaced windows, and was emitting a humming sound. After it descended another six feet, a door slid open between the windows, and about ten small, helmeted figures descended a 'ladder' to the ground. They were wearing one-piece garments, and he estimated their height as being three-and-a-half to four feet.

O'Barski admitted to being terrified, and kept his car idling as he watched the little creatures using 'spoon-like' implements to scoop dirt into some bags they were carrying. After about four minutes, they re-entered the craft, which ascended and moved off to the north.

The next day, O'Barski returned to the site, and found the holes the entities had dug. Bud Hopkins was later able to find other witnesses in the area, who had seen a strange object in the sky that night.

Nearly fifteen years later, they were still 'at it'! In late 1991, the Camacho family, from Puerto Rico, grew the 'Split Leaf Philodendren' in their garden. More commonly known as the 'Swiss Cheese Plant', it was popular as a medicinal herb.

During the year, neighbours had reported seeing a UFO hovering over their house, and Albert Camacho had seen it on one occasion. One evening, his wife, Marisol, heard voices coming from the porch. She looked out the window and noticed 'two little creatures, big shiny white egg-shaped heads, skinny.'

When she saw that they were stripping the leaves off her Swiss Cheese Plant, she opened the window. The little beings ran off, only to return, to gather more leaves, a few nights later.

On the evening of 23rd September 1996, Mary Morrison and her ten-year-old son drove to their local shopping centre, in Fife, Scotland, to buy some coffee.

Researcher, Malcolm Robinson, related how, on the way, Mary and Peter saw some strange bright lights in the sky. At times they illuminated the ground below, and appeared to be coming from a silent, black 'triangular' object above. After a while, it seemed to move away.

Mary was curious, and before going home, she called in to see her friend Jane. Along with Susan, Jane's fifteen-year-old daughter, they all set off in the direction of the earlier sighting.

They were startled to see, on the other side of a ploughed field, a huge bright white light on the ground, beside of group of trees. More spinning coloured lights appeared, and then all four witnesses could see the silhouettes of small grey figures that were running around, further back in the woods. They appeared to be picking up cylinders and boxes or cubes, and taking them back to some 'triangular structure'. A short distance away was a taller 'being', a sort of 'tan-brown' in colour, who seemed to be in charge.

Suddenly, another beam of light shot down from the sky, and illuminated the road ahead of them. Mary, Jane and the two children took fright, and drove back to Jane's house.

After a while, they regained their courage, and went back out, armed with a pair of binoculars. Returning to the scene, the 'little beings', along with their taller 'supervisor', were still busily at work. This time they could discern the unusual features of the larger person. He seemed to have a large, 'bulbous' head with a very flat face.

A mist arose, and a lot of the 'little guys' seemed to be moving towards them, so they jumped back into the car, which Mary drove at some speed back to Jane's house.

Researchers later investigated the possibility that the witnesses may have experienced further interaction with the 'beings' after the event.

Sometimes aliens, especially the 'little guys' take an interest in humans' domestic animals. Do they want them for companionship, as 'pets', or for more sinister purposes?

Usually most dogs either become aggressive or whimper and hide during an extraterrestrial encounter. Some have run away, never to be seen again, and others had been found later, either injured or dead.

There has been more than one case where the 'visitors' have tried to dog-nap somebody's pet.

On 23rd December 1977, a farmer in New Zealand's Waimata Valley was woken to the sound of his dogs barking. He raced out the back door with his rifle, and was stunned to see a landed flying saucer to his right. It was forty feet across, with a brightly glowing blue metallic shell, and looked similar to a 'bowler hat',

There was an unusual 'boomerang' shape icon on the outside, and two open rectangular doors. To the left of the object he saw two humanoid figures, just under five feet tall. They were wearing close-fitting silver, metallic overalls, cuffed at the bottom over red, glowing boots. Their helmets, which extended across their shoulders, were white and opaque, and their hands were covered with flared 'gauntlets' which extended halfway up their forearms.

Between them, they were carrying the limp, upside-down body of one of his sheep dogs. The farmer shot at the beings, winging one, who dropped the dog and ran into nearby bushes. The second being ran for the craft, which took off vertically, at great speed, after the doors closed behind him. The dog got up, rather groggy, and started jumping around and barking.

There was an interesting turn of events. Bryan Dickeson, who investigated this incident, received another report. Six days later, at 7pm on 28th December, a man driving down Waimata Valley Road, saw a 'small man', just under five feet tall, trying to flag him down from the side of the road. He described the hitch-hiker as wearing red boots and a silver suit, but there was no mention of a helmet.

The 'little guy' was jumping up and down and frantically waving. There had been several sightings in the Waimata Valley during the past few days. Were the visitors looking for their missing comrade?

Coral and Jim Lorenzen wrote of two similar cases in the USA, which occurred twenty years earlier.

At 6.30 am on 6th November 1957, when Everett Clark of Dante, Tennessee let his dog Friskie outside, he saw a long, round object about 100 yards away in the field near his home. About twenty minutes later, when he went to bring Friskie back inside, he found him, along with some other dogs, across the road and in the field next to the strange object. They were all just sitting there, staring up at the craft and its occupants.

There were two men, and two women, dressed in strange clothing, who gestured at him to come over, but he refused. They then grabbed at Friskie, who growled and backed away. One man then got hold of another dog, who promptly bit him. They appeared to give up, and got back into their craft which silently took off – 'straight-up'. Investigators later found markings in the field where the 'ship' had landed.

That same evening, at dusk, John Francis of Everittstown, New Jersey, went outside to feed his dog. He saw a brilliant white light hovering in front of his barn, and was confronted by a three foot being with a 'pasty face', noticeable nose and 'frog-like' eyes.

"We are peaceful - people – we only want your dog;" it said.

"Get the hell out of here!" John said, and the being fled back to its craft, which took off – straight up!

In his book, *'Unearthly Disclosure'*, Timothy Good wrote about a report originally investigated by Antonio Ribera. This more benign encounter was experienced by Julio Fernandez and his dog, Mus, on the 5th February 1978.

Early in the morning, Julio and Mus had set off in his car, to go hare hunting in an area west of Madrid in Spain. For some unknown reason, he pulled off the main road onto a dirt track, where his car engine and electrical system failed. Mus was growling, and after he got his shotgun out of the boot, Julio saw two 'quasi-human beings' approaching.

They had broad shoulders and muscles, exceptionally long arms and legs, pale skin and large bony heads with long thin noses and huge eyes. They were both wearing tight fitting pastel-green overalls, and yellow, satin hoods, which left their faces uncovered.

They asked him not to panic, and to follow them. For some reason, he complied, and soon they arrived at a saucer-shaped craft, hovering just above the ground between two 'hillocks'. It had a smooth surface and a matt, silvery metallic colour, about 15 to 20 metres high, and 60 or 70 metres in diameter.

A cylinder, with a sliding door, descended and Julio stepped in, dragging a reluctant Mus behind him. When he was given a tour of the ship, and its technology, he had his gun over his shoulder, and the dog tucked under his right arm. There was a third crew member on board, and after Julio put Mus on the floor, the dog ran around, sniffing at everything, including the aliens, who seemed quite surprised.

They indicated that they would like to examine Mus, and take blood samples. When they had finished, they requested that Julio also submit to a physical examination. Julio found this more disturbing, as they took many more samples from him as they had from Mus.

Afterwards, Julio watched the crew operating the craft. They communicated telepathically with him, but spoke an unknown language amongst themselves. They showed interest in his cigarettes and also his gun, but appeared to be disapproving when he said it was used to hunt animals. Suddenly, he could hear a brief 'whistle' and the three crew seemed a little flustered. The image of an older looking man appeared on one of the screens, and spoke in a strange language. This seemed to provoke some activity, and soon Julio and Mus were escorted back to their car.

There have been occasions where it ended badly, for both the dog and the alien. Christopher Montgomery wrote about such an occasion, which happened on 19th October 1998.

Dr. Jonathon Reed was taking his dog, Suzy, a seven-year-old golden retriever, for a hike in the US Cascade Mountains. At about 3pm, Suzy 'went crazy', and took off, barking. Reed became concerned when her barking changed to yelping and howling. He ran towards the sound, picking up a large 'stick', about the size of a baseball bat, as he went....perhaps she had encountered a 'big cat' or other wild animal.

When he reached her, the air was 'vibrating' all around, and Suzy was wrestling with a short being, about four-and-a-half feet tall. She had sunk her teeth into its arm, and in an attempt to free itself, the creature had ripped off half her jaw. Suzy's injuries proved fatal, and in a rush of emotion, Reed swung his 'stick' at the alien, crushing its skull in the process.

The creature let out a terrible scream, and fell prostrate, dead on the ground. He examined it, and noted it was very skinny, with a light-beige or brown coloured skin, and a skeletal system very similar to our own. Its eyes were an angular, large bulbous shape, with a slit for a mouth, and a nasal ridge terminating in two holes.

Reed was severely traumatised, and it took him about an hour to recover. He heard a humming sound, and further on he found a black 'obelisk' shaped craft, about five feet wide and ten feet long. He took a couple of photographs, but the negatives were not very clear.

Perhaps the visitors have learned that cats are very feisty creatures, which are better not messed with. Rabbits, on the other hand, are docile little animals, often kept as pets for small children.

The Italian, *'Settinama Incom.'*, reported that on November 14th 1954, farmer Amerigo Lorenzini found a bright craft, shaped like a cigar, landed on his property. Three 'dwarfs', wearing metallic 'diving suits' emerged, and were speaking a language that Amerigo did not understand.

They had apparently stolen some of his rabbits, out of their cages. He grabbed his rifle, and aimed at the thieves. Upon pulling the trigger, he discovered that not only would his gun not fire, he suddenly grew so weak he could not hold onto it, and it fell to the ground. The little men jumped back into their craft, and along with his rabbits, flew away leaving a bright trail in the sky.

ALIEN ARTEFACTS

Although some researchers insist that all the unidentified flying objects during World War II were advanced German technology, the United States was already aware that some were of extraterrestrial origin.

William Jones and Dr Irena Scott detailed a very credible report received from the daughters of a Rev Turner Holt, who held a Doctorate in Theology, and was a community leader and minister at his local Christian Church in Ohio.

Rev Holt's cousin was Cordell Hull, Secretary of State under Franklin Roosevelt, and winner of a Nobel Prize for Peace. One day, whilst he was in

Washington, Cordell swore Turner to secrecy and took him to a sub-basement in the Capitol Building. There he saw a wrecked round craft of some kind, and four large glass jars, each containing some unknown four feet tall creature in formaldehyde.

The 'metallic material' was of a silvery colour they had never seen before; and appeared to be a 'vehicle' which apparently had been taken apart and was in pieces. Rev Holt never referred to them as extraterrestrials or if he knew where they came from, and said Cordell told him they were afraid it could start a panic if the public ever found out.

This had been a family secret, which Rev Holt wanted revealed after he and Cordell died. His daughters also wanted publication delayed until they had passed away.

(It was only later that I joined the dots together. There is a report that in April 1941 a craft crashed in Missouri and was retrieved and stored underneath 'the largest, most important building in Washington.' Further, it happened during the Presidency of Franklin Roosevelt who was aware of the incident and the hidden artefacts.)

The 1941 incident was later reported by UFO researchers Raymond Fowler, Len Stringfield and Ryan Wood. The very thorough investigations they initiated led them to conclude the event most probably occurred as stated.

The witness was the widow of another ordained and more trustworthy witness, Rev. William Huffman, a Baptist Minister who was called out by the local police to what they thought was a plane crash outside of town. What they found was debris and the remains of a shiny metallic 'saucer'.

There were three bodies, not human, each about 4' tall, with very long hands and fingers. Their bodies were hairless and limp, with oval slanted eyes, slit mouths and two small holes for a nose. He provided the requested blessings for the three dead occupants, and then walked up to the wreckage. He looked inside a broken portion of the 'command module' and could see a small metal chair and gauges and dials he could not recognise. He also noticed there was some kind of hieroglyphic inscriptions and writing inside. When the authorities arrived he was instructed "not to talk about this", however he told his wife and family when he returned home.

Were these the retrieved artefacts later seen by Rev. Holt?

THE 'GRAYS'

The 'Grays' were initially reported in the 1950s and 60s, and even then, only in small numbers. In the 1970s, the incidents increased dramatically, and from the 1990s onwards, these particular aliens comprised the majority of contact cases, especially from the USA. In fact, when the Russian investigator, Felix Zigel, spoke of UFO occupants in 1976, they did not get a mention. He only referred to the 'human' looking entities, the 'little guys' and the seldom seen nine-foot giants.

I believe, as the Italian's W56 advised, the taller, emotionless 'Grays' were soulless, biological robots, who had fought, and escaped from their creators and 'masters', and are now embarked on an agenda of their own.

Tall and skinny, with large heads and 'wrap-around' black eyes, they often seem linked to a common 'directing' mind, indicating that they are not the ones in control.

Col. Philip Corso aptly described them when he said they weren't benevolent alien beings who had come to enlighten human beings, and were; – *'genetically altered humanoid automatons, cloned biological entities, actually, who were harvesting biological specimens on Earth for their own experimentation.'*

They have the ability to manipulate the human mind and most contactees, who usually only remember them under hypnosis, express fear and apprehension. Many times they show little regard for their captive's emotional well being, and concentrate on their task of physical examination and the taking of body samples and fluids.

In 1998 Dr. David Jacobs articulated his views on the alien intrusion into our society. He had investigated many later cases involving the abduction phenomena and the 'Grays', whom I have also said I believe to be biological robots, and not the more friendly humanoid 'little guys'.

Since 1986 he had been employing hypnosis to better understand the apparent 'abductee' experiences. Jacobs did not like what he uncovered. The more he learned the more confused and distressed he became, and subsequently wrote the books *'Secret Life'* and *'The Threat'*. He did not necessarily agree with the opinions of other academics such as John Mack and Edith Fiore.

"I do not think that these beings are here to help us overcome our problems, both physical or mental or whatever it is. I don't think they are here to help us build a better world for ourselves through ecological and environmental rebuilding. I agree that there is an environmental message in these abductee accounts. I think that's true, but I think that's for different reasons....

"I am more and more convinced that we're involved with a program that has a beginning, a middle and an end.....and I think that this program is going to an end not to our liking. I think this is a secret phenomenon because they don't want us to know what they are doing, and we might try to take steps to prevent them."

Jacobs felt that the government was not really aware of what was happening, and in his opinion although there were four distinct species of aliens reported, they were all working for the same purpose. I, and many other researchers do not agree with him, and feel he has ignored the evidence and data on the early friendly contacts with the 'Nordics' and human looking visitors. However, in all honesty none of us really know the truth, and we all base our opinions on the available evidence.

Jacobs went on to say; *"This is a physiological program of exploitation of one species by another. Sperm and egg and the production of hybrids is what they want....I have a very bad feeling that this could be a take-over program. This could mean an integration into society somewhere along the line where normal humans would be in a subservience group."*

Walt Andrus, the founder of MUFON, had been involved with UFO research since the 1960s, and was aware of the differences between alien visitations and intentions. In 2002, when speaking of alien abductions, as distinct from the earlier pleasant contacts and interactions, he also thought there was a process of 'hybridisation' occurring.

Whilst he would not necessarily classify these particular visitors as hostile in the conventional sense he considered that they had their own agenda, of which we are a part and possibly an unwilling part.

"I believe these alien creatures are hybridising a species to create a generation of hybrids. With each succeeding generation of abductees they perfect the hybrid species....recycling the DNA until they have a race of human hybrids that

look no different from the way we do. However they are still aliens endowed with an alien intelligence and whatever other powers aliens possess.

"What's their mission? To insert themselves into powerful positions in government, industry, communications and in the financial industry with each new generation. There will be what I call a 'zero-force' takeover. Therefore the threat may not be a threat of violence, but rather a loss of what we consider our freedoms in a takeover of our planet.

"What is happening is a gradual infiltration of our institutions with individuals who possess incredible powers....with each generation, very gradually over the years, the infiltration takes place as these young aliens move up the ranks and make room for their successors."

While I do not necessarily agree with him, Walt believed that these aliens were not 'beings' in the way we understand 'beings', and that their agenda was more specific to a complete takeover of our culture and planet.

He considered that their aim, as they centralise their power, was to have their hybrids walk down the street, and not be recognised for what they are. He sadly felt that we did not have the capability to detect them.

THE ALIEN AGENDA

There are many reports regarding the true reasons behind alien visitation. These explanations can be as many and as varied as the contacts themselves.

Author George Andrews quoted an elderly lady, who wished to remain anonymous. She said that she had been abducted by 'little guys' who safely returned her afterwards; *'Fear and panic are very important to the alien. If you become panic stricken, you will be of no use to their Earth project. A person must be able to stay calm under all situations. The aliens must work with people who do not panic. They are not here to get us out of fights, to end our wars, to change our governments or to physically save us.*

'All they do is to pass on information about what their instruments are recording to those willing to listen and able to understand. We must save ourselves. We must protect ourselves. We are not really their concern. They have problems enough of their own.

'If somehow their information can help us, they are glad to be of service. When the time of disaster arrives, they will pull out of our Solar System. They refuse to become entangled with our war-like planet.'

───────────────────────────────

CHAPTER TEN

COME FLY WITH ME

Have you ever wondered what happens when our 'visitors' tour of duty ends, and they return to their home planet?

One such report came from Arlington in the USA. A college student, working in a paint shop, said that one peculiar client had claimed alien encounters on several occasions. They became friends, and the customer told him about these beings from other planets, who'd shown him their spaceships and advanced technology.

The man told him that he had no family, and intended leaving this Earth to live on another planet. Before he departed, and knowing the student was struggling to support a young family, he wished to deed his house and land to him. The student didn't believe a word of it, but agreed to the older man's request. A few days later he transferred his house, land and all his assets to the young man, who then received a call to go to a certain field on the property that evening. His friend said he was leaving Earth with the spacemen, and would never return.

The student drove up to the property, parked his car, and walked over to the field. He could see a strange mist-like green light ahead, and a saucer-shaped craft hovering a couple of feet above the ground. His friend was there, and after giving a wave, entered through an opening which appeared on the saucer. In a matter of seconds the craft shot up into the sky and disappeared from view. Once he realised his benefactor really wasn't coming back, he moved his wife and children into the house, but didn't stay long. He told the researcher that many strange, eerie things happened there, but added that some of the advanced technology, which the painter had told him about, and seemed so far-fetched at the time, exists in today's world.

In his book *'Alien Base'* Timothy Good wrote of 'Rose' and her contact on 11th April 1952. Rose, who lived with her father near the French town of Nîmes, woke one night to the sound of their dogs barking. She went outside, and saw four strangers. Three were very tall, and the other of normal height.

The shorter man spoke in French, and seemed to be acting as an interpreter for his three colleagues. He said they had come from a 'far-away world', and showed her their craft which was enormous, shaped like a straw hat, and slate grey in colour.

They asked her if she would like to go with them, but she declined, saying she had her daughter and father to care for. The normal man said that he had met these 'beings' twenty years earlier in 1932. He had been a twenty-five year-old schoolteacher at the time, and having no family, accepted their offer to go and live with them. He reassured her there was nothing to fear, and she allowed him to go into her father's outhouse library to take a few books.

Once inside, the visitors showed their abilities to levitate, teleport and dematerialise objects. The leader also demonstrated his telepathic powers.

He explained that thousands of years ago some extraterrestrials, from whom humans are descended, were banished to our planet. The reason for their visit now, was to analyse what damage we had done to Earth with our atomic explosions.

He mentioned their concern for the destructive, senseless behaviour of humans, and disregard, not only for our contemporaries, but also for future generations on this beautiful planet. They had tried to intervene, without success, in the past.

They said they could not stay for long, and asked her to step back from their craft, and hold the dogs. They entered the saucer, which took off making a droning noise, and creating a strong draft of warm wind.

In May 1955, a 74-year-old vagrant, Charles Jevington, ('Old Charlie'), suddenly went missing from the British Cumbrian village of Thursby. He was well known and liked by the locals, many of whom would buy him a pint of ale at one of the two pubs.

After a while, villagers became concerned, and determined that the last person to see him was Meg Crompton, the daughter of a local farmer. She said he had been wearing a haversack and hurrying across a field towards the woodland. An intensive police search failed to find him, and they could not locate any possible relatives.

Five years later, in August 1960, Charlie suddenly turned up, alive and well, in the local pub. He explained to the villagers that he had been on board 'one of those flying saucers' all that time. He told of how, five years ago, he met some aliens, who had been collecting plants in the woodland. They invited him to go on a 'long trip' with them, and even waited for him to collect some basic possessions.

He detailed some incredible voyages across the galaxy, and weird and wonderful worlds he had visited. One amateur astronomer scoffed at his tall tales, and when Charlie mentioned planets other than Saturn having 'rings', he disputed the whole account. This prompted disbelief in all the other drinkers, who laughed when Charlie stomped off and said he may go back with his alien friends in a fortnight.

Charlie did go permanently missing two weeks later, and around the same time, five discs were seen across the sky in Carlisle. In later years, NASA discovered that Charlie was correct, there are faint rings, not discernable by Earth's telescopes, around Jupiter, Uranus and Neptune.

'The Flying Saucer Review' discussed an interesting incident which occurred at 4am on June 5th 1964. An Argentinean Doctor and his wife were in their car, about thirty kilometres from the Pajas Blancas International Airport, when they found the road blocked by a huge, extraordinary object. After they stopped, its very powerful light went out, leaving only a violet coloured hue coming from the craft.

They sat in stunned silence for about twenty minutes, when suddenly a stranger appeared and asked in Spanish; "What's the matter, my friend?" The doctor told him that his engine had failed, and when the man suggested that he try again, both the engine and headlights came on.

The stranger said; "Don't be afraid. I am terrestrial. I am carrying out a mission on Earth. My name is R... D.... Tell mankind about it in your own fashion."

He then slowly walked away, and was joined by two beings dressed in grey. Along with the stranger, they entered the machine, which rose rapidly and vanished, leaving a violet coloured trail.

Salvador Freixedo wrote about an interesting account, (translated by Gordon Creighton), from the Dominican Republic in 1972.

At 9am, on a deserted road near San Cristobal, an insurance company director was flagged down by a man wearing a light-green overall, which covered his entire body, including his feet. The driver pulled up, and the stranger asked him if he recognised him, which he didn't.

He identified himself as F...M...., a person well known in San Domingo, who had mysteriously disappeared at sea fifteen years earlier. Everyone had thought that he had drowned, along with two colleagues, however he explained that he had been saved by a UFO.

He nodded to two people some distance away, who were slim and over six feet tall. They stood, with their arms crossed, silently observing They had short, brown hair, and light coloured skin, similar to that of the Chinese. F.M. said they had rescued him because of his intelligence and knowledge of radio techniques, and then drew their attention to a nearby small craft, which was the shape of an American football, with a 'nickelled' surface.

F.M. thought his companions came from Venus, and that they were 'investigating', with a special interest in the Milwaukee Depth, which is the deepest part of the ocean, to the north of the island. F.M. then told the director to step back, as they were about to leave.

Timothy Good contacted Puerto Rico investigator, Jorge Martin, who advised that the incident took place on 22nd September 1972. The company director was Virgilio Contreras, and the mysterious stranger, Freddie Miller, a Dominican Republic television broadcasting pioneer, who was thought to have been lost at sea.

In his book *'Alien Agenda'*, Jim Marrs spoke of contactee Lyn Buchanan, who revealed his experiences after retiring as a military intelligence officer.

In the mid-1960s he was a young student pastor, living with his wife and family in the parsonage at a Methodist Church near Huntsville, Texas. He had been assigned to a new position in another church, and at 2am, he was alone in the house. Everyone else had already moved to their new accommodation, and he had been packing up any remaining items, before bedding down with some blankets and a pillow.

Suddenly he heard the noise of something coming over the house and down into the backyard, followed by the sounds of 'people' moving up the sides of the building towards the front window. He was terrified, but unable to move.

The next thing he knew, it was morning, and he was standing in the living room, completely disorientated. For years he was haunted by the feeling that there was something he had forgotten, and suddenly the memories came flooding back.

He didn't remember how he got there, but he recalled sitting on a 'ship' with a large window in the front. There were about fifteen other people in the 'room', and there was a very scared little old lady sitting beside him. There was a tall person walking around, and a smaller guy, with weird eyes, who appeared to be the pilot.

The craft appeared to lift off and set down several times before they reached their destination, and Lyn was allowed to sit at the controls during part of the trip. There was some discussion about Lyn's hands, unlike those of most humans, being large enough to manipulate the ship's control mechanisms.

When they landed he could see two other saucers sitting there, with two lines of people, 'one embarking and the other disembarking'. As he and the other passengers started walking up a hill to a large, open-sided, pavilion, the small pilot of his craft, pulled him out of line and they sat together on the hillside. He could hear sounds of both laughter and screaming coming from the building, and was glad he had not remained with the other passengers.

After a while, another man came up and offered Lyn a job flying the saucers. Lyn was excited, but when he learned that meant never being able to come back or see his family again, he declined and returned to the line of people boarding his ship. The pilot told him he would not be allowed to remember the experience, and the next thing he knew he was back at the parsonage and standing in the middle of the living room.

Lyn continued with his life, and after joining the Army, was assigned to military intelligence at Fort Meade in the early 1980s. Later that decade, he was questioned by two intelligence operatives about his earlier experience, and he thought, judging by their reactions, some of the information confirmed what they already knew. A year later, whilst on a classified tour of a mock-up exhibition of aircraft crash-sites, he saw a control-panel which was on display.

Without thinking, he exclaimed; "That's not out of a plane. That's out of a flying saucer!" Within four minutes his group was hastily rushed out of the building, and told not to talk about their visit. It was enough to convince Lyn about his earlier memories.

Sometimes we cannot be sure of the authenticity of a report, however researcher John Keel said people felt that, the witness, Carroll Watts was beyond reproach. The incident was also investigated by the Air Force, who noted one of their personnel was, for some time, chased along a road, by a similar craft, only a week earlier.

It was 10.30pm on 31st March 1967, when Carroll Watts was driving home in Wellington, Texas. He noticed a clear fluorescent light coming from what he thought was an abandoned farmhouse, and drove over to investigate. He stopped about twenty feet away from a strange object, about one hundred feet long, and eight or ten feet high.

He walked around the side of the strange machine, and knocked on a port or door, which then opened. A strange voice asked him if he would be prepared to undergo a physical examination. When Watts asked why, the voice said if he passed, he would be able to take a flight with them, however this privilege was only for men – women and children were not allowed.

He was directed to a machine opposite the doorway, and told that all he had to do was stand in front of it. He also saw a large-scale unknown land map, and was told that they had a machine that when they flew within three hundred yards of a building, they could tell how many people were inside and even their ages. (Something we can also probably do now.)

They said they were stationed all over the world, and could come and go whenever they pleased. Watts was encouraged to take the physical – several people had already done so, and made the promised flight. He became nervous, and declined. After jumping back into his car, and turning on the headlights, he saw the craft rise silently into the air and fly south.

I have come across a couple of cases of women, who following a contact on board a spaceship, have been asked if they would like to go away with them. These were genuine offers of comradeship, which were declined due to their families back at home.

Some cases seem a little more insidious in their intention. South African researcher, Cynthia Hind, thoroughly investigated the following incident; On January 3rd 1979, Meagen Quezet of Mindalore, near Kugersdorp, South Africa, ran as fast as she could when after she, and her twelve-year-old son, Andre, encountered a brightly coloured craft on a lonely road.

It was just after midnight, when Megan had heard their own dog, 'Cheeky', and a couple of others, barking. She tried to bring the dog into the house, but he ran off. She called Andre to come and help bring 'Cheeky' back home, as he had previously been injured by a passing car on the road.

They followed the dog, and came across a 'thing' standing in the middle of the road, about twenty metres away. Their immediate thought was that it was a light aircraft, which had landed due to an emergency, but soon realised that was not the case. Perhaps it was some sort of experimental craft. Megan had trained as a nurse, and wondered if anyone had been injured.

The craft was a smooth metallic colour, egg-shaped, and cut straight across at the bottom, with four long 'spindly' legs supporting it on the road. It was about fifteen feet wide, nine feet high, and encased in a very bright pink glow, which seemed to be emanating from within an opening on the side. There were two other lights on either side of the 'door', and another on top.

Megan and Andre quietly edged closer, and five or six 'men' stepped out of the opening onto the ground. They all looked quite normal, just over five feet tall, of slender build, with darkish coloured skin, and wearing white suits, with shoes attached to the trousers. One of them, who had thick .dark curly hair and a beard, appeared to be the leader.

Once the men, who had been quietly talking in an unknown language, noticed Megan and Andre, the 'leader' stepped forward, and was very charismatic. He bowed to Meagan, trying to speak in a high pitch voice. She couldn't understand everything he said, but he kept staring into her eyes. She suddenly had the feeling that 'something was not quite right'. Something was 'not normal'.

Cynthia Hind realised there was about thirty minutes of 'missing time' and arranged for a reliable psychiatrist to do a regression, during which she remembered him asking her to 'go with them,' saying it was 'very nice where they came from'. That was when she became frightened, and told Andre to run quickly and bring his father.

Andre sped off, but came back after the men jumped into a sliding door on their craft, which made a humming noise and disappeared up into the sky within seconds.

There are other cases, involving women and children, where the poor 'victims' do not have any choice in the matter. Three such 'candidates' had a very lucky escape in 1989.

Two women, along with one's six-year-old daughter, were walking in a park, beside the Dnieper River in Kiev, Russia, when they encountered three silver clad, blond haired beings. They said they came from another planet, and intended taking one or more of them back to their home world.

The women felt overpowered by their presence, but regained their senses after the aliens conducted them to a silver craft with a circular antenna. After the little girl started crying, and the women protested, the aliens decided they had changed their minds, and would not take them after all. They got back into their craft, and zoomed away.

A similar case occurred over twenty years earlier. Dr Walter Buhler, investigated an incident which occurred on 25th February 1966, at Quipapa, Brazil. Just after 10pm, three young women were walking home when they saw a strange, round craft in the middle of a road, next to the railway line. It looked like a large dish, or reversed cup, about four metres long, and one-and-a-half metres high, with what appeared to be two large, pale yellow headlights.

At first they thought it must be a broken down vehicle, but suddenly three small individuals approached. They looked quite human, and were wearing peculiar large 'headgear', and one-piece grey garments. Near them was a very tall 'luminous' being, standing motionless and erect.

The three little people approached, silently gesturing to them, as if wanting to engage in conversation. The girls became frightened, thinking they may be robbers, and hid until another car came from the opposite direction. At that stage, they took the opportunity to rush past the craft and beings, only to find the saucer had landed, much closer to the railway track ahead of them.

They managed to get home and tell their mother, who went outside to have a look. Suddenly the craft came racing towards them, only about six metres above the ground. All four women raced back to the house, and the UFO circled overhead a few times before it climbed higher and higher and vanished from sight.

A couple of other female contactees I have interviewed have also been offered the chance to 'go away with them'. Two of the women were married with a family, and the aliens accepted their refusal due to not wanting to leave their husbands and children.

CHAPTER ELEVEN

TELEPATHY, CHANNELLING AND COMPULSIONS

Telepathy is the ability for one mind to communicate, often instantaneously, to another. Just as we have individual finger prints, each person possesses a unique energy field and 'frequency'. The ability to manipulate this mental power can be taught, and occasionally comes naturally. Some refer to telepathy as a 'biological radio'.

Contactees, who from the mid-fifties, worked with the Amicizia group of visitors, claimed that although they could converse naturally with the visitors, sometimes telepathic communications occurred, although thought transference did not come naturally. The aliens used specific methods to induce telepathic abilities in their human counterparts.

Usually this consisted of a small, black implant, called an 'ania'. Once inserted under the skin, immediately behind the ear, it dissolved into thousands of minute biological robots that dispersed in the body. That way it couldn't be detected by X-rays or any other conventional methods.

In *'The Days of the Space Brothers'*, I wrote about New Zealand contactee Mr. X. In the early 1960s he originally had a couple of rare physical contacts with the 'visitors', who usually left him written messages, and urged him to practice and develop the art of telepathy.

This was a different approach from the open contacts practised by the 'Space Brothers' during the previous decade. Perhaps it was to avoid detection or capture by the authorities, who by that time were well aware of their presence.

In 1960, Mr. X, after being told not to publicly reveal his identity, received his first note, which said in part; *'We cannot openly reveal ourselves because of hostile surroundings, and request that you do likewise, and that is why we say 'tell no man'. Other things will be revealed to you according to your progress. Time is now fast running-out, and our responsibilities become heavier as the focal point is reached.'*

Contactee, George Adamski, who more recently had been making outlandish statements, had fallen out of favour with the visitors. He wrote to a colleague; *"There is a new group of space people that have replaced those who have been here for quite some time.... When new groups come in to help us, they present differently than the groups before them....I have not been informed what their ideas are, but I will sooner or later."*

In October 1961, the Space Brothers wanted to negate some of Adamski's claims. They wrote; *'...We are not from your System, but from a constellation or system near what earthlings call Sagittarius, which is very far from your position in space.....There is too much sensationalism written about us of which we are not capable. We again stress that we do not take earthlings for rides into the Creator's Heavens, and as you already know, if we have business to arrange, it is always done by appointment on your solid Earth, and we wish all earthlings to know this truth.*

'No humans exist on any of your neighbouring planets, and we say again that your planet is the most favoured. - Your Two Friends.'

Mastering telepathy took Mr. X some time, but eventually he channelled, and wrote down, telepathic messages, which I reproduced in some detail.

He wrote another poem, which I wonder is conveying the sad opinion of the Space Brothers.

We're all fellow travellers upon this speck of dirt,
Which swings around the heavens, I verily assert;
It carries a special cargo, of crazy human life,
Which is ever aggressive, and the cause of much strife.

Humans are not happy till they're at each other's throats,
Or causing human misery, and all which that denotes:
They ravage and smash city after city,
Blasting homes of the innocent, more is the pity.

If there is such a thing as a madhouse of Creation,
Then the dirt-speck we live on is surely its foundation;
For I know of no other which can lay claim to the name,
Where there is pitiless mass murder, and everlasting shame.

They blast and burn, and kill many mothers,
Leaving children as orphans to be cared for by others.
The way they maim the children is an everlasting disgrace,
So therefore I term them 'A DESPICIBLE RACE'!

In 1964, Australian researcher Fred Stone was visiting Timaru, and spent an evening with Mr. X and New Zealand researchers - the Dickesons. He later commented;

'Mr. X is a great musician and composer. He claimed the 'Space People' had inspired many of his compositions. Half way during the evening he said he felt moved to improve a piece of music – a simple composition which had just come floating through his mind. He went to the piano and began playing. Suddenly I felt myself also being moved, and as each note was played, I knew what was coming and began to hum the tune as though I had known it all the while. At the end I asked Mr. X if he knew the name of the tune, and he replied that - no he didn't know – what was it?

'Without thinking I said "Dedication'- there are verses to it. Play it again." He returned to the piano, and as he replayed the theme, the verses came into the mind telepathically from the Space Brothers, who were unseen, yet present. This was witnessed by everyone present at the time.

'Surely this was evidence that we two men were being moved together in unison to be instruments of service. Maybe you may not be impressed by this account, or feel it was a proof of the genuineness of either party, but one had to be present to know what was felt and transpired in that room. We were not being moved by our own powers, but from those of a much higher source.'

Mr. X's 'music' has intrigued me. Perhaps he was unwittingly channelling it and passing on more information and inspirational contact from his two friends. Our bodies and cells react to sound – their vibrations and frequencies. Perhaps there were more messages being secretly transmitted within the pulse and harmonics of the notes.

In the US, George Van Tassel and his family also sang popular songs, and sometimes hymns to their guests under the Giant Rock. A couple who were visiting commented; "On one occasion they sang a certain song which Van had obtained directly from one of his space contacts. To us the music was very unusual, and the words were both simple and beautiful."

As an investigator, I have always found the claims of self-professed 'contactee', Howard Menger, to be very dubious. It is, however, interesting that he also claimed that although he could not play the piano, he was able to play music that the Space Brothers had taught him.

They explained that every note had a specific density and frequency which causes a sympathetic vibration when created at the correct frequency and in certain combinations. People hearing the themes would react in their conscious state with increased understanding and brotherly love toward one another.

In *'The Alien Gene'* I discuss the events on Waiheke Island, which is just off the coast of New Zealand. In the 1970s several islanders witnessed many visitations by, and had contact with, humanoid aliens who were working with scientists on a secret project. Patty, one of the contactees, said that sometimes the 'visitors' would walk around, unrecognised, in the town. The project closed down later, when Waiheke's population increased, and as the children reached adulthood, many left the island.

In 1999, during the Christmas holidays, Patty and her companion, Mark, went back to visit her father, and they met up with all their childhood friends, who had also returned and were congregating in the local pub, where Mark and Patty were singing in a band.

When I was speaking with their friend, Gillian, she reminisced; "It was so strange, a lot of others were there, people we had gone to school with. It was like something had simultaneously drawn us all to come back at the same time. Many of our contemporaries were very musical. It was something in the notes and rhythm, and we all felt this tremendous bond and connection with each other."

Throughout history we have been aware of the hidden elements in sound and music. Acoustic phenomena – sound, pitch, rhythm, frequency, vibration, resonance – have all been known to produce an amazing effect and outcomes in unimaginable ways. In fact, these subliminal forces are far more powerful than most people realise.

The Egyptians, Greeks and Romans all incorporated music in their sacred rituals and ceremonies, as did the Sumerians before them. The Gregorian Chants of the Catholic Church were believed to impart spiritual blessings when sung in harmony during religious masses. The Tibetans use sound and vibration in their religious practices, including the art of levitation. Native cultures also have songs and instruments for their traditional ceremonies.

Two modern 'New Age' composers, Steve Halpern and Medwyn Goodall, both credit their music to 'higher sources'.

Steve Halpern said; *'As my life and career have unfolded, I've had a number of experiences that suggest some of the insights I've received in vision, meditation and dreams had an extraterrestrial dimension. This is not something I have spoken about publicly, but in light of the contributions made to my latest release, 'HIGHER GROUND', I feel compelled to share some of the background. This may help explain why this recording has been providing the extraordinary experiences that it has for so many listeners.*

'In October 1988, I received an unexpected call from a woman I met on tour in Egypt in 1980. In the years since we had spoken, she had become a very attuned psychic, and was in direct contact with the Pleiadians. She said she had some information that I needed to have concerning my next recording.'

The woman flew over from Egypt, and Steve felt the several hours they spent in the recording studio were rather fruitless. She had little musical vocabulary, and both of them became very frustrated at the concept and melody she was trying to communicate. The venture was put to one side for several months.

'Back in the studio for another project, I decided to listen to the song we had co-composed. I really didn't remember what it sounded like, but this time I was knocked out! I truly heard the music as if for the first time, and was transported to a place that transcends words. I also received an instant vision and complete understanding of how the rest of the album would unfold.

'I was directed to purchase a new instrument that provided sound textures never before available. As soon as I began playing it in the studio, I entered a place of deep silence.....evocative harmonies and motifs virtually played themselves. Even my recording engineer, who doesn't believe in such things, knew something special was in the air.

'....Is this what Pleiadian music sounds like? Or is it what Pleiadian-Terrestrial duets sound like?....Does this represent just one of many off-planet possibilities? I don't have the answer to those questions.'

Musician, Medwyn Goodall, was also forthcoming; "I have four guides who assist me with my music. They act as a single entity. They do not communicate with me verbally, and there is nothing written down, we communicate through music.

"Today, I have a clearer picture of the guides. There are four entities who appear to be humanoid males. They pool their talents together and act as one.

They have a spokesperson whom I now know by name. He has long white hair, blue eyes and a youthful appearance.

"I have now come to understand that their work with me is to inter-weave light and high vibrational frequency into the very fabric of my music. The albums are light encoded and have the divine capacity to spiritually awaken people, to heal, to trigger dormant artistic talents and to ground light into Mother Earth.

"I have come to understand that other guides assist on a program which is very specific. If I wanted to produce a very ethnic album, a guide who has experience of that culture would join in the influencing of the music."

'TELEPATHIC' TECHNOLOGY

I am reminded of the memoirs of William Tompkins in *'Selected by Extraterrestrials'*, where he was later subjected to ridicule when he claimed that whilst working on secret military projects, with large corporations, there were several pretty little 'blond Nordic alien' secretaries who were telepathically giving them technical information.

In *'Contact Down Under'*, I noted that whilst my research has not concentrated on paranormal events, it is evident that there is more than a casual connection between these phenomena and UFOs – be it by inter-dimensional or other mechanisms. Colin Norris, editor of *'Australian International UFO Research'*, advised of an interesting episode which occurred to a Northern Territory colleague who had some previous experience with unidentified objects.

Roger, (pseudonym) was highly intelligent – a background in Mechanical Engineering, Science, Technology and Psychology. He had not been feeling well for a couple of days, and although he went to bed early, couldn't sleep.

"At first it was this horrible headache, like my brain was exploding with an 'energy' or 'force rays' which penetrated through my head, and then my whole body. It lasted for about an hour or two and then subsided – believe me, I was awake the whole time.

"Suddenly I could see in my mind a picture – like a large movie screen – with writing projected onto it. It looked like a complicated formula, the letters like some kind of numbers and brackets etc. I exclaimed out loud - 'What the hell is that?' I heard a male voice saying that it was a formula for a very special material used for making certain parts and components, used in the building of spacecraft, flying saucers and advanced technology.

"Hearing that, I asked out loud 'what does it look like?' and the screen showed a large, round oval object. It was some kind of component part of a sub-assembly, a grey-metallic colour. It had a very smooth, glossy surface, like metal – melted together – with no visible signs of screws, bolts or welding.

"The screen and voice disappeared along with my headache. I lay in the dark with the picture of that space component/material remaining in my mind. It occurred to me that whoever was showing me all this and giving me the formulae must be very advanced in their technology, perhaps more advanced and intelligent than we Earth people.

"Some things still bother me today. My head hurt so much, and felt so heavy, was it caused by energy or rays of some sort projected into my head by some genius, aliens or something or someone else? Why would someone pick me up to be a messenger for a specific material? I do not know, but I do believe it was not human from the planet Earth.

Anything in this world or universe can be questioned, and for most things there would be logical answers – but not all."

Preston Dennett, in his Case No. #036, reported on a similar case which occurred on May 10th 1975; *'Chuck Doyle of Florence, Kentucky, went outside to check his horse, when he encountered a twenty-foot long metallic object, shaped like a 'manta ray', hovering over his neighbour's garden. The object had coloured lights and was emitting a green beam of light.*

'Suddenly the light began moving towards Chuck. He described it as a "straight shaft of light that didn't get wider at the bottom, like a laser...then the beam came at me. When it hit me, it was like being hit by a bucket of ice-water. I suddenly felt frozen. I couldn't move."

'Chuck was actually frozen in the position of trying to run away. Although he was leaning forward, he was held in position by the beam. To his surprise, a flood of strange symbols and images filled his mind. He saw mathematical equations, images of a strange planet and a kaleidoscope of strange colours.

'Then the beam retracted, and Chuck fell to the ground. The UFO disappeared with a purple flash and a loud bang. He returned to his house in a state of shock.

'It wasn't until he returned inside that he noticed something strange. Before the encounter, he had been suffering from a miserable head cold. Immediately afterwards, all traces of the cold had disappeared. Chuck saw a doctor a week later, making no mention of his UFO encounter. The doctor pronounced him perfectly healthy.'

THE 'KNOWING'

Many UFO contactees claim that they just 'know' things – and often inexplicable compulsions control their actions and lives. They don't understand how or why.

My book *'The Alien Gene'*, discusses some of this phenomenon. In the latter half of 2015 Elizabeth, Leesa, Vera and one other contactee, all followed an inexplicable compulsion and bought inflatable airbeds, and Vera a collapsible bed. None of them knew why. They were not expecting visitors, and had spare beds if any arrived. All have extra supplies of long-life or non-perishable food, and several had the ability to grow their own. They wondered if this was related to their alien connections? Sometime in the future would there be some emergency where they would have to be self-sufficient, and accommodate unexpected friends or refugees?

Lydia had gone one step further, and had bought and kept a caravan she never actually used – she didn't know why. Patty had gone to extremes. She and her mother suddenly purchased a farm and old house, inland to the west of the mountains behind Sydney. She wasn't even living in it!

ALIEN INFLUENCES and COMPULSIONS

Sometimes I am contacted by an eccentric witness. It is unwise to dismiss them out of hand. Often an in-depth investigation into their individual claims and their family history can prove very interesting. One such case was Roy Wallace, who privately approached me in 2010, when I was managing a charity bookshop. He came in looking for science and technical books, and when he saw the UFO books I had donated, we got talking. I also became acquainted with his wife, Lorna, a professional psychologist who was concerned about her husband's behaviour and compulsions. She confirmed he was definitely a quite sane and intelligent scientist, and that she believed him when he spoke of his UFO experiences. She was a little out of her depth when it came to the alien influence on him, and the possible harassment, or worse, by unknown persons to both Roy and previous contacts.

Lorna said: "He has this weird idea that he has certain objectives in life, but doesn't know why. One is a compulsion to build a library. He has been acquiring books, mostly scientific and technical, and has literally ended up with a warehouse full. He joined forces with another man, Peter Roach, who is a biomedical engineer specialising in cryogenics. Roy and Peter discuss very little with me except that they are working in tandem."

Lorna sighed; "Between them they purchased thousands of technical and scientific books. Then they bought two mountain properties in the country to house the collection, insisting they had to be more than six hundred metres elevation, a reasonable distance from Sydney and the coast, and away from any main road. Then, after all that, the structures have to be partially underground and covered with earth and concrete."

My interest was aroused by his wish to house a multitude of reference books in an area and manner reasonably safe from natural disasters or modern warfare. Was he expecting some form of cataclysm where there would be no more electricity or digital technology?

Roy and Lorna had moved inland in the 1990s, away from the coast. He had a dread of being in Sydney, and commented that he was not alone in this. One of his workmates, a physicist designing electronics, computers, etcetera, was quite manic, saying he had a feeling or intuition, and moved his family to an elevated area up the north coast. (Quite a lot of witnesses and contactees develop a similar impulse and move away from coastal areas.)

Roy confided he had seen unexplained craft several times in the past. One event really interested me. When he was a young biologist in the 1960s, he was conducting surveys with three other colleagues in a bushland area near Wauchope, New South Wales.

"We had been spotlighting wildlife, and at about 7.30 pm. decided to pack up and head to town for a meal. We were driving back down the winding dirt road when a bright light came up fast behind us. Thinking it was another car, that couldn't pass, we sped up. After another ten kilometres, it was still there. The light shining in our back window and rear vision mirror was starting to affect our eyes. We managed to pull over into the verge so it could get by.

"We checked the dashboard clock – 8.30 p.m., still time for dinner. Things became a little hazy. I suddenly jumped up, as if I'd been asleep, but I didn't remember anything about going to sleep!

"My mate said; 'Those headlights are gone! I don't remember that car overtaking us.' We got out of the car and looked – nothing. It was weird, the dirt road was wet, but there were no other tyre tracks besides ours. We thought maybe the other vehicle had broken down, and did a U-turn to go back and check. No-one there! Better get back for dinner!

"We continued on our way, and as we were going down the hill towards Wauchope we saw another light. This one was up in the air, not at road level, so we knew it wasn't a car. We got to the bottom of the hill, had dismissed the light, and were talking about other things. Everything was closed in town. We were dumbfounded when we saw that it was now 4.30 a.m. on the dashboard clock!

"It was afterwards that I started to get ideas – a sort of telepathic communication - an intuition and compulsion to start beneficial and worthwhile activities."

I could not contact the three other witnesses who had been in the vehicle. One had moved to Darwin, and the other was killed in New Caledonia. I suspected the remaining witness was his colleague, involved in the 'technical/scientific project', but Roy was not prepared to give me his details. Naturally a missing-time scenario came to mind. Lorna was a qualified psychologist, and if she had conducted regressive hypnotherapy, she was not prepared to admit it or discuss any details.

Lorna herself, is now not so sceptical about unidentified craft, although she is undecided about their origin (whether alien or terrestrial). They had never told their daughter about UFOs, but in 2006, when the girl was fifteen, she and Lorna were together in Cowra one night and saw a black triangular craft which hovered overhead. It was silent and had a hexagonal back, which looked like a crystal.

"This frightened me," Lorna said, "especially with regards to my daughter's wellbeing. I often wonder about her in relation to her father's experience. She is super-bright, almost a genius. I was driving from Bathurst home to Cowra late one night, between 2 a.m. and 4 a.m., and there were strange lights in the sky. I had seen them before, and was scared. A friend who lives on a rural property, near Grenfell says he sees them quite often."

> **Dr Miran Lindtner**
> Dr Lindtner was a respected scientist, a fighter pilot in World War 2, and President of UFO Investigation Centre in Sydney (UFOIC). In the late 1960s he 'fell' under a train in Germany. Colin Norris, veteran South Australian researcher once wrote to me: "The sad ending of his life was not necessary – an accident when he fell under a train in Munich. Was he pushed, as he was going to a conference back in his original country?"
> Alan did locate some of the missing paperwork in a university basement, where he found letters and magazines dating back to the 1950s in a couple of dusty bins.

Lorna was also uneasy because of the unknown fate of a colleague, Alan, which had made Roy very wary of the authorities.

"Alan told us that, in the 1960s, he once saw a UFO and contacted the Department of Defence. After the sighting he went in search of information on alien craft. He also sent a report to Dr. Lindtner of UFOIC in Sydney. On following up, and hearing of Dr. Lindtner's untimely death, he wanted to access Lindtner's files, for some reason."

Lorna said, "I don't know what Alan was looking for, or why, but he took a lot of the letters. Alan said that he 'should have kept quiet', and claimed he was being followed by cars and his credit card was blackened. He was really frightened. A short while later he moved to South Australia and then just disappeared. I don't want something like that happening to my family."

Sometimes ufology can be a dangerous business. We will never know what it was Alan witnessed or reported to UFOIC, or what was in the paperwork he smuggled out of the University. Did it have any connection to his disappearance or Dr Lindtner's death?

The connection and corroboration between UFO sightings can often be quite uncanny. It was some years later when a friend from Blackheath, in the Blue Mountains, who knew of my interest in UFOs, told me of a classic flying saucer she had seen travel over her house when she lived in Blacktown in 1971.

Recently she rang again, to tell me about a rather 'eerie' event, which really 'spooked' her. She saw her sixty-four year-old neighbour, Kyle, walking along the road with a strange figure which suddenly 'dematerialized into thin air'. She asked him about it, and when they both realised they had seen the same UFO, hovering over the forest three months before, he agreed to contact me and lodge a report.

We got chatting, and I was astounded when Kyle started talking about his friend in Cowra, who had collected many thousands of technical and scientific books. I immediately recognised the previous case from Wauchope in the 1960s. One witness subsequently died, one went to Darwin, and the third fled the area for Canberra after being harassed. It was mainly the fourth, to whom I gave the pseudonym, 'Roy', whom I had worked with documenting the case. Since their strange possible encounter, Roy and his family had several other UFO experiences, and he had succumbed to an overwhelming compulsion to purchase and store, (safely inland), every technical and scientific book he could get his hands on.

Kyle gave me 'Roy's' real name, and it didn't take me long to realise that Kyle was the fourth student who was in that car in the 1960s. He had long since returned from Darwin, and led an almost hermit existence in his house in Blackheath.

Kyle talked about other 'findings' during his studies in the Northern Territory and out west. One day he tripped over a rock, and noticed there were others, in a definite geometric placing. There were also many hieroglyphs there, and he wondered about their relevance to the Egyptian glyphs at Kariong, on the NSW Central Coast. (See *'Contact Down Under'*.)

Kyle's life experiences differed from those of Roy. His family had several instances of generational alien interaction on his mother's side of the family. He also had vague memories, dreams and psychic abilities going back to his childhood. The incident in the 1960s at Wauchope was not his first or last experience of missing time, and I wondered if he was actually the main target of that encounter.

Kyle was highly intelligent, as were the rest of his family. The alien experiences, and apparent genetic interference had taken an emotional toll, and I decided not to take the investigation any further. I did, however, realise that since the 1960s, all four of those young men had, like many other experiencers, moved away from the coast and settled on a much higher elevation.

LANA McDONALD

In *'Contact Down Under'*, I wrote about the unusual, and disturbing case of Lana McDonald, from Victoria, Australia. Lana rang me in late August, 1996, not knowing quite where to turn. In mid-July she and her husband Mark were travelling from Ballarat to Geelong. They had dropped Mark's two children at Ballarat at 9pm and were driving back to Geelong – a trip taking one hour, so they were due to arrive home about 10pm.

Lana said; "We were driving our station-wagon along a two lane highway – one lane each way – and we thought there was a car behind us, 'zapping' its high beam. Other cars were overtaking us in a hurry, and the light behind us was affecting my glasses. Suddenly this bright, sparkling silvery light shot over the top of our car – over the bonnet - and then shot up into the clouds on the other side of the sky.

"It looked something like one of those 'modelling/photographer's spotlights', and it was big – about the size of a 'room' – much bigger to the eye than a car or full moon.

"Mark looked at his watch, and neither of us could believe it was 11-30pm! We were concerned as we had left my two children with my mother, and as expected, she was very angry when we were late getting back. After we got home, every time I shut my eyes all I could see were silver lights and dark black eyes – like 'cat's eyes' – no eye whites or pupils. There were little bruises all over my buttocks and thighs, and I couldn't understand where they had come from. They were so bad I couldn't wear a short skirt.

"I had epilepsy as a child, but it has been under control for many years – I even have a driving license. Since this happened a few weeks ago, I have been getting 'blackouts' three or four times a week. These 'blackouts' are weird, they come with dreams of future events – like some type of psychic prediction. I am getting headaches, which I never had before, and I have to take pain killers to get any relief. Two weeks ago I got an infection in the reproductive area, requiring antibiotics."

She was also worried about Mark: "He has developed nose-bleeds, and gets occasional bad dreams he cannot remember. We both get very lethargic, and suffered a strange 'two-day flu' with high temperatures. I get sick if I go near radios or TVs – and there is 'static' if I sit in the car. I get dizzy quite often, and the doctors want to attach an EEG monitor to test for a 'leak', but I'm a little hesitant about this.

"A few weeks after the encounter the whole house seemed to become 'hot' and then very cold. We used to go to bed at 9.30pm, but now stay up until 1am, often going out onto the balcony and look at the stars 'like dick-heads'.

"A couple of weeks later, something flew over our house, and a whole lot of 'metal stuff' came down – like short, fat silver 'chips'. There was one large piece, like a 'half-an-egg' shape. I picked them up – but something made me throw them away."

Lana started getting dreams of the future, and some of her 'predictions' came to pass. Lana was also getting some 'flashes' of memory – of lying on a table, surrounded by white light. She could see a 'being' about 5ft 8in tall – white skin – a head that look human – no hair – and totally black eyes.

Lana was wearing a pendant, with a symbol and an amethyst centre, which she thought she once found, and she could see a similar symbol around the 'being's neck. The only other memory she had was the 'being' reaching out and touching the pendant and saying in English, (no accent) "You're one". She didn't remember where she got the pendant – but the jeweller couldn't get the stone out, and said he hadn't ever seen the symbol before.

I asked Lana questions about her psychic 'dreams' and asked if she was getting any more 'recall' of what had happened during the apparent 90-minutes of 'missing time'. It seemed to me as if some of what she considered 'dreams' were in fact 'flashes' of 'recall'.

"I asked the 'being' on the road – 'who was she?' She said her name was 'Zenna' – and they were 'visiting' me. They had a base in Peru, and it took them an hour to get to Australia. They are 'in a glass ball' on their ship, and must sit in the 'glass ball' to contact Earth people. They work through the 'minds' of people."

(The reference to a base in Peru interested me, as it corresponded with the terrain another contactee, Penny, had described when she was taken on her 'Space Ride' after being abducted at Roma Qld. It also matched a place described by two other contactees during a possible inter-dimensional experience; - detailed in *'Contact Down Under'*.)

"I was told when I understood how to contact them, I could call them anytime, and they would send me a message. I asked if they believed in God, and they said he was 'the master of all' and that they prayed. They also said that they would teach me how to use modern medicine and cure people – and I was to keep notes."

She said they told her they are here to take our uranium as there was none anywhere else. (Lana couldn't even pronounce uranium correctly, and apparently hadn't a clue what it was.)

Lana said that she had been 'directed' to 'ring' me. – 'Me? - Why me, I thought. It was after this that things got really interesting. Given her obvious naivety, I later asked her if she could get the 'aliens' to answer some questions for me. At times she obviously didn't have a clue as to the implications or meaning of my questions – and yet the answers were logical.

"Is the genetic 'collection' for their benefit or ours?" – Both.

"Are they the only ETs here?" – No not the only ones – but the others will not reveal themselves – the world is too violent. They are very angry as we have tortured some of their people. (This complaint kept surfacing – we tortured their people alive.) Further the US had two of their bodies – and they wanted them back now! They 'reprogram' human minds - and test abductees, but never harm them – it is other humans who hurt the abductees, and this also makes them very angry.

"Why are they here?" – (This is an overview of a lot of answers) – They don't eat food, but need a clear atmosphere to live in. Their planet is dying – they come in peace – but need our planet for all their people to emigrate to. (At this stage I was becoming aware that Lana may had been 'implanted' with messages and beliefs – and as I appealed to her logic – she realised some of the information was misleading, and not as peaceful as she thought.)

After that the communications became more aggressive. Lana herself was not aggressive – just the content of the messages. They said there was another planet – many years of travelling – to which they would move the Earth's population – but then as they added the chilling comment – 'Two of everything' – I couldn't help but wonder about 'Noah's Ark'! The messages became quite adamant that they are going to move 'wholesale' onto the Earth very soon, and all humans will have to go.

It all became a little garbled but essentially I understood what some of the messages were about. In one part it got mixed with what were essentially predictions. Keeping in mind that these discussions with Lana occurred in 1996, some predictions have proven correct. In hindsight I suspect that at one stage, she was referring to Assange, Snowden and others when she mentioned London and America and said – "Those that tell what they know won't come back."

By this time I was beginning to doubt my own sanity. Was I talking to Lana or some alien or entity channelling through her? Often her answers would contradict her own opinions and reasoning. I decided to go along with this, even though both of us might be crazy. I had to speak-up even if there was the remotest possibility that somehow I was providing feedback to her alien contacts.

I advised that the aggressive takeover of another planet and relocation of its population was not peaceful and something akin to an intergalactic 'Hitler'. Further, if they couldn't retrieve two bodies from the US, how could they expect to take a whole planet? Thirdly – according to Biblical and other prophecies they would be defeated. I suggested their course of action would be disastrous for all, and suggested another alternative – on a galactic basis be sought – such as a different suitable planet for their people.

Given her history and all the information, I felt that Lana may well have had more than one encounter, possibly long before this recent incident. She had mentioned the subsequent 'reproductive' infection was in her only remaining ovary, the other having been removed due to a cyst. It is common for quite young abductees to have ova removed from one only ovary, causing a cyst to develop. I did not suggest any of this to Lana, as it would only distress her and contaminate any later investigation. Having counselled her regarding the careful consideration of any hypnotherapy, I referred her to a very qualified colleague, with the comment – "I think Lana needs help urgently – regardless of authenticity"

During our long interviews Lana had given me some prophecies which have come true during the intervening twenty years, one of the reasons I have decided to relate this story. I had also asked her three 'trick' questions, relating to a different totally unrecorded UFO event, to which she could not possibly know the answers, or my reason for asking. I was 'floored' when each answer was correct.

How much of what Lana said was actually communications from 'aliens' (who've been known to lie) – how much may be psychic communication with another dimension – how much may be the product of some form of 'mind control' or even the distinct possibility of an implant - and how much may be delusional ravings or an elaborate hoax? - I really don't know. In some ways I wondered if she was the victim of a sort of 'possession' – a conduit for channelled messages.

A few years later, I was amazed by what British researcher Tony Dodd wrote in his book *'Alien Investigator'*.

'I also know, from my own experience. That the alien abductors do communicate with their victims by telepathy, and not necessarily simply during abductions. As I question the abductees during hypnosis, on several occasions a truly remarkable event occurs. I find myself talking not to them, but their abductors.

'Through their mouths come the words and messages of the aliens who are monitoring them, and who are, obviously, able to be present at any time. It is as though the alien intelligence finds a voice to communicate directly with me through the hypnotised contactee. It does not happen often......the decision to talk directly to me is always theirs – never mine....

'The room was quiet, and the abductee breathing slowly and steadily. The hypnotherapist signalled to me that she was ready to be questioned. I was asking the young woman questions about her last abduction when her voice changed, becoming higher and acquiring a slightly metallic tone. I knew, without being told, that I was talking directly to her abductor, but the policeman in me made me ask the logical question; "How can I be speaking to you now, when her last abduction was several weeks ago?"

'The voice replied: "You do not understand the nature of things. Time is only something that has been devised by humanity to create an organised society, but in truth time does not exist."...

"What gives you the right to take people without their knowledge or authority and do these things to them?" I asked. - "We have every right," said the voice. "Do you not do these things to your lower animals?"

'Once again, the implication that we were inferior creatures, and I asked; "Are you what we call Gods?" - "This is how some of you perceive us, but you do not understand the nature of things."

"If this is the case, do you require us to worship you?" - "No, this is not necessary."

I asked if they were responsible for all the strange machines we saw in our skies, which we called UFOs. The reply came; "Some of these things are our vehicles."

"Are some belonging to other entities?" I asked. - "Yes"

"Are all these entities friendly?" - "No."

'When I asked what the purpose of the abductions was, the voice avoided answering by telling me again that I did not understand the nature of things. Then the abductee was talking in her own voice again. When she came round from the hypnosis she had no memory of the conversation.'

Researcher, Kevin Randle, brought a third incident to light when he discussed the much investigated case of Betty Andreasson, who was a contactee from Massachusetts.

During a hypnosis session, organised by Raymond Fowler in 1977, she began to 'channel', and one of the aliens began 'speaking through her'. Fowler commented that he didn't know if they were actually speaking to an alien or to Andreasson's subconscious.

Later, Tony Dodd, who was a retired police officer, and a sane and sensible investigator, began to develop his own telepathic abilities. He started asking many questions as to who the visitors were, and why they were involving themselves in the life of this planet.

He received the following response; *'Our presence within your solar system is to observe the evolutionary progress and environmental changes occurring not only to your planet but to its people. Using this observation technique enables us to foresee potential future difficulties which may arise, and if necessary give you advice on the course of action needed to overcome them. To achieve these aims we employ the use of many types of monitoring equipment, each with a responsibility for a different area of scientific investigation.*

'Telemeter discs of all sizes used as remote-controlled sophisticated recording and analysing vehicles, are one of the many types of drones. We observe every aspect of your world and its inhabitants, from the environmental changes and pollution levels to the microbiological disease potential of mankind. Our techniques also enable us to record and analyse thought patterns and therefore anticipate man's course of actions before he embarks on it. There is nothing about your world and its people that we are not aware of.'

In my research, I usually only employ the use of hypnosis to 'fill-in' the blanks in conscious memory, and always avoid Ouija boards, psychics and mediums.

Ken Llewellyn, a retired British RAF Squadron Leader, and Senior Public Relations Officer for the Royal Australian Air Force, published a most interesting book – *'Flight into the Ages'* – before he returned to England in 1991.

He mentioned how he knew several people in high positions who consulted psychics, and he talked about paranormal events which have affected many airmen. He included a most interesting chapter about a 'channelling' communication he had with several aliens during sessions with his medium Monica.

They spoke of some entities being on a different vibrational level, and made a most interesting comment regarding Ken's question on 'transportation': *'Can you not transport sound through a telephone? Can you not, this minute, pick up your telephone, and speak with someone on the other side of the world, in a few seconds?*

'How long would it take you to travel by aeroplane, if you wished to visit that person to whom you are speaking? Consider this, then consider how you could transport not just a voice but a full human the same distance in the same time......It is difficult with your limited knowledge to accept it, but it is so.'

This communication occurred more than thirty years ago. Since then our image can also be instantly transmitted to someone on the other side of the world. In

1989, Ken asked Monica if they could get more information from the guides about UFOs. An entity called 'Tarloc' came through, and his voice was extremely slow and deliberate, unlike any guide who had advised them before.

When asked where spaceships came from, he said; *'From ancients times, ships have traversed time spans. Many dimensions exist that are not physically visible. Those of us, who are, as you term it 'immortal', have learned the secrets of the Universe. We exist in another time-frame. We have a different technology from yours, based on anti-gravity. Some of these secrets are entombed in the pyramids. We are able to project our ships onto your wavelength; we then become visible to you, and return almost instantly from galaxies in a very short time.*

'Our cities are vastly different from yours, and would be difficult for you to comprehend. There are many different kinds of beings on different planets. Some of your more progressive scientists have experimented with what we would term very elementary spacecraft. Often these experimental craft, and other less sophisticated craft, cause damage and trouble. Our spaceships are more sophisticated.'

The complete communications are most interesting and informative, and Ken's book is well worth reading.

Although many may scoff at the thought of the government employing psychics, in 1995 the US Congress investigated the cost of expending tax money on psychics for top secret military projects.

Joe Lewels quoted an *'ABC News'* report which said that the Central Intelligence Agency and Defense Intelligence Agency had spent twenty million dollars, over a twenty-five year period, on psychics who were primarily 'remote viewers'.

They were used for several purposes, including detecting wanted people, enemy submarines and military bases and activities. While some witnesses claimed the program had spectacular successes in many instances, others claimed that only twelve out of five hundred cases produced accurate results.

Although several times the remote viewers described typical 'flying saucers' hovering over nuclear vessels and installations, the conclusion was that no further use of psychics for defence purposes was warranted. It was suggested that 'such experiments were better explored in an academic setting.'

There could be yet another reason for the 'authorities' exploring the benefits of telepathy, perhaps from a technological perspective.

Some witnesses, who claim to have viewed captured alien space craft, said the little pilots lay on the floors of their ships, and controlled them with their minds. Researchers, John and Ann Spencer, were told by one witness, who crept into a downed saucer, that the control panel seemed to be alive, somewhat like a 'biological computer'.

CHAPTER TWELVE

OUT IN SPACE

The possibility of aliens already being in our Solar System or on our Moon is very controversial. In his 1957 book, *'The Flying Saucer Conspiracy'*, Major Donald Keyhoe was convinced that there was an alien base beneath the rocky surface of the Moon. He also thought that there could be one on Mars.

He found a quasi-confirmation when speaking to Paul Redell, an aeronautical engineer. When Keyhoe asked if there was actually a saucer base on the Moon, Redell mentioned the observations and reports of astronomer Dr. H.P.Wilkins, and J. O'Neill, science editor of the *'Herald Tribune'*. Redell suggested that Keyhoe read their articles, and then added; "You won't find *all* the dope....after O'Neill and Wilkins let it out, they were put under pressure to stop talking. But you'll find enough."

On 15th May 1954, the *'New York Herald Tribune'* published an article detailing how, in 1953, astronomer Clyde Tombaugh had confirmed the discovery of two unknown artificial satellites orbiting the Earth. Until then, the government had also kept the information secret.

One cannot blame the aliens if they were concerned about our venturing into space. A couple of senior US military had unsuccessfully proposed 'nuking' the Moon, as part of a scientific project, 'A119'. In the 1950s, the 'boffins' were also designing a craft with nuclear fuel, where their 'Orion Drive' would propel a craft through space with a series of nuclear explosions. Thankfully, this idea was also abandoned in 1964.

In 1959, New Zealand Scientific Space Research Group, who referenced both the British *'Flight'* and American *'Aviation Week'* magazines, reported that on January of that year, a Soviet Lunar rocket, the last of a series of eleven or twelve, was fired towards the Moon. Some of the rockets carried thermonuclear warheads, and none reached their destination. The official reason given was that unexpected strong magnetic fields, prior to third stage cut-off, prevented the rockets from hitting the Moon.

Dr Steven Greer, interviewed retired US Air Force Colonel Ross Dedrickson in September 2000. In his testimony, he confirmed that in the late 70s or early 80s, the Americans had also attempted to put a nuclear weapon on the Moon, and explode it 'for scientific measurements'. He claimed that the extraterrestrials destroyed it before it reached its destination, as they did any nuclear weapon we sent into space.

Officially, the first Soviet Sputnik went into orbit in October 1957, so there was no question as to the non-Earthly origin of satellites before that. However, a tracking station in Venezuela, which was photographing Sputniks 1 and 2, said that one of them was being followed by an unknown object, a claim also made in relation to a 1959 VANGUARD photographic satellite being tracked by Akron Canton.

Not long after, Yuri Gagarin, with his epic flight, was our first real 'astronaut'.

Both the Russians and Americans realised that whoever controlled the space around our planet, had the 'upper-hand' in any future war. The Russian technology was primitive, and any crashes or accidents were kept secret, even from their own people. One such occurrence happened in 1958, when a moon rocket killed leading space scientists on the launching pad.

Russian Dr Medvedev told the *'New Scientist'* magazine that the launching pad was near the Ural town of Blageveshnsk, where nuclear waste had been buried for many years. He said; *"Suddenly there was an enormous explosion, like a violent volcano. The nuclear reactions had led to an overheating in the underground burial grounds.*

"The explosion poured radioactive materials high into the sky. Tens of thousands of people were affected, hundreds dying, though the real figures have never been made public."

The first space casualty was a Russian dog called 'LAIKA', who was sent aloft in Sputnik 2. It was said that then, between the end of 1957 and the beginning of 1959, the USSR made four attempts to place a human in orbit. The Italian News Agency, *'Continentale',* was the first to announce the sad results.

The first was aspirant was Alexel Ledowsky who reached a height of 300 kilometres before his transmission failed, and no more was ever heard from him.

Serenty Schiborin went aloft in February 1958, and his fate is also a mystery. Andreij Mitcow, a leading test pilot, lost his life when twenty minutes into the mission the rocket exploded. Mirija Gromov, the only female, went aloft in a 'space aircraft'. All that is known is that the mission 'ended tragically'.

An unconfirmed report also detailed a Soviet man and woman exploration team, whose rocket was launched on May 17th 1961. It was tracked for a week by stations all over the world, until it mysteriously disappeared on the 24th May.

In 1967 Soviet cosmonaut Vladimir Komarov plunged to a fiery death when Soyuz 1 crashed to earth. In 1971, astronauts Dobrovolski, Volkov and Patsayev suffocated when their Soyuz ferry capsule returned them from the Salyut Space Station. Although not related to his space voyage, Earth's first man to orbit the globe, Yuri Gagarin, died aged 34, in a plane crash in 1968.

The Americans also had their fair share of accidents. In 1961, Virgil Grissom nearly drowned after making a Mercury sub-orbital flight. When he landed in the ocean, the hatch on his capsule blew prematurely, causing it to sink.

On 27th January 1967, astronauts Grisson, Chaffee and White were incinerated when their Apollo 1 capsule caught fire and exploded during tests on Pad 34, at Cape Kennedy. A similar fate befell Soviet cosmonaut Valentin Bondarenko in 1960.

One Apollo Mission was struck by lightning on the launch pad, and another suffered an explosion which demolished its power system, and nearly caused the flight to end in disaster.

Nobody can forget the disastrous Challenger explosion, which killed seven NASA astronauts in January 1986.

By the 1960s, despite the fact that they must have had other accidents of their own, the American technology appeared to be giving the US an advantage in the race to the Moon.

On 4th July 1960, American *'Newsweek'* detailed the eleven US satellites and one Russian object known to still be in orbit. The Air Force Space-Track program, at the National Space Surveillance Control Centre, also noted one US and one Soviet probe circling the Sun, and Pioneer V heading towards Venus.

Many scientists considered that there was one other object, which was neither Russian nor American. Some speculated that the Russians had sent two men up in a capsule, and failed to bring them back. Were they still up there?

In the early 1960s, Western publications were rife with reports of secret Soviet satellites. In 1963 the *'Sunday Telegraph'* published an article by John Delin. It claimed that twelve Russian space efforts had failed, and speculated about the number of possible lost cosmonauts. Russia responded with public denials.

The Royal Aircraft Establishment produced an amazingly accurate *'Table of Artificial Satellites'* which noted a tentative identification of six 'Sputniks' launched between September 1st 1962 and January 7th 1963. They had unknown or uncertain orbital data, however neither the USA nor the Russians admitted to launching these craft. Just who or what was orbiting our planet?

In 1979, Soviet scientist Professor Sergei Bosich and two colleagues made the startling announcement that ten large pieces of metallic space debris had been detected orbiting 2,000 kilometres above the Earth.

This was not a new assertion, as rumours had been circulating, since 1953, of these unidentified objects being discovered. Some researchers claimed that United States radar had detected at least ten objects, all around two to five thousand feet in diameter, and in 1954 *'Aviation Week Magazine'* also wrote about 'two mysterious satellites'. In 1957 Italian astronomers reported a huge mystery satellite three months before the launching of Sputnik-1, the first ever satellite of our own, which was a Russian achievement.

Boshich claimed that some pieces measured as much as seventy metres by thirty-five metres, and they were the result of one large body breaking up in orbit on 18th December 1955. The general consensus was that these objects were not in a 'natural' orbit, and must have been 'man-made'. The problem was that, at the time, no country had technology advanced enough to manufacture or launch them. Further, we did not have the capability to conduct a close-up investigation.

The Russians were not alone in their belief that unidentified objects were circling high above our Earth in the late fifties. In January 1960, the US Navy had tracked an unknown object, weighing about fifteen tons, in a near Polar orbit, and dubbed it the 'Black Knight', noting that it did not emit any kind of radio signals.

At first the Americans, who considered it to be 'man-made', thought the object may be of Russian origin. This was soon disputed by Russian Professor Alla Masevich, who was responsible for the USSR Sputnik tracking stations. She 'very much doubted' that the mystery object was a Russian satellite or any remains of a payload launch rocket. At that time, all Russian satellites were launched into orbits of 65 degrees to the equator, taking them well clear of the Poles.

Later, it was discovered it had a 'twin', approximately the same size, and also in Polar orbit. While the Americans were persistent in their belief that the mysterious objects were Russian, nobody mentioned that the safest place, at that time, for an alien intelligence to monitor Earth would be from over our Polar Regions.

In the following decades, several countries have launched numerous known and secret satellites, as well as Space Stations and ventures beyond our planet. Most are highly classified with military significance, and the true nature of the 'Black Knight' or the objects discovered by Boshich may never be known. Both the Russians and Americans have remained silent on the matter.

Many of the early satellites went 'missing', including the Soviet 'Molniya' satellite. Of the thirty-four US 'Explorer' satellites, not all could be considered a success. Five simply 'vanished' from our tracking systems, two failed to achieve orbit, and one, which was sent to the Moon, missed its target due to a velocity error. In 1965, a Soviet communications satellite also 'disappeared'.

Other satellites and probes, including 'ANNA', 'TELSTAR's 1 and 2, 'MARINER' 2, and 'RANGER'3, inexplicably stopped transmitting, only to mysteriously start working again. In 1968, an Australian ground station turned off the transmitter on the American scientific satellite, 'PEGASUS'. Nine years later, in August 1977, it mysteriously resumed sending radio signals.

Years later, the much feted 'Mars Observer' inexplicably became 'deaf-mute', and all attempts to restore communications were futile. Experts were unsure as to where it was. Some sceptics claimed that it was engineered to prevent any discovery of alleged artificial artefacts on the planet's surface.

NASA launched a satellite for RCA, which was designed to relay telephone and television transmissions. It was working perfectly, when it suddenly vanished.

Neither NASA, NORAD, nor the North American Defense Command, all of whom had excellent tracking equipment, could locate the satellite or explain its disappearance.

In November 1964, the US launched Mariner 4, destined for Mars, where it was to take photographs and transmit them back to Earth. In July 1965, it reached its destination, and took 24 pictures. Once it passed behind the planet, it mysteriously took over twelve minutes longer than anticipated to reappear, when it commenced sending the photographs back to the Australian Tidbinbilla tracking station. There were other bothersome signals – termed 'anomalies' – interfering with the transmission, and at the same time a glowing, oval-shaped UFO was reported, by many witnesses, to be hovering only a few miles away, between the tracking station and Canberra Airport.

Paul Dodd, of the Meteorological Bureau, said it appeared to be a steel revolving disc, and Air Traffic Controller, Tony Frodsham, agreed that it was a metallic object, glinting in the sunlight. Scientists at the neighbouring Mount Stromlo Observatory could not identify it, and the instruments at the nearby Goldstone tracking centre were recording strange irregularities in the messages from Mariner.

As long as it was there, the tracking station was plagued by anomalous signals. An Air Force jet was scrambled, but the pilot reported that as he neared the object, 'it flipped up' and left him, vanishing at a great altitude. At the same time, the anomalous signals ceased to interfere with Tidbinbilla's reception.

Reports from Russian astronauts are rare. On 12th October 1964, Voskhod 1 brought its three cosmonauts back to Earth in Central Asia after only twenty-four hours and sixteen Earth orbits. Since Soviet officials had been predicting a 'long flight', there was speculation as to the reason for the early landing.

Some suggested that there had been a defect in the craft's radio transmitter, and others noted a rise in the cabin's temperature, indicating a faulty orbit, too close to the Earth's atmosphere.

The next day the astronauts commented that they regretted being brought down so soon as they "had seen many interesting things, and wanted to investigate them more fully."

Investigator, Major Donald Keyhoe later wrote; *"In Moscow there are, in fact, persistent rumours that the last manned satellite was repeatedly overtaken by extremely fast flying discs which struck the craft violent, shattering blows with their powerful magnetic fields."*

At a later press conference, a Western journalist asked the Voskhod 1 Commander if they had encountered any UFOs during orbit. He and the other two crew members immediately got up and left the room, and the meeting was abruptly terminated.

On 18th March 1965, Pavel Beljajev and Alexei Leonov, the crew of Voskhod 2 reported two strange cylinders which they could see in space. They were perfectly formed and had no apertures, and it was assumed that they were 'man-made satellites.' Leonov also became the first man to 'walk' in space, when for ten minutes he 'stood' in space, with a thick cable linking him to the cabin.

They were given instructions to land as they completed their seventeenth revolution, but they made an unexpected eighteenth, and descended manually to an equally unexpected spot in the Urals. It was nearly nine hundred miles away from the designated landing place in Kazakhstan.

Newspaper reports claimed that the craft had come down in flames, and its radio antennae were burned off. The astronauts had apparently lost contact with their mission control for several hours before their crash landing in the snow.

On 27th March, at a press conference they said that their solar orientation system had failed, causing them to make an additional orbit and overshoot the nominated landing area. They also mentioned an 'unmanned mystery satellite' they had sighted only a few orbits before they landed.

Moscow suggested that this object may have been of American origin, designed to monitor Voskhod, something which was strenuously denied by the USA.

One contemporary Western researcher commented; *"It sounds far more as though this were another UFO. And the big question is, did they come down in a hurry to get away from it, or did it 'assist' them to come down, and by driving them out of orbit down on to the edge of the Earth's atmosphere, and give them both a very narrow escape from death?"*

Over the years, the Russians also sent probes into the Solar System, including a series of at least ten to Venus. Some were successful, however on the 30th July

1967, Venus 4 unfortunately landed on top of a 24 kms high mountain. They developed and launched several space stations, including Cosmos-557, and seven of the Salyut series between 1971 and 1982.

In 1973, on April 3rd, the Russians launched their space-lab Salyut 2. It was planned to house three cosmonauts, who would be conducting tests for nearly a month. German space expert, Harro Zimmer, head of the Wilhelm Foerster Observatory in West Berlin, reported that, in between Salyut's 22nd and 24th orbits, it was joined by eighteen unidentified objects, which accompanied it along the way. On April 14th, it was badly damaged by an unexplained accident, and began to disintegrate. The cosmonauts were never sent aloft to board their space station, and the Russians never gave any explanation.

US astronauts rarely made comments, however Gordon Cooper and Edgar Mitchell both stated that UFOs, alien visitations and technology are a very real occurrence. Gordon Cooper, who flew the Mercury 9 Mission, and was the commander of the eight-day Gemini 5 Mission, only admitted to a 1951 sighting when piloting a plane over Germany. He saw a group of 'double lenticular –shaped' objects, flying in formation, higher and faster than any plane of the day.

It was thought that Cooper, being one of the most experienced astronauts, would have been chosen for an Apollo Mission, however Maurice Chatelain, in his book, *'Our Ancestors Came From Outer Space,'* suggested that Cooper had already seen too much, and his nature was such that he would want to talk about it.

When the United Nations held a debate on UFOs Cooper wrote to them and stated the following; *'I believe UFOs exist and that the truly unexplainable ones and are from some other technically advanced civilization...I believe that these extraterrestrial vehicles and their crews are visiting this planet from other planets, which are obviously a little more advanced than we are here on Earth......I feel that we need to have a top-level, co-ordinated program to scientifically collect and analyse data, from all over the Earth, concerning any type of encounter, and to determine how best to interface with these visitors in a friendly fashion.'*

In so far as the sightings by astronauts are concerned, I have an interesting 1976 letter, sent by arch-sceptic James Oberg to New Zealand's Fred and Phyllis Dickeson. He reminded them of his access to NASA's files, and engaged in his usual dismissal of all reports. He then noted; *'Have you heard of the Apollo12 'moon pigeons? Have you seen the Skylab-2 photo of the thousand foot UFO solid object (NOT a light in the Dark). How about the recently released X-15 photos from fifteen years ago?...I'm sorry your summary didn't include Gemini-4 and Gemini-11, two of the strongest astronaut UFO cases on record.'*

Apollo 14 astronaut Edgar Mitchell, who became quite spiritual after his Moon landing, did not testify as to any sightings, but made this cryptic comment to Richard Thieme; "If we could do what they can do, they wouldn't have sent me to the Moon in a 'tin-lizzie'."

In October 1998, when addressing the 'UFO Experience Conference' in North Haven, he called on Congress to grant immunity to officials who have taken an oath of secrecy so they can acknowledge the existence of UFOs and aliens.

He was ninety percent sure that many of the UFOs observed over the years belonged to aliens, and added; "...this suggests that there are humanoids manning craft which have characteristics not in the arsenal of any nation on Earth."

That same year, in an interview with Steven Greer he said; *"Yes, there have been UFO visitations. There have been crashed craft. There have been material and bodies recovered. And there is some group of people somewhere that may or may not be associated with Government at this point, but certainly were at one time, that have this knowledge. They have been attempting to conceal this knowledge or nor permit it to be widely disseminated."*

The authorities were quick to explain away nearly all reports made by American astronauts. Scott Carpenter, piloting Mercury VII, is reported as having confirmed that while in orbit on 24th May 1962, he photographed a UFO, which authorities later claimed was a 'tracking balloon'. Carpenter said; "At no time when the astronauts were in space were they alone. There was constant surveillance by UFOs."

A few days later, on May 30th, it was reported that Joe Walton, an X15 pilot, claimed to have photographed five disc-like objects. Authorities dismissed this as being fraudulent, as the real pilot's name was Joe Walker, who refuted the statement.

On July 17th, another X15 pilot, Robert White, also photographed objects that were about thirty feet away from his craft, which was at an altitude of about fifty-eight miles. These were dismissed by NASA as being 'flakes of ice'.

On October 3rd 1963, Mecury VIII's pilot reported large, glowing lights over the Indian Ocean. 'Lightning lit clouds!' said the authorities.

On 3rd June 1965, James McDivitt and Ed White, in Gemini 4, lifted off from Cape Kennedy on a sixty-two orbit, four day mission. At 3am the next day, during its 20th orbit, McDivitt saw a cylinder with an arm-like protuberance, which at first flew above, and then below them. He took a photograph and motion pictures. NORAD explained it all away as being the Pegasus satellite, which was in fact twelve hundred miles away at the time.

Later that year, on December 4th, the Gemini-Titan VII lifted off, and astronaut Frank Borman reported a 'bogey at 10 o'clock high' flying in formation with their space craft. When questioned by Houston Flight Control Centre, he confirmed that it was not the GT-VII booster rocket, which he could also see at the same time.

At a later press conference, no description of the UFO was released, nor were the photos taken by Borman and Lovell mentioned. An official explanation, given by the authorities, was that the photos were 'fakes', and someone had 'airbrushed' away any vehicular structures around the objects.

On September 12th 1966, Charles Conrad and Richard Gordon were orbiting the Earth in Gemini-Titan XI. Conrad reported observing a large unidentified object, and both astronauts took pictures. NORAD identified it as the Russian Proton III satellite, but NICAP later calculated that this object was twenty times the size of Proton III.

In 1968 and 1969, astronauts on Apollo missions 8, 11 and 12 all allegedly reported unidentified objects.

Apollo 8 – the initial mission, was to fly around the Moon, without attempting to land. NASA had arranged this trip to occur at Christmas 1968, with astronauts Borman, Lovell and Anders to send a Christmas message back to Earth, however they were not told what to say, as long as it was 'appropriate'. Once the manoeuvre was successfully completed, Commander Lovell announced; "Please be informed, there is a Santa Claus!" NASA claimed it was never meant to refer to anything alien or extraterrestrial.

After completing their mission and taking many colour photos, they made a final orbit of the Moon. They had to 'burn' the engines to propel them out of orbit, and head for home. Any mistake would render them stranded, and there would be insufficient oxygen to last until any rescue attempt could reach them.

In May 1969, Apollo 10, with astronauts Stafford, Young and Cernan, also flew to the Moon. It was designed to test the Lunar Module, close to the surface, without actually landing. Stafford reported hearing strange 'whistling' and modulated sounds, for which no definitive explanation has ever been given. During their trip, they also experienced some guidance system malfunctions.

Did the astronauts Armstrong, Aldrin and Collins on Apollo 11 see UFOs on the Moon? This is still a contentious issue.

Despite conspiracy theorists saying we never went there, I personally believe that, from 1969, we did make several successful Apollo missions to the Moon. In those days I was a very junior employee working with government engineers who were assisting NASA with the project.

Further, Armstrong and Aldrin had deployed an Early Apollo Scientific Experiment Package on the Moon's surface. It was designed to transmit, back to Earth, data on temperature and seismic activity, which it did for about a month.

(Already there were signs of comradeship among astronauts, no matter what their nationality. Before Apollo II departed from the Moon, they left, on the surface, the medals of Yuri Gagarin and Vladimir Komarov, two dead Russian astronauts, and the insignia of Virgil Grissom, Roger Chaffee and Edward White, the three American astronauts who perished in a fire in an Apollo spacecraft during training on the ground.)

At the time, a copy of the original magnetic data tapes, from the Scientific Experiment Package, were sent to the Australian designer, physicist Brian

O'Brien, who left them in the care of a colleague at West Australian Curtain University. In 2006, after discovering that, in the 1980s, NASA admitted 'mislaying' the original video tapes of the historic Moon landing, O'Brien went in search of the data tapes. They had also apparently gone 'missing', but there was nothing suspicious about it this time. After being safely stored for 25 years, they were moved due to a change in premises. A thorough search finally located the boxes – some under the students' lecture room seats, and others under some outdated electronic equipment.

They were still in good condition, and O'Brien was happy, because he considered that they were further proof that we really had landed on the Moon.

Pilot-Cosmonaut Leonov has also confirmed that Soviet radars monitored everything, and were able to observe the Americans, with Leonov and his colleagues 'rooting for them.' Obviously they also monitored all the original, unedited transmissions which came from the Moon during that time, including the mention of UFOs.

The *'National Enquirer UFO Report'* quotes Soviet Dr. Valdamir Azhazha, in a telephone interview, as saying; *'According to our information, the encounter was reported immediately after the landing of the module. Neil Armstrong relayed the message to Mission Control that two large, mysterious objects were watching them after having landed near the moon module. But his message was never heard by the public – because NASA censored it."*

Another Soviet scientist, Dr. Sergei Boshich said; *"It's my opinion that other civilizations learned of the proposed moon landing...and two spaceships probably were dispatched so there would be back-up in an emergency. Undoubtedly, their objective was to learn the extent of Earth's technological know-how. Having verified the landing, they departed without making contact."*

On November 24th 1977, the Novosty Press Agency was present when Vlagyimir Georgijevic, Assistant Head of the Oceanographic Department of the USSR National Academy of Sciences, gave a lecture regarding UFOs.

He said; *"The report of the American astronauts, (Armstrong, Collins, Aldrin), who landed on the Moon is extremely interesting. The Apollo11 crew noticed two UFOs shortly after their take-off, but considered this to be a part of the Saturn 5's stage rocket. But the object escorted them, then advanced on their craft. The size of the ship was about 1.5 km.*

"When Armstrong/Aldrin's landing manoeuvre was completed on the Moon, they observed a few saucer-like UFOs on the opposite side of the crater. Armstrong cries; "Damn, they are already here!"

"According to the orders of the Control Centre in Houston, the UFO's code name was 'Santa Claus', but Armstrong and the crew were so shocked at the sight, that without coding it, reported; 'straight ahead, on the opposite side of the crater, spacecraft of cosmic origin are pacing and watching us."

"Houston ordered them to stay in the Lunar Module. Five hours later, when convinced that the UFOs had no hostile intentions, they were permitted to step on the Moon. Aldrin filmed the UFOs, and the movie became Top Secret. This communication was released much later, and I hope the film will eventually be shown.

"The astronauts left a box on the Moon, which contained the Declaration of the United Nations in 72 languages, related to outer space and the celestial bodies. But, this action to contact extraterrestrial civilisations had no result at all. It was kept Top Secret for a long time, but the manufacturer of the box blundered out the secret.

"The encounter on the Moon with the UFOs bewildered the astronauts. Aldrin has had a nervous breakdown, and as of today, his health hasn't been totally restored. Collins has become a virtual monk.

"The Moon seems to be a permanent base of the UFOs, and all the Apollo crews to the Moon were under UFO examination. Also, the Apollo 10's American astronauts' scientific explosion on the Moon failed. Namely, they tried to induce a moon quake, but couldn't trigger it."

Timothy Good claimed that a university professor reported a conversation he supposedly had with Neil Armstrong during a NASA Symposium. Armstrong had said that they were warned off by the aliens, so there was never any question then of a permanent Moon space station. Their ships were big and menacing, and far superior to ours in both size and technology.

Armstrong has never confirmed this conversation, however in 1979, Maurice Chatelain, the former head of NASA Communications Systems, confirmed in an interview that Neil Armstrong had reported seeing two UFOs on the rim of a lunar crater.

Allen Hynek, in his book *'The Edge of Reality'*, also commented about this; *'The astronauts? Some of the NASA movie frames that I examined were most interesting – particularly those taken on the Apollo II flight, one of the few for which NASA has come up with some sort of explanation. And several astronauts have stated that they definitely saw things in space which they could not identify. Thus - it satisfies the definition of UFO! Unidentified!'*

It must be remembered that the television film footage from Apollo 11 and 12 were not 'live', and came 'second-hand' from NASA, who claimed the original was of poor quality, which had to be 'improved' by an 'optical system'.

(At the same time Apollo 11 was heading towards the Moon, Russia's unmanned Luna 15 was also in orbit, apparently in an effort to collect samples of lunar soil and rock and return to Earth before the US mission. It was tracked by Jodrell Bank Observatory, who noted it crashed on the surface shortly before the Americans arrived.)

In November 1969, Conrad, Bean and Gordon made a successful landing in Apollo 12. In 1999, the British 'Contact International UFO Research' organisation published an alleged transcript of a conversation between the astronauts and Houston.

They claimed they were being followed, through space, by two shiny spinning objects, one in front, and one behind their craft. After seven hours, Houston came back with a couple of lame, possible explanations. Basically, nobody could identify what the objects were.

The astronauts could also hear strange noises, like static or a whistling sound in the background, both in the craft and on the lunar surface. On their way back to Earth, they saw a sharp, bright light, which has also never been identified.

Apollo 13, although it orbited and took photographs, was unable to land due to an explosion in one of the oxygen tanks. Lovell, Swigert and Haise luckily returned safely to Earth.

In February 1971, Apollo 14, carrying Shepherd, Mitchell and Rossa had a successful mission, as did Scott, Irwin and Worden on Apollo 15 in August 1971. In his book *'Cosmic Top Secret'* Jon King quotes NASA's former data and photographic documentation supervisor, Ken Johnston, who claimed his superiors erased film footage taken by the Apollo 14 astronauts. It showed structures of unnatural origin on the Moon, and also five or six lights in a crater on the far side.

Apollo 16, with astronauts Young, Duke and Mattingly, landed in April 1972, with some more experiments being conducted on the Moon's surface. Young and Duke spent seven hours exploring the 'highlands' in their electric 'Moon Buggy', and planted the fifth American flag on the surface.

Apollo 17 followed soon after, in December 1972. This was, unexpectedly, the last landing mission. Schmitt, the only scientist/astronaut to walk on the Moon, was a geologist who conducted a survey of the minerals there, and before leaving set some explosives to test the Lunar crust. Cernan, Schmitt and Evans set-up a sixth measuring station, and were also engaged in intensive lunar back-side photography, with the King Crater area of specific interest.

Suddenly, despite three more craft having been built and ready to go, and an increase in Mars Probes, there were no more astronauts officially sent to the Moon.

In 2003, the late Stanton Friedman made this interesting observation; *"A question for which I have never had a satisfactory answer is why the USA didn't launch Apollo 18 and 19? The hardware was all built. The crews had been selected and trained. President Nixon said it was to save money. But almost all of the bills had already been paid. Yes, I am aware that some have suggested that the aliens secretly told us to stay off their moon......At best an idea in my grey basket.*

"So the big question is, do we Earthlings want to take dominion over the Solar System, or do we wish to continue to be a primitive society whose major activity is tribal warfare? I am certain that the lost astronauts had greater vision than that."

Were there further secret Apollo missions to the Moon? According to William Rutledge, who claimed, in 2007, that in 1976, he worked at NASA on the two failed missions, Apollo 19 and 20, which were launched from Vandenberg Air Force Base. They were classified joint operations, between the US and Soviet governments, to further investigate a large object which had been photographed by Apollo 15 on the far side of the Moon.

This report cannot be verified, but if Stanton Friedman was correct, we already had the craft built and ready to go. Further, investigator Richard Boylan said that the late USAF Colonel Steve Wilson told him military astronauts trained at a separate secret aerospace academy, and operated out of the Vandenberg Air Force Base, in Northern California. This information begs another question. Was there an Apollo 18, and if so did it also go to the Moon?

In Aldrin's book 'Return to Earth' he mentions a strange occurrence at a 'pin party' held later for the astronauts from Apollo 10 and 11 who had landed on the Moon.

'The highlight of the evening was a film showing Fred Haise...stumbling around on the surface of the Moon until, in desperation, he retreated to the lunar ladder which, the moment he stepped on the ladder, tumbled into pieces around him.'

Wait a minute! Officially, Haise was only on Apollo 13, which never landed! So, when was this film taken? Could there have been an Apollo 18?

Also, if even one of the reported UFO/alien encounters is correct, it lends credence to another statement made by Dr. Richard Boylan in 1998. He said; *"The reality is that in the 60's, a space station was sent up and manned by US and USSR personnel, and has been operating ever since. Among its tasks is keeping tabs on incoming extraterrestrial traffic, and outgoing, and other matters."*

Dr. Clifford Wilson wrote about a 1969 report in the Calgary, Alberta *'Herald'*, which stated that Dr. G. Henderson, the Senior Space Research Scientist with the General Dynamics Corporation at Fort Worth, Texas, had said that American astronauts had not only sighted UFOs, but also taken photographs. He claimed that the astronauts had been instructed to say nothing about the sightings, and their photographs had been locked up.

My colleague Rosemary Decker said an astronaut once admitted to her that he was not allowed to answer certain questions on what he saw and learned on the Moon. Despite reports of intercepted transmissions, or comments made by astronauts, when openly questioned, everything is denied.

What happened to out astronauts after their voyage to the Moon? They are the only humans who have officially gone there, and their experiences were many and varied.

Neil Armstrong, who became a little reclusive, did not seek publicity, and left NASA in 1971 to become a professor in aeronautical engineering at the University of Cincinnati. Buzz Aldrin found the attention too much to cope with, and also left NASA in 1971, returning to the Air Force as a commander of future astronauts. He still suffered psychological problems and sought professional help in 1975. He wrote two books, and eventually became the chairman of the National Association for Mental Health.

Pete Conrad, who was known for his sense of humour, coped well. He extended his contract with NASA, and in 1973 flew into space for the fourth time as commander of the first manned Skylab mission. He once said; "Nobody seems to remember what Skylab was. I do. For me it was the most beautiful thing in the space program. The moon was a great adventure, but that was it."

Alan Bean, from Apollo 12, flew Skylab 3, and then left NASA to pursue his favourite pastime – painting. Al Shepard, who commanded Apollo 14, and is remembered for hitting two golf balls into infinity, left NASA in 1974, to concentrate on his already thriving financial business.

Ed Mitchell, although a scientist who spent twenty years helping the US conquer space, was very spiritual, and actually conducted private telepathy experiments whilst on Apollo 14. He left NASA in 1972, wrote three books, and founded the 'Institute of Noetic Sciences' in Palo Alto, California.

Apollo 15's Dave Scott resigned in 1975, and founded his own company, 'Scott Science and Technology'. Jim Irwin was a committed Christian, who admitted to praying to God for guidance, rather than contacting Houston, if any problems occurred during their Moon mission. After leaving NASA, his later evangelical preaching proved too onerous, and he suffered two heart attacks requiring surgery. After recovering, he wrote his autobiography, and continued his religious pursuits.

John Young, commander of Apollo 16, and the ninth American to set foot on the Moon, was once asked if UFOs exist: "If you bet against it," he said, "you'd be betting against an almost sure thing..." He was also present on Gemini 3, Gemini 10 and Apollo 10. He considered going to the Moon – 'just a job' - and after being in charge of eighty astronauts, commanded two more shuttle missions before retiring.

Charlie Duke said his trip to the Moon led to the beginning of a deep religious conviction. He left NASA in 1975, and after some difficult times, psychologically, travelled around the world giving lectures on the need for peace. Jack Schmitt, the only astronaut who was essentially a scientist, and not a pilot, later became a politician, and then a lecturer.

In 1973, Apollo 17 Commander Eugene Cernan, was the eleventh man to set foot on the Moon, and had also been on the Apollo 10 dress rehearsal for Apollo 11. He left NASA in 1976, and founded his own firm, the 'Cernan Corporation'. He was quoted in an article published by the *Los Angeles Times*, as saying; "I've been asked about UFOs, and I've said publicly I thought they were somebody else, some other civilisation."

While their Russian contemporaries were usually silent on the matter, before his death, cosmonaut Yuri Gagarin was also reported as saying; "During my space flights, I saw something that is far beyond any fantasy. If I am ever permitted to tell this publically, I am sure that the world will be in shock."

In the intervening years we have launched many more satellites, several permanent space stations, and probes throughout and beyond the Solar System.

In 1979 Victor Afanasyev noted being followed by a UFO while on route to the space station Salyut 6. "It had an engineered structure, metallic, about forty metres long with inner hulls, and it followed us during half our orbit." Given our own technological advances by that time, it cannot be automatically assumed that the craft was of extraterrestrial origin, but it is unlikely due to its size.

In 1992, *'Rabochaya Tribuna'* and *'Soviet Youth'* contained an interview journalist Leonid Lazarevich had by radio with cosmonauts Manakov and Strekalov aboard the Space Station Mir.

They said that, during their stay, they had seen a huge, iridescent silvery sphere hovering about twenty-to-thirty kilometres over the Earth. The sky was absolutely clear, and there was no doubt as to what they had seen.

Later, Alexi Limov interviewed two Russian cosmonauts, who, for their own safety, preferred to remain anonymous. They said that whilst aboard Mir, they saw unidentified craft on several occasions. At a later date, cosmonaut Alexandr Baledrin verified some of these claims.

Several times, whilst they were setting up experiments to measure solar radiation winds, a craft would come very close, affecting both the probes they had deployed and the instruments in the station. Once they aimed a powerful torch at the intruder, only to receive identical flashes back in return.

They also saw other 'comings and goings', including some 'formations' which were definitely under intelligent control. They performed astonishing aerobatics, sometimes in tight formation. On one occasion, they seemed to disappear into a huge black cylinder, only to reappear five minutes later.

Antonio Huneeus wrote about another incident which apparently occurred on the space station 'Mir'.

'While there are numerous sightings of, and statements regarding UFOs by cosmonauts, practically no footage has been released by the Russian space program. The one significant exception was filmed on March 31st 1991, by cosmonaut Musa Manarov. He was able to capture a remarkably clear cigar-shaped UFO for more than two minutes while filming the approach of a Progress cargo flight to the Mir space station.

'The video clearly shows how one end of the cylinder-shaped object lit up. This is undoubtedly one of the best known examples of UFO footage ever taken in space because it shows an unknown, and rather large structured, object in space, and not just mere white dots near the spacecraft, as is the case with a lot of NASA footage taken from space shuttles in the last several years. While we don't know for sure what it is, the object certainly looks artificial and not like some kind of unexplained natural phenomenon.'

In my opinion, the problem is that by 1991, several countries could have secret spy satellites and vehicles also orbiting the Earth.

Sometimes, there have been extraordinary claims occasionally coming from the Soviet Union. In January 2000, several newspapers published statements made by astrophysicist Boris Rodionov, where he claimed that; "...a highly developed extraterrestrial civilisation existed on one of the satellites, (Europa), of the planet Jupiter."

The Russians said that the Americans had also encountered similar phenomena, and even requested that one of their astronauts, who belonged to a security service, be placed onboard to gauge the amount of harassment they could expect on the new joint adventure space station.

Considering that there was a 'space race' occurring at the time, I have often wondered why the Russians, who certainly had the technical expertise, didn't follow up their initial Sputnik program with their own planned Moon landing expedition?

In those days, speculation was also circulating about who or what may be on our Moon. While attending a meeting, over forty-five years ago, a young teenage girl approached me during a supper break. She showed me a letter she had received from her uncle, who was in the USA, working for NASA. He said they were all very excited as they had received photographs from the far side of the moon showing the remains of massive, unnatural structures rising miles into the sky. I checked all kinds of clues on the correspondence, handwriting, stamp, postage marks, and stationery. It all seemed genuine, and certainly confirmed later reports.

In 1965, Airman Karl Wolfe worked for the Director of Intelligence at Langley Base, Virginia. There was a NASA installation on the base, but he did not possess the security clearance required to enter it. One day, when NASA's own technician was not available, he was called over to fix a problem with some malfunctioning equipment.

He saw, to his surprise, that there were several international scientists working in the facility, and noticed many photographs which had been downloaded from a lunar orbiter. He was told that they were working on a reconnaissance project to determine the best landing spot on the Moon for the forthcoming Apollo missions.

Karl asked why there was so much security, and was told that they had discovered a 'base' on the dark side of the Moon. It was then that he spotted the massive artificial structures, some with circular antennae, clearly depicted on the enlarged pictures. He later commented that they were all different shapes, some tall and thin, and others spherical and domed. They didn't compare with anything we have on Earth.

This was four years before our astronauts first landed on the Moon, and being too scared to ask any questions, he never found out if this 'base' was alien or our own.

The Russians would also have been aware of the anomalies. Years before their Lunik 3 had upgraded technology which enabled it to take forty minutes of photographs of the far side of the Moon. At that time astronomer Boris Kukarkin announced many more rockets would be sent to photograph the Moon and nearby planets. However, to date, no known manned missions have been deployed there.

There have been some Russian successes and some failures. Luna 21 landed on the Moon in 1973, and released the Lunokhod 'moon-buggy' which travelled across the surface for more than four months, sending information back to Earth. In 1974 Luna 22 orbited the Moon, relaying information back to the Soviet Union. Later that year Luna 23 crash landed on the surface, damaging much of the equipment, however in 1976 Luna 24 made a successful landing.

In 1971, cosmonauts Georgi Dobrovolsky, Vladislav Volkov and Viktor Patsayev were found dead in their landed re-entry capsule after they had undocked from a 24 day mission in Soyuz II, one of the world's first orbital laboratories.

NASA had also spent many years surveying the Moon, partly to discover who or what may be up there, and partly to designate the most suitable landing spots for future missions.

One of their projects, 'Operation Moon Blink', included a *'Chronological Catalogue of Reported Lunar Events',* which listed the locations of mysterious lights and clouds observed by astronomers for more than a century. Later unmanned space probes were launched, and five Lunar Orbiters successfully photographed virtually all of the Moon's surface. The authorities were fully prepared to ensure that the public only ever got to see photographs of a bleak and desolate rocky outpost.

Richard Dolan wrote about remote viewer Ingo Swann who, in 1975, was taken to a secret U.S. base, and spent about a week remote viewing certain co-ordinates on the Moon. He was startled to see structures, buildings and people.

Dolan also commented that in later years, Russell Targ, a scientist involved with the government's remote viewing program in the early to mid-1980s, confirmed that he had been tasked to train remote viewers to concentrate on the far side of the Moon, especially to look for extraterrestrials.

THE MISSING MOON SLIDES

Before my dear friend, Australian researcher Paul Norman (USA) passed away, he sent me copies of some amazing correspondence, dated 1971, between NSW researcher Bill Moser (deceased) and a colleague in the USA.

It related to three sets of slides showing some unexplained items on the Moon:

SLIDE Z 6/78 FW: *Taken by Apollo 10 crew, showing crater I.A.U. No.302. A very bright blue object – height estimated at over 20 feet – showing clear against background and looks a bit thicker on top.'*

SLIDE Z 20/96 MD: *Taken by Apollo 11 crew, showing South-West part of Mare Tranquillitatis with crater Maskelyne. Again a bluish looking globule was noticed, shaped like an orb.'*

Moser had shown the slides to an Australian radio-astronomer, a Government astronomer and a Deputy Director of the CSIRO, and all had considered *'a proper research investigation could be done much easier in the United States than anywhere else.'*

He requested a US colleague forward the slides to Professors Hynek and McDonald, noting he could make more copies available for any other scientists, as required.

In 1995 Paul Norman wrote to Bill Moser's colleague in the States – who subsequently contacted seven different investigators in America trying to locate these slides and the final appraisal by the two professors. He replied to Paul in rather mysterious terms, asking how Moser had come by the slides – who had initiated his request to on-forward them to Hynek and McDonald, and why hadn't he sent them direct? He also wanted to know the involvement of the Australian scientists and went on to say he had enjoyed meeting and talking to Dr. Lindtner and *'his death was a most unfortunate thing.'* (Dr. Lindtner had been pushed under a train in Europe. Was this a hidden warning?)

Paul Norman wrote to me later in 1995, and asked me to follow-up the slides and publicise it at a later date, (after he, Paul, had 'passed-on'.) I wondered if Paul was scared, due to the reference to Dr. Lindtner's 'accident'. Paul was a little non-committal, but said that given the circumstances there was the distinct possibility this may have been considered a 'sensitive' matter. I did not pursue the missing slides, as obviously someone 'on-high', did not want them released or scrutinised.

Why, in all the following decades have astronauts not officially gone back to the Moon? It has always been of utmost priority to the USA, Russia and probably China today, to not only to establish a manned, habitable Lunar Outpost, but also to mount a manned expedition to Mars. Some whistle-blowers claim that 'photos of UFOs on the edge of a crater' were genuine, and that aliens already there had warned us off.

According to some journalists, NASA has proffered several plausible, but questionable, explanations for the cessation of manned journeys beyond our own planet.

1. They were suddenly concerned about the biological effects of space radiation on astronauts.
2. There were problems with the 'take–off' of craft returning from the Moon and Mars – (despite several successful Apollo missions and the fact that both have a lower gravity than Earth).

3. There were multiple technical risks, including vibrations on the craft structure and the inability to recreate the material used for the Apollo Thermal Protection System, which provided a heat shield for craft re-entering our atmosphere at hypersonic speed.

(One must wonder why we cannot recreate something utilised fifty years ago? Also, if our probes travelled to the Moon and Mars and reduced speed to land or orbit, why could our craft not adopt the same procedure when returning to Earth?)

While there could be some truth in the conspiracy theories, it could be something so simple as the more recent realisation that solar flares are far more dangerous and unpredictable than previously thought. If the enormous cost of venturing into space is a factor, then perhaps George Adamski had a point when he noted that our economy is based upon spending enormous amounts of money on wars and armaments; money which could be better used for space exploration.

In 1998, *'The Times'* published an article detailing the statements of Father Balducci from the Vatican. He expressed his beliefs that although extraterrestrials probably existed, and would be superior to us, that would not negate the teachings of Christ.

The Vatican astronomer, Dr. Christopher Corbally, had already been outspoken in 1997, when he urged mankind to become an integral part of a cosmic community, and told a science meeting in Seattle; *"We have always believed that God created all things. If he created life elsewhere, then fair enough."*

In 2001, it was reported that Italian astronaut, Umberto Guidoni, on board the space shuttle, 'Endeavour', wanted to read a message from the Pope. Just as the space shuttle was deployed alongside the International Space Station, to install a new cradle arm, Guidoni was forbidden to read the message, which would have been transmitted on a 'live' TV link. NASA later said that the message may have 'offended non-Catholic astronauts'.

While there have been several NASA task forces to plan our return more permanently to the Moon, I have a feeling they are prevaricating. In September 2005, the *'Sydney Morning Herald'* featured an interview with Michael Griffin, the space agency's administrator, who detailed a plan which would get them to the Moon by 2018, serve as a stepping stone to Mars and beyond, and stay within NASA's existing budget. It would be similar to the Apollo program, but bigger and safer.

In the intervening years our space missions have been unmanned ventures to the Moon and Mars, with robotic technology. Closer to home our manned programs have all been contained to a low earth orbit, and it is only logical to assume some of these projects would contain an element of space control and defence.

At the end of 2001, Mars Odyssey set off for the 'Red Planet', only one of the unmanned probes we have been sending to Mars. Some have been successful, and some have mysteriously failed or disappeared.

Our jointly operated manned Space Station orbits the planet, and as of 2019, the European Union and nine other countries can independently launch spacecraft. Although in 1967 over one hundred nations, including the United States, signed the 'Outer Space Treaty', forbidding the militarisation of space, Russian, US, and possibly Chinese plans to create a 'Space Force' means this consensus is unlikely to continue.

The actual purpose of a 'Space Force' is debatable. Is it for defence against earthly or alien enemies? Perhaps both! In the 1960s and 1970s, many American and Russian satellites went missing. Others experienced interference with their electronic control systems. Russian probes to Venus and Mars mysteriously vanished, as did the US Explorer III and Syncom I. The strange behaviour and disappearances of our probes and satellites continued, and despite reports of UFO activity above the Earth, nobody would admit that perhaps our ventures into space were being stymied by the aliens.

Many years ago, rocket scientist Werner Von Braun advised against the weaponisation of space, however it seems his warnings have 'fallen on deaf ears.' Now, in the 21st century, multiple countries have satellites, many of which are integral to their defence systems. Occasionally a country will shoot down one of its own satellites, saying it has gone 'rogue', with adversaries claiming they were practising for possible future conflicts.

The entire international community is dependent upon the current array of over five thousand satellites currently orbiting the Earth. They serve military, commercial and communication purposes. We all unwittingly rely upon them, and if they were to suddenly fail, or be sabotaged, we would have difficulties functioning in our everyday lives. It only stands to reason that, in time of conflict, opposing countries, or even less than friendly extraterrestrials, would try to disable our communication and other capabilities.

Nearly every facet of our society is controlled by satellite facilitated digital technology. Many contactees, who have a premonition of a future disaster, have moved inland, above sea level. Whilst not 'Doomsday Preppers', they do stock extra provisions – 'just in case'. They also reject the concept of digital currency.

Twenty-first century space observatories are becoming much more powerful, and our robotic probes have gone far and wide. Plans are coming to fruition to return to the Moon, and land manned vehicles on Mars, perhaps installing a permanent habitable base there. The planets and asteroids in the Solar System are rich in minerals and rare substances, and resource poor but technology savvy nations are anxious to avail themselves of these resources.

America's NASA and private corporation Bigelow Aerospace have already announced, in advance, the intention to build a lunar base. It may only be coincidental, but CEO Robert Bigelow has held a fascination for UFOs and aliens since early childhood. He has spent millions of his own money on research projects, including The Bigelow Foundation and the National Institute for Discovery Science. A couple of years ago, while appearing on CBS's '60 Minutes', he reportedly said that he was absolutely convinced that aliens exist and that UFOs have visited Earth.

Due to its internal problems, China was a little slower to venture into the Cosmos, however it has now caught up with its 'Great Leap Forward', and a technological advancement that matches its Western competitors. As early as the 1990s Chinese scientists were planning their own space station, missions to Mars, and landings, with a possible later mining base, on the Moon.

China's first known manned venture into space was in 2003 when Shenzhou 5 carried Yang Liwei aloft. On June 16th 2012, Shenzhou 9 was buzzed by two glowing unidentified objects a few minutes after its launch in the Gobi Desert. Its crew of three included China's first female astronaut, Liu Yang.

In 2008, India launched its first Lunar mission when its unmanned, Chandrayaan-1 was launched from its Satish Dhawan Space Centre. With China, Japan and India entering the race, the 'competition' to return to the Moon is heating up, and there is already legal debate as to individual mining rights and resource ownership. The actual definition of the 1967 'Outer Space Treaty' is also coming into question.

In 1984 only thirteen nations ratified the *'Moon Agreement of 1979'*, which states that *'Neither the surface nor the subsurface, nor any part thereof or natural resources in place, shall become the property of any State, international intergovernmental or non-governmental entity or of any natural person.'* It sounds very good, but in fact is essentially meaningless as so few countries have agreed to abide by it.

Today, besides thousands of pieces of 'space junk', there are countless military and commercial satellites orbiting our planet. Some are extremely scientifically advanced, with amazing capabilities. There are both known and secret Space Stations, with 'shuttle' craft ferrying personnel to and from.

Also, the major powers are finalising urgent plans to land an astronaut on Mars. The race is on! But the question still remains. How did we get this sophisticated technology, and is anyone else out there?

Of course, what goes up usually has to come down, and many satellites and other man-made objects have been mistaken for UFOs when re-entering our atmosphere.

In December 1977, Soviet spy satellite, Cosmos 954, malfunctioned and splattered its debris across northern Canada. It led to intensive searches, and accusations that it was carrying a dangerous payload of one hundred pounds of enriched uranium 235.

Was radioactive material, or worse still, nuclear weapons being shot into space? No wonder the extraterrestrials were concerned. The atomic bombs dropped over Hiroshima and Nagasaki, and subsequent testing, signalled that mankind was playing with some very dangerous toys.

The inevitable development of the hydrogen bomb would have created even more concern. In November 1952, the Pacific island test led to the complete disappearance of Eniwetok Atoll, and its replacement by a crater 175 ft deep and one mile across. More tests followed, culminating in the explosion in near space of a bomb over Johnson Island, which sent electrified particles into the upper atmosphere, and caused auroras over large parts of the world.

In 1998, a huge American Titan IV rocket, carrying a top-secret spy satellite, crashed off the coast of Cape Canaveral. It started to self-destruct at 6,000 metres, forty-two seconds after launch. Controllers blew up the rest of the rocket to prevent a serious accident, and officials warned the public not to handle the debris, as it may contain 'hazardous material'.

In 1979, the 'Home Office' circulated a restricted document which outlined the problems, and procedures to be followed, if a nuclear powered satellite crashed on British soil, and whether the public should, or should not, be advised of the danger.

In 2001 space station Mir crashed back to earth; however the most memorable was Skylab's fiery fall, when it landed in the West Australian desert in 1979. Another West Australian crash, at Marble Bar, in 1981, was possibly Cosmos 434, a Russian satellite which authorities feared was nuclear powered.

In 2004, NASA's Genesis space capsule, bringing back a container of solar wind particles, smashed into the Utah desert, after its parachute failed.

While we discuss our ventures into space, and what has been discovered and seen out there, we must not forget our astronomers, in powerful observatories, who are scanning the skies every night.

In 1965, long before our first manned Moon landing, my late friend and colleague Paul Norman released the following report he had received from the Adhara Observatory in Argentina, where they were not only pursuing their normal astronomical pursuits, but also scanning the skies for our new satellites.

'As it was your wish, the last object of which you received news, I would like to tell you the following: On November 14th 1964, at 20.35, 20.45 and 21 hours in my observatory in the city of San Miguel, Province of Buenos Aires, Argentina, while observing the space with Messers Nerster Flores (Optician), Horis Roz (University Student) and various others, with a clear sky and a first crescent Moon, we were able to follow the movement of a solid object with orange borders and a brilliant white centre. It was cigar-shaped and the size similar to Saturn with borders clearly marked and a speed superior to that of Echo2. It first followed a N to SSE course, with no audible sound, illuminated by its own light, because as it entered the cone of terrestrial shadow it remained brilliant.

'Three times we saw it pass. The first time it appeared at 20.35 hours under Pegaso Constellation, crossing over the direction of Echo2 going towards NW-SE disappearing into the Orion Constellation. The second time it passed at 20.45 hours from the Centauro Constellation, ascending to our local zenith, where it crossed Echo2, travelling from horizon to horizon in four minutes, until it disappeared near the Andromeda horizon.

'The third time it appeared at 21 hours near the Altair Star, diving straight up to the Orion Constellation where it crossed Echo2 near the SE horizon, and after four minutes disappeared in the Southern horizon.

'On another occasion which occurred on October 17th 1964, the telescope at this same observatory was focussed on the Moon at 20.45 hours when a cigar-shaped object crossed in front of the Moon in route from E to W (of the concavity of the convexity) taking twelve to fourteen seconds to sweep over the disc of the Moon.'

Then, and at other times, there have been more less specific reports received of unidentifiable objects being seen in the vicinity of the Moon.

In his book *'Flying Saucers – Where Do They Come From?'*, Richard Tambling, a former Air Force photographer, discusses a photograph taken by a member of the Ballarat Astronomical Society on 4th June 1969, forty-eight days before Armstrong set foot on the Moon.

It was five hundred kilometres long, with a metallic mirror-like hull, and cast an immense black shadow on the lunar surface. Another member of the Society independently took two further photos of it, surrounded by haze.

The roll of film contained other local pictures, and when developed, it was analysed and pronounced genuine by independent photographers and laboratories.

As our telescopes and exploratory probes venture further and further into space, our view of the galaxy, and indeed our own Solar System are constantly being reshaped.

Minor planets, such as Makemake are being discovered, and the 'heliosphere', the Sun's zone of influence, is asymmetrical, not spherical as previously thought.

Many do not realise the vast distances covered to even reach the outer limits of our own Solar System. It takes years for our craft to travel the Solar System, and dozens of hours for commands, travelling at light speed to reach our far flung probes.

CHAPTER THIRTEEN

AMERINDIANS

My interest in the American Indians basically started when I met a young Indian at UFO research meetings. He was highly spiritual, and well motivated in his search for knowledge, with an instinctive connection with the natural world.

Born of a single native Indian mother, he had been adopted by an Australian couple, and despite their kindness, was desperate to find his roots and tribe. He returned to the US, and upon finding his people, was very disappointed at the poverty and drug abuse. His elders must have recognised his special ancestry and heritage, and trained him, as much as was permitted, in shamanistic arts.

A few years later, I met and became friends with a second contactee, 'Leonard', who, appeared to be another one of the Native Americans whose family had been 'selected'. Leonard's father, who was born in 1930, only passed away, in Sydney, a couple of years ago. He was an American Indian, part of the Hopi Nation, who had married an English woman, (born in Chile). When Leonard's father was nine, he was a sickly child, and rather a burden to the tribe.

One day he was left alone, and started walking until he came to an old oak tree. He sat under it for ages until two tall beautiful people came up. The man and woman were both blond, and at first he thought they were Germans.

He felt a hand on his shoulder, and they said; "Come with us, we will heal you."

His father didn't feel scared, and went with them to a 'spaceship', which looked like a traditional 'saucer' on three legs. He followed them up a ramp, and once inside, it took off at a fast speed. He could see through the walls and the Earth was disappearing behind them.

He was reasonably sure that Mars was their destination. The craft orbited then went down into a tunnel below the surface. When he alighted, he was greeted by normal people, wearing three different types of military uniforms. They all spoke English, and he assumed some were from the US and Britain, and was unsure about the third. There were also other different alien races present.

His father couldn't see this base from above, but once inside he could see the sky through the roof. It was similar to a one-way mirror. The rooms were like compartments, and the floor glass. He was healed of his disease, and remembered having blood on his ears and nose. When they brought him back to Earth and his family, the visitors told him they would come back for him much later in life.

He migrated to Australia, and got married. Leonard was born in 1960, and became a mechanical engineer in his early adult years.

When he was in his twenties, Leonard met his first wife, and during that time he saw more than one unusual object. On each occasion, it was as if the surrounding area was in a 'cocoon'. There was no noise or wind. Once he called out, and his brother-in-law, David, thinking he was hurt, rushed outside and saw the craft. Leonard commented that David had been a very aggressive man in the past. Since that incident his personality had changed. He became much more positive, and seemed like a different person.

After his first marriage broke down, Leonard moved to the isolation of the country, and purchased a property thirty-five kilometres north of Tamworth in NSW. It was situated in a valley surrounded by hills, and the cliffs were rich in quartz and granite. He became self-sufficient, and enjoyed 'stone-making', and often designed his own hydro-electric machines.

Late one dark night he looked out of the window, and saw some bright orange/yellow lights approach in the sky above, and thought it was a plane that might crash. He turned on all the lights and his torch so that it could safely land.

When he walked outside he realised it wasn't a plane. He saw two craft, which were slowly moving, side by side. They came overhead and hovered, and Leonard felt intense love, and the 'feeling' that 'we are all a part of everything.' He mentally communicated that they could use his property if they wished, and they landed. Perhaps that came from his connected Amerindian heritage and genes.

For several years after that, many craft came, sometimes four or five at a time. He never once recalls ever seeing the occupants, but seemed to have a telepathic connection with them. The saucers themselves were of varying sizes. Most had a clear dome and were a dark, smooth, seamless aluminium on the underside.

Leonard returned to Sydney, and met his second wife Henrietta in the strangest of circumstances. He was just visiting his friend's cousin, whom he had never met before, but when he walked into the lounge room he saw a woman he instantly recognised. In 1996, when he was still in the valley, he had what he thought was a 'flying saucer' dream.

He and Henrietta had both been in a 'park', surrounded by a white glow. Wherever they were, they were sitting back-to-back, and could only see each other's profile. All he could remember was one of them saying; "Don't forget me."

Before he could regain his composure, Henrietta jumped up and stared at him. "You're the Indian with the very long hair!" She recalled having exactly the same 'dream'.

So.....what about Henrietta's family? Her mother, who migrated to Australia in 1954, came from England. Her maternal grandfather had fought in the War, and often mentioned seeing strange lights in the sky.

Henrietta's father was from Austria, and had also come to Australia in the 1950s. In the early years he worked behind the counter of a shop/garage in the NSW country town of Hay.

One day two very tall men came in. They were both fair skinned and in their thirties. They were wearing hats and tan suits, which looked brand new, and he thought their car was an old Buick, gold in colour. He cannot remember anything else until he reappeared behind the counter one week later. He had been missing, without a trace, for a week, and the police and emergency services had been searching for him.

When Henrietta's parents married, they desperately wanted children, but she had several 'false' pregnancies where the babies just 'disappeared'. Eventually, in 1977, Henrietta was born premature, and lucky to survive.

In 2004, six weeks before Henrietta and Leonard married, they were driving back to Sydney with a friend. They were towing a trailer they had borrowed to help Henrietta move, and stopped at Singleton to get petrol. They checked the receipt later - it was just after midnight.

Back on the road, they saw a huge orange ball of light. At first Leonard thought it was the headlights of a goods train, but it was moving to the side and behind the car. They had their cat in a carry basket, and it was 'going crazy'. Despite covering the carrier with a blanket, 'Pussy' has never been the same since.

Everything seemed 'fuzzy' for two or three minutes, and suddenly they saw the Newcastle/Sydney sign on the Pacific Highway. It was 4.20am – where had four hours gone? They took the roundabout to the Freeway, and a short while later, a lady called out from a passing car; "You've got no wheels!" They stopped and got out. Two wheels, the nuts and all fittings were missing off the trailer.

Leonard and Henrietta moved to Werrington, in Sydney, and had two daughters. The youngest walked at nine months, and by the time she was one, could put her blocks in alphabetical order. Like other gifted children, she could read and write by the age of four. She would mumble or sing to herself, and yet rarely spoke. Leonard wondered if she was telepathic.

Late one night, in early 2016, Leonard took the dog for a walk in the local park. He saw a strange object through the trees, and although he thought he was only there for a few minutes, he 'lost' over two hours. Later that year he was diagnosed with incurable cancer. His young daughter put her hands on him and said; 'You'll be here a long time Daddy." Later X-rays showed the cancer had gone!

The older girl was not quite so bright, but very clever. In January 2018, she drew pictures of her family under an apparent saucer. When asked about it she said that she had seen 'lights' two weeks ago.

Leonard and Henrietta's case had an exceptionally interesting generational aspect to it. There was possible long-term alien interaction on both sides of the family.

Looking into the legends and ancestry of American Indians is, at times, a 'delicate' quest. When well known researcher, John Keel, also tried to pursue this line of inquiry, he said the following; *'.....several Indian tribes on the North American continent have ancient legends about the saucers and the saucer people, but Indians are not a communicative group, particularly today. There have been many sightings of UFOs descending into or near Indian reservations in recent years....and the Indians refuse to comment upon them.'*

This could be, in part, because the United States Government had, in the past, tried to convert the 'pagans' to Christianity, often with threats of imprisonment to their spiritual leaders if caught conducting ceremonies or praying in their native language. This changed when the 'Freedom of Religion Act' was passed by President Carter in 1978.

Keel also noted that some Indians, like the Gypsies, tended to live amongst themselves, outside of our society, and the origin of their languages have never been completely traced.

In 1823 Ozark historian, Haywood, wrote that several Indians had mentioned ancestral legends of white men living in a string of fort/settlements. The Cherokee had said that these people were already there when they migrated 8,000 years ago. Other Indian legends speak of these people who brought civilisation, and were often treated as 'Gods' by the tribes.

One place which was a source of great mystery and speculation, is 14,000 feet high Mount Shasta in California. In the mid-1800s, gold prospectors told of flashes of light over the area. This was often during clear weather, when it was definitely not lightning. In 1931, a forest fire swept up the mountain, only to be contained by a mysterious 'fog'. A circular demarcation line showed the fire had been mysteriously halted in a perfect curve around the central zone.

(Mark Davenport wrote of a similar incident in Brazil in 1963. As a crowd of witnesses watched a wildfire in the Paraná Forest, a 100ft shiny saucer came down from the sky and silently hovered 165 feet away inside the fire. It was only thirteen feet above the ground, and remained there for fifteen minutes.

It seemed to have some form of protective barrier, or invisible 'bubble', around it. Before flying off, two or three tall, 'good looking' people got out, unhampered by the smoke and flames, and walked around collecting rocks and vegetation.)

The fire at Mount Shasta created some interest, and in 1932, the *'Los Angeles Times'* featured an article by Edward Lanser, who investigated the matter, and claimed that a strange community existed there, which the locals had known about for decades.

In 1962, Australian author Andrew Tomas, who, at the time, was mainly interested in Atlantis, also researched the reports from Mount Shasta, and the book, *'A Dweller on Two Planets'*, written by Fredrick Oliver in 1884.

It speaks of vast underground 'halls' and tunnels within the mountain, all with secret entrances. The people who lived there were Caucasian in appearance, and wore white robes. The locals said that in the old days these strange people would come to town, for brief periods, often blending in with the population, and paying for their purchases with gold nuggets.

During World War I, civic records of old San Francisco state that a deputation from the community, headed by a white robed patriarch with several younger men, made an official visit bringing greetings and goodwill, along with a generous gift for the American Red Cross.

Professor Larkin of Mt. Lowe Observatory testified that once, when he was testing out his telescope, he spotted something on the slopes of Mt. Shasta. He said it was; "....a marvellous work of carved marble, and onyx rivalling in architectural splendour the magnificence of the temples of Yucatan." After learning of Mt. Shasta's 'colony' Professor Larkin also commented; "...Their display of light far excels our modern electrical achievements, and I am, for one, consumed with curiosity to know how these people can produce such amazing light effects..."

In later years, cars on the roads at Mount Shasta, had developed ignition problems, without any apparent cause. In 1956, Shasta resident, David Williamson, saw fourteen lights, making unusual sky manoeuvres over the mountain. One then descended, and appeared to land right on top of Mt. Shasta.

Are these strangers still living there today? Possibly not – the old-timers are all dead, and no-one else seems to know the secret entrances to the halls and tunnels.

The legends and environment of the native Indians of North America's plains and Rockies, to the jungles and Andes of the South, vary to a great extent.

From time to time, further evidence of a 'lost' civilisation emerges. On December 17th 1869, the *'Los Angeles News'* published an article about an amazing discovery made by Captain Lacy of Hammonville, Ohio. His miners were making an entry into a coal bank, when about one hundred feet below the surface, a mass of coal collapsed, revealing a large slate wall. Several lines of unknown hieroglyphics were carved onto the smooth surface, and there was much speculation as to their age, and who had made them.

In 1971, the Canadian publication, *'Saucers, Space and Science'*, wrote about Navaho Indian Oge, who, following the publicity regarding flying saucers, made a visit to the Paiute tribe to ask about the legendary craft in Death Valley.

Their chief said they had known about the flying ships for untold generations, and spoke of a sacred plateau, out west, where the gods resided. After the 'Hav-Musuvs' arrived they initially lived in great caverns, later building hidden cities. They ruled over all, and allegedly had magic rods, which caused the skin to 'prickle', including paralysis, and rode the night skies in great, metal 'birds'.

Many years ago, Professor E. Clark of the Washington State University, wrote an interesting book – *'Indian Legends of the Northern Rockies'*. In 1969, the *'Flying Saucer Review'* followed up with an article by Richard Hack, in which he compared the legends with modern day ufology.

He was also interested in the unique stories which spoke of the 'Little People', who were similar to some of the UFO occupants reported today. Nearly all these tribes knew about the smaller entities, 'strange dwarfs', who apparently lived in some of the deep forests. These were not pleasant beings, fairly vicious and primitive, and there is no suggestion that they arrived or flew in spaceships, neither did they have the 'magic rods' reported by the Paiute. One does wonder whether they had originated, like the Chinese Dropa, from the survivors of a crashed craft, or had merely been abandoned here.

Another Indian legend refers to the San Luis Valley, and Mount Blanca being a sacred place, from where the 'Star People' emerge, having arrived aboard 'flying seed pods'.

Around the world, almost all ancient cultures claim their knowledge and civilisation came from benevolent aliens who arrived from either the sky or the sea. These 'Gods' were always responsible for their advancement. In Mexico their 'benefactor' was 'Quetzalcoatl', the Maya referred to 'Kukulkan', and the Inca spoke of 'Kon-Tiki-Wira-Kocha'. The Kayapo Indians of Brazil revered 'Bep Kororon', who arrived from the sky carrying a 'thunder weapon'.

Some Indians claim they were aliens who have been reincarnated with the assignment of raising earthly awareness. In 2008, author Brad Steiger wrote of one such case; *'A Cherokee physicist, who now lives in Alabama, not only had a recall of a past life in the Pleiades, but he was also able to fit his alien memories together with tribal legends that his people had come from another world.'*

The Yakima Indians, who come from rugged terrain in south Central Washington State, claim that a long time ago, a red-eyed man, with great healing powers came to live with the tribe. Just like us, he grew old, and when he was dying, he asked to be taken out to a particular place. Soon after his death, a craft came from the sky, landed, took his body on board, and flew back into the heavens.

The North American Hopi Indians, have a culture which believes in the 'Great Spirit', who comes from the sky, (possibly Orion), and the existence of several previous civilised 'worlds'. They prophesise another, which may be catastrophic, is soon to come.

'Black Mesa' rises 3,300 feet above the desert floor, in northern Arizona. It is the home of the Hopi, whose legends and myths have been passed on in cave paintings, legends and ceremonial dances. They also believe they are descended from an ancient people, the 'Kachinas', tall, blond-haired, blue eyed beings, who lived in an inner city called Palatkwapi, and flew in fantastic aerial craft.

They speak of their 'Ancient Fathers', who were masters of all spiritual knowledge and judgement, and dedicated their lives to the laws of their 'Great Spirit'. The prophecies and instructions handed down, were guidelines to use and live by on Earth. A great disaster, created by the wilfulness of man, is foretold, at which time the 'Ancient Fathers' will return to reclaim the land. Only the 'true sister and brother' will give rebirth to the earth, and recycle and renew its life.

In years gone by, Hopi chief, Dan Katchonogya, and other elders, unsuccessfully tried to present a petition to the United Nations. They wanted to share their prophecies and findings, regarding the 'End Times', and ask that the 'white man' mend his ways before it was too late.

In North America, ruins of what seemed to be an ancient city, was discovered in 1804 by Daniel Boone and Missouri Governor Boggs, when they were on their way to Washington County. They were built of rough, but substantial masonry, and enclosed within the walls were several large basins with strange carvings. They were still there in 1834, but the remains have since gone.

.One person who searched for the gods and extraterrestrials of South American Indian legends was George Hunt Williamson. After serving with the Army Air Corps during World War II, from 1945 until 1952, besides studying anthropology at University, he spent time with the Indian Hopi and Chippewas tribes in North America, and was awarded an honorary degree for his thesis 'Ethnology of the Modern Sioux-Chippewa Indians'. He learned the ritual North American Indian Dances, and often participated in their 'pow-wows'.

I wrote about Hunt Williamson in my book, *'The Days of the Space Brothers'*. Williamson was, for several years, involved with a group of ham radio operators, who were in contact with aliens. He wrote extensively about this in his books, *'The Saucers Speak'*, and *'Other Voices'*. In 1952, after receiving a specific ham radio message, he, along with his wife and another couple, the Baileys, immediately travelled to make their first contact with George Adamski, and lead him to the place in the desert, where the famous meeting with the extraterrestrial, Orthon, occurred.

Everybody has always assumed that Adamski was the intended recipient of the resultant contacts and messages. However, after Orthon had left his footprints on the ground, Williamson examined them carefully before making a plaster cast, sketches and photographs of the symbols which had been on the bottom of Orthon's footwear.

He was apparently able to decipher and translate them. Investigator, Michel Zirger, who obtained many of Williamson's manuscripts, quite rightfully wondered for whom were the symbols intended - Adamski or Williamson? Which one was better qualified to interpret them? After this, Williamson had very little contact with Adamski, although whilst in Arizona, he and his wife, Betty, saw two UFOs on the night of 3rd February 1953. The symbols obviously had some meaning for him, and he soon made more trips into the jungles of South America.

In 1955-56, whilst in Peru, he heard of many reports of UFOs going in and out of unknown and unexplored jungle areas, and the Indian legends of ancestors who communicated with these 'sky people' in the 'great road in the sky'. He was searching for these lost cities of the Amazonian Empire, and soon after claimed to have discovered a 'hidden city' deep in the Andes, near Lake Titicaca.

He explored several countries in South America, searching for lost cities, and in 1957, ventured into the Peruvian jungle with the Machiguenga Indians. There he found a huge stone cliff face, covered with many strange ancient petroglyphs. It had originally been reported as the 'Rock of Writings' by British explorer Colonel Percival Fawcett, who had never divulged its exact location before vanishing in the jungle in 1925.

In an interview with a Miami newspaper, in October 1957, Williamson said; "I believe these lost cities have a definite 'tie-in' with flying saucers. As an anthropologist I have become fully convinced that the Earth was visited by outer space objects in civilization's past."

Williamson wrote many books including *'Other Tongues–Other Flesh', 'Secret Places of the Lion', 'Road in the Sky'*, and *'Secret of the Andes'*. He lectured to numerous groups, and wrote scores of articles, including his own publication, 'The Telonic Research Bulletin'.

Hunt Williamson combined his knowledge of the American Indians, UFO and alien contacts, along with developing mystical beliefs and practices of his own. However, in 1961, something apparently 'spooked' him. He dropped out of sight, and changed his name to Michel d'Obrenovic, the name of his mother's Serbian ancestors. He died in 1986, and some people claim the movie character, Indiana Jones, was based on his life. His third, and last wife, had been a movie star, and involved with film producers, so this is quite possible.

The 'hieroglyphs' on Orthon's footwear, and the film negative shown in Adamski's book, also had meaning to archaeologist, Professor Marcel Homet. They were identical to the symbols he had found on a plate in Argentina. He later reported discovering engraved boulders at Pedra Pintata, in northern Brazil, which also bore a striking resemblance, and sometimes were identical, to these symbols.

In his book *'Les Fils du Soleil',* Homet details his world-wide explorations, many of which were in the Amazon region of Brazil, searching for the lost continent of Atlantis. Homet said that he had become certain that space people had visited Earth in previous civilisations, and in 1961 he personally saw a 'space-ship' in the skies of Brazil.

In Peru, locals still claim they have had direct contact with extraterrestrials, who have a hidden base inside the surrounding mountains. It is reputed that there are vast networks of hidden underground tunnels, stretching across the continent, something which both Hunt Williamson and Professor Homet were anxious to discover.

At that time, explorations into the South American jungles were a very risky business. In April 1960, three well-equipped expeditions disappeared without a trace in the rainforest. The first was a 22-man party of surveyors and engineers, who were studying the proposed layout of the Trans-Amazonian Highway. A second search/rescue party also disappeared. The next time a more experienced six-man patrol was dispatched. They had all been trained in jungle fighting and counter-insurgency, but none-the-less, they also never returned. What happened to them? We can only speculate.

The Indian populations of the central regions of the Americas were usually more advanced than their northern neighbours, and their practices more bloodthirsty and vicious. They had ancient settlements and fortifications built from massive blocks of stone, some of which were nearly fifty feet high. In 1920, one archaeologist said that some of the ruins appeared remarkably similar to the buried cities he had excavated in North Africa and the Middle East.

As archaeologists learn more about these ancient megalithic structures in the Andes, it is still a mystery as to how they were built. Also the Peruvian architecture was different to that of the Mayans and Aztecs. Amazonian elders and 'shamans' insist these massive stone settlements were built long before the Inca civilisation.

In 1969, the *'Flying Saucer Review'* published an interesting article by Gordon Creighton, detailing the reports of UFO bases he believed were still in existence in the mainly uninhabited mountains of Peru and Argentina in South America. There were also rumours of undersea bases in the Atlantic, off the coasts of Brazil and Argentina. In all cases, the saucers leaving and entering these areas, were described as resembling the smaller 'scout' type craft, and not gigantic 'mother-ships'.

In 2001 the *'Chicago Tribune'* discussed the discoveries made by Northern Illinois University anthropologists, Jonathan Hass, Winifred Creamer and a Peruvian colleague.

They had been excavating a site in a remote desert area, near Caral, along the Rio Supe River, which was originally discovered, but later abandoned, by archaeologists in 1905. The local farming village was still quite primitive, with no electricity or running water.

The scientists had found large, stepped pyramid structures, dating back to 2627 BC, at eighteen sites in the area. The largest was five hundred feet on two sides, and four-hundred and fifty feet on the other two. The flat top had rooms, chambers, stairways, halls, altars and hearths.

Unlike their Egyptian counterparts, they had been built with woven reed sacks, filled with river pebbles, and the piles increased with trimmed, flat-faced rock. A final coat of plaster was painted over in 'earth tones'.

There have been other interesting artefacts discovered in North America. In Wyoming's Bighorn Mountains, there was a mysterious 'Medicine Wheel', which was discovered to have astronomical alignments, which may have been used as an observation tool by the nomadic Plains Indians.

At Cahokia, near St. Louis, Illinois, on the banks of the Mississippi River, are similar mounds, one ten stories high. There are the remnants of cedar 'rings' which were apparently a solar calendar. The Indians claim that one thousand years ago, a large population of their ancestors lived there.

Previously unknown ruins and civilisations are still being discovered in the South and Central American jungles. On June 6th 2002, *'BBC News'* announced that Britain's Royal Geographical Society had reported the discovery of the ruins of a 'lost city' hidden in a remote jungle in south-eastern Peru, about fifty kilometres from the better known Machu Picchu in the Andes. It was well hidden, in dense jungle, at the bottom of a near-inaccessible river canyon. It is 1,850 metres above sea level, and any approach impossible except for coming down from the mountains above.

The area included about thirty stone buildings, one of which was more than twenty metres long, around a central plaza. The expedition, co-led by Hugh Thomson, named the site 'Coca Coca', and said the 'constructed area' was more than twice the size of another Inca ruin they had discovered a short time before.

Like ancient Egypt and other sites across the world, many of the ancient ruins, which have been discovered across the Americas, comprise massive blocks of stone, some weighing over 100 tons, which have obviously been moved considerable distances, often up steep mountains, then lifted into place. How was this done? We still don't know, and most theories don't adequately explain these massive monuments.

What kind of aliens were frequenting both North America and the Amazon and Andes? Maybe more than one species. Certainly 'humanoids' were being reported, and Cynthia Hind wrote of South American people who tell of a non-human race whose blood was not red.

One correspondent noted that the people who live in the high altitudes of the Andes, some twelve to twenty-thousand feet above sea level, have one or two pints of blood more than most people, and their hearts beat at a slower pace. If there are, or have been, extraterrestrials living in the Andes, apart from their inaccessibility, perhaps the atmospheric conditions are similar to those on the planet from which they came.

Recent carbon tests have confirmed the presence of human beings in that area at least 9,000 years ago, and other experts claim that there was an advanced civilisation in the area as long as 30,000 years ago.

In July 1965, Gordon Creighton translated an interesting report from the Argentine newspaper, *'Córdoba'*. It detailed an amazing occurrence which happened in the February of that year at Chalae, near Formosa on the Argentina-Paraguay border.

The local population, who were South American Indians, from the Toba tribe, were amazed when several saucers flew around in the sky. One of them landed, and three 'beings', enveloped in 'luminous halos' emerged from the craft.

All fifty witnesses fell to their knees, with arms uplifted in the traditional manner of salutation to their ancestral Sun God. The three figures came slowly towards them, and used friendly gestures to indicate that the Indians should keep away from their ship.

A voice came from one of the visitors, urging them to remain calm as there was nothing to fear. They would always remember this moment, for the Space People would return in order to convince Earth men of their existence and to bring to this world the peace it so badly needed.

The Space 'Beings' slowly returned to their saucer, which took off, emanating luminous beams which almost blinded the witnesses. Local police had taken photographs of the craft, which added credibility to the Indians' report.

Do the native American Indians still have contact with extraterrestrials? This is something we may never know, and something they would never tell us.

In 1996, during Queensland's International UFO Symposium, investigator, Wendelle Stevens spoke at length about Pleiadian ETs, who looked entirely human. They were in contact with several people in Argentina, Venezuela, Peru and Mexico. These witnesses kept the meetings and information secret, but said they were told the 'visitors' had been coming here for a very long time, often establishing colonies.

Reports were also coming in from North America. The *'Arizona Daily Star'*, July 26th 1974, reported on an airborne, disc-shaped object landing on the San Carlos Indian Reservation, a settlement of about six hundred people, thirty miles north-west of Stafford. It was had a rounded top, surrounded by an aura of blue light, and a second light was beaming down on the ground. At about 9pm it hovered several hundred feet above the ground, and then landed near Mt. Turnbow, seven miles south-west of the village. Shortly after it darted upwards and disappeared into the sky. The San Carlos Indian Police in Bylas, said over fifteen witnesses had confirmed the incident.

One more mystical event, which occurred in the seventeenth century, still has me wondering.

In 1622, both Prince Philip IV of Spain and the Pope, were contacted by Father Alonzo de Benavides, after he had been sent to Mexico to convert the Indians to Christianity. He discovered the natives were in possession of crosses and rosaries, and celebrated Mass with an unusual chalice. They claimed that they had been given to them by a mysterious 'nun', the 'lady in blue', who had already visited them.

When he returned to Spain, Father Alonzo heard about a young nun, Sister Mary, who lived in a convent in Agreda. She claimed she had taken 'flights' to several parts of Central America to convert the Indians to Christianity, and was able to accurately describe their living conditions and customs. She also described the Earth as rotating on a north-south axis, something only known by a few scientists and navigators at the time.

What astounded everyone, was that while the convent superiors said the young nun had never left the convent, they immediately recognised the Indians' chalice as having come from their convent.

The Native Indians of North and South America, have a long history of interactions with the 'Sky Kachinas' or 'Star Elders'. Ancient folklore, petroglyphs, artefacts and ruins tell of their coming from the skies in past times. There are numerous legends of interaction between these space beings and humans, including 'marriages', with some of the visitors staying on, and sometimes people from the tribes going away with them.

Dr. Richard Boylan, a much respected researcher, was asked his opinion regarding the American Indian 'Star Nations'. He said; "The term 'Star Nations' really says what it's about. It's about people from the stars, not our stars but other stars, and nations, whose cultures, civilisations, organised groups of people are from other star systems....The 'Nations' refers to a number of things that have been held very closely by the prophecy keepers, the tradition keepers of the various tribes until the last several years."

When discussing contactee reports, he wrote; *'It is my surmise that Native Americans are more likely to be selected because of their culture – at least the tribes I have studied the most, the Hopi and Lakota (Sioux) – had a tradition of visitors from the sky who bring important messages and have special powers.'*

At the beginning of the twenty-first century, Richard Boylan was also asked what we should be doing in preparation for the new millennium.

He said; "I defer to the Native Americans who are much older, more spiritually and environmentally deep, and on the whole, particularly among the 'traditionals', a much more balanced people in our modern 'go-go', technological, morally bankrupt society of the US white world.

"They suggest a prayerful, a sensitive, a thoughtful and open-to-mind kind of mind and heart of people. It is a time for prayer. It is a time for study. It is a time for opening heart and trying to attune very carefully to where the hearts of those around you are. And to be discerning and trying to inform self about what the traditions, that are worth learning from, have to say."

During a conference, I met Robert Morning Sky, who was half Hopi, half Apache. His parents had died when he was young, and his grandfathers, from both tribes, had helped raise and educate him. I was very impressed with his humble, but intelligent demeanour, but unfortunately, there was no opportunity to embark on any meaningful discussions.

Morning Sky later wrote of his peoples' beliefs and society. He explained that contacts with extraterrestrials, or 'Star Beings', had a long tradition among his people, and much of their knowledge had been taught to them by the 'heavenly teachers' who visited their forefathers.

There has been so much written about UFO crashes in South Western USA, that although I am aware of the various reports, I don't repeat them ad-nauseam in my books.

Morning Sky believed that a Roswell documentary he had seen was 'real', and in an interview he said; *"I know that many people won't believe me, but that being in the film looked exactly like the Star Elder about whom my grandfather had told me.*

"In August 1947, more than a month after the famous UFO crash near Roswell, my grandfather and five of his friends went on a vision quest. That is an old ceremony, a technique to learn about one's own future, to find out what the stars have in store for you.

"They saw a light in the sky which descended and crashed. With us, the Star People are part of our daily lives. We believe in them, know that they exist, we talk to them, dance with them. So it is no wonder that my grandfather was interested in this light and that he knew there were Star People in it.

"These young men were very naïve, and ignored all the rumours that went around the reservation; that if a star fell from the sky, one should keep off, for soon soldiers would come there. Soldiers and Indians just did not belong together!

"My grandfather and his friends went looking for the star, and found it before the soldiers arrived. When they examined the wreck, they discovered one

survivor, but he was injured. They decided to take him back with them to their vision-quest camp.

"There they nursed him. Sometimes he was conscious, sometimes not, and whenever he could, he gave them instructions. After a few months, he had recovered his health. During this time they had won his confidence, and they called him 'Star Elder'.

"One day he produced a small, green crystal. It was round and flat, and fitted into his little hand. When he held up the crystal, he was able to project pictures into it. Through these pictures, my grandfather and his friends learned who he was, from where, and what he was doing here.

"They decided not to talk about him to anybody, for they were anxious about his safety. Curious people would come, ask questions, and finally the soldiers would get to know of him and come to take him away. When he was in full health again, and could have been picked up by his people, he decided nevertheless to stay on for a short while."

Morning Sky's grandfather told him about the many things that 'Star Elder' had explained about Earth's history, his own people, and their interactions with us.

He stayed for a while, and then felt it would be dangerous if his colleagues came to pick him up. So he eventually waited for five years, until he thought it was safe to go. One day he left the camp, but actually appeared a few more times after that.

In more recent years, since the 1960s, the US has shown an increasing interest in the tropical regions of South America. At first it was assumed to only involve the search for precious minerals.

In the 1970s and 1980s, parts of the Amazon were abuzz with rumours and reports of much nastier, vampire type, ugly entities.

Scott Corrales reported that;.....*'in the summer of 1993, South American newspapers published articles discussing the Bolivian and Peruvian governments' discomfit at the prospect of a large contingent of US forces setting up a 'semi-permanent' base in the Bolivian Amazonas part, allegedly, of the vaunted 'War on Drugs'.*

'Over a hundred US troops from the 37th Airborne, stationed at Fort Bragg, have been engaged in the construction of facilities at Santa Ana, a small Amazonian village in the Beni region of Bolivia....A powerful transmitter, also under construction, will enable direct communication with the Panama based Southern Command and the Pentagon itself.

'The Bolivian parliament, incensed by the presence of the foreign 'garrison' questioned President Jaime Paz Zamora over the matter. The official explanation, given to all and sundry, was that the soldiers 'are building a school'.

'Independent investigators, appointed by the Bolivian parliament, visited the jungle area in question, stated in their report that the weapons systems being brought into the country were of a power in excess of anything needed to fight drug traffickers or insurgent groups like the Sendero Luminoso terrorists.'

Corrales then asks the obvious question; *'Could the avowed purpose of these troops be to monitor the increased UFO activity that is taking place throughout Amazonia?'*

In 1994 the US facilitated the building of an advanced radar system – SIVAM – which would relay their information to 'jungle processing centres'. This was purportedly for the war on drugs and also defence purposes, and probably have gone unnoticed by the rest of the world, except for members of the Brazilian senate levelling accusations of bribery when the contracts were originally awarded.

Steven Greer interviewed Lance Corporal Jonathon Weygandt, who was stationed in Peru in 1997. His duties included providing perimeter security for a radar installation which supposedly tracked drug aircraft moving in and out of Peruvian and Bolivian airspace.

Early one morning, he was sent with other Marines to investigate what was a possible plane crash in the jungle. When they reached the site, he and the two sergeants were the first to find a huge metallic craft which was buried in the side of a cliff. They had not seen anything like it before, and knew it was not from Earth. It had a couple of gashes in the rear, and Weygandt thought it might have been hit by a surface-to-air missile. A strange, greenish-purple 'goo' was dripping from the object, which had a slight hum, and a light slowly going around.

His sergeant started yelling at him to 'get the hell out of there', and suddenly he found himself taken into custody by government officials in containment suits. They 'cuffed' his hands and legs, took away all his gear, and transported him to a base where he saw a lot of personnel of different nationalities. For three weeks he was segregated with Air Force personnel, and constantly threatened and intimidated about ever speaking about what he saw. The two sergeants had families, and were scared to even discuss the matter with him, but Weygandt thought the Command Centre had equipment, like large telescope laser range finders, which were used for more than just tracking drug aircraft.

What do the Indian Nations have to say about their ancient Gods, and their inherited wisdom? The *'Techqua Ikachi'* is a native Hopi Indian publication written by some of the village leaders. Their words, dedicated to the 'survivors', are so wise and beautiful, I know they will not mind me sharing them with you here.

'...to those to whom the task was set, not only to preserve the ancient wisdom and knowledge, but in so doing, had to preserve the physical body in order to see their goal achieved. Many lost the way. Feet strayed from the path, but throughout all – famine, fire, drought and flood, the coming of other races and creeds – the old ones gave love and courage to the newly born, so that their children, and their children's children would see the light of truth and love and justice in the new world to be.

'The world that is now was once before a beautiful home for God's creations. The Great Spirit has preserved that knowledge to make it so again, so that all of creation can look again at the rainbow jewel set in God's firmament – shining with love and hope for future mankind to see.'

More wise words have been written by Sun Bear from the Bear Tribe; *'I saw that the time drew near when, for the sake of Earth Mother and all of our evolution as human beings, we must return to a better and truer understanding of the earth, and all our relations on her. I saw that we would have to put aside the petty fears that divided us, and learn to live as true brothers and sisters in a loving way.*

'I saw that we would have to find others who shared our hearts' direction, whatever their racial background, and join with them into groups that always

remembered that our purpose was to be instruments of the Great Spirit's will, and helpers to our Earth Mother. I saw that such groups could greatly affect the cleansing of the cleansing of the earth that is now occurring.'

CHAPTER FOURTEEN

SOUTH-EAST ASIA

We do not receive a lot of reports from South-East Asia, and who knows what activity is hidden in the thick tropical jungles.

KOREA

The Korean War lasted from 1950 to 1953, and involved both Western and Communist forces. Even earlier than the Vietnam War, some Korean War veterans reported unidentified aerial objects, which had capabilities far beyond our own airpower. In his book *'Advanced Aerial Devices Reported during the Korean War'*, author Dr Richard Haines discusses the electromagnetic effects on US Air Force and Navy planes. The description of these strange craft did not correspond with anything Soviet or American, and they were certainly not the tired, old official excuse – 'lighted enemy balloons'.

Many Korean veterans never reported the strange craft they saw in the skies. Richard Hall, in his book *'Uninvited Guests'*, wrote; *'When I was on the faculty of the University of Minnesota, a student came to me, having heard I had some interest in this question. He informed me that his father, a colonel, an artillery colonel in Korea....had flown over a hill in Korea in his observer plane, and found (right next to him virtually) a characteristic unidentified flying object with the usual kind of configuration.*

'It had promptly retreated upwards. It had frightened him, but he was an experienced and trained observer, so he took notes on it....When he returned he was so ridiculed and laughed at for a long period of time that he completely gave up trying to have this taken seriously. He refused to talk about it.'

Richard Haines also documented several incidents, including one in 1950, when a US Navy aircraft reported two flat discs, shaped something like a 'coolie's hat', which had a silvered mirror appearance, with a reddish glow surrounding them. They had oblong 'ports' which emanated a copper-green coloured light. At one stage they halted, backed-up and began a jittering or fibrillating movement.

In 1951, at least fourteen US Navy ground and airborne radar sites tracked a UFO for seven hours as it circled the ships at sea off Korea. It was reported as often being at a very low altitude, and travelling at speeds ranging from 'slow' to over one thousand miles per hour.

Don Jernigan, a researcher from Ohio, became interested in UFOs after a mind-boggling incident in Korea. In 1952, he was in a military unit fighting close to the enemy lines. At about 9pm they were taking enemy fire, when a large, one hundred feet diameter, glowing disc-shaped object came out of the sky, from the direction of the hills.

The men in his platoon were frightened, thinking it was some new communist weapon, but the other side also stopped shooting. It was low, only about 600ft up, and it remained for about twenty minutes before rapidly shooting straight up into the sky, leaving a small streak behind it.

In 1952, during the Korean War, when many US soldiers were stationed in Japan, other unusual craft and saucers, travelling up to 6,400mph, were sighted by ground observers, pilots and tracked on radar. On December 29th, Wing Commander Blakeslee was sent up in a F-94 Interceptor to investigate a report from the crew of a B-29, flying over northern Japan.

He reported visual contact, and described the object as having rotating red, green and white lights, and three fixed beams of white lights. Blakeslee tried to close in on it, but within five seconds it had sped out of sight.

Not all pilots were so lucky. C. Hawke, a US Air Force meteorologist, was on duty in the Combat Operations Centre, in Japan, during 1959. Suddenly there was some excitement, with one operator calling out – "They're back!"

A colleague explained; "There is an unidentified flying object here. We've seen them quite frequently. They travel at 2,000 miles per hour, and for some strange reason, quite frequently, they stop and hover, stationary, for up to two or three hours."

At that stage, the radar operators advised the target was stationary, and two special aircraft, from Masawa, which had equipment designed to track and fire on the intruders, were scrambled. Some of their navigation aids were strangely malfunctioning, but they headed into clear skies above the cloud.

One pilot had the UFO in sight, and described it as being a circular, metallic object, with a cockpit on top. He was ordered to make a 'firing pass', which was unsuccessful. Their rockets had detonated before reaching their target, as if there was some invisible shield protecting the strange craft.

At that stage the pilot started screaming that he was under attack; "Oh my God, they've turned on some kind of beam and they're turning. They're coming after me!"

The radar operators could see the UFO closing in on their pilot, until the two 'blips' met. The 'F-106' plane was gone, and a four day intensive search failed to find any trace of the plane or its pilot.

Many years ago I knew two Australian ex-Korean POWs – they were always very silent and 'tight-lipped' when it came to the subject of UFOs. Francis Wall, who had, in 1951, been a G.I. in the US Army in Korea, told researcher John Timmerman of a harrowing experience he never wanted to repeat.

His unit was making an artillery attack on a village in the 'Iron Triangle' region when a glowing, disc-shaped craft approached them. Wall took a shot at it with his rifle, and he could hear the sound of the armour-piercing bullet hitting the metal of the object. The UFO 'went wild', moving erratically, flashed its lights off and on, and 'revved-up some kind of generator'.

Wall said; "And then we were attacked, I guess you would call it. In any event, we were swept with some form of a ray which was emitted in pulses, in waves that you could visually see only when it was aiming directly at you."

The soldiers all felt a burning, tingling sensation penetrating their bodies. After the disc departed they felt no lasting ill effects from the attack. Three days later the entire company of men were too weak to walk, and had to be evacuated by ambulance.

VIETNAM

Apparently, in South-East Asia, opposing troops didn't fare very well either. The *'Australian UFO Bulletin'* published a 2001 report by Erich Aggen, which told of an incident in the summer of 1965. A special unit of two hundred Russian soldiers, stationed near Hanoi, fired upon a UFO which appeared in front of their headquarters. It retaliated with a laser-like weapon, and the Russians were 'completely dematerialised.'

The *'Flying Saucer Review'* published a report made, on January 13th 1966, from the SS *Morgantown Victory,* which was part of 'Task Force 34', a supply ship convoy, which was northeast of Marcus Island, en-route to the war zone in South East Asia.

A 200ft, silent, cigar-shaped object, hovered about four hundred feet above the sea a mile away. It was visible for about three minutes, and the ship and its crew searched for over an hour, but found nothing. The Air Force later noted that the area of the sighting was just north of the Marianas Islands, and some of the deepest depths in the Pacific.

On June 19th 1966, hundreds of American GIs at the Nha Trang camp were outside watching movies, when suddenly a bright light appeared out of nowhere.

It was at an altitude of about 25,000ft, and at first they thought it was a flare, but its speed was inconsistent. It suddenly dropped to about four hundred feet overhead, and lit everything up, making the little valley and mountains around look like the middle of the day.

The generators, lights and movie stopped. Everything 'went black' and there was mass panic. The object shot back up into the sky and out of sight within a couple of seconds.

At the air base, half a mile away, all power was cut, and two planes which were getting ready to take off had sudden engine failure. A later check could find no fault with any of the affected equipment.

An anonymous report was made in the January 2013 edition of *'The Ufologist'*. In the spring of 1969, a twenty year old soldier in 62nd Maintenance Battalion, was manning a thirty feet gun-tower in Plieku, South Vietnam. For five minutes he watched a yellowish glowing object about three miles away over the rice paddies. Within a split second it moved from that location to within 300ft of his position, and hovered at a very low altitude.

It appeared to be a thick 'cloud', with the glow coming from inside. Over the next five minutes he watched as the 'mist' got thicker and thicker. Three or four orbs were around the perimeter, just floating at different heights and locations to the razor wire. He did not hear any noise, and did manage to take a photograph before they all 'simply disappeared.'

At 2am on 17th April 1967, a member of the U.S. Military Intelligence Unit was on the roof of the Saigon Field Office when he saw five large illuminated oval objects. They were glowing a steady white, and travelling in formation at very high speed, much faster than any known plane. They passed overhead, and were temporarily lost from view in a cloud formation. As they disappeared towards the horizon, they turned to the right. Several planes raced across the sky, following the same course, and obviously in pursuit.

The witness referred the incident to Project Blue Book, but never received any answer or evaluation.

WALTER MORGAN

I knew Walter for several years, and assumed his psychological problems and bouts of depression were post traumatic stress caused by his war service, but after he confided in me, I wondered if there was more.

"I was serving with the Australian Army in1968/6, and early one morning, I was on patrol with D Company in Phue Thue Province. It was a clear night, with a full moon on the horizon. We came to a clearing in the jungle, where there was a building and a bizarre object outside, about a hundred meters away. It was quite clear, but kind of fuzzy at the same time. It was silent and had steady lights shining from it. It was hard to say whether it was actually on the ground or hovering just above.

"Our nerves were already on edge, so this made us quite jittery. We were ordered to withdraw to 'consider the situation'. The officer in charge broke us into two sections, and we tentatively advanced, not really knowing what to expect. As we edged closer we could see it was round – like an egg – and about the size of a double-decker bus.

"I felt weird, we all did. Maybe it was something coming from this craft or just our own fear. Every hair on my head was standing on end. It started sending out tremendous vibrations and humming and disappeared, I assume 'straight up.' There were burn marks on the ground where it had been.

"There was no explanation forthcoming from HQ – there never was. Strange objects were often seen in 'Nam, especially during battles, and they were not known aircraft."

The 1989 *'The UFO Enigma'* Newsletter, contained an article which discussed an incident the next year, in September 1971. A US Army 'Special Forces' unit was on a mission into Cambodia. This was a secretive mission, as it was, at the time, a country out-of-bounds to US troops.

Peter Bostrom, who interviewed the witness, noted that there was mention of MJ-12, a 'government entity' that was involved in the gathering of information regarding UFOs in the airspace in and around Thailand.

Peter, gave the witness, who had been a Lieutenant at the time, the pseudonym 'Joe', and published a transcript of their interviews.

Joe began by saying; *'I was stationed with the Army in Thailand. Originally, it was a routine mission in Cambodia, close to an area called Tonie Sap, just south of Angkor Wat, where the temples are. We had gone on a previous mission in answer to some problems and had gone back on a search-and-destroy mission. The area we were mainly concerned about was insurgents from the Khmer Rouge – Pol Pot's people, who were wrecking havoc with the local indigenous personnel'.*

'We were after one group and when going through the jungle, we heard some noises coming from a hidden area. It sounded like equipment running.'

When they entered a clearing, they saw a spherical, metallic craft, about a hundred feet in diameter, and as tall as a 'five storey building', suspended close to, or on the ground on four legs.

There were about sixteen to twenty 'humanoids' around it. They were no more than five feet tall, well built, with greyish-white skins, and wearing one-piece silver jumpsuits. There was one, possibly the 'leader', who was taller, perhaps five feet six or seven.

They were carrying some kind of instruments and an inexperienced young corporal thinking they were weapons, fired. As one of the beings fell to the ground, Joe immediately pushed the corporal's arm and weapon down. The taller 'humanoid' walked over. He put up his hand, in a sign of peace to the platoon, and struck the corporal across the face. Both the corporal and the injured alien, who were initially lying on the ground, appeared to recover, and the humanoids picked up their equipment and returned to their craft. A 'door' slid down, and after the 'beings' entered, the craft lifted straight off the ground.

Three days later, when they returned to base, all the soldiers were confined to quarters. For over three weeks they were subjected to intense questioning by military and civilian officers, he said came from the 'firm'. After a while they were all given drugs during hypnosis sessions. This left a few of the men confused, and it took some time before their memories regained some clarity.

Years later Joe heard about two other incidents which occurred just after their encounter. In one case, some US soldiers were pinned down by the Phaphet Lao. Two of the 'little fellows' stepped out of the woods and threw a small object between them and the enemy. It was like a 'darkness grenade', a 'dark gas' and it gave sufficient cover to enable the Americans to escape. When they returned to base they experienced the same confinement and questioning as Joe's men had.

In late 1970, William English was stationed, in Vietnam, with US 'Special Forces'. They were ordered to infiltrate the jungle of neighbouring Laos, to recover survivors and flight recorders from a B-52 bomber which had reportedly come down following a report that it was under attack by a 'bright light'.

After four days they reached the plane, which was sitting, intact, on its belly on the ground. Only the bottom of the fuselage showed any damage. There was no apparent damage to the surrounding jungle, which tended to rule out the 'crash' theory, and it still had a full load of fuel and bombs. The soldiers, who had to 'blow' a hatch to gain entry, were appalled by what they found inside.

The crew, who were all dead, were still strapped into their safety harnesses, and had injuries which we now know were reminiscent of the later 'cattle mutilations'. Although they were hideously mutilated, it had been done with surgical precision, and there was no blood anywhere. The horrified troops took photographs and collected whatever items they could, before they placed explosives which destroyed the doomed plane and its occupants. Researcher Peter Brookesmith also discussed this case in *'UFO - The Complete Sightings Catalogue'*.

There is now a great deal of information now available about the 'damnable nuisance', to the US military in particular, of countless radar plots and metallic discs hurtling and hovering over the ocean.

HMAS HOBART

Researcher Jon Wyatt wrote in the *'Australasian Ufologist'* that in 1968 the HMAS Hobart had been hit by 'friendly fire' in Vietnam. It was claimed that it occurred during a night operation against 'enemy helicopters', but Wyatt suggests it was in reality a 'UFO story'.

He relates how, on 15th June 1968, after seeing strange lights in the sky over the demilitarised zone, the Allied Command, assuming they were North Vietnamese helicopters, feared another Tet-Offensive style build-up, and placed forces on stand-by, including the HMAS Hobart.

More lights appeared in the sky, and air, sea and land forces sprang into action, firing at the 'enemy helicopters' which moved down the coast and out to sea. That is when things 'went wrong'. Just after mid-night a US navy swift boat PCF-19 was sunk by 'friendly fire' – three air-to-air missiles. There was great military activity over the next few hours, and at about 3.30am the Hobart, (blacked out and maintaining radio silence), was struck by a Sparrow air-to-air missile on the starboard, and then by two more missiles.

There were many subsequent enquiries. It appears that there was no evidence of enemy helicopters being present or shot down. The 'lights' were sighted for some weeks later, but were left 'unchallenged'. Wyatt quotes the US Commander in Vietnam at the time – General George Brown – as saying; "UFOs plagued us in Vietnam. They weren't called 'UFOs', they were called 'enemy helicopters', and were seen up around the DMZ in the early summer of '68. This resulted in quite a battle, and an Australian destroyer took a hit. There was no enemy involved, but we always reacted after dark."

Wyatt also quoted another retired US serviceman who claimed that upon the first 'friendly fire' the target 'disappeared in a flash of light'. This corresponded to a report I received from a retired navy colleague who told me – "My mate was on the HMAS Hobart that night. He said 'heat-seeking' missiles were being fired at a UFO – but they deviated and hit the Hobart instead."

During the Vietnam War, not all strange phenomena were UFOs. The US maintained a massive base on the Pacific island of Guam, and although no unidentified craft had been seen, many were tracked on radar. The matter was considered very serious, and the Pentagon sent a team of high ranking officers to investigate the matter.

After about two weeks, an electronics task force solved the mystery. There is often an explanation for unidentified phenomena. 'Second-trip echoes' were being relayed by aircraft flying far beyond the horizon. Panic over – better to be sure than sorry!

THE PHILIPPINES

Colonel Aderito de Leon, the APRO representative in the Philippines, noted several sightings, of apparently the same object and occupants, near the communications satellite station, thirty miles east of Manila.

At 4am on November 1st 1968, a farmer saw a white object, about the size of a Volkswagen car, descend with a hissing sound. It had a red light in front, and six big exhaust tubes at the rear. He could see two Caucasian looking men, wearing 'headphones' and dressed in white overalls, inside a clear canopy on the top. When he approached the craft, it emitted a loud roar, moved across the ground, and then silently took off.

Two hours later, a similar craft and occupants landed behind another frightened farmer, who promptly reported the incident to the local mayor. At 8am, a third farmer and his son, who were ploughing their field, in a more mountainous region, noticed the object silently hovering overhead.

The last incident occurred at 11am, in the same place as the first sighting. This time a different witness was riding his bicycle, and saw an identical object down the bottom of a hill. As he passed it, he noticed one of the 'men' was inside the 'canopy' and the other 'looking around' outside. He stopped twenty yards further on, and when he looked back, the 'man' got back into the craft, which took off with a roar.

Whilst there is no evidence to determine where this craft and occupants originated, I submit it was much more likely to be an 'earthly' encounter rather than alien.

The Philippines Atmospheric, Geophysical and Astronomical Services Administration (PAGASA), actively participated in the investigation of UFOs and Close Encounters.

One case they were unable to explain happened in 1984 when several children saw a disc-shaped craft which landed in Ormoc City on the western coast of Leyte Island. Three different sightings were reported, and 'bulbous-non-human beings' were seen alighting from the saucer. Details were sent to investigators in the USA, who were also unable to provide an explanation.

INDONESIA

Timothy Good, in *'Need to Know'*, noted that many other Asian countries have also had their fair share of UFO encounters. Several active periods were in the 1950s and 60s when there were hostilities between Indonesia and Malaysia.

Indonesian Air Commodore Salutun confirmed that their forces had fired upon the alien intruders with perhaps 'the heaviest anti-aircraft barrage in history'.

He added; *"I am convinced that we must study the UFO problem seriously, for reasons of sociology, technology and security. The study of UFOs may lead to new and revolutionary concepts in propulsion and space technology in general, from which our present state-of-the-art may benefit. The study of UFOs is a necessity for the sake of world security in the event we have to prepare for the worst in the space age, irrespective of whether we become the Columbus or the Indians..."*

In 1976, several strange objects were seen over the oil-rigs off the coast of Southern Herwang, West Indonesia. Paul Dong obtained some photographs from J.Salatun, an Indonesian Air Force Air Vice Marshall.

CHINA

There are many cases of UFOs being seen in Chinese legends, but due to the Communist regime, not so many have been reported in the twentieth century.

Antonio Huneeus researched ancient Chinese records, and discovered some interesting cases. One occurred during the Tang Dynasty, (618-907).

'...a celestial ship, over fifty feet long, was found and placed in the Ling De Hall. The ship gave out a metallic sound when struck, and was of very hard material which was rustproof... The Tang Prime Minister later chipped a piece from the ship, and carved a Taoist figurine.....However, in the year of the Emperor Daoming, the figurine disappeared, and the ship also flew away.'

China also has some other unsolved mysteries from its past. Colonel Maurice Sheahan, the Far Eastern director of Trans World Airline, was flying over Shaanxi province when he reported seeing an enormous pyramid, and multiple burial mounds, at the foot of the isolated Tsinling Mountains.

Several newspapers mentioned the matter, but although Sheahan claimed to have taken a photograph, it never materialised, and the Chinese government denied the existence of any such 'pyramid'.

Investigator/author, Hartwig Hausdorf, later discovered much smaller, and more primitive pyramids in 1994, but not the one reported by Sheahan. Hausdorf did, however, uncover an incident from the beginning of the twentieth century.

Apparently two Australian traders came upon over one hundred much older, and more primitive pyramids, on the plain of Qin Chuan in Central China. The custodian of a local monastery told them that they were thousands of years old, and were the product of the 'old emperors', who did not originate on Earth. Rather they were the descendants of the *'sons of heaven, who roared down to this planet on their fiery metallic dragons.'*

This myth makes more sense when one examines the reports of the Dropa Tribe and their stone discs allegedly found in 1937-8 by an expedition led by Chi Pu Tei, an archaeologist with the Chinese Academy of Sciences in Beijing. He and his team members were in the Kunlun-Kette mountains, and sought shelter in a cave.

They noticed inscriptions on the walls, some of which appeared to be astronomical. Further inside they found several tombs and strange looking skeletons, buried with unusual stone discs, which had spiralled grooves of closely written characters going from a hole in the middle to the outer rim. Eventually over seven hundred grooved discs, in some ways similar to a LP record, were uncovered in the same caves. It was not until the 1960s that academics were able to decipher them. Chemical analysis showed the discs contained large amounts of cobalt and other metallic substances.

They told of the crash of an extraterrestrial spaceship 12,000 years ago. Unable to repair their craft, many of the survivors were hunted down and killed by the terrified local Ham tribe. When the Hams realised the aliens meant no harm, the Dropas, who could not return to their own planet, remained on Earth and inhabited the cave area later discovered by Chi Pu Tei.

In 1938, at the time of the discovery, the area was still inhabited by two tribes, known as the Hams and Dropas. Anthropologists were unable to match their genes to any other known race. They were not Chinese, Mongolian or Tibetan, and had thin bodies and disproportionally large heads, similar to the skeletal remains found in the caves.

Soviet archaeological scholar, Vyacheslav Zaitsev, wrote an article in the *'Sputnik'* magazine. He detailed the seven hundred plus discs, found in the mountains at the Tibetan-Chinese border. He claimed they were estimated at being at least fourteen thousand years old. Zaitsev also said they were covered with only partially deciphered pictographs, which tell of the Dropas, or 'sky people', who came down from the sky in their 'gliders'.

When Russian scientists noticed that a disc would vibrate when unusual musical notes were played, they tested one with an oscillograph. A surprising rhythm was recorded, as if it had once been electrically charged, or had functioned as an electrical conductor.

Due to a 1978 irresponsible and sensational 'Dropa' science fiction book, *'Sungods in Exile'*, many dismissed the research in its entirety. Other respectable investigators have found a great deal of corroborating evidence.

In 2000, Zhang Hu, a research fellow of the Xinjiang Museum in Uramqi, investigated many sites of 'stone circles', some 2,500 years old, close to the Mongolian border. He noticed that many of the sophisticated geometric patterns resembled the crop circles of today,

---

The Himalayas, Nepal, Tibet and Mongolia lie on the northern borders of China. No conventional explanation can account for the report made, in August 1927, by Russian explorer Nicholas Roerich and his party, when one clear day they saw a fast-travelling metallic disc shaped object at high altitude over the Himalayan Mountains.

Roerich himself described it as a huge big oval object, with a shiny surface, one side of which was brilliant from the Sun. It was moving very fast from north to south, and as it went overhead it changed direction from south to southwest, and quickly travelled out of sight.

Roerich was fascinated with the reports of, and locating, the mythical Shambhala, (Shangri-la), and wrote several books, including *'Altai Himalaya'* in 1929, where he documented this event. Shangri-la was a mystical realm where powerful, spiritual lords were rumoured to reside, although I have also wondered about the myths regarding ancient Atlanteans retreating to little known parts of the Himalayas. One of his companions, a Tibetan lama placed a spiritual connotation upon the event, because at the time of the sighting it was a clear day, and they had been gazing at an unusually large black eagle flying overhead.

We know very little about UFO sightings and encounters in China, however in November 1661, Belgian Jesuit missionary, Albert D'Orville, was exploring Tibet with a Lama guide. He wrote in his diary that he saw an unusual object in the sky. It was the shape of a 'Chinese double-hat', and circled over the city twice.

He asked the lama if he had also seen it. He nodded his head, and said; "My son, what you witnessed just now was not magic, because beings from other worlds travel across the oceans of space, and it was they who breathed the spirit into the first people who lived on this earth.

"These beings condemn all violence; they counsel mankind to love one another. Their teachings are like seeds, but if these seeds are sown on rocky ground, they cannot germinate. These beings, who are light-skinned, are always received by us in friendship, and they often come to earth near our monasteries. They have continued to instruct us, revealing truths that were lost in the centuries of cataclysm which have changed the face of the earth."

In 1941, members of the Chinese People's Liberation Army saw and photographed a saucer-shaped object, with a dome-like hump on its upper side. It hovered over a major road in Tianjin, Northern China.

Gordon Creighton, editor of the '*Flying Saucer Review*', was multi-lingual and had served in many diplomatic and intelligence posts for the British government. That same year, during the summer of 1941, while stationed at the British Embassy in Chungking, China's wartime capital, he also saw a flying saucer over the far western part of the country, near Tibet.

Thanks to Lin Win Wei's, (writing as Paul Dong), thorough research in his reports, and also his books '*The Four Major Mysteries of Mainland China*', and '*UFOs Over Modern China*', some other older, and more recent cases have come to light.

One early case, on 8th May 1880, a local farmer, Ju Tan, was walking home when he saw a glowing object in the bushes. There was a rushing and humming in the air, and he felt paralysed - 'numb and floating'. The next thing he knew, he woke on a mountain, two weeks later. He had no idea where he was until a forester told him that he was three hundred miles away from home in Guizhou Province.

In April 1968, on the Gobi Desert, Gu Ying and his companion were working on an irrigation scheme. A red-orange, illuminated, disc-shaped object, with a diameter of about one hundred feet, appeared to land about half–a-mile away. The military commander in charge of their engineering project, requested the regiment to send out investigators.

As the troops, on motor-cycles, approached the landing site, the object took off and headed towards the northern border with the USSR. Everybody thought it must have been a Russian reconnaissance craft, but all they had left to examine were some burn marks on the ground.

Paul Dong also mentioned a report from Sheng Shuhui who, in Mid-September 1971, was a ten year old young cadre from Beijing. His group was on assignment in a valley in Ulasutai, Inner Mongolia.

At 10pm one night, he and two other friends saw a bright, round luminous object moving slowly from east to west, across the night sky. It radiated a yellow light from a hazy, luminous red corona, and suddenly turned and accelerated out of sight.

The local peasants were unperturbed, saying that this was a common occurrence in the desert, as a **UFO Base existed out there**.

Other reports from the northern border area were quite frequent. In late Summer, 1976, Li Lingpei was a teacher in an Inner Mongolian school. One evening, at dusk, he and several students were working in the fields when they saw a strange object in the sky, flying from south to north towards the China-Mongolian border.

It was a metallic, silver-grey, with a cylindrical tail which spurted out a white, misty 'gas'. It flew slowly across the sky, at an altitude of about 3,000 metres, and rotated horizontally on its own axis. After a couple of minutes it disappeared across the northern horizon, and Li was unable to proffer an explanation to his students.

In the 1970s, late at night, two farmers saw a bright, shining object land silently on a hilltop in Tai Yu County in the Fujian Province. As soon as they told the army, about three hundred troops arrived and surrounded the hill.

The captain in charge originally thought it was a secret American weapon, bound for Taiwan, and determined to capture it. He sent an advance party up the hill to investigate, but when they neared the object it became brighter. The light affected the vision of some soldiers, and others became dizzy.

The object emitted an indescribable noise, and after his men retreated, the Captain ordered the soldiers to open fire. Amid the sound of gunshots, the UFO rose slowly into the air and then vanished into the night.

In 1978, a worker at the Karamay Oil Field Headquarters saw a silver, oval shaped object, silently moving up and down the desert grassland. Believing it may be an enemy attack, the army was notified.

Soon a group of soldiers, with anti-aircraft weapons arrived, and along with oil field workers, surrounded the object. Their hopes of capturing this strange craft were also in vain. It suddenly took off and vanished into the sky.

The Chinese are proud of the bravery and nationalism of their people, and they have spoken about one such occasion which happened on 13th October 1979. It was 4am when truck driver, Wang Jian Min was driving near Lan Xi in Cheking

Province. He nearly ran into a parked car, and when he approached the driver, learned that he was scared to go any further, because there was a flying saucer on the road ahead.

Wang announced he would lead the way, and slowly drove up the hill, only to find that a strange dome-shaped craft was really at the top. It was emitting an odd blue glow, and standing beside it were two silver-suited beings, each about five feet tall, and wearing bright lamps on their heads.

Wang decided that attack was the best form of defence, and rummaged around in his truck's cab until he found a crowbar. He turned around to confront the 'aliens', only to find that they and their craft had gone.

Researcher Jenny Randles told of a British woman, Dawn, who had been crossing Nepal and Tibet, west of the Chinese border, in November 1947. She was in the company of her husband, a British Colonel and a Ghurkha guard, who were travelling in a convoy of trucks.

They had stopped for supper on a desert plateau when a vibrating noise shook everything, including the vehicles. Everybody suddenly felt 'icy cold' and an enormous pressure, pushing down from above. A grey, floating mass, which was spinning like a top, swooped down towards them. Her husband ran towards it, only to be struck down by some invisible force, later recovering in a very disorientated state.

Dawn felt only a hazy recollection for some period of time before she picked her husband up. She looked around and the object was gone. That night, all the witnesses suffered pounding headaches, nausea and a rash on the exposed parts of their bodies. The Ghurkhas, who were on the way to see the Dalai Lama, were so frightened they refused to continue the trip.

The Mongolian border between China and Russia, has seen many severe skirmishes, some of which nearly led to serious confrontations between the two countries.

By the 1950s, territorial and other disputes led to a serious breakdown in relations between China and Russia. By 1965, Russia had withdrawn all technical and financial aid, and deported all Chinese students.

On 24th April 1970, a Soviet bomber, on a secret mission, disappeared on its flight from Vladivostok to Moscow. The Russians blamed the Chinese, and for a while both countries were on war-footing and moved troops to the border.

At the same time, multiple flying discs were seen over the Sino-Soviet-Mongolian frontier area, and salvos of ground-to-air missiles were fired at the intruders. Apparently both the Russians and Chinese thought the new 'aircraft' belonged to the other, and several serious border hostilities ensued.

Paul Dong said that although no photographic proof or documentary evidence was available, a British correspondent and also a group of German tourists, in Mongolia at the time of the incident, reported that the Soviet Union had destroyed a secret UFO base, of immense proportions, in Northern Mongolia. It consisted of dozens of pyramid-like structures and many miles of subterranean tunnels.

The Soviets maintained their normal veil of secrecy, however, years later, a retired Red Army General from the People's Republic of China would only affirm that there had been heavy border activity in the vicinity of Mongolia at that time.

Gordon Creighton translated an interesting case from Beijing ufologist Zhang Ke-Tao, which occurred in the autumn of 1975.

A unit of the People's Liberation Army was stationed in Jian-Shu County in Yunnan Province. Two guards, stationed at the gates to the army barracks, were startled to see a huge saucer-shaped flying object, emitting beams of soft, orange-coloured light, circling above their heads. The one soldier ran to the camp to sound the alarm, while the other stayed to observe it.

The Camp Commandant, along with several armed soldiers, soon arrived at the gates, only to find both the strange object, and remaining guard were 'gone'! A search party, of all personnel, officers and enlisted men, was immediately instigated, but they could find no trace of the missing soldier.

Several hours later, four soldiers, taking over sentry duty, heard a moaning sound behind them. They looked around, and there was the missing guard, who had miraculously reappeared. When he recovered, he had no memory of what had happened, but his eyebrows, hair and beard had inexplicably grown very long.

It is not known if this was due to a 'time-slip' as suggested by some researchers, or a possible effect on the 'victim's' hormones, however a similar incident occurred half-way across the world, in Chile's far north desert, less than two years later, on 25th April 1977.

Six members of an army cavalry patrol, who were conscripts on a training mission, were sleeping around a campfire, while two of their comrades stood guard. Suddenly, at 4am, two brightly lit objects descended from the sky. Although one UFO dropped out of direct sight, behind the Andes foothills, they could still see the glow of its light.

The second object descended, almost to the ground, about five hundred metres away. At that stage it emitted a violet light with two intense red points. Corporal Armando Valdes, extinguished the fire and ordered his men into defensive combat positions. He told them to keep him covered while he took his rifle and set out, up the slope, to investigate an area of undergrowth where they thought the object may have landed.

When he was halfway up the slope, there was a blinding flash of light. After the troops were able to focus their eyes again, it was dark all around, and the UFO and Corporal Valdes had disappeared. After twenty minutes, the Corporal reappeared, and came stumbling back down the hill towards his men. Before passing out, he mumbled; "You do not know who we are, nor where we come from. But I tell you that we will soon return."

When dawn came, the conscripts carried Valdes to the nearby town of Putre. They noticed that his previously clean-shaven chin now had several days of 'stubble', and his digital watch had stopped at 4.30am on 30th April, five days into the future.

He was immediately transferred to a military hospital, where he recovered quickly, but had no memory of what had happened on that lonely mountainside.

There are many reports of UFOs causing massive blackouts, not only in the USA and other Western countries, but also in China. In the early evening of 12th September 1979, a brilliant, silent UFO, emitting white rays, was seen over the towns of Huaihua and Xuginglong in the Hunan Province. Before it departed, there was a massive power failure in the area, but the government did not comment on the event.

China, like Indonesia and many other countries, received reports of UFOs over their oil fields. In 1978 a worker at the Karamay oil field headquarters reported a silent, silver, oval shaped craft moving up and down over the desert grassland.

A group of soldiers, armed with anti-aircraft weapons, arrived and surrounded the strange object. As they closed-in, it suddenly took off and rapidly disappeared into the sky.

On 7th July 1977, at Zhang Po, Fujian, a large audience, of about 3,000 people, had gathered together to watch an outdoor screening of a Romanian movie, *'Alert on the Danube Delta'*. At about 8.30pm, two massive fiery UFOs swooped down out of the sky and buzzed the assembled movie audience. They came so low and close, people could feel a radiated heat coming from the craft. In the crush and ensuing mass panic two children were unfortunately trampled to death, and over two hundred people injured.

The Chinese have always been very secretive about UFOs. In the late 1990s I met Chinese researcher, Professor Sun Shili, at a UFO conference. During his lecture and subsequent conversations, he imparted very little about events in his home country.

He mainly discussed an incident from the Red Flag Tree Farm in Heilongjiang . Peasant worker, Meng Zhaoguo was abducted, and forced to have sex with a female alien. He said that it was not pleasant the first time, but subsequently 'much better'.

During the lecture, photos were shown of a rather unattractive man with a big grin form ear-to-ear. I wonder why?

The Chinese are still very uncommunicative about UFO sightings, many of which could either be their own latest weapons and experiments, or spy missions from western countries.

They now have their own 'UFO Groups' but membership is limited to professionals. Occasionally, in the past, some official comments have been made. In 1976, Chen Yu-Ching, editor of the Chinese Air Force magazine, when asked his opinion, said; "I believe that they are controlled by some other intelligent beings on certain planets other than the Earth. Consequently, the saying that UFOs are interplanetary should be recognised."

The *'Shanghai Hebei Daily'* reported on a dramatic encounter on October 19th 1998. Four radar stations had detected an unknown object above a military base near Changzhou City. Many witnesses on the ground described it as being a 'mushroom-shaped dome, with a flat bottom, and covered with bright, rotating lights'.

An armed jet was immediately sent up on an intercept mission, but every time it got near, the UFO would shoot up out of reach, only to outdistance and then reappear above its pursuer. A request for permission to fire upon the intruder was denied, and the jet was forced to return to base when it ran low on fuel.

JAPAN

On 17th October 1975, multiple witnesses saw a bright, golden disc-shaped UFO over Akita airport in Honshu. It descended to an altitude of about 1,500 feet, and hovered for a few minutes, about five miles away. Airline pilot, Captain Masaru Saito also saw the strange craft, which he described as resembling two plates put together, face-to-face. As the UFO flew away, out to sea, it was also tracked by air-traffic control.

Japanese Air Force and civilian pilots have also had many encounters with UFOs. In the late 1960s, Colonel Fujio Hayashi, Commander of the Air Transport Wing, commented; "UFOs are impossible to deny. When we pilots scramble, we have to identify the object clearly, whether it is an enemy or not...Though it is said that these unknown objects might be the secret weapons of some powers, it is very strange that we have never been able to find out the source for over two decades."

In 1967 Japan's Chief of Air Staff, General Kanshi Ishikiwa said; "UFOs are real and they may come from outer space......UFO photographs and various materials show scientifically that there are more advanced people piloting the saucers and mother-ships".

In 1974 Air Force Major Shiro Kubota was ordered to intercept what was thought to be a Soviet bomber. When they approached the intruder, it was not what they expected. Straight ahead was a red-orange disc, about ten metres in diameter, with square-shaped marks around the side, which were either windows or propulsion outlets.

His colleague, Lieutenant Colonel Toshio Nakumora, aimed their 20mm cannon at the object, and closed in. The UFO reversed direction, and headed straight for the Japanese plane, forcing them into a sudden, violent dive. The intruder then made several rapid, high speed passes, coming closer and closer until it struck their aircraft.

Kubota and Nakumora ejected from the plane, however Nakumora's parachute unfortunately caught fire, and he plunged to his death. The Japanese Air Defence authorities determined that the crash was caused by a collision with an aircraft or object unknown.

In 1976, Gen. Kanshi Ishikawa, former Chief of Air Staff, said; "We must establish systematic study for UFOs more sincerely, surely resulting that visitors are coming from outer space to the earth."

His comments were supported by Col. Fujio Hayashi, Commander of the Air Transport Wing of the Irma Air Squadron; "Even if it is a small number who have sighted UFOs, they are unable to be denied by anyone. It is very easy for us to deny something with ignorance, but it is a great mistake."

The Japanese have always been interested in UFOs, and when Toshiki Kaifu became Prime Minister in 1989, he said that he had been interested in the subject since 1967, and encouraged the establishment of civilian UFO organisations and a museum.

After his term in office ended in 1991, Kaifu said; "When you ask me if I believe in UFOs, I'll say I'd like to, though I've never seen them, because the existence of UFOs is a perfect dream....It's been one of my desires to watch a UFO, but it has never materialised. I hope my dream to encounter a UFO comes true in the future."

CHAPTER FIFTEEN

THE CHILDREN REMEMBERED

In my book *'The Alien Gene'* I examined many cases where several members of one particular family have experienced alien encounters and interference. This can cause enormous trauma and confusion for the affected contactees, many of whom are reluctant to divulge any details.

Sometimes I have come across cases where the 'visitors' have affected an adult contactee's memory, but somehow forgot about the children, who were also present, and remember many, if not all, details of the encounter.

<u>JOCELYN FRAZER</u>
One case of interest was that of Jocelyn Fraser, who remembered childhood incidents, but none of those from later years. Like many other experiencers I have worked with, Jocelyn was born in Britain, where her male ancestors served in the military.

Jocelyn's father was a highly intelligent man, who served in the British RAF as an aircraft mechanic, and later in the Merchant Navy. After migrating with his family to Australia, in 1968, he worked as a civilian aircraft engineer, before taking his skills on to a position in a power production plant.

I asked Jocelyn if her father had ever discussed aliens or UFOs, and her reply was interesting; "My father, who was an atheist and highly sceptical, only mentioned one possible incident from when he was ten years-old. He recalled something being present in his room, and pressing him down on the bed.

"When we discussed this a while ago, I thought he would jump at my explanation of 'sleep paralysis'. Instead he became adamant that something had been present in the room, and only left when he 'screamed blue murder', and adults came running."

Jocelyn's mother was also quite brilliant, and after graduating from London University, worked both in a laboratory and as a science teacher.

When Jocelyn was ten, her mother became mentally distraught, and was fearful that someone was going to steal her children, Jocelyn in particular. At one time she was worried that people would come over the roof to kidnap her. When

Jocelyn asked her if someone was overhead in a helicopter, her mother suddenly 'clammed-up'. She suspects that her mother had experienced some form of UFO or alien encounter in the past.

One interesting family 'generational' anomaly is a scar on the top of Jocelyn's right foot. Her mother had an identical scar – same appearance and location - as has her daughter Sonia. She is sure it was not there when Sonia was born, and medical colleagues have assured her that scars are not an inherited feature of three generations.

Like many other female experiencers, Jocelyn only reached out to contact me after she became concerned for the well-being of Sonia. She confessed as to once sharing her mother's irrational fear about aliens taking her own daughter.

Sonia (who is now in her teens) has always been physically healthy, and was exceptionally intelligent from an early age. When she was young, Jocelyn only allowed her to watch ABC type 'kids shows' on television, usually with animal characters – certainly nothing 'creepy' or any mention of 'aliens'. She was very unsettled when the following conversation occurred;

'When my daughter was four, and had just started kindergarten, she suddenly announced from the back seat of the car; "Mum, there are good aliens and bad aliens. You see those lights - (pointing to a particular shaped street light) – I like to think they are the space ships of the good aliens, and they can use these to win against the bad aliens." I responded by asking her what the spaceships of the bad aliens looked like, and she shrugged and said she didn't know.'

Jocelyn convinced herself that Sonia must have got this idea from something she picked up at kindergarten, but she naturally still felt uneasy. Like most of the third generation children, Sonia was very articulate and bright, even as a young child. She had always been creative, thinking outside the box, and enjoyed art and music. Whilst she can be a bit dreamy, and highly imaginative, Sonia has already displayed psychic abilities.

Jocelyn's own earliest childhood memory of an unusual event was not long after the family arrived in Australia. They were living in a rental home on a bush block. Her father strode over to the couch, lay down, and appeared to instantly fall asleep. His head was on Jocelyn's rag doll, and she tried to pull it out from under him. The doll's hair became damaged by the time Jocelyn dragged it out, but her mother just stood staring out the window, 'in a very unsettling way.'

"Don't worry about the doll," she said. "They are coming now."

Jocelyn remembers going across to her mother's side, and telling her that her younger sister was asleep on the floor. Instead of picking her up, her mother kept silently staring out of the window. She recalls a massively bright white light appearing and expanding to 'a huge level of brightness' in front of the window, but cannot remember anything after that.

'Later, I asked my mother why she thought Dad fell asleep on the couch so quickly, and showed her my damaged doll. She said I must have dreamt this happened. In retrospect, I think she truthfully believed this to be the case, and her memory of preceding events had somehow been erased.'

A year later, when Jocelyn was five or six, her grandmother became ill, and she returned to London with her mother and sister for a period of time. She has a vivid memory of attending a childcare centre with her sister. She cannot exactly recall travelling to or from that place, just what happened whilst there.

Jocelyn's report of this incident, and her mother's reaction, is interesting;

'The teacher was a young-looking woman, with light skin and fair hair. There were boys and girls involved in all sorts of activities, which seemed to be organised around the room. I was overwhelmed by the degree of noise and frenetic activity....I noticed a cubby, the like of which I have never seen since. It resembled a small cottage made of some hard moulded plastic. I convinced my four year-old sister to go in with me, and bolted the door shut. I was tense as the noise outside was still very loud.

'Soon I heard the other kids saying 'knock, knock', and asking to be let in. I was replying; 'You cannot come in,' but not in words.

'I did state verbally to my sister; "They are knocking, but don't let them in." She looked baffled, and said that no-one was knocking. At that point I heard the teacher, as clearly as if she was standing next to me, stating; "Jocelyn, it is nice to share with the other children, you should let them in the house."

'Again, my sister obviously did not hear this, and protested when I told her we had to get out.... The teacher got everybody to hold hands, and soon we were moving in unison and weaving spiral patterns. It was as if we were all connected mentally, quietly working together. I found this peaceful and

enjoyable, and almost regretted the arrival of my mother to take us home. I remember the teacher saying, "We will see you next time."

Jocelyn doesn't actually remember leaving the place, and later asked her mother not to send them there again. She was bewildered when her sister said the other children made no noise at all, and no one spoke, except once when the teacher held her hand.

'Mum looked genuinely confused. She stated she had no idea what we were both talking about, and that we had gone to no such place, cutting short any disagreement between my sister and myself. I believe all communication in this place was happening telepathically, and that for whatever reason, my sister was not able to tune into this form of communication, at this time at least.'

Jocelyn's next memory was much more disturbing. After her grandmother died, they returned to Australia. When she was about seven she noticed a vaginal discharge, and her mother took her to the doctor – but it was not the surgery or doctor she normally attended, and she doesn't remember travelling there.

They were met by a different fair-haired woman, who showed them into a room with a metallic floor and walls. This 'surgery' was very spacious, with an arch but no actual door. The 'doctor' wore a white gown and mask, so Jocelyn is unable to describe his face.

Jocelyn was made to undress, and assisted onto a metallic table. She noticed what looked like several metallic surgical instruments, but the doctor produced a large syringe, with a very long needle. She was asked to remain very still, and slowly and carefully he inserted it into the general area of her urethra. She cannot remember what else was done, but the doctor said to her; "You are very special to us Jocelyn." She did not know why.

Back in the 'reception' area Jocelyn, her mother and the fair-haired woman were joined by a tall man wearing what seemed to be a white robe. He had long dark hair and a beard, and she recalled him lifting her up as she hugged him around the neck. She also remembered that after this she lay on his lap, and listened to his low resonant singing before she drifted off to sleep.

Later, Jocelyn wanted to ask her mother further questions about the weird nature of this visit to the doctor. Much to her incredulity her mother had no memory of them going to the doctor, or of Jocelyn having an infection.

Like many other experiencers, by the time she was fifteen Jocelyn had become a vegetarian, and developed an interest in animal welfare, ecology and peace and justice issues.

For many years after that Jocelyn's life was mostly uneventful, but during her late twenties to thirties, she began to experience inexplicable 'missing time' episodes. She would go for what she thought was a short drive into the country, and arrive home, to an angry and frantic partner, hours later than expected.

On most occasions she has no recall of what happened, but has partial memory of one instance when she was in her early thirties. She was working as a nurse at the time, and decided to visit her parents on her day off. She arrived at about 9am, planning to stay until at least mid-afternoon.

Suddenly, about thirty minutes later, for some reason she could not comprehend, she felt an urgent need to leave. She got into her car, and followed a strange compulsion to drive to a lookout in an isolated area.

'I recall parking and going up a small flight of stairs to the lookout. Once there I saw another car pull up, and a family get out. I remember communicating telepathically with someone that there were other people present. A reply came that they would soon be gone. Sure enough, they got back in their car and left.

'My next actual recollection is driving down the freeway to Melbourne. I got home about 7pm. I entered the house to a very angry husband. He wanted to know where I had been, as he had rung my mother, the police and every major hospital. I honestly did not know, and made up some excuse. I felt angst ridden, confused and just wanted to shut the whole incident down and get on with life, which eventually happened – until the next time!'

Jocelyn was not always aware of her 'missing' episodes. In 1999 she was the overnight nurse in charge of an elderly residential facility. Occasionally she would see a tall, thin shadowy entity. It seemed to be watching her, often for considerable periods of time. She told herself that she must be suffering from sleep deprivation due to the night duty. She nearly lost her composure when one of the residents asked her about the tall, thin man, and gave her an accurate description. One night another resident told Jocelyn that she was 'physically' missing from the facility for several hours, but she cannot recall being anywhere else.

Strange things were also happening in Jocelyn's home. The radio would turn itself on in the middle of the night, often fluctuating the volume from soft to ear splitting levels. Electronic toys would self activate at odd hours. This frightened Jocelyn so much she bundled them up and gave them to a charity shop.

On the health side, Jocelyn was quite well, with only one disturbing issue. While she did not give birth to Sonia, her only daughter, until she was forty, from her early twenties she suffered from persistent lactation, which could be quite embarrassing. Despite a medical investigation, the doctor's could offer no explanation for this occurrence.

In 2010, when Jocelyn was in her early forties, she began to hear strange 'frequency' noises, and also developed a disturbing 'precognition' on a couple of occasions. Just like many other experiencers, she sensed 'some impending cataclysmic event'. At that stage she was unaware of other abductees' reports, and thought she may be losing her sanity. She felt an inexplicable fear, started stocking-up on non-perishable provisions, and is still considering moving inland to higher ground.

In 2017 Jocelyn had a disturbing experience which caused her to re-evaluate her past memories, many of which she had dismissed or pushed to the back of her mind.

'With echoes of my father suddenly falling asleep on the couch all those years ago, one night my husband suddenly announced he was off to bed. I was surprised at both the suddenness of the decision, as well as by the fact he was heading to bed so early. He tends to be a night owl, and often retires after me.

'I lay down to relax on the couch, and must have drifted off to sleep. My mind was dwelling on earlier mundane household events that evening, when suddenly I fully woke up. There was a profound level of silence. I couldn't hear the heater fan or the clock ticking.

'I was not able to determine whether I was dressed or not, but I was totally immobilized, in a state of paralysis. I didn't feel afraid, or in any state of panic, and somehow this scenario had the feel of some well-worn routine. I tried mental communication, reaching out with my mind and asking who was there, but got no response. I could not open my eyes, and at one stage felt pressure on my brain, and a jerking on my neck.

'I finally awoke at about 3am, and took myself off to bed, convinced I must have experienced some form of sleep paralysis combined with lucid dreaming. The next day I noticed a small stinging sensation on my left forearm, and noticed a smear of blood and small puncture wound. There was a small track mark with a slightly palpable donut shape object at the end.

'Three days later, when I was sitting on my daughter's bed, to tuck her up for the night, I noticed an identical object in the same spot on her left forearm. There was no puncture wound scar, so I wondered if it had been there for some time. I was even more concerned when, a few months later, at a family get-together I noticed an identical thing on my father's arm. I surreptitiously checked my husband's arm and could not see one.'

Jocelyn had always ignored her periods of 'missing time', and didn't consciously associate it with any problem until it caused ongoing difficulties within her own family. Finally, something else happened which prompted her to contact me in 2018.

She sometimes had vivid dreams, which she always considered to be just that – dreams. During one of these episodes there were grey type 'beings' and also tall blond men. They all wore greyish/blue jumpsuits with the same insignia. She was astounded when Sonia was testing out some new school highlighters, and started absent-mindedly drawing an identical insignia on the scrap paper.

Jocelyn is a sane, no nonsense medical professional. She does not know what occurred during her 'forgotten' experiences, and while she cannot discount some form of alien involvement, is just as prepared to entertain the thought of earthly mind-experimentation or something else she has not yet considered.

LYDIA

I wrote about this case in my book, *'The Alien Gene'*. I have still given Lydia a pseudonym, although due to publicity some may realise who she is. Originally she had never reported any of the incidents, and it was a concerned relative who advised a professional. From there she was referred to researcher, Ken Phillips, and later hypnotic regression. She had never wanted the limelight, however the hypnotist who assisted with the initial and ongoing investigations, participated in documenting her experiences, along with those of other witnesses, in a book. Unfortunately when the initial press releases were sent out, Lydia's true identity was revealed.

"I had no idea," she bemoaned. "One morning I opened my front door, and there on my doorstep, front path and out on the street, were journalists, photographers and TV crews. It was all so confronting, and there was no way I could retreat into anonymity! After that I agreed to give interviews and speak at meetings, but I also attracted unwanted attention and even threats and stalking. In hindsight, sometimes I wish I had never told anybody what happened to us all.

Lydia has developed an increased psychic ability, but only uses it privately, and not for commercial purposes. She now has five grandchildren, all very intelligent – one could write and draw before the age of two. Amazingly, she still remained close friends with the hypnotist – perhaps he was one of the few confidents she could talk to now that Ken was gone – he still rings her frequently. Unfortunately, due to dementia, he was not really able to assist with any further follow-up.

CHILDHOOD

I became acquainted with Lydia in the early 1980s, and our still firm friendship has lasted nearly forty years. Once we got talking, I discovered Lydia had a strange experience as a small child, although at that time she was living at Weymouth in the south of England.

"I was outside playing with the other kids, and although there was one of the parents keeping an eye on us, I suddenly went missing. Everyone was searching, and the police were called. Just as suddenly they found me back in the same place I had been 12-15hrs earlier. It is strange that I can remember every detail of my mother's kitchen in those days, and have no recall of those missing hours."

"I can also remember one evening, when I could see a fairground across the park, and kept asking if I could go. I could see the ferris-wheel, all pretty with coloured lights. I thought Mum was lying when she said there was no fair. If it wasn't a ferris-wheel – what was it?"

Lydia also mentioned that her mother's youngest brother, Daniel, was only six years older than her. There was another day - she was four and he was ten – when they had a strange 'missing day' experience together.

(This reminded me of Jane and Christine's case from my book *'The Alien Gene'* – when Sylvia, Jane's mother, told me how she had gone missing one morning when playing with other children in a park in Eastern Europe, and was located back in the same spot that evening. All she could recall was being with a 'lovely blond angel'.)

"My mother was also psychic, and Tony, my husband, never quite understood when she started rambling on about something to do with aliens and 'flying carpets' in the early 1940s. She said one didn't want to meet them – it was worse than war! I later wondered if she was talking about the time she spent in the military on the Isle of Man during the War."

OUT OF PLACE AND TIME

"I will never forget an incident on my birthday in July 1972. Tony and I were still courting in those days. He brought me a bunch of flowers and took me for a night out in his brand new E-type Jag. It was about 9pm, and we pulled up at a red traffic light. I remember seeing a light behind us, which I thought was a police patrol, and told Tony be careful as they targeted sports cars.

"It was a clear starry night, and suddenly the car seemed to be 'spinning' just like those ones at the fairground do. Next thing we were still sitting at the red traffic light, and we both urgently wanted to go to the toilet! Tony drove to the pub, but it was closed – everything was closed! We looked at our watches in amazement – it was 3am! What had happened for six hours? We couldn't have been stationary at the lights all that time – other motorists would have done something. When I picked up the bunch of sweet-peas they had grown! It may not be connected, but two months later I discovered I was pregnant, but had a subsequent miscarriage."

Another strange episode occurred in 1978, when Lydia and Tony took her daughter Annie to stay at their nearby caravan, where a relative was holidaying. After they had dropped her off, they just can't remember 'travelling', but found themselves in South Wales!

"We regained our composure, and made our way home. Both Tony and I rushed upstairs, both vomiting, but our son young Martin, who had also been in the car, remained unaffected."

FAMILY ENCOUNTER

Lydia's next experience, in 1979, when she was thirty-six, brought her a lot of unwanted publicity when researchers released details of her case and her identity.

"My friend James had been over for the afternoon, and the kids and I walked along with him through the fields as he cycled home. (It was only much later that James confided in me that he too had been 'taken' at the same time, and the 'aliens' had done something to his pineal gland. I was just so glad, for James' sake, he hadn't told anyone else about that fateful evening in 1979. At least he was spared all the unwanted publicity that I endured).

"It was dusk by the time we left him at the road on the other side, and as we were ambling back, about a ten minute walk from home, Martin claimed the Moon was coming down out of the sky.

"Of course, I thought he was being ridiculous. I looked, and got quite a start when I saw this bright spinning object coming down out of the sky towards us. I initially thought it was a plane about to crash, and made the children crouch down in the tall grass with me for protection. When we didn't hear any impact I looked up and saw this object pass overhead, and drop silently and vertically behind a nearby embankment.

"Everything all around was eerily silent and still, like some unseen barrier had eliminated all the previous background noise. Thinking it might have been some kind of a small plane crash, I had a compelling urge to go and look behind the embankment, and the children and I took a few steps closer. Everything seemed safe so we hurried up to the top of the rise.

"We all stood there and stared. It was a crescent shape object, about sixty feet across, hovering a couple of foot off the ground. It was hard to see the details – the massive white light around it was so bright. At times it didn't appear to be totally solid, it was like a dark, grey pewter intricate lattice, and I could still see the field through it. It was pulsating – moving backwards and forwards - and seemed to disappear, then reappear, then disappear again.

"I was mesmerised – transfixed – and it must have come back into view because I could see this separate white light above it, which still seemed to be part of the overall structure. I felt drawn to it – like a moth to the flame, and it seemed to get brighter as I moved closer. A slowly rotating orange ball of light came from the far side of this 'thing', and began to move towards me. I still kept walking towards it, as if in a trance.

"My daughter Annie started screaming at me to come back, and she jolted me back to reality. It was weird, I had this strong feeling of fear and déjà-vu. In hindsight I wonder if this was somehow connected to my previous 'episodes'? I grabbed Martin and Annie by the hand and started running down the embankment.

"Poor Martin was having trouble keeping up, and Annie was screaming that the 'thing' was now at the side of us. I scooped five-year-old Martin into my arms, and ran like hell, dragging poor Annie along with me. Everything seemed to be in 'slow-motion' as Annie called out again –"'Look Mum – there are two of them." I was close to exhaustion but told Annie not to look back – just keep running.

"We were now running along the riverbank path, and the surrounding area was starting to look surreal. The grass was folding flat upon itself, as if being pushed down by some strange force from above. We kept running until we reached the house, and I was surprised to find my Tony was home from his evening shift. It was well after 10.30pm – there was over an hour and a half I couldn't account for since we saw the strange object at 9pm.

"Whilst he did not mention the two previous episodes in the car, I'm sure he must have recalled it when we told him what had happened. He got us all to draw a picture of what we had seen. Tony also made me look in the mirror – the skin under my eyes was all red and scaly. Also Annie and I both had violet scars on our left legs.

"Tony was also very understanding, because a few years before his younger brother, now deceased, had a sighting on the Yorkshire Moors. He was with his kids, and there was some missing time. The one boy is very intelligent.

"It's strange, and rather worrying that of my two kids, now adults, who were also there, **remember everything quite clearly**. Martin can talk about it privately, but is so terrified he always sleeps with the light on." (Martin also spoke of other 'people', with heads shaped like 'raindrops', being on board the craft, and I know several other witnesses who cannot sleep in the dark since their experience. Many also keep the radio or TV quietly playing.)

I asked Lydia about Annie, who was fifteen, and very traumatised at the time: "She just totally avoids the subject, and I can't ask her what, if anything, these 'beings' did to her."

In 1979, about a month after the experience, their neighbours, a few doors down the Manchester street, mentioned seeing a large, silent, orange 'ball' bobbing up and down over Lydia's roof and the house next door. Another three different neighbours confirmed seeing a 'thing', through their windows, about the same time as Lydia and the kids' abduction. Their descriptions were similar – a 'dark grey disc'.

"We hardly told anyone about it, but a friend persuaded me to have a couple of hypnotic regressions, which I found so disturbing I couldn't even watch the tapes. Later I started to get more conscious recall and 'flashbacks' and knew that sooner or later I would have to face what happened to us and 'come to grips' with it.

"I recalled that at the point of turning to run away I saw, and bumped into, a person - a human figure - standing next to the main object, then everything 'blurred'. It was like I was in a dream, and I felt myself 'floating'. The next thing I was in a room and six people came in. They were human, but Oriental in appearance, with yellow/olive skins, very dark hair and slanted eyes. They were all dressed the same, wearing dark suits but with high necks.

"I recall being laid on a table, with very bright lights shining in my eyes. Someone was examining me and something cold, like pieces of ice, were being put on my legs. I don't want to know or remember what was done to me on that examination table.

"After that my periods stopped, and a few weeks later I had a slight 'show', and a waxy discharge which I took to my doctor. He told me I'd had a miscarriage. I was flabbergasted – I'd not been pregnant – I couldn't have been, and there was no blood loss or any sign of a miscarriage. What was happening to me?

"My menstrual cycle did not return, and I was referred to a gynaecologist who ran a series of tests. He said my fallopian tubes had scar tissue, which may have been caused by an ectopic pregnancy. Of course, he said he was only speculating as to a possible cause, but I knew I had never had an ectopic pregnancy or anything like it." When Lydia told me this I immediately thought of other women, who had similar problems with their Fallopian Tubes and ovaries after their experiences.

"Of more concern was his inquiry as to when and why I had my ovaries removed. **I hadn't!** What was he talking about – how could he say that 'somehow they were *gone*? Then it dawned on me – I hadn't had a period since that encounter in 1979! What is even more inexplicable is that, at the age of **60,** in 2002, I started to menstruate again – at least that's what I thought.

"Later, in 2005, the specialists said 'something' was lodged in the lining of my womb – but they weren't sure what it was – but it had been there a very, very long time. They wanted to investigate, but for some reason I was not only terrified of anaesthesia but also 'needles', so I still don't know. I couldn't tell them why I was scared of 'not being in control', they would have thought I was nuts."

After the encounter, in 1979, Lydia also noticed strange marks would appear on her body, only to vanish the following day. Seven years later in 1986, she was required to wear a plastic name badge at work, and within hours her name just disappeared from it. After this happened three times they were tested by a scientist who felt the anomaly may have been caused by 'radio waves'.

There had been strange 'happenings' before on the riverbank from which Lydia and her children were abducted. The houses, in the street where she lived, had fields, at the back, going down to the river.

"One of my neighbours told me that during the War, he was walking out there with his wife, and saw massive lights up above, like bright spotlights. They thought it must be some form of film set, and saw some people on the ground. Thinking they must be actresses, as they were wearing robes, similar to 'nuns', they went up and asked them what was happening. They got no reply, and after walking away they turned and looked back – everything was 'gone'!"

"There was a lady, who used to mind my son, and the first time I met her she said – 'I've seen you before'. It transpired as a child she had lived much further down the same river, and used to also cycle along the bank. On several occasions she had gone out in the morning, and the next thing it was dark and she was coming home on her bike with no lights. She also made vague references to 'aliens.'"

CONTINUING PHENOMENA

Lydia was naturally concerned regarding her other 'altered or missing time' episodes; "I know I wasn't suffering from what one would normally call 'amnesia' because on more than one occasion I was physically 'missing'.

"In 1992 I went out into the garden at about 1pm. It was a nice sunny day and I sat at a table out on the patio. Tony had dropped in for lunch and gone back to work, and I was expecting a friend at 1.30p. My mother, who lived with us was expected back from the Day-Care Centre at 3.30p. The next thing I knew I was still sitting at the table, but it was **7pm**.

"I thought I must have fallen asleep, but the thing is – I wasn't there during the intervening time! My friend had called and left when she couldn't find me. The assistants from Day Care had brought Mum back, and finding no-one home had left her at the local hospital for us to collect later. After we picked her up I looked at my bare arm – it had a round area of tiny pinpricks of dried blood – similar to an inoculation site!

"Another time I was visiting some relatives in Somerset. It was 9.30p, in winter, and when I went out into their backyard, half of it lit up like sunlight. I ran back inside, recalling that a similar thing had happened back home in the West Midlands."

THE LATER YEARS

It was to be another twenty years before an implant was discovered and removed from behind Lydia's ear. No-one had been aware of it until her body started to 'grow' a protective membrane around it.

Lydia has developed an increased psychic ability, but only uses it privately, and not for commercial purposes. She now has five grandchildren, all very intelligent – one could write and draw before the age of two.

PORTLAND, N.S.W. AUSTRALIA - 12th MARCH 1997

Linda and her two children, Lucy and Peter, were living on a recently rented property just outside Portland. Linda was a university graduate, working in a respected profession at the time; Lucy (11) and Peter (9) were both intelligent and mature for their age.

"It started as a normal night," Linda said, "much like any other. At about 9.30 I was on the phone to my friend Donna. My daughter had gone to the toilet before bed. This was located outside at the end of the veranda, and as Lucy was spooked by the dark and the quiet, Peter kept watch by the door to the veranda. My conversation was interrupted by their excited voices yelling - 'Mummy, Mummy, come and see the UFO!' Thinking it was a fuss about nothing, I asked Donna to wait a minute, and put the phone down.

"I went outside to see what all the commotion was about. The entire back of the property was lit up like day. Hovering over the far side of the garden some fifty feet away, was this huge oval ball, about thirty-five feet high and twenty feet across, of silver-blue sparkling light.

"On later reflection, I behaved totally out of character – as if mesmerised. I casually went back to the phone and said; "It's OK, they're just watching a UFO in the back garden." Donna thought the object might be affecting me strangely. I kept talking for about another fifteen minutes, and just left my children out on the veranda watching that thing!"

Suddenly the phone cut out. Donna told us that she became concerned, as the family lived in a very remote place. Linda was worried that someone may have cut the phone lines, as she was living incognito to avoid a violent domestic situation. She considered calling the police, but didn't know how to explain the UFO. (When checked later, we found the phone cable to the house is an underground one, buried about a metre deep!)

Linda had also thought there might be an intruder; "There was no dial tone or anything, so I loaded the gun which I kept under my bed, went outside, and checked around the house. I ignored the UFO and remember thinking – 'all clear, no need to worry, there must be a logical explanation for it'. I was only concerned about the phone being out of order. Looking back now, my behaviour then seems very odd.

"For some inexplicable reason I felt very tired, and just walked back right past the kids, into the house and went to my bedroom. I lay down fully clothed on the bed. It must have been about 10.30 p.m., and I just blacked out. At about midnight I woke up, had a shower, and went to bed. It was as if I was in a trance. I had not even thought about Lucy and Peter, let alone gone to check on them.

"The next morning I woke at daybreak, in sheer terror. Memories flooded back and my first thoughts were for the children; 'My God, I left the kids out there with that thing!' I breathed a thankful sigh of relief when I checked and found them peacefully asleep in their beds.

"I ventured outside. The morning was quiet and peaceful; nothing amiss or strange in the sky. I crossed over to the fence beyond the garden, where the 'thing' had been hovering, and stopped at an odd eight-foot patch of swirled grass. The grass seed heads were bent over and flattened some forty centimetres above the ground, but the plants were otherwise unaffected.

"Over breakfast I tentatively asked the children about the previous night. Lucy described the object as being similar to what I had seen – a large blue light, hovering over the ground, with air and light emanating from all sides. She noted the entire back area was lit up, and went on to say the grass underneath the object was moving and swirling. I was taken aback when she mentioned a door in the middle of the craft.

"Peter's recollections were essentially similar, but far more detailed. He said he first saw a star sized light in the sky, which seemed to get bigger and come close very quickly."

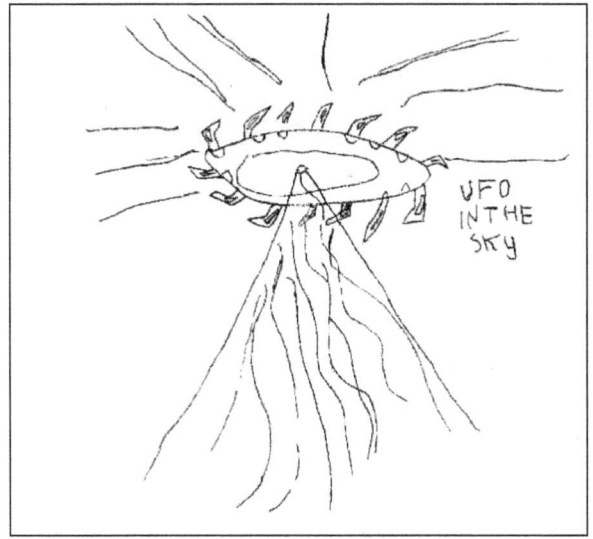

His description indicated that it was a more traditional type saucer object with claws around the circumference, which descended after hovering just over one hundred feet from the ground. Both kids mentioned that the object bobbed around when hovering, and travelled at incredible speed when moving.

"I felt a growing concern as I began to realise that Lucy and Peter did not seem to have any immediate recollection of what happened later that night. They could not say when or how they got to bed, but both mentioned a beautiful blue light and a floating sensation. It was as if their memories had been blanked out, with just odd flashes of something else."

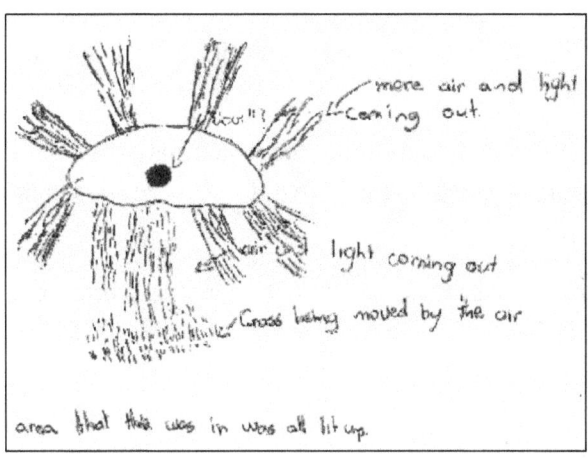

(A few days later, Linda rang me, and my colleague Bryan Dickeson visited the property a week later, to sight the strange ground traces and gather other evidence.)

"My sense of trepidation worsened two weeks afterwards when I had what appeared to be a dream, in bed one night. There was a loud humming sound, and the whole house seemed to be vibrating. I was petrified and calling out 'Go away – don't touch us!' and asking God to help me."

Before Bryan could follow-up on his preliminary interview, and conduct more tests on site, Linda had moved out, and we could not gain access to the property.

Linda and the children moved in with her mother down on the New South Wales South Coast: Linda said; "It is not so remote; I feel safer with another adult in the house and neighbours all around."

During the next three months other disturbing factors were becoming apparent. The children, especially Peter, were starting to recall more and more on a conscious level, including the entities. (They had no exposure or access to alien or ufology literature at any time.)

Neither of the children seemed to have further conscious recollections of what happened after they had been on the craft – the next thing they recalled is when they woke up in their beds the next morning. They did not remember leaving the craft or indeed any other details of that night.

They both agreed they did not like the strange beings, and did not want to see them again.

Linda said, "I don't recall any of this at all, and more than what may have been done to me, I am indignant and angry that some unknown force or entity should interfere with my children.

"Both children had three strange red spots on their inside ankles, forming a triangle, and Lucy mentioned someone 'doing something' to the back of her neck. I knew she had never had any operation or accident involving the back of her neck, and felt a sinking sense of disbelief when I lifted her hair to see a small scar, complete with 'stitch marks'. She also claimed there had been a strange 'person' outside her window one night."

I visited the family in their new home, and the children seemed to be regaining some of their memories of that unusual

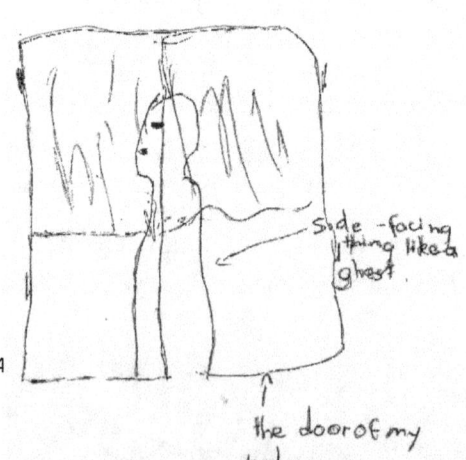

night at Portland. In order to prevent any cross-contamination of details, I separated Lucy and Peter during interviews. I sat in the garden with each one, playing with the rabbit, and only inserting crucial questions into normal conversation.

Both had consistent memories of the craft having some form of door in the middle, and being floated into the UFO without their feet touching the ground. They both drew pictures of the beings they had seen, and had clearer memories of what happened inside the craft.

Peter said there were creamy-blue walls inside. He mentioned bright white lights on the ceiling, and a table in the middle. He described the beings as being quite tall, whitish in colour, with big round black eyes and no mouth.

Lucy's memories were slightly different. She drew a picture of what she initially saw "after the UFO came." It resembled a window, with a side-on figure, and she has written "side-facing thing like a ghost." Lucy recalled a continual electric buzz and said that the middle door to the craft looked like a black hole in which five beings were standing – looking out at them.

She described "skittle-shaped" entities (she didn't notice any arms); they seemed to be wearing some form of silver-green strap around the lower half of their faces. She also detailed them as being creamy-white with large black eyes. Their heads seemed too large for their bodies. Lucy recalled that while nothing was said and they made no gestures, there was some communication "in her mind."

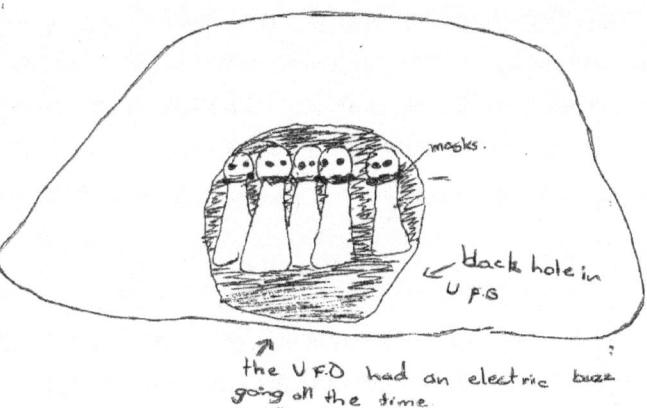

She spoke of "a needle on a cord which was attached to a wall." It gave her an "electric zap", and said the beings were doing something to the back of her neck, like an operation. She also saw her mother, Linda, lying on a table. One entity was standing next to her "with something metallic in its hand, like a clipboard – which it appeared to be looking at."

The children were seeing a fully-qualified psychiatrist for counselling about the family break-up, and he was quite satisfied that they have had a genuine experience. I also found them to be a very credible, well-balanced family, and have remained in contact ever since. While Linda and Lucy have adjusted well to their unfortunate experience, Peter (now in his thirties) has become more distant and refuses to discuss it.

In his book *'Close Extraterrestrial Encounters'*, Dr. Boylan also mentions an incident in 1992, when a contactee recognised a woman from 1952. They had both lived in California, within sixty-five miles of each other, and they remembered sitting together on a 'spacecraft' all those years ago.

During the 2000 Intruders Foundation Conference, abductee Anna Jamerson spoke of her chance meeting with Beth Collings, whom she was sure she had seen before.

Beth described how she still remembered that during her childhood 'experience', she had sat, on the spaceship, next to a shy little girl with an English accent, who was wearing a school uniform. Beth drew a picture of the emblem on the uniform, not knowing that Anna had attended a school in England, and the emblem matched the one on her uniform.

Anna described how she and Beth, as children, were abducted from different locations and placed together, possibly in an attempt to see how they would interact socially. Anna did not believe the aliens were 'good guys', and thought they are here 'for their own purposes'.

Kevin Randle wrote about a case from 1973, when divorcee, Pat Roach, was living with her children in a Utah house. One night, after she had dropped off to sleep on the couch, she heard a noise, and thought it may be a prowler. Her two daughters recalled what had happened, and insisted that 'spacemen had been in the house'. She didn't believe them, and a later police search showed no sign of an intruder.

Later hypnosis indicated that a few days after the initial incident, Pat had woken from the couch to see several small creatures. They had captured her, along with Debbie and Bonnie, and floated them out of the house and into a craft which had been standing in a nearby field.

The only person who consciously remembered the encounter was the youngest daughter, Debbie, who said an 'Indian girl' put her on a machine. She also commented that a couple of neighbours were also there, who later said they didn't remember anything.

All the family described the creatures as being short, about five feet tall, with pasty white faces, long fingers, big eyes, no nose and a slit for a mouth. They were wearing shiny suits, which looked like uniforms. There was also a 'man' present, who seemed to be totally human.

Pat was subjected to a medical examination, and they were all asked questions about their lives, thoughts and feelings. As with other similar contactees, it was only Debbie, the youngest child, who had retained any memory of the event.

CHAPTER SIXTEEN

OF SCHOOLS AND TRAINS

SCHOOLS

During a seminar I was conducting on the NSW Central Coast, a middle-aged man hesitantly approached me, and related an event he has never forgotten from his childhood.

In 1963, when Alan was eight years old, his family suffered a difficult break-up, and for a couple of years, he was placed in a Boys' Home in North Parramatta, a suburb of Sydney.

It was the Friday night of a holiday weekend, when the cooler June weather allowed for Saturday bonfire and firework celebrations. The children had been sent to bed early, at 6.30pm, so they would be well rested for the big day to come.

At about 8pm, Alan and his room-mate heard a humming sound outside their second floor room. At first they were frightened, and huddled together under the bed. After the strange noise had continued for about ten minutes, they gathered up enough courage to peek out of the window.

It was a clear night, and for thirty minutes they watched in awe as, some distance away, a strange object hovered about fifty metres above the ground. It was 'cigar-shaped', pink in colour, with a red light on the top. Suddenly, the humming sound became louder, and the object's brightness increased as it 'shot off like a bullet'. Just as quickly, it came to an abrupt halt behind the Boy's Home, and descended directly behind some nearby trees.

The next day, several of the boy's were sent out to collect wood for that night's bonfire. Alan and his mates made their way to the spot where they had seen the object descend. The trees had broken branches, as if something had 'pushed them down from above'. The grass below was flattened in a ten metre diameter circle, which was quite warm, despite the surrounding area being covered with frost.

A few days later, there was great excitement at the Home. Several reporters were congregated at the front gates, wanting to interview Alan and his mate about what they had seen on Friday night. While they were standing in the driveway watching, Alan and his friend were approached by the headmaster and a uniformed policeman, who told them that if they ever wanted to see their families again, they must not talk to the reporters or anyone about what they had seen. They were pressured into silence; "When one is a small boy," he said, 'large police officers and housemasters can be very intimidating."

Less than three years later, another incident was witnessed by children from a combined primary/high school, several hundred kilometres to the south in Victoria

On 6th April 1966, a disc was seen by pupils and teachers at Westall School, Melbourne, Victoria. I wrote about this event in *'Contact Down Under'* and also received one unverifiable report that a couple of school children, who got too close to the landed craft, were later monitored by a government medical team.

Rather than repeat my previous account, perhaps the incident is best told by a High School student who, shortly after, wrote the following article for their school magazine. It was privately authenticated and passed on by one of the teachers.

'I was in class when a disturbance occurred outside. I didn't take any notice and when the bell went for morning recess my classmates and I went to our lockers and then walked out into the yard. We noticed that all the girls who were doing physical education were gathered right down near the end of our playing field.

'Suddenly, the school came alive with excitement, and everybody began running down towards where the girls were. I was among the surging mob. I had seen something that looked very unusual in the sky.

'As I looked up I saw a dazzling, silvery object, flying around some pine trees which grew on a ridge about a quarter of a mile directly behind the school. It then flew across some open paddocks, also behind the school, and returned to the pines. On the other side of the ridge there is a small field. The thing hovered over the pines and descended behind them, and must have been directly over the field. I then lost sight of it because of the pines.

'As the thing was out of sight I began to notice many private aircraft, mainly Cessna, flying towards the pines. It was then the thing reappeared and rose to

the level of the approaching aircraft. This enabled me to get a rough idea of its size. It was a silvery object, as long as one of the Cessnas, but very thin.

'As the aircraft approached, the thing tilted on about a 45-degree angle, and started to move into the distance, gradually gaining height. The planes increased their speed and began to follow it, but the object streaked away, leaving the planes far, far behind. The planes turned back, but we all stood, hoping it would return, but it didn't, so we all went into school, fifteen minutes late.

'After school, two friends and I went to the field where the object had descended. In a few minutes we were crawling under a barb-wire fence which surrounded the field at a height of about four feet. We waded through the waist-high grass, making a gap in it. Suddenly, we were there. We found ourselves standing in a spot where the grass had been utterly crushed against the earth It was an area of about 20-30 feet in diameter. Cows could not have done it because the fence was barbed, and also the cows would have left a track in the grass. There was no track. The object had descended over the field; could it have done this? It all leads back to the same question. What was the object? Some people say it was a weather balloon, but do weather balloons go up and down quickly, crush grass and fly across the sky faster than reasonably speedy aircraft? Otherwise, your guess is as good as mine.'

Note the number of 'private aircraft' initially accompanying the disc. 'Authorities' arrived much quicker than expected, the area was 'ploughed over' and cleared of any evidence, and the same day children pressured into not discussing the subject, with those who did speak to the press being punished with 'detention'. Another investigator who actually attended the scene soon after, believed this was one of our own experimental prototypes. I tend to agree, however, these are our personal opinions, not shared by many other researchers who also put a lot of time and effort into this case.

This case also has similarities to the USA – 'Cash and Landrum' case, which had several helicopters following the disc. I began to wonder if both the Australian 'school' incidents were due to our own prototypes either accidentally or deliberately landing near school children. Perhaps, just perhaps, it was an attempt to gauge public reaction? After all, children are not always believed, and easy to silence.

I searched my friends' and colleagues' files and records, and discovered that there were several incidents involving schools, during the 1950s, 60s and 70s.

In 1976, on 15th July, ninety children and four teachers, from the Treleigh CP School, at Redruth, Cornwall in the UK, watched as a spherical object crossed high in the midday sky.

At least, this one didn't land, but everybody in the school yard saw the white, saucer-shaped object, quietly and slowly, spinning overhead. Everyone said it resembled two dinner plates, face-to-face, and had silver and yellow flashes coming from it at a ninety degree angle.

In 1977, British researcher, Norman Oliver, wrote an article for the *'BUFORA Journal'*, detailing several incidents over the past few months, and asking if our schools were being 'singled out'.

On 4th February, at the Broad Haven County Primary School near Pembroke in Wales, fifteen children, most of whom were playing football, saw a silvery, metallic object on the ground within a quarter of a mile away. It was there between 1pm and 3.45pm, and the pupils described it as being a disc at the bottom and a sort of dome with a red light at the top. Some students said they saw three or four windows, and others heard a humming sound.

Several children claimed to have seen a silver-suited figure near the craft, before it 'moved behind some bushes and vanished.' A few of the boys were so scared they ran inside to tell the headmaster, who didn't believe them at the time.

After school, a couple of students crossed a stream on the school's boundary, and made their way to the field where the craft had last been seen. The area was very wet, muddy, and 'boggy', but they saw the object from about four hundred yards away. They said it was about the size of a 'coach', and looked like two saucers, stacked one against the other to form a dome.

It suddenly moved over the ground, becoming obscured by a hedge, and the frightened boys ran away. On the Monday morning, the headmaster was besieged by reporters. He took the kids more seriously, and got them to draw and relate what they had seen.

Two canteen workers said they had also seen the object, but were sure it was only a sewage truck. Later investigations proved this to be impossible – the field was a muddy bog, which no truck could enter.

Was this craft alien, or one of ours? To the north was a top secret rocket testing station at Aberporth, while at Brawdy, near St. David's, was a military base which trained pilots, and also housed both a Tactical Weapons Unit and a US Navy underwater research station which tracked Soviet submarines.

The following week there were two more reports from England. Twenty children from the Herbrandston School at Hakin, Milford Haven, watched from their playground as a white, cigar-shaped object flew noiselessly overhead, at an altitude of about five hundred feet.

The other report came from Edenhurst School in Newcastle, when most of Prep II form watched a silent object for about ten minutes, before it disappeared into a cloud.

It was described as – *'a silvery-blue, cigar shaped object'* – *'a cigar shape of silvery-grey colour'* – and – *'a circular sausage-shape with a sort of a round dome on top, changing colours from brilliant white to orange, blue and red.'*

On the afternoon of 16th February, back in Wales, nine girls, and their teacher, were playing netball in the yard of the Anglesey Rhos-y-bol County Primary School.

Gwawr Jones said; *"Mrs Williams was showing us how to throw the ball in the net, when I saw an object high in the sky. I shouted to the others, and they all looked up and saw it. It had a black dome on the top, and a silver cigar-shaped base. It was travelling smoothly across the sky in a northerly direction...it went behind the only cloud in the sky, and reappeared again, then disappeared. Mrs Williams took us inside and without conferring, we got a piece of paper and drew what we saw..."*

Ron Halliday, in *'UFO Scotland'*, also discussed a couple of similar cases: In the summer of 1952, Joan Torrence and several other students were leaving Elder Park Primary School, in Glasgow. It was 4pm, and due to the long daylight hours, they were planning what to do for the rest of their free time.

Suddenly a dark shadow blocked out the sun, and the pupils, along with a teacher and the school janitor, looked up. They could see a rotating, sombrero-shaped object hovering one hundred feet up, just above the school steeple. It was slightly tilted to one side, and after a short period of time, a distinct whining sound could be heard. The disc shot of across the city, where it was also reported by other witnesses.

In 1978, another incident occurred at Glasgow's St. Mark's Primary School in Muiryfauld. Again, it was a bright summer's day, and a group of schoolchildren, enjoying their playtime games, were startled to see a strange object hovering about twenty feet over the school fence. It was glistening in the sun, and not very large, only a few feet across. It looked like 'two fedora hats joined together', was sharply defined, and silver-coloured, like shiny metal.

Witness, Euan Riley, didn't report the sighting until many years later. He said at the time they didn't think the teachers would believe them, and he couldn't remember how the saucer left – just that it 'vanished'.

The next year, across the Channel, another incident occurred in France. Jean Sider translated the following report for *'XENOLOG'* in New Zealand.

On 14th May, at Eyzin-Pinet, near Vienne, sixty school children, and their teachers, were coming out of the canteen after having lunch. They stared in awe as an oval disc, shining in the clear sky, came from the north, and passed directly over the school, at an altitude of about sixty metres.

The children rushed to the other side, in order to follow the object's path. They were all shouting; "The Martians are landing! They are Martians!"

M. Paul Viallet, the school director, said his nineteen-year-old son, Jacques, ran towards a field located near the Sallin Housing Estate. It was there that they had lost sight of the object, and he spotted it as he reached a barbed wire fence.

The craft was in the field, about seventy metres away, and silently hovering five or six metres above the grass. It was an oval shape, not that large, at an incline, and changing in colour from 'black to brilliant'. The cows did not seem to be disturbed, but as Jacques tried to climb the barbed wire fence, the object slowly rose, accelerated in speed, and disappeared into the sky at an incredible rate.

An incident, at the Santa Leonor College in Callao, Peru, was probably not an intentional visit by an unidentified object, and more likely one of our own prototypes. At 10.10am on 25th August 1965, three hundred pupils, and several teachers, were startled when a strange noise was heard from the roof, and the desks and walls shook as if there was an earthquake.

They all raced outside to see what appeared to be a 'space-craft' on the roof. It was oval, shaped like a dish, terminating in a pointed top and emitting two red beams of light from the sides. Everyone stared in amazement as it took off, with a loud noise, and circled around as it gained height. There was fire and smoke coming through two vents on the side as it shot away and vanished towards the north-east.

Three years later, across the Pacific in New Zealand, was another incident, reported in the *'Panorama'* publication.

Students at the Te Mata School, Havelock North, were quite frightened when they saw a strange craft hovering over an orchard near the school. Some of the children, who were near the pool, where the teacher was giving swimming lessons, drew everyone's attention to the object, which they estimated to be half the size of the pool.

It was touching the top of a tree, about one hundred yards away from the playground, and making a 'clicking' noise, 'like a clock'. The craft was saucer-shaped, with lights around the bottom, and a 'diamond-shaped' light on the dome. It was white on the bottom with a black band around the side, where there appeared to be a hatch.

Suddenly it shot upwards, and travelled towards Hastings, leaving a vapour trail in its wake. A teacher said it was too round to fit the description of any aircraft he knew, and the Bridge Pa aerodrome and Napier's Civil Aviation Department said that there were no aircraft in the area at 11.20am – the time of the sighting.

Nancy Usjak, in Canada, was also discovering that sometimes strange craft are interested in our children. On 10th January 1979, a UFO landed, in full view of a teacher and three students, in the playground of the Queen Elizabeth Public School in Kitchener.

During later interviews, another teacher could only recall a lightning strike in the January, however all the witnesses drew detailed sketches of the craft they had seen.

Perhaps some UFO sightings over schools are inadvertent, and not actually meant to be witnessed. Researcher Ted Phillips reported several cases of 'levitation' to the *'MUFON Journal'* in 2006. One involved the students at the San Francisco de Chiu-Chiu School in Chile.

On 19th October 2000, a large craft, surrounded by multi-coloured lights and about three hundred feet in diameter, hovered close overhead. It was first seen by the school's custodian, Fresia Vega and student Valentina Espinoza, who saw a door open in the middle of the object.

Mrs. Vega said a bright, blinding light came out, and she experienced the sensation of being paralysed and 'sucked in' through the door. There was a tingling sensation over her body, and people's voices seemed to be far away.

At the same time, a loud blast was heard, and teachers and children ran out and also saw the object, which moved away. Valentina had been hiding behind Mrs. Vega, who didn't seem to be able to speak. Both of them felt very cold for some hours after.

Following the 'blast' the village dogs started barking continuously. Some people fled on foot, and television signals were lost all over town. The State Police noted that the other children did not experience any side effects, however two residents had eyesight damage due to the glare.

In April 1998, students from the Adikaran school in Bandarawela, Sri Lanka, reported seeing a strange object landed on the playground.

It was large, disc-shaped, about eight feet in diameter, and sitting on legs. It suddenly flashed bright red and yellow lights, and took off at a tremendous speed.

It was only 6.30 in the morning, and maybe it hadn't intended to be observed. Only two students, Indika Dissanayake and Harsha Ellawalagdera were present. Harsha was a promising child, who was entrusted with opening the classroom doors early each morning.

The headmaster believed them, as there had been previous reports of a similar object often flying overhead early in the morning. Other local residents, of good repute, had also recently sighted unidentified craft both in the sky and on the ground. Was this an alien object, or a terrestrial craft, thinking it wouldn't be noticed, making a quick landing?

There are instances when landings near schools are most likely extraterrestrial in origin.

On 14th September 1994, there had been multiple reports of bright lights and objects traversing the African night sky over Zimbabwe. Most were attributed to either a meteorite shower or the re-entry of one of the stages of a Russian satellite. Due to the massive discrepancies in the size, speed and altitude of the objects, investigator, Cynthia Hind, doubted both of these explanations.

The Ariel School was a private primary school, about twenty kilometres from Harare, and taught students from a variety of races and cultures. Two days later, on 16th September, all sixty-two pupils were on their morning break in the playing field.

They noticed three silver balls of light moving in the sky, and suddenly one came much closer, and appeared to land about one hundred metres away, from where they were standing on the edge of the school grounds. This area was very rough, and out of bounds, due to the thick vegetation, thorn bushes and snakes, spiders and other less than pleasant wildlife.

The older children were very curious, and described seeing a small man, about four feet tall, dressed in a shiny, tight fitting, black suit, appear on top of the object. He had a pale face, huge eyes, shoulder length black hair and a long scrawny neck. He walked a little way through the bush, and upon seeing the children, promptly disappeared. Either he, or someone similar, re-appeared on top of the object, which soon took off very rapidly and shot away into the sky.

The younger children, having been told legends of 'tokoloshies' eating them, ran back to the school building calling for help. All the teachers were at a meeting, and didn't come out. The mother in charge of the tuckshop didn't believe them, and later said she was not prepared to leave the food and money.

Cynthia took several investigators to the school four days later, and interviewed many of the students. In advance of her visit, Mr. Mackie, the headmaster, had over thirty drawings from the pupils. Some were better than others, but many depicted a typical flying saucer. Some mentioned three or four smaller objects in the sky above.

Despite an extensive search, the investigators could find no radiation or other traces on the 'landing site', and Cynthia wondered if the object had hovered just above ground level.

In early December, Dr. John Mack along with colleague Dominique Callimanopulos visited the school and interviewed the children, whom he believed. Many, who were standing at different vantage points in the playground, reported telepathic messages, or 'feelings', that mankind was not caring for the planet. Since the children have attained adulthood, their memories and evidence have remained consistent.

TRAINS

UFOs also seem to show an interest in our railway trains and tracks. In the late 1950s, my Scottish relatives were very excited when they were travelling to the west coast for their summer holidays. A 'flying saucer' had buzzed their train for some minutes, and all the passengers had watched in awe and astonishment.

That same decade, in 1954, across the English Channel, in France, Marius Dewilde also saw an unusual object on the National Coalmines railway line which was adjacent to his home, at Quarouble, near the Belgian border.

At 10pm, he heard his dog barking, and suspecting a prowler, went outside with his torch. He could see a dark mass on the railway tracks, which were only eighteen feet from his house. At first he thought it was an abandoned farm cart, but then noticed two 'creatures' walking in single file towards the 'object'. He turned his flashlight on them, and saw that they were small, less than four feet tall, and wearing suits similar to those of divers, with large helmets made of either glass or metal.

He rushed to the gate, but when he was only six feet away from the beings, a powerful light, similar to a magnesium flare, shot out from a square opening in the object on the tracks. It left him paralysed, and he was only able to move again after the strange craft rose slowly above the ground, hovered, and then ascended vertically into the sky. As it disappeared from sight, it displayed a reddish glow, which was also reported, at the same time, by other people living in the area.

There have been other times when UFOs have landed on or near railway tracks. Gordon Creighton reported on an unusual incident, which occurred on October 21st 1963, in Argentina, near the town of Trancas in the Tucumán Province.

At 9.30pm, Dr. Moreno, one of the leading citizens, and his family, were preparing for bed when their maidservant pointed out that something intensely luminous was on the railway line, which was about 300 yards away from the house. There appeared to be a number of men moving to and fro around it.

It was not feasible that track maintenance would be operating at that time of night, so the Morenos thought there must have been an accident. Julia, the daughter, looked out and saw the same thing, so she and her mother walked across the garden, and then returned to the house to get a lantern, which they set up near the gate.

Suddenly, one half of the luminous 'train' shot away from the rest, and flew above the ground for about half a mile. At this time they could see that it actually consisted of three circular objects.

Once the women had set up the lantern, it was as if the visitors were aware of their presence. A beam of light, emanating from one of the objects on or above the railway tracks, turned from white to violet, and swivelled around to play upon the two witnesses in the garden. They were immediately overcome by suffocating heat and prickling or tingling sensations in their bodies.

As they ran for the house, the light changed from violet to red, and focussed the beam on their home. For the next forty minutes, the family hid in terror and anxious silence. The temperature had risen, and everyone was experiencing the same burning, needling and prickling sensations in their bodies. The dogs were behaving out of character, listless and depressed, only growling when the light beam fluctuated or moved away.

Donã Teresa, the matriarch of the family, wandered around the house, taking peeps from various windows. She claimed there were at least five discs, two of which were only seventy yards away, thirty or forty feet above the ground, and apparently supported by a 'jet of gas'. She and her husband estimated the discs as being about twenty-six feet in diameter, with six brightly illuminated portholes in the centre. Señor Moreno was sure he could see figures silhouetted inside.

There were two tubular luminous beams, one red and one white, which seemed to be solid, sweeping the house, which now felt like a furnace inside. One witness claimed that these beams gave off a whitish gas, and made a 'sort of howling noise'.

After forty-five minutes, the UFO on the railway tracks rose into the air, and started to move away, followed by the other discs. They moved, at low level, over the house and towards the Sierra de Medina range.

The three dogs started howling and the house and garden were full of a thick sulphur smelling mist and abnormal heat, which was still noticeable the next day.

The police who attended the scene the following day, had received independent reports of six discs passing across the sky, and also the extraordinary illumination of the railway embankment. Some researchers have speculated that UFOs land on railway tracks at night, so they will be less conspicuous whilst effecting minor repairs to their craft.

What about the many occasions when UFOs have merely 'buzzed' railway trains, usually freight engines and their cargo? These events were occurring in many parts of the world. It is unlikely they intended to 'grab' such large objects.

I was reminded of the 1970s, when an Air Force Officer told me of a dispatch motor-bike rider who was regularly sent from one Australian RAAF Base to another with classified documents. One day, the poor 'mailman' was 'buzzed' by a flying saucer until he fell into a ditch - either some human or alien pilot's idea of 'a bit of fun'. Perhaps the following incidents, first publicised in the 1950s, were also 'just a lark', by either terrestrial or alien 'hot shot' pilots, to frighten the living daylights out of unsuspecting train crews!!

In the USA, Bob Teets reported an October 1954 event from Stonewood, West Virginia. The witness's job was to ride in the back car of the train, and to signal the engineer when it was in position to take on a load of coal. As he swung his lamp, he noticed a light in a nearby deep hollow. It became larger and brighter, and soon he saw an oval, twenty-five feet wide, hovering craft with blinking lights across the front.

It moved over the train, and its heat appeared to be igniting the coal dust in some of the empty rail cars. The poor man was terrified, and hung onto the side rail of the last car until the object flew off. He said the engineer had not seen the UFO, but believed him when he saw his burned glove and hand.

Another incident happened a few months earlier, on April 28th 1954, at 7.20am, in Australia. It was reported by the *'Melbourne Argus'* on 10th May.

It was a clear morning when engineer Ted Smith, and fireman Colin Beacon, were driving their goods locomotive, and were between Duverney and Berrybank, forty-five miles west of Geelong, in Victoria. An enormous, dark blue or black saucer, without any visible doors or windows, rushed down out of the sky, and headed straight down towards the train.

A.L. Smith, the train driver said; "I nearly keeled out of the cabin when I saw that huge, round, dark mass plunging down at the train." Both of the men were terrified, when it came within 350 feet of them, and then suddenly raced upwards again.

They watched for about four minutes as it 'careened' about the sky. It halted, stationary over them, 'like a huge monster', before moving higher and higher until out of sight. They said it was about a 'quarter-of-a-mile' in diameter, with no visible windows or doors.

Two years later, in 1956, a New Zealand freight train was about ten kilometres south of Gisborne, on the east coast of the North Island. They were running behind time, and after rounding a bend, speeded up.

Ahead of them, at a height of about five hundred feet, and to the right of the track, were four large, circular balls of intense white light. Each one was 'the size of a small room', and they were flying in formation, with one ahead, two abreast and one astern. They seemed to be rising, as if to fly above a hill, and cross the bay to Gisborne. Suddenly, they changed direction, shot off high in the air, and passed over the back of the train.

In 1958, another locomotive crew were frightened by four similar unidentified objects which stalked their train for a considerable period of time.

It was at 3.20am on 3rd October, and the five crew of a freight train, owned by the Monon Railway, were just outside the US railroad crossing settlement of Wasco, Indiana. Four big, white, soft fluorescent lights, about forty feet in diameter, manoeuvred back and forth, in various formations, above the freight train, which was travelling forty to fifty miles per hour.

They were soundless, at about tree-top level, and in sequence, increasing their brightness with speed, and dimming to a yellowish orange when slowing down.

Author, Brad Steiger, reported a 1965 event from Lincoln, Nebraska, when a train crew working near Weeping Water noticed a strange craft which was in the sky, ahead of the train, but returned, descended slightly, and hovered overhead for some time.

It was also seen by the conductor, engineer and brakeman of the nearby work-train, who described it as having an outer rim with several lights which steadily 'blinked' in a clockwise direction.

BOLIVIA

Early in the morning, on 10th March 1983, a diesel locomotive, hauling fourteen cars and more than seventy passengers, encountered an enormous cloud of light over the town of Ventilla. It flew towards the train, and emitted such a blinding light that the engineer, Sixto Churaz, slowed the train to fifteen kilometres an hour.

The oval shaped object, about 120 feet in diameter, changed colour from white to orange, and hovered over the train. A ray of yellow light struck the locomotive, bringing it to a complete halt. At that time, all the passengers woke up and started screaming.

The crew were unable to start the train for fifteen minutes, when the object started to move away. The train was not damaged, and the local police, who had also seen the UFO, investigated the incident.

CANADA

The *'Yukon News'* reported an incident on 13th October 1967, when a strange craft showed inexplicable interest in a freight train. One of the crew first saw the object as they were a mile north of Elnora, and thirty-five miles south of Red Deer.

The train was travelling at about 50 mph, and a forty feet diameter object was flying alongside, at a distance of about one hundred yards. At one time, it dived towards the train, and came much closer. When they stopped at Alix, to drop off a car, the strange craft also stopped and 'just hung there'.

By this time, all the crew were watching, and said it had coloured lights, which flashed red, green, orange and yellow around the rim. Its top was black, and underneath was another circle of glowing lights.

When they got to Mirror, it was also seen by the station attendant, who said it remained in the sky, about fifteen miles to the east, for the next two hours before it left. The next night, the engineer of another freight train also reported a similar object.

AUSTRALIA

Several, or similar, incidents since the 1954 Victorian case have been documented in Australia.

Darwin's *'Weekend News',* reported that on 27th July 1961, dozens of people, from Darwin, Tennant Creek and Wonarah, including an airline pilot, had described seeing a brilliant object, with a 'flashing red-and-white jet tail'. G. Holstabek said it seemed to have a controlled flight as it moved and headed inland, and Mrs R. Parker commented that it was so low, she was sure she could see what she thought were cabin lights.

When a train from the North Australian Railway arrived in Darwin, the driver, Douglas Clark, and George Firman, the fireman, gave a graphic description of how it had 'buzzed' their train. They were 285 miles south of Darwin when the object came right up behind them, and descended until it was no more than one thousand feet overhead. It had given them 'quite a start' as, at one stage, they thought it was coming 'straight at them'.

The RAAF compiled a list of all the witness's report, but no explanation seems to have been forthcoming.

NULLABOR TRAIN - 16th JANUARY 1985

The Trans-Australia Railway Line runs from Adelaide to Perth. This incident occurred 740k northwest of Adelaide near a remote railway siding at Ooldea, near the restricted Woomera military base and only a short distance from Maralinga.

An Australian National goods train was crossing the Nullabor Plain when the driver and his offsider saw a bright light descending from the sky to the ground.

It then disappeared from sight. Their first thought was that it was an aircraft crash, but fifteen minutes later they saw the same light very close to their engine, which suddenly started to lose power. They turned off the train's headlights so they could better observe the object in front of the engine. Whatever it was, the craft possibly thought better of trying to 'take' a fully laden goods train, (not so easy as a sedan car!), and departed.

They were forced to detach/unload most of the cargo to get up a steep incline, and left half of the wagons at a siding. The train continued west to Cook, where it was handed over to a new crew. The engine had only malfunctioned whilst the strange light was present, and no fault was found when checked out at Port Augusta.

The driver was most upset that the station clerk – not present during the incident - had told the media that the object was just a reflection of the engine's headlights on a sand dune. He contacted VUFORS researcher, Paul Norman, who felt this was just another case of 'debunking' a genuine sighting. The driver, who had been a South Australian police officer for seven years before becoming a train driver, said he and his offsider were scared when the engine had started to lose power. A man of his experience and employment history is a trained observer and 'does not scare easily'.

This was not the only case of trains being accosted by mysterious craft. John Pinkney reported that four trains, hundreds of kilometres apart, were 'buzzed' at exactly the same time, 9pm on 9th September 1989. This was confirmed by the Port Augusta Rail Control Centre, whose memo on 14th September. logged reports from Zanthus, Hesso, Watson and Manguri. All the drivers and witnesses described essentially the same experience.

The Perth Observatory dismissed it all as 'probably space junk re-entering the atmosphere,' which the witnesses hotly disputed; "It's easy to sit at a desk and make pronouncements like that – we were on the spot and we know what happened."

Transline express driver Lou Becarrelli, and his offsider Mick Yuryevitch were about 14km east of Zanthus when they noticed a vertical pencil-shaped light in the western sky. They realised it was just the exhaust trail of an enormous 'contraption' which was initially travelling at incredible speed and then suddenly 'swooped' the train within twenty seconds.

Lou said; "In twenty-five years on the railways, I've never seen anything like it. It was totally silent and ringed with six white lights – each of them pouring white smoke which made me cough, and blacked out passenger windows for several minutes. It was obviously intelligently controlled, because it kept pace with the train. I got on the two-way to the guard, Greg Bourne, and we stopped the train to report what was happening."

The moment the train came to a halt the intruder vanished leaving a vast cloud of exhaust smoke which dissipated into thin mist which was evident all the way to Zanthus.

Even the Soviet Union was not exempt from strange 'train spotting' craft.

During 1961, forty kilometres from Moscow, a strange object was sighted by drivers of locomotives. They stated that it was disc-shaped, and seemed to be 'topped by a cupola'. It followed a goods train towards Golytsino for a few minutes. All the statements, taken one-by-one, dwelt upon the fact that the 'saucer' seemed to reduce its speed to match that of the train. After one kilometre of escort, the locomotive stopped without visible reason, and could only be restarted after the mysterious object left.

Antonio Huneeus reported another event which happened years later at Petrozavodsk. In February 1985, locomotive driver, S.Orlav, and his assistant were operating an empty, kilometre long, foreign train, when they saw, to the side, a shining sphere above the forest.

It flew alongside of them for some time, but when the train approached a steep hill, and slowed down, the object irradiated a bright light, moved ahead of the locomotive, and positioned itself across the train's path.

Suddenly, the train began to gather speed on its own. When it started the descent, on the other side of the hill, Olav tried, with no effect, to apply the brakes. The sphere appeared to be pulling the locomotive along, at a steady fifty kilometres an hour, and Olav radioed the nearest station, Noviye Peski, saying he was unable to stop his train.

The station master ran out onto the platform, and could see a fiery red disc, resembling a transparent and glowing sphere, moving back and forth in front of the approaching train. It flew off, but as soon as Olav had passed the station, it returned and resumed its position ahead of the engine.

The train came to an unexpected halt, even though Olav had not applied the brakes, and he and the engineer fell against the windscreen. After that the train started moving again at normal speed. After a while, the object disappeared into some nearby woods. When Olav and the crew arrived in Petrosavodsk, they found that the train had more diesel fuel than expected. They had used three hundred litres less than what was normally needed for the same journey.

The years went by, and then a 2002 incident in Kentucky, reported by US researcher, Peter Davenport, is more difficult to explain. Were these earthly or extraterrestrial objects?

It was 2.47am on the 14th January, when a two-engine coal train, en-route from Russell to Shelbiana, rounded a corner in an area referred to as 'Wild Kingdom'. The crew saw lights coming the other way, and thinking it was another train, dimmed their own lights, so as not to blind the oncoming driver.

Their onboard computer began to flash in-and-out, the entire electrical system went haywire, alarm bells began to ring and both locomotives 'died'. The crew could see at least three objects, each with several 'search lights' trained on the nearby river. One was hovering about ten to twelve feet above the track. It was metallic silver, about eighteen to twenty feet in length, and ten feet high. There were multiple coloured lights near the bottom and in the middle, but no sign of any windows or openings.

The train, still in motion, hit the object, only stopping nearly two miles away, after the emergency brakes brought the locomotives to a halt. When the impact occurred, the train had still been travelling at about 30mph, with 16,000 tons of coal trailing in the cars. The lead engine's top was damaged, and chunks sliced out of the trailing unit and first two coal cars. The cab of the rear locomotive was demolished and smoking. They could not see the other aerial objects anymore, and once their power was restored, the crew notified the dispatcher in Jacksonville, Florida.

They were ordered to proceed to the mostly defunct Paintsville yard, and when they arrived, they noticed the huge overhead surrounding lights were unusually dark. What they assumed were railroad officials' vehicles were parked near the end of the tracks. They were not railroad officials, but seemed to be an army of unknown workers, in weird outfits, running in all directions.

A man called 'Ferguson' took the crew into the old yard office, and began to ask a lot of questions, without really giving any information back in return. They were told, for their own protection, that they would be medically tested before they left. He would not let them talk to their superiors, and confiscated the conductor's cellular phone.

After several hours the crew was led outside, and noticed the two locomotives and lead cars had been removed, probably to a spot four tracks over, and covered with a huge, tent-like structure which was 'buzzing with activity'. Before being led away, and put on a railroad vehicle bound for Martin, Kentucky, they were told that 'due to national security, their silence on this matter would be appreciated.'

When they arrived in Martin, they were questioned and drug tested by railway officials, before being sent on to Shelbiana. After an eight hour rest period, they worked another train back to Russell. When they passed Paintsville it was deserted. There was no sign of the engines, cars, tents or people.

ARGENTINA - DECEMBER 1963

Jenny Randles published a more unusual report made by a three-man, freight train footplate crew as it arrived from Presidencia La Plaza. As their train came thundering down the track, they saw a seven feet tall being on the tracks ahead.

Except for the unusual height, it looked completely human, and had long, blond hair. Just as the train crew were bracing for a tragic disaster, the being floated upwards into the sky, as if 'picked up by a whirlwind'.

Their report to the police was substantiated by Justo Masin and his son, who lived a few hundred yards away in the nearby town. They were having a meal in the garden, when they were astonished to see a tall, strange man, with long blond hair, floating above their heads.

CHAPTER SEVENTEEN

WHAT REALLY HAPPENED?

Sometimes we may never really know the truth about some incidents.

At 1.20pm on 7th January 1948, a strange, unidentified object was seen hovering in the sky close to the Godman Field Army Air Force Base in Kentucky, USA. In the hours before, several military bases had already reported seeing a UFO travelling overhead. Many witnesses described it as a round object, metallic in appearance, the lower side comparatively flat, the upper part conical, and showing an intermittent red glow at the top.

At 2.45pm four P-51 Mustang fighter planes, who were on a routine training flight at the time, were ordered to divert and investigate the unusual object. One plane, which was running short on fuel, had to return to base. The three remaining planes remained on course, until another pilot requested permission to also break away. He claimed he was losing his bearings, and was fearful of becoming lost.

He was also granted permission to return to base, but would have to be accompanied, and safely guided, by one of the two remaining pilots. This left Air National Guard Capt. Thomas Mantell piloting the only remaining pursuit aircraft.

At an altitude of about 15,000ft he advised the control tower that he was climbing and closing in on the object, which was a 'metallic object of tremendous size'. Soon after his plane apparently went into an uncontrolled downwards spiral and crashed into the ground 130 miles away. About two hours later, an unidentified object, travelling at incredible speed, passed over the military base at Lockbourne, Colombus, Ohio.

Thomas Mantell had been killed, but the official report did not attribute the crash to the UFO. It concluded that at such a high altitude, he had as lost consciousness due to oxygen starvation. It also determined that his plane had exploded and disintegrated, however, even though some reports said he had crashed on a farm, no remnants or photographs of the wreckage were ever seen. This explanation was widely accepted by the public and many UFO researchers.

In 1957, author Aimé Michel thoroughly investigated the Mantell crash. Both he and Donald Keyhoe suspected a 'cover-up', as they were unable to obtain any meaningful records regarding the incident; *'The photographs of the remains of Mantell's aircraft are still secret....The medical report on the examination of Mantell's remains have also been kept secret...The same course has been followed in the case of two other essential documents – the official evidence of Mantell's two companions and the verbatim report of Mantell's own conversations with the Goodman control tower...Nothing has been disclosed beyond a few sentences which are incorporated in the meagre communiqué of the Saucer Commission dated April 27th 1949.'*

One of the subsequent official explanations was that he had been chasing Venus, and another, discovered later in declassified documents, was that the Navy had been conducting secret balloon experiments as part of its Skyhook project, which sought to measure radiation levels in the upper atmosphere. It is hardly credible that a decorated World War II veteran, with over 2,800 hours of flight experience, would misidentify what he was seeing.

Further hints of a 'cover-up', were later disclosed when his family told researchers that the authorities didn't inform them immediately about his death. The first they knew of it was when a neighbour, who heard about the crash on the radio, came over and told them. They waited for days for an explanation from the military, and were never given access to his body.

Almost fifty years later, another witness came forward. Capt. James Duesler was now an elderly retiree living in Britain, when he contacted my late friend and colleague, Tony Dodd.

Duesler was not happy that the US government had attributed part of a flawed official statement, regarding Mantell's death, to him. He had not made, nor signed, this report which attributed pilot error to the crash, and decided that it was time to reveal the true facts of what happened that day.

On 7th January 1948, Duesler was on the Godman tarmac conversing with his friend, Capt. Warren Carter, who was suddenly asked to go to the control tower. Duesler accompanied his colleague, and they both saw a strange, grey-looking object hovering some distance away.

Duesler said; *"Because of its shape, we described it as an inverted ice cream cone. The widest part pointed towards the ground, and the narrow part pointed towards the sky. We also noted that the object appeared to be rotating because it had a black line, running from top to bottom, which moved around, giving the appearance of rotation. The wide bottom of the object was a red colour."*

He confirmed the return of three of the planes to base, and the last message from Capt. Mantell that he was at 15,000ft, and climbing to get a better look. At that time, the object was becoming obscured by cloud, and Duesler lost interest. He left, and went to a BBQ, later returning to his quarters.

It wasn't until early the next morning that he heard any more about the object. At 1am, the control tower woke him up, saying there was something else strange in the sky. He went up there, and his attention was drawn to an object, in the distance, which was circling in a large arc. Control tower operators at St. Louis and Wright Patterson had received reports of the same cigar-shaped object, which was also seen by several military bombers.

Duesler went back to bed, only to be woken again, at 3am, with the news of Mantell's plane crash. As a member of the accident investigation board, Duesler was required to attend the crash site.

When he attended the scene with two other investigators, they were told that Mantell's body had been taken away. The military personnel who were present, and later the coroner, commented that whilst Mantell's skin showed not a single puncture wound, all of his bones were crushed and pulverised.

"On inspecting the aircraft I found that it was very strange how it had come down. The wings and tail section had broken off on impact with the ground, and were a short distance from the plane. There was no damage to the surrounding trees, and it was obvious that there had been no forward or sideways motion when the plane had come down.

"It just appeared to have 'belly-flopped' into the clearing. There was very little damage to the fuselage, which was in one piece, and no signs of blood whatsoever in the cockpit. There was no scratching on the body of the fuselage to indicate any forward movement, and the propeller blade bore no tell-tale scratch marks to show that it had been rotating at the time of impact. One blade had impacted into the ground.

"The damage pattern was not consistent with an aircraft of this type crashing at high speed into the ground. Because of the large engine in the nose of the plane, it would come down nose first, and hit the ground at that angle. Even if

it had managed to glide in, it would have cut a swath through the trees, and a channel into the ground. None of these signs were present. All indications were that it had just belly-flopped into the clearing. I must admit, I found this very strange." Duesler was also surprised that there was no sign of any fire, and he had never seen a crash like that without having a fire.

"The next day a Dr. Loading came in from Wright Field, Ohio. He was an aeronautical engineer with a Ph.D, and was in charge of what he called the 'Saucer Project'. He told me about the many files they had on record about flying saucers, and said they were aware that the highest number of sightings were in the areas of high industrial and high military activity....Dr Loading also indicated to me that they were aware that these craft were of extraterrestrial nature, and said, 'Thank God they are not hostile, otherwise we wouldn't stand a chance."

Duesler said he wasn't exactly silenced, but his commanding officer, an 'idiot Colonel', told him to 'shut-up' about it, as he (the Colonel) didn't want to be laughed at.

In 1994, another group of researchers spoke to Glen Mays, a witness who said that, all those years ago, he was just a boy, waiting for the school bus when he witnessed the crash, and later saw military personnel burying some of the wreckage on the nearby farmland.

Investigator Larry Tabor, and his team, claimed they then searched the area with metal detectors and a Geiger counter, and dug up over two dozen pieces of what appeared to be only some of the wreckage of Mantell's aircraft. Several pieces, positively identified by serial numbers, registered strong levels of radiation. They asked the obvious question; - Why was part of it found buried in an unmarked trench by the same military that had promised to do a thorough investigation?

Fourteen days after Thomas Mantell's crash, 'Project Saucer' was officially established as part of a government investigation into UFOs. Although it concluded that the saucers were extraterrestrial, its findings were rejected on the basis that they 'lacked evidence'.

Duesler was still mystified by the event, but Gordon Creighton and other investigators have reported that in 1961, a similar incident occurred half way across the world near Tobolsk, Siberia, in the Soviet Union.

An Antonov An-2P Kurgan bound mail plane disappeared from the radar screen when it was about 150 kilometres from its destination. There had been the crew and four passengers on board, and a huge air and ground search was immediately undertaken.

The aircraft was found, completely intact, in the middle of a dense forest. Investigators concluded that there was no way it could have landed there unless it was gently lowered from above. Further, although all the mail and luggage was intact, there was no sign of the crew or passengers. There was enough fuel in the tanks for another two hours of flight, and when a puzzled technician tried to start the engine, 'it fired first time'.

One hundred metres away from the plane was a well defined thirty metre circle of depressed grass and scorched earth. In addition, at the time of the aircraft's disappearance, strange radio signals were heard, and an unidentified object was tracked on radar.

On November 23rd 1944, during World War II, British military, manning an anti-aircraft battery in a Belgian field, saw an American B-17 aircraft swoop down and make an emergency landing.

The soldiers raced over to rescue the crew, only to find nobody on board. All ten parachutes were still there, and later examination of the plane showed it was apparently undamaged, with the engines working perfectly. The aircraft had apparently landed itself, and it still remains a mystery as to how all the airmen had 'vanished' mid-air.

Sometimes, there have been mysterious disappearances of the entire population of American Indian villages, such as the Anasazi, and much speculation as to a possible extraterrestrial involvement. Little is known about this ancient Indian nation, which apparently inhabited the south-west region of the United States. Some ruins of this civilization have been uncovered, but when the local Navajo people have been asked about the Anasazi, they have provided little information, merely referring to them as 'the ancient ones'.

John Keel wrote about one incident in his book, *'The Disneyland of the Gods'*; - *'Soon after Virginia Dare, popularly referred to as the first American, was born in 1587, she, her parents, and the entire Roanoke Island colony disappeared into thin air. When supply ships arrived from Europe, they found the island deserted. The nearest Indian tribe were not hostile, and were also baffled by the mass disappearance. The only clue left behind was a meaningless word carved into a tree: 'CROATOAN'.*

Nigel Blundell wrote about an incident which occurred in 1930, and still remains a mystery today.

Trapper Armand Laurent and his two sons were travelling towards Lake Anjkuni in Canada, when they saw a huge, bullet-shaped craft, which seemed to continually change shape as it passed them and moved across the sky.

A few days later, another trapper, Joe Labelle, contacted the police. He had arrived to find the entire Lake Anjkuni settlement deserted. The village, which was normally buzzing with activity, was undamaged but silent. None of the 1,200 population, or their animals, were to be seen. Their clothing and rifles were still there, and inside the huts, pots of mouldy caribou stew hung over long dead fires. There were no signs of violence, and their boats and kayaks were still tied up at the shore.

The Canadian Mounties initiated an extensive search, and after a few days, found the missing sled dogs tied to trees. They had apparently died from cold and hunger. One of the graves in the Anjkuni burial ground had been dug-up, and the corpse was missing.

There were no trails out of the village, and no known means by which the people could have left. Canadian authorities searched for years, but never solved the mystery'

In 1900, thirty years earlier, across the ocean, in the Outer Hebrides, another mysterious 'disappearance' occurred.

Three fishermen arrived at the remote Flannan Isles beacon, to relieve the three lighthouse keepers who had been on duty for some time. Although facility was working well, the three attendants were missing, and never found. There was no sign of any disorder or panic, and no messages or indications of any accidents or damage. The boats and fuel were still there, but not the three lighthouse keepers. It was as if they had 'vanished off the face of the Earth'.

Gordon Creighton also documented another mysterious case from Russia during 1961;

*'A woman parachutist jumped from a height of nine thousand meters. The pilot of her aircraft saw her floating down, with her chute extended, so he landed to wait for her. She came down...at Saratov ..**three days later**. Her explanation? She had been caught mid-air by a saucer. Its three occupants had treated her well, and had taken her out to an immense distance in space so as to view the Earth. They had given her a message for the authorities. The envelope containing the message was given to the local Chief of Police. We are told nothing of its contents,'*

Bob Teets, in his book, *'West Virginia UFOs'*, reported on a strange 1992 case from Beckley.

It was 3am, and Bull was driving home after going to the midnight showing of 'Batman' at the local picture theatre. A short distance along the highway, his headlights illuminated a blond-haired woman running alongside the road. She appeared to be heavily pregnant, so he immediately stopped and asked if he could help.

She jumped in his car and begged him to – "Get out of here! They're after me!' As he sped away, he could see, in his rear vision mirror, 'headlights' swooping up behind. The woman screamed, saying they were right behind them, and urged him to go faster.

By this time, Bull was getting very nervous. The woman kept screaming, and the 'lights' were still on his tail. He went back through the town, and was heading towards the main highway, when his passenger yelled – "Turn here!"

He skidded around, and went down a side road. The lights were still behind him, so he threw on his brakes. Suddenly the lights flew over the top of his car, and hung low overhead. Bull reversed and drove back through the town again. When he went under a bridge, his pursuer went over it.

By this time he realised it was no irate husband or boyfriend following them. Suddenly, his passenger screeched; "Turn here! It's my grandfather's house."

As soon as he pulled into the driveway, the woman jumped out, ran across the yard, and disappeared into an old, decrepit house. The lights came up from behind, flew over his car, hovered for a couple of seconds, then shot off into the night at incredible speed.

Bull left as quickly as possible, and it was a few weeks before he returned to the place he had left her that night. There was no-one home at the old house. He said it looked abandoned, and that nobody could have lived in it because of its condition.

He began to wonder about the woman he had rescued. She was very pretty, but her clothing was unusual. She was wearing a bright green blouse, which seemed to absorb rather than reflect light. Her slacks did not have a wrinkle or crease, even when she was sitting in the passenger seat; "It was like the material in the slacks was solid of some sort, or a liquid."

We will never know if she was a human, escaping aliens – or, given her 'Nordic' appearance, an alien in distress.

MUFON, Southern Ohio, investigated a similar interesting case on 21st November 2003.

Between 9pm and 10pm, several witnesses saw a soundless, oval-shaped aerial object hovering over an open field. It moved around the sky for a time before settling in another field, when its lighted colour changed from white to orange. At that time all the neighbourhood dogs erupted into frenzied barking and howling. The object turned red, and 'shot off like a dart'.

About twenty minutes later, twenty policemen and the rescue squad turned up in the field. They were responding to several reports of a woman heard screaming; "Help me, oh my God, help me!"

One woman, whose husband was a volunteer with the Fire and Rescue squad, was told that 'a woman with a baby was seen walking around on a hill'. Another man told the police he saw a woman in a field. 'A spaceship had come down and taken her.' A third person had called the police station, saying that a child, about two years old, and wearing only a diaper, was walking down a nearby road.

The police combed the whole area with searchlights, but no trace was found of the woman, child or strange craft. Further, no report was received by the 'missing persons' unit.

Paul Stonehill is a respected investigator on Soviet incidents. He reported that in May 1981, Russian cosmonauts, Savinykh and Kovalyonok, when aboard the Salyut 6, saw another unidentified craft which came within three hundred feet of the space station. It was a spherical, metallic object, with no visible appendages or markings. There were eight 'windows', with sixteen other strange, transparent illuminated spheres arranged throughout the hull.

When the craft approached, some beings showed maps of a Solar System through the porthole, and the cosmonauts asked the Soviet space flight control centre if they could initiate close contact. This was refused, and all they could do was to reply by displaying mathematical symbols. The aliens responded by also showing them symbols which may have been some form of formula.

Salyut's crew then observed, and filmed, three brown-skinned beings who had emerged from their craft. They had slanted blue eyes, straight noses and bushy eyebrows. It was thought these may be mechanical robots, as their faces were expressionless, and they were floating outside their ship without protective suits or breathing apparatus. The alien craft moved around quite erratically, and eventually it 'floated away' into the distance.

I have my doubts about this report, which was also published by Latvian, Henry Gris, in the *'National Enquirer'*. While Gris spent some time in Russia, the *'National Enquirer'* had a reputation for sensationalism and was not considered reliable source. There is no way of verifying the accuracy of their original account. However *'Pravda'* quoted Vladimir Kovalyonok as saying he did report seeing an unidentified object which exploded in space. He also said; "I do not believe it when astronauts say they have never seen anything extraordinary in space."

In 2012, researcher, Antonio Huneeus, published a very different version of the incident. He said that in a later interview, Kovalyonok elaborated on the sighting, but never once mentioned any alien beings or interaction. He said; *'On May 8th 1991, we were in orbit and I saw an object that didn't resemble any cosmic objects I'm familiar with. It was a round object which resembled a* melon, round and a little bit elongated. In front of this object was something that resembled a gyrating, depressed cone. I can draw it, it's difficult to describe. The object resembled a barbell. I saw it become transparent and like with a 'body' inside. At the other end I saw something like gas discharging, like a reactive object.

'Then something happened which is very difficult for me to describe from the point of view of physics....I have to recognise that it did not have an artificial origin. It was not artificial because an artificial object couldn't attain this form. I don't know of anything that can make this movement....tightening, then expanding, pulsating'

'Then, as I was observing, something happened, two explosions. One explosion, then 0.5 seconds later, the second part exploded. I called my colleague, Victor,(Savinykh), but he didn't arrive in time to see anything.

'...The object moved in a sub-orbital path, otherwise I wouldn't have been able to see it. There were two clouds, like smoke, that formed a barbell. It came near me and I watched it. Then we entered into the shade for two or three minutes after it happened. When we came out of the shade, we didn't see anything. But during a certain time, we and the craft were moving together.'

In another interview, Kovalyonok elaborated on some details. They were about 350 kilometres above the Earth, and the object about 150 kilometres lower. He said; "*it seemed to be over the bottom of the Earth. After the explosions I could see a white smoke, like after a magnesium combustion. There also you could see a head in front and behind the barbell.*'

While most people would dismiss the initial report of 'aliens floating in space', it is hard to determine the truth. As Huneeus wrote; '*The Russian space program was a highly controlled state system that brought enormous prestige and revenue to the country, and UFOs were not part of the script, especially during the Communist era.*'

One enigmatic character from our past was Compte de St. Germain, who lived in Europe in the eighteenth century. Often the guest of the French Court of King Louis XV, he was a reputed alchemist who claimed to have discovered the secret of eternal life.

Nobody knows his real date of birth, or even if he really died, but legends date his appearances in France, England, Germany and other countries over both the eighteenth and nineteenth centuries, making him well over one hundred years old.

The French Bibliotheque de Troyes has preserved St. Germain's manuscript, *'La Très Sainte Trinosophie'*, which contains the following passage; *'The velocity with which we sped through space can be compared with nought but itself. In an instant, I had lost sight of the plains below. The Earth seemed to me only a vague cloud. I had been lifted to a tremendous height. For quite a long time I rolled through space. I saw globes revolve around me and earths gravitate at my feet.'*

So who was the mystic St. Germain – human, alien or contactee? We may never know!

Probably some of the most discussed, and controversial series of incidents in Britain are the 1977 'Ripperstone' sightings. The Ripperstone Farm itself lies within a region that local investigators had nicknamed 'The Welsh Triangle'. In Dyfed, Pembrokeshire, on the coast of West Wales, the area encircled St. Brides Bay, and encompassed several military facilities and bases within a twenty mile radius.

To the north was the top secret rocket testing station at Aberporth. RAF Brawdy, near St. Davids, trained pilots on Hawker Hunter planes, and also housed a Tactical Weapons Unit. Also in the area was a US Navy underwater research station, which tracked the movements of Soviet submarines. (To the west, across the sea, is the Isle of Man, which I mention in my book, *'The Alien Gene'*.)

There were several disused mines in the area, and also a small civilian aerodrome at Haverford West, which was used infrequently due to the bad weather conditions over the coast.

In the February of 1977, many students at the nearby Broad Haven School had reported seeing a silver cigar-shaped UFO in a bordering field. Over the following couple of months, several school children plus students from Haverford West Grammar School also reported seeing UFOs, either landed or hovering.

On 26th March, Josephine Hewison, of Lower Broadmoor Farm, saw a massive object, fifty feet wide, standing in a field at the front of their home. She was a qualified scientist, and studied the object intently before it went, leaving no traces behind, after ten minutes.

On 16th April, Pauline Coombs was travelling home, just after dark, with three of her children. As she reached the driveway, her car stalled, and the lights failed, leaving her to 'coast' all the way back to the house. Her son, Keiron, who had been in the back seat, claimed a strange light in the sky had been following them. Billie, her husband, and their elder son, Clinton, raced out to see the object heading out to sea.

Early in the morning of the 23rd April, the Coombs family, who were watching a late night movie on TV, at their home on Ripperstone Farm, claimed that they saw the head of a tall figure, in a 'spacesuit' peering through their window. They called a rather perplexed policeman, who said the family seemed terrified, although he couldn't be sure what they had actually seen.

Early one evening in October, Pauline Coombs was driving with her mother, and some of the children, when they saw a disc-shaped craft overhead. It flew to Stack Rocks Island, which stands out in the sea, half a mile from the mainland. The island was uninhabited, and had three jagged cliffs, rising to eighty-seven feet above sea level. The object dived into them through what appeared to be sliding doors. Shortly after, they saw two 'men', in silver suits, emerge and walk up and down the rock, as if looking for something. They went back up to the 'doors' which were open. The family saw somebody else moving about inside, before the other two re-entered, and the doors slid shut.

At the same time, Mrs Granville, from the Haven Fort Hotel, having seen a flash in the sky, got her binoculars, and saw some figures climbing about on the rocks, before disappearing back inside. On another occasion, she had also seen a strange craft come down on the island and disappear through sliding doors.

As interest in the events grew, several investigators descended on the area, and even more locals reported seeing strange craft.

Other, more inexplicable, or even supernatural events were being reported. Frightened cattle were found some distance away from their securely fenced and locked fields. The Coombs family reported strange paranormal activity in and around their house, and their electricity bill sky-rocketed. (In *'Contact*

Down Under' I mention a rural West Australian family, who after a sighting, also received inexplicable and excessive power charges.)

Some witnesses reported being interviewed at length by RAF officers, and asked not to talk about the matter. Other local folk said that after they were told that the RAF was leaving the area, and their housing would revert to the local Council, the situation changed. Quite a few Americans, who were often seen in civilian clothes around town, had taken their place.

Several months later, in September 1978, further up the Welsh coast, at Llanerchymedd, on the Island of Anglesey, a woman and several boys, saw a white, illuminated object come down from the sky, and hover over a copse of trees.

Described as a 'bullet-shaped object', it descended to the ground, and they saw three 'figures', each about six feet tall and wearing greyish, one piece suits. The cattle in a nearby field were running away in panic, and the 'men' soon disappeared into the early evening gloom.

The little village was in an uproar, and the authorities were called. Another woman, who had come out of the vicarage, saw the object moving slowly in the sky, and at the same time her horses began to stress and sweat profusely.

When the police arrived they could find no sign of the strange craft or its occupants. They noticed the distressed horses, and spent some time controlling the frightened cows.

Theories about the 'Welsh Triangle' ranged from an underground alien base and activity in the area, to misidentified terrestrial military exercises and covert operations. What really happened? Again, we may never know!

EPILOGUE

What is the purpose of the visits from these strangers from the skies? There is more than one kind of alien, and probably several varied reasons for their arrival, some beneficial and some more ominous.

It is naive and simplistic to think that all Visitors are benign. Some may wish to conquer and dominate the Earth. If they are essentially like us, they will have various motives and agendas. In the past, when we have colonised new countries, we have given the natives beads and simple goodies to win their trust and friendship. Is this perhaps the equivalent of the primitive alien technology we have been given?

One may well ask why extraterrestrials did not liaise directly with our governments, however if tried, it was not successful. National sovereignty rarely exists. We now live in a world of global finance, military and industrial liaisons, and political systems controlled by 'big business'.

In 1949, and the following years, Dan Fry, in the USA, assisted the visitors when they wished to integrate, incognito, into our society. When conversing with Alan, his extraterrestrial contact, Dan Fry asked him why the need for secrecy? Could they not just land on the White House lawn?

Alan did not think this was a good idea; 'If we were to appear as members of a superior race, coming from 'above' to lead the people of your world, our arrival would seriously disrupt the ego balance of your society. Tens of millions of your people, in their desperate need to avoid being demoted to second place in the universe, would go to any lengths to disprove, or simply deny, our existence.

'If we took steps to force the acceptance of our reality upon their consciousness, about thirty percent of the people would insist on considering us as Gods, and would attempt to place upon us all responsibility for their own welfare. This is a responsibility we would not be permitted to assume, even if we were able to discharge it....

'Most of the remaining seventy percent would adopt the belief that we were planning to enslave their world, and many would seek means to destroy us. If any great and lasting good is to come from our efforts, they must be led by your own people, or at least by those who are accepted as such...'

Some interesting and thought provoking insights were provided by the alien entities contacted by Ken Llewellyn's medium Monica. He detailed these 'conversations' in his book 'Flight into the Ages'.

When asked about their presence in our skies, they said; 'The best place for us to be visible is in the air. The best communication is on a one-to-one basis. Then there is not the same opportunity for you to attack us. But our presence will gradually become more accepted.'

Another communication was much more enlightening. Ken had asked that when we are also able to travel in space, will we get a better understanding of God?

'Not necessarily so, for God is not on the far side of the Universe. It is not necessary for you to travel vast millions of miles past many stars to reach God. God is on a different dimension.

'You may reach God only by entering within the inner places of your soul and venturing upwards towards the Godhead. This is not outward travelling but rather travelling to the centre of the centre. Your awareness of God's magnitude will obviously be heightened as you are able to travel and see the magnificence of the Universe which he has created. The beauty, peace and tranquillity; the order and magnificence will all be yours.'

Magdalene Graham from Ragnarok considered the purpose of all these visitations and contacts. What have they achieved?

'If they are the 'Sons of God', what have they done to help us, beyond uttering vague warnings about nuclear war and pollution dangers, of which we are already aware, and about which we can do practically nothing. If they have offered any solutions to the problems, they have not communicated them to the right person, and very few of the people they have selected have been psychologically or otherwise equipped to receive their message. Inept is a fitting word for some of their communications. There are other words, such as baffling, contradictory and infuriating. The debate rages.

'Leaving aside the imponderable - 'what are they trying to do?' Let us consider what they have done. They've got Terrestrial Man metaphorically tearing his hair in bewilderment and exasperation – puzzling, investigating, studying, thinking. Maybe that is what they are trying to do. To get man to THINK. To reactivate all of his atrophied brain, instead of muddling along with the tiny percentage of cells he at present uses. When that happens, Man can say to the Gods, thanks for the helping hand, but I'M grown-up now, I can stand on my own feet.'

Magdalene went on to comment that personal contact is the only way one can discover the secret of UFOs, and if that happens, no-one believes it!

INDEX

A

Aborigines 45,163,187
Acevedo Carlos 158
Adamski George 50,127,184,201,257-8,299,314
Afanasyev Victor 294
Africa 66
Agelu Senor 222
Aggen Erich 328
Akhaltsev Vladimir 115
Akkuratov V 80,106
Akisionov Lex 113
'Alan' 368-9
Aldrin Buzz 29,288-9,292
Alonzo De Benavides – Father 319
'Amanda' 223-4
American Astronauts Chapter 12
American Spacecraft Chapter 12
Amerindians Chapter 13 + 213, 391-2
Amicizia 172-3,181,246,256
Anders 287
Anderson Gerald 217
Anderson Lt.Col. William 9,204
Andreasson Betty 273
Andrews George 245
Andrus Walt 22,224
Anfalov Anton 94-5,123-4
Antarctic 197-200
Antonio Jose 185
Apollo Missions Chapter 12
Apraskin Arkadly 109
Ariel School 376-7
Argentina 58-9.125,131-2-146-182,-186,197,249,315-9,377,386
Arlindo 206
Armstrong Neil 29,288-9,293,305,
Artis Movich 106
Aston Warren 175
Auchettl John 4

AUSTRALIA 12,33,37-8,172,187

Adelaide 382
Alice Springs 34
Armidale 8
Ballarat 156
Black Creek 157
Blue Mountains 12,147,156,266
Broken Hill 37-8,40,42-3
Central NSW 224
Coonabarrabran 155
Cowra 265,267
Darwin 382
Eucla 39
Geelong 380
Gilgandra 37
Grenfell 266
Gundiah 140-1
Gympie 34
Hay 306
Hervey Bay 33
Hughenden 135
Kempsey 144
Kununarra 154
Kurrajong 159
Maryborough 30
McKay 141
Melbourne 3,69,352
Moree 163
Mount Isa 45
Mundrabilla 148
Northern Territory 34,261.267,382
Parramatta 368
Portland 361
Singleton 308
South Australia 12,39,42,193,282-3
South Coast NSW 8
Sydney 264
Tamworth 306
Tasmania 151,153-4
Victoria 268

Wagga Wagga 38
Wauchope 264,267
West Australia 34
Wilcannia 37-41
Woomera 35-6,39
Woy Woy 218
Zanthus 383-4

Austria 16,129,172,308
AVRO 22
Azhazha Dr. Valdamir 288

B
Bachurin Emil 98
Balanchikov Nikolai 119
Balducci Father 300
Baledrin Alexandr 295
Barker E 130
Barnett Barney 218
Beacon Colin 380
Beames Kenneth 12
Bean Alan 290,293
Belarrelli Lou 283
Belgium 226,391
Belk Capt 20
Bezac 88
Bigelow Robert 302
Birdsall Graham 73-4,199
Blakeslee Wing Cdr. 327
Blondeau Claude 45
Blundell Nigel 110,392
Boan Dr. 26
Boggs Governor 313
Bogolepox Igor 111
Bok Dr. Geunther 21
Bolivia 222-3,381
Bonham James 69
Boone Daniel 313
Borman Frank 286-7
Bornholm 9
Bosich Prof. Sergei 280,288
Bowles Joyce 165-7
Boyd Cdr. 25
Boylan Richard 66,292,320,366

Bradburn Dave 12
Brazier Maurice 53
Brazil 57-8,62,126,130,132,152,161-2,
182,185,210,214,223,232,234,254,310,312
,315-6,323
Breccia Stefano 173,181
Brezeanu Leonida 92

BRITAIN 16,48,61,69,168,184
Anglesey 372,399
Birmingham 145
Broadhaven 371,397
Carlisle 249
Channel Islands 68
Cornwall 371
Cumbria 248
Derbyshire 186
English Channel 64
Glasgow 372-3
Gloucestershire 16
Haverford 397
Kent 64,158,160
Lakes District 70
Liverpool 63
London 350
Manchester 359
Milford Haven 372
Newcastle 372
Newmarket 61
Northamptonshire 160
Outer Hebrides 392
RAF Cosford 59-61
RAF Shawbury 61
RAF Stradishall 61
Ripperstone 397-9
Scotland 377
Skerries 16
Wales 14,397
Weymouth 355
Winchester 165-7
Windsor Castle 11
York 10

Bronk Dr. 216

Brookesmith Peter 332
Brown Gen. George 333
Brown Townsend 23
Bruns Edward 158
Buchanan Lyn 250
Buhler Dr. Walter 162,254
Bulgaria 87
Bull 393-4
Burea Emil 92
Burgess Bruce 210
Burns William 104
Burt Harold 104
Bush Dr. Vannevar 216
Buskirk Dr. 28
Bykovsky Col. 108
Byrd Admiral 197-8

C

Caldwell H 26
Caldwell Jonathon 20
Callimanopulos Dominique 377
Camaboau Gianni 24
Comacho Albert & Marisol 236
Cambodia 331-2
Canada/Canadians 10,22,49,50,66,
115,130,153,168,303,374,381,392
Candless Jerome 9
Cardenas Filberto 136
'Carmina' 188
Carpenter John 217
Carpenter Scott 285
Carter President 85,310
Carter Capt. Warren 388
Cash & Landrum 72,370
Cashell Sandra 168-9
Castillo 189-90
Cavallo Tiberius 11
Cayce Edgar 136
Cernan Eugene 287,291,294
Chaffee Roger 279,287
Chatelain Maurice 284,289
Chen Yu-Ching 345
Chilkoski L 130

Chile 1,58,161,169,172,182,197,343,
374-5
China/Chinese 302,328,335-45,385
Clark Douglas 382
Clark Everett 238
Clark Jerome 15,56
Cohn Norman 71
Coleman Tom 163
Collings Beth 366
Collins (astronaut) 29,287-9
Collins Francis 157
Collins 'Snowy' 37
Compt De St. Germain 396-7
Conrad Charles 286
Conrad Pete 290-293
Contreras Virgilio 250
Coombs Pauline 398
Cooper Gordon 284
Coppersmith Joshua 29
Corbally Dr. Cristopher 300
Corrales Scott 322-3
Corso Col. Philip 243
Coyne Lawrence 170
Creamer Winifred 316
Creighton Gordon 47-8,79,96,101,112, -
114,116,122,136,139,175,215,225,250,316
,318,339,342,377,390.393
Crinon Kathy 66
'Crister' 184
Crompton Meg 248
CTR 1,174,181,187
Czechoslovakia 88

D

'Daniel' 183
Daniels Wilfred 60
Darnhyl Col.Gernod 48
Davenport Marc 157,310
Davenport Peter 385
Davis Isabel 220
Davydof V. 79
Decker Rosemary 50,292
De Costa Olmiro 234
Dedrickson Col.Ross 277

De Leon Coladerito 334
Denmark 55,184
Dennett Preston 262
Dewilde Marius 377
Diaz Carlos 131-2
Diaz Dr. Leopoldo 207-8
Dickeson Bryan 238
Dickeson Fred & Phyllis 5,127,258,285
Dickinson Terence 122
Dillon Floyd 15
Diorville Albert 338
Dissannayake Indika 375
Djorkovk Peter 93
Dobrovlsky George 297
Dodd Paul 282
Dodd Tony 3,272-3,388
Dolan Richard 297
Dominican Republic 250
Dong Paul 335-9,342
Dorado 125-6
Doyle Chuck 262
Drake Francis 80
Drake Rufus 9,204
Dropa 213,312,336-7
'D.S.' Mr & Mrs 235
Duchon 88
Duesler Capt. James 388-392
Duginov 102
Duke Charlie 291,294

E
Ehricke Dr. 1
Eisenhower President 79,215
'Elizabeth' 263
Ellawalagdera Harsha 375
Elliot Megan 169-70
Ellis David 158
Espinoza Valentina 375
Esposito Maurizio 179-80
Evans Castro 291

F
Facchini Bruno 225
Fadden Sir Roy 18

Fahrney Rear Admiral Delmar 2
Farcas Dan 90,134
Farish Lucius 15
Farrell Mike 164
Fawcett Col. Percival 315
Fengolio Alberto 80,139
Fernandez Julio 239-40
Ferraz Marcilo 161-2
Ferraudi Orlando 181
Filer George III 202-3
Filipov Lachezar 88
Finland 184
Fiore Edith 243
Firman George 382
Fish Marjorie 122
Fowler Raymond 242,273
France 10-11,24,71,172,186,207,222,225,228,247,373,377,396
Francis John 239
Frazer Jocelyn 347-354
Freixedo Salvador 48,202,250
Friedman Stanton 122,217,291-2
Frodsham Tony 282
Fry Daniel 174-5,185,400
Fry Margaret 13,137,165
Fuentes Cpl 56
Fumoux Jean 222

G
Gagarin Yuri 278-9,287,294
Galli Luciano 177
Gardner Norma 215
Gatland Kenneth 1
Gennadiy 116-7
Georghita Florin 92
Georgijevic Vlagyimir 288
Germany/Germans 8,16,17,18,20,22,31,172,186
Gerrard Steve 105,119,285
Ghibaudi Bruno 175-6,181
Gilroy Rex 12,37,146,154,156,163

Good Timothy 3,45,78,117,175,186, 188-190,207,210,214,220,239,247,250,289,335
Goodall Jim 27
Goodall Medwyn 259-60
Gorbachev Mikhail 102-3
Gordon Richard 286,290
Graham Magdalene 401
Granchi Irene 62,126,206,223
Granville Mrs 398
Greenland 80
Greer Dr. Steven 221,277,323
Griffin Michael 300
Gris Henry 108,395
Grissom Virgil 279,287
Gromov Mirija 279
Guidoni Umberto 300

H
Hack Richard 312
Haines Dr. Richard 326
Haise (astronaut) 290,292
Hall Evonne 56
Hall Richard 155,203,326
Halliday Ron 372
Halpern Steve 259-60
Hardasty Col. 31
Harvey Luis 58
Hass Jonathan 316
Hausdorf Hartwig 336
Hawke C 327
Hayashi Colfujio 345-6
Haywood 310
Healey Sgt. John 170
Henderson Dr. G 292
Hernandex Alejandro 69
Hesseman Michael 76
Hewison Josephine 395
Hill Betty & Barney 121
Hillenkoetter 215
Hind Cynthia 253-4,318,376
Hinfelaar Henk 111
Hobana I 86
Hobart HMAS 333
Holstabek G 382

Holt Rev. Turner 241-2
Homet Prof. Marcel 315-6
Hopkins Bud 236
Huffman Rev. William 242
Hull Cordell 241-2
Huneeus Antonio 172,295,336,384,395-6
Hungary 86,89,92,160
Hu-Zhang 337
Hynek Dr. Alan 171,201,290,298

I
Iatan Florin 92
Ilyin Vladim 97
Ilyumzhinov Kirsan 117
India 83,168,302
Indonesia 335
Irwin 290
Ishikiwa Gen. Kanshi 346
Italy 11,17,19,30-1,172,175-7,181,224-5,241
Ivanku Petrovszky 130

J
Jacobs Dr. David 243-4
Jamerson Anna 366
'Jane' 230
Japan 65,83,302,327-8,345-6
Jareacki Franciszek 9
Jernigan Don 327
Jessup Dr. M 128
Jevington Charles 245
Jezzi Lt. Arrigo 170
Joelle 186
Johannis Rapuzzi 224
Johnston Ken 290
Jones Sir George 2
Jones William 241

K
Kadmenski Prof. Stanislav 114
Kaifu Toshiki Prime Minister 346
Kamarov Vladimr 79,287
Katchonogya 313
Kzavtsev Prof. 106
Kean Leslie 68

Keel John 115,252,309-10,391-2
Keleti George 89
Keyhoe Donald 8,49,65,277,385
'Khan' 173
Kilagallen Dorothy 46
King Gustavuus 201
King Jon 296
Kirzhakov Oleg 119
Kylatkovo 79
Knowles Admiral 49
Knowles family 148-151
Kopal Prof. Zdenek 1
Korea 32,326-8
Korolyov Segei 78
Kosygin Prime Minister 84-5
Kovalyonok Vladmir 395-6
Krilov V 102
Krushchev 79
Kubota Major Shiro 346
Kukarkin Boris 297
'Kyle' 267

L

Labelle Armand 292
Lacy Capt. 311
Laika 278
Landeira Andres 148
Langelaan George 78
Lanser Edward 310
Larkin Prof. 311
Laurent Armand 292
Laxton Eddie 61-2
Lazarevich Leonid 294
Lebedev Nikolai 97,117
Ledowsky Alexel 278
'Leesa' 263
Leir Dr. Roger 210
Le Marqunda 130-1
Lenin 77-8
Leonard & Henrietta 306-309
Leonov Alexei 283,288
Lerch Oliver 128-9
Lesiakiewicz 17
Lewels Joe 275

Li Wei Yang 302
Liabeuf Inspector 11
Liapunov Prof. 76
Limov Alexi 295
Lind Dr. James 11
Lindtner Dr. Miran 266,298
Ling Pei Li 339
Linke Oscar 51
Lippisch Alexander 17
Llewellyn Ken 274-5,401
Lorenzen Coral & Jim 232-3,238
Lorenzini Amerigo 241
'Lorretta' 135
Lovell 287,290
Luis 132-3
Luisi Mario 70
Luftwaffe 16,31
'Lydia' 263,354-361

M

Machado Tiago 232
Macieira De Linda 133
Mack Dr. John 243,377
MacRae Gordon 217
Maltsen Igor 103-4,118
Manarov Musa 295
Maney Prof. Charles 2
Mantell Tomas 387-391
Mantle Philip 94,145
Marchetti Victor 78
Marconi 1,17
'Mark & Val' 186
Marrs Jim 250
Martin John 3
Martin Jorge 250
Martin Leticia 159
Masevich Pro. Alla 281
Masin Justo 386
Massey General 31
Mattingly 291
Mays Glen 290
McDivitt James 286
McDonald Lana 268-272
McDonald Prof. 298

McKay Glennys 45,187
McLaughlin Robert 19
Medvedev Dr. Dimitry 117,278
Melderis Ian 102,108
Meng Zhauguo 344
Menger Howard 184,258
Menzel Dr. 216
Metrodorus 1
Mesnard Joel 227
Mexico 207,312,319
Michel Aimé 388
Miller Freddie 250
Mitchell Edgar 284-5,290,293
Mitcow Andreij 279
Mongolia 337,339-342
Monica 275,401,199
Montgomery Christopher 239
Montiero Wayner 162
Moore Olden 56
Moreno Dr. 377-379
Morentsen Larry 68
Morgan Walter 336
Morningsky Robert 321-2
Morrison Mary & Malcolm 236-7
Moser Bill 298
Moulton Howe Linda 199
Mountbatten Lord 47,201
Moya Miguel 158
Mr.X 180,256-8
Murray Derek 35
Mus 239-40
Mussolini 17

N

Nagy Tibor 164-5
Nakumora Lt.Col. Toshio 346
Nepal 27,83,337
Netto Severino 126
Newfoundland 55
New Zealand 54,55,127,192,230,238,256, 259,374,380
Nielsen Olaf 139-40
Niemtzow Dr. Richard 223
Nixon President 291

Norman Paul 298,304,383
Norris Colin 43,261
Norris Peter 44
Norway 31,47,184
Noury Leo 185
Novoa Enrique 186
Nukarinen Rita 77

O

O'Barsky George 236
Oberg James 285
Oberth Prof. Herman 2
O'Brien Brian 287-8
Octavian Bota 92
Oge – Navaho Indian 311
Oliver Douglas 63-4
Oliver Fredrick 310
Oliver Norman 64,371

P

Paget Peter 112,165
Pallman Lugwig 190-2
Papua New Guinea 68
Parvu George 90
Patsayev Viktor 297
'Patty' 192-5,231,263
Pauchet Dr. Victor 207
Payne Debbie 36
Pena Afriano 162
'Penny' 269
Penrose Horatio 145
Pereira Jader 214
Perez Prof. Calixto 203
Perisse Lt. Daniel 198
Peru 269,314-319,373-4,322-3
Petersen Hans 55
Petit Jean 165-7
Petrova Svetlana 124
Petrovich Sergey 95
Philip IV Prince 319
Phillips Don 221
Phillips Ken 354
Phillips Ted 374
Phillipines 26-7,334-5

Pike George 37
Pinkney John 383
Piri-Reis Admiral 196
Pisani Adolfo 157
Poland 9,94,220
Ponce Jose 227
Pope Nick 61
Powell Dr. 26
Pratt Bob 130-2
Pratt Ted 165-7
Prince Phillip 201
Pro Hart 38
Puerto Rico 182,188,203,236

Q
Queen Juliana 201
Quezet Meagen 253
Quick Andy 155

R
Raffy Claude 228
Rall Dr.Yuri 204
Randle Kevin 273,366
Randles Jenny 13,16,47,70,160, 224,341,386
Reagan Fred 137-9
Reagan Ronald 26,102-3
Redell Paul 277
Redfern Nick 16,60
Reed Dr. Jonathon 239
Reino Maj.Gen. L 106
Reshetnikov Gennadij 81
Reynolds Andrea 140-44
Rhodes William 39
Ribera Antonio 239
Rich Ben 27
Richards Barry 167
Riera Pedro 209
Riley Euan 373
Roach Pat 366
Robb Carter 218-9
Roberts Keith 154
Rodionov Boris 295
Roerich Nicholas 337-8

'Roger' 261
Rohrer Joe 21
Romania 89-91,134
Roosevelt Franklin 241
Roque Dolor 162
'Rose' 247
Rossa 290
Roswell 19-21,39,78,215,217
Rubtsov Dr. 96
Ruppelt Capt. Edward 22
Russell Senator Richard 52
Russia (Russians,Soviets) Chapters 3-4 17,19,22, 23,29,31,32,48,52,66,168,187, 189,254,341-2,384,391,393,395
Russian Spacecraft Chapter 12
Ruth 173
Rutledge William 293

S
Sagan Carl 80
Saiji Capt. Masaru 45
Salutun Air Commodore 335
Salyut 395
Sammaciccia Bruno 173
Sandby Thomas 11
Sardinia 24
Satu-Ra 190-1
Savinykh (astronaut) 395
Schiborin Serenty 279
Schmitt 291
Schuessler John 73-4
Scotland 53,236
Scott Dave 290,293
Scott Dr. Irena 241
Sheahan Col. Maurice 336
Shertzer Beau 115
Shepherd (astronaut) 290
Sichenkoc Dr. 105
Sicily 178
Sider Jean 207,373
Siragusa Eugenio 178-9
Sister Mary 319
Smith Ron 115
Smith Ted 380

Smith Wilbur 49-51
Smith Willy 56
Sochevanov Nikolay 96
Sokolov Colboris 81-2
South Africa 283
South America 187,189-92,206,318,322
Spain 31,148,161,185,222,239,319
Spencer John 182,184,276
Squires Hayden 147
Sri Lanka 375
Stafford 287
Stalin 78
Steiger Brad 312,381
Sten 182-4
Stephens Peter 37
Stevens Wendelle 319
Stewart Alan 151
Stokes Paul 60
Stolyarov Gen. P 106
Stone Clifford 27
Stone Fred 258
Stone Rueben 185
Stonehill Paul 77-8,96-7,123,395
Stringfield Leonard 65,203,219
Stroganov Yuri 78
Subbotin Nikolay 98-9,105
Sudan 27
Sun Shi Li Prof. 344
Svechkov Maj. Germai 99
Swann Ingo 297
Swarz Tim 123
Sweden 8,139,182-4,225
Sweed Richard 15
Swigert 290
Switzerland 172
Sylvester Ellen 42
Szachnowski Antoni 30,91

T
Tabor Larry 390
Tambling Richard 305
Tanda Francesco 24
Targ Russell 295
Tatar Jill 2

Teets Bob 379,393
Tei-Chipu 336
Terechkovax V 108
Teriski Vladimr 18
'Thomas' 220-1
Thomson Hugh 317
Tibet 83,337-8
Tichit Germain 227
Timmerman John 328
Tite John 137
Tomas Andrew 310
Tombaugh Clyde 277
Tompkins William 261
Totten Darrell 62-3
Transylvania 91
Trembath Wayne 154
Troitsky Dr. 95
Truman President 201
Tshechanovich 102
Tunguska 75-6
Twining General 216

U
Uhouse Capt. Bill 221
Ulster Jack 155
UMMO 185-6

UNITED STATES AMERICA
17,19,22-24,26.29.32,48-9,168,189,321
Andrews AFB 9,204
Arizona 21,68,213,313-4,319
Arlington 247
California 8,15,19,21,39,62,70,
125,204,292,310,366
Cascade Mountains 239
Chicago Great Lakes Naval Base 205
Death Valley 311
Edwards AFB 24
Florida 15,26-27,136
Fort Dix 202-3
Fort Hood 73
Fort Meade 251
Godman Field Army AFB 387
Hawaii 205

Illinois 153,317
Indiana 128,380
Kentucky 219,262,385-6
Lake Ozarks 163
Langley Base Virginia 296
Maryland 9,20
McGuire AFB 203
Minnesota 158
Missouri 242
Mount Blanca 312
Mount Shasta 175,310-11
Nebraska 381
Nellis AFB 10
Nevada 27,48
New Jersey 202,236,239
New Mexico 73,216,219
New York 152,235
North Carolina 153
North Dakota 15
Ohio 56,65,115,170,241,311,394
Oklahoma 13,61
Pennsylvania 152,233
San Francisco 311
San Luis Valley 312
Tennessee 238
Texas 13-15,72,169,250,252
Vandenberg AFB 291-2
Virginia 9,204
Washington 15,64,242
West Virginia 167,379
White Sands 19
Wyoming 317

Uravov Dr. Valery 81,119,123
Uruguay 56
Ustal Nancy 374

V

Valdes Cpl. Armando 343
Valentich Frederick 156
Vallee Dr. Jaques 3,111,186
Van Tassel George 258
Var Lamov 85
Vega Fresia 375
Vegas Dr. Sanchez 208
Venezuela 157,182,208,227,235,319
'Vera' 263
Vesco Renato 19,125
Viallet Paul 373
Vietnam 17,329-334
Villela Dr. Rubens 199
Vincente Enrique 220
Visani Umberto 173,181
Vitolniek R.E. 102,107
Volkov Vladislav 297
Von Braun Werner 300
Vysoky Dr. 97

W

Wall Francis 328
Wallace Roy 263
Walton Joe 283
Walton Travis 213
Wang Sian Min 340
Watts Carroll 252
Wei Lin Win 339
Wells H.G. 77
Westall School 369-70
Weston Keith 40-1
Weverberg H.J. 86
Weygandt Jonathon 323-4
White Edward 279,286-7
Widman Dr. 213
Wilcox Garry 235
Wilkins Dr. H.P. 277
Wilkins Harold 10,13-4,20-1
Williamson David 311
Williamson George Hunt 314-6
Wilson Dr. Clifford 292
Wilton Raw Eater 153
Wolfe Karl 296
Wood Ryan 242
Wooley Dr. Richard 29
Worden (astronaut) 290
World War I 14,18,311
World War II 16-17,19-21, 30-31, 39,172,189,196,198,201,227,241,391
Wyatt Jon 333

Y
Yanacsek Sgt. Robert 170
Yeend Maggie 151
Yevgeniy Gen. 105
Young John 287,291,293
Yugoslavia 93
Yuryevitch Mick 383

Z
Zaitsev Vyacheslan 337
Zayas Jose 203
Zhang Ke-Tao 342
Zigel Dr. Felix 76,85,106-111,243
Zimbabwe 376
Zirger Michel 314
Zoccoli Count Gian 175
Zolotov Dr. Alexel 76,124
Zverev Boris 113

www.ingramcontent.com/pod-product-compliance
Lightning Source LLC
Chambersburg PA
CBHW081352290426
44110CB00018B/2354